# Quantitative Methods
# for Computing Students

**Brian Catlow**, Cert Ed., B.Sc., M.Sc.

Brian Catlow is a Senior Lecturer in Mathematics and Computing at
Bedford College of Higher Education where he has taught for the past nine
years on a variety of diploma, degree and post-graduate courses. He has
over twenty-five years teaching experience at all levels within school and
college settings.

DP Publications Ltd
Aldine Place
London W12 8AW

1993

## Acknowledgements

I would like to thank all those students and staff at Bedford College who have contributed directly or indirectly to this book. They, and the college itself, have been an endless source of ideas and inspiration for the case study and associated material. Particular thanks are due to Maggie Roddis, Steve Wilson and Dave & Irene Wooldridge, my colleagues in the Mathematics Section; working alongside them has been a tremendous learning experience for which I shall be ever grateful. A special mention is also due to my wife Carol for her unflagging support and encouragement; without it, this book would never have seen the light of day.

A CIP catalogue record for this book is available from the British Library

ISBN 1 873981 17 1

© Brian Catlow 1993

First edition 1993

Printed in Great Britain by The Guernsey Press Co Ltd, Vale, Guernsey

# Preface

## Aim

The aim of this book is to provide all the support needed for a student on Higher National or the first or second year of a degree course in Computing.

A Computing student has to be able to translate needs into workable computer applications. Many of these needs are practical problems requiring **quantitative techniques** for their solution. In turn, it is necessary to possess a broad range of skills to deal with new problem situations. Some of these skills are based on practice and experience, others on intuition and common sense. Those encountered in this book are the most common ones, which can be developed by practice; these include:

1. Handling information (collecting/recording/processing/presenting)

2. Interpreting information (in the form of: words/tables/formulas/diagrams/graphs)

3. Number (approximation, calculation)

4. Algebra (translation, manipulation)

5. Graphs (plotting, sketching, interpretation).

Quantitative Methods is concerned with *applying* Mathematics; so, knowing *where* and *how* to use the mathematics is just as important as learning and understanding the mathematics itself. The listed skills are all useful ones to possess; however, it is also vital to develop the ability to recognise problems where those skills might be helpful and how they can be applied to produce satisfactory solutions.

So, through an applications approach, this text aims to:

1. provide an understanding of necessary mathematical concepts as a basis for realistic problem-solving with the aid of computer technology;

2. develop confidence and competence in analysing numerical information;

3. support other Computing core subject areas;

and also aims to:

4. develop analytical and modelling skills;

5. broaden the range of problem-solving techniques available to you;

6. develop the ability to choose the most appropriate problem-solving technique for any given situation.

## Need

The ever-increasing range of uses to which computers are being put places extra demands on students of computing disciplines in tackling practical problems. The ability to use Quantitative Methods effectively in new problem situations requires a broader range of skills than is usually taught within the confines of a traditional Mathematics course.

For instance, the effective use of a spreadsheet package demands that students have a sound understanding of the underlying Mathematics in order to construct accurate and workable spreadsheet models. Complementary to this, however, are the skills of mathematical model formulation and validation, interpretation of results and model evaluation. So, this book aims to balance technique acquisition with technique application in a way that emphasises the full range of skills appropriate to Computing students.

Further, the vast majority of Quantitative Methods texts currently available to students entering post-school Computing courses do not take into account the revolution that has taken place in school

Mathematics education in recent years. Students now leaving school have come to expect an investigative and problem-solving approach based on well-presented, stimulating, relevant and practical problems. This book aims to build on these previous experiences and uses a broad spectrum of applications as the basis for discussion, investigation and solution.

The book satisfies the increasing need for texts that can be used to replace a proportion of lecturer-contact time, rather than merely to support it.

## Approach

The approach has evolved over a number of years from that taught by the author within the Quantitative Methods components of a variety of Computer Studies courses. The book has been designed to encourage lecturer-student and student-student discussion/investigation of key ideas as well as to provide consolidation of skills on an individual basis. This is achieved by dividing the material into three related sections which provides a flexible structure, taking into account variations in existing knowledge/experience and the lecturer's preferred method of organisation.

### Section 1 – Discovering quantitative methods

This section is made up of a series of units relating to a single case study of a typical educational institution. Each unit presents a realistic problem which requires the student to respond at a variety of levels:

1.  Tasks

    These require that the student consider, discuss and investigate points raised in the book. This can be done on an individual, small group or whole class basis (see lecturer's supplement below). References are given to those parts of Section 2 which are of particular help in completing the task in hand. **Outline answers where appropriate are provided in an appendix.**

2.  Extended tasks

    These build on the earlier tasks and normally require:

    (i)   more time for completion;

    (ii)  the use of computer facilities to introduce and develop spreadsheet/programming skills;

    (iii) the student to undertake some investigative/practical work.

    Outline answers to these tasks are provided in the lecturer's supplement (see below).

### Section 2 – Information Bank

This section provides the background information, principles and examples needed by Computing students.

Students only need to use this section when directed to a particular topic from Section 1. Every part of Section 2 is cross-referenced from Section 1 so that all principles and practice of the subject are covered via a problem-solving route.

### Section 3 – Further tasks and extended investigations

This section contains:

1.  tasks based directly on the material in Sections 1 & 2 and providing **consolidation** of skills and techniques developed in those sections;

2.  extended investigations which provide the stimulus for the student to research information, undertake further reading and answer additional questions. The extended work is related to topics developed in Section 2 but not necessarily dealt with explicitly within that section.

Outline answers to appropriate tasks are provided in the lecturer's supplement (see below).

## How to use this book

The structure of the book allows it to be used in a variety of ways according to the demands of the course:

### Open/Distance learning programmes

Students studying on their own are advised to work through the units in Section 1 in sequence and tackle Section 3 tasks as directed by the text.

### Taught courses

Lecturers can use the book in either of the following ways:

1. **As a support text for a course of lectures.** Once a lecture on a particular topic has been given, students are directed to work through those units of Section 1 covering the topic in order to practice and confirm their skills and knowledge.

2. **As a supported self-study text.** Students work through Section 1 units in sequence, covering the topics in Section 2 as directed, and freeing lecturers to 'manage' the learning process.

3. **As a combination of (1) and (2),** to suit particular courses.

## Lecturers' supplement

A free lecturer's supplement is available to lecturers recommending the book as a course text. It contains answers to the extended tasks in Section 1 and to **some** of the further tasks in Section 3. The supplement also gives guidance on group work and the extended investigations in Section 3.

# Contents

# Background information for Section 1 – Dale Institute

*Section 1 is a single case study of a typical educational institution, Dale Institute. In each unit in Section 1 the problems arising are given in the context of the Institute. You should therefore read the following background information before starting so that all the problems can be seen in the appropriate context.*

*This is an extract from Dale Institute's prospectus. It gives some details about the Institute itself, the town in which it is situated and the courses it offers to prospective students.*

## The Institute

Dale Institute is a new educational establishment which has recently been formed by the merger of two colleges of higher education and a college of further education. It is a thriving, well-equipped institution situated in pleasant urban surroundings. The Institute offers a range of courses, including non-vocational courses, GCSE and 'A'-level, degrees, post-graduate certificates, in-service training for teachers and social workers and higher qualifications such as Ph.D. and M.Phil. There are over ten thousand students enrolled, both full-time and part-time.

There are three main Institute campuses – Wentworth, Brooklands and Harper. These are the names of the three colleges which have merged to form the new Institute and which will continue to provide the venues for the courses. They form a triangle around the town of Chelford (see the map below for more detail). The Wentworth campus provides the bulk of further education courses, whilst Brooklands and Harper will be the focus for degree and teacher training activities.

Each campus has comprehensive library facilities containing a large collection of books, periodicals, and audio-visual materials including slides, records, film-strips and computer software. The libraries also subscribe to a number of on-line databases including Prestel, Campus 2000 etc. Each campus is well equipped for information technology. A large selection of stand-alone microcomputers (IBM, Apple, Archimedes, Amstrad, Elonex, RM Nimbus and BBC) is available as well as a VAX 11/750 minicomputer capable of supporting approximately 40 users. In addition, each campus has microcomputer laboratories containing networked IBM, Apple, RM Nimbus and Archimedes machines. These hardware facilities are well supported by a comprehensive range of software.

## The town

Chelford is an attractive prosperous town on the River Dale. The river is a central feature of the town and features in the annual regatta as well as a colourful river festival which takes place every two years.

Chelford has a spacious library and excellent specialist bookshops. The shopping centre has a modern precinct and there is a wide range of entertainment and recreation. Drama, music and film flourish in the active cultural climate. Many different ethnic groups have settled in Chelford and their presence encourages a lively cosmopolitan atmosphere.

Sporting facilities in the town include a superb Olympic-size swimming pool where Institute students stage an aqua-pantomime each year. There is a modern leisure centre with squash courts and water sports on the river. Chelford has a top-class rugby team, rowing and canoeing clubs with national reputations.

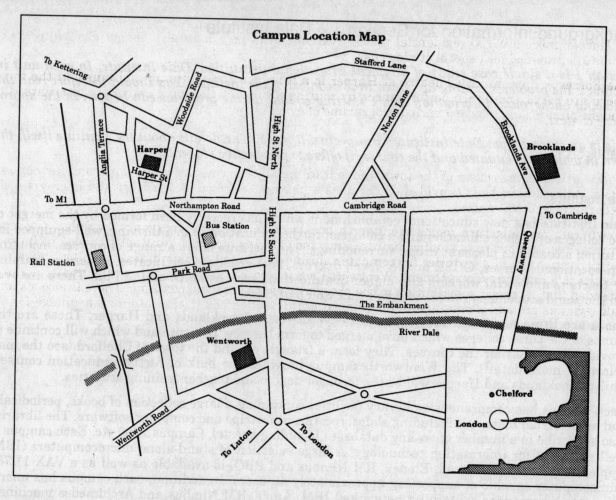

## Brooklands

Brooklands is to the east side of the town in a modern residential area. It is the base for Primary Education and the Humanities.

Brooklands has many pleasant lecture rooms with a recently opened Primary Centre. There are two halls, one of which is used as a conference centre. Brooklands is a major venue for in-service training. A comprehensive programme attracts large numbers of teachers and social workers. The campus has a modern gymnasium and is set in extensive playing fields. There is an excellent library with a specially developed resource centre used by both students and tutors. Brooklands has a day nursery where qualified staff look after children whose parents work or study at the Institute. There is a large well-appointed lecture theatre which is regularly used for outside speakers, some with national or international reputations.

There are residential places at Brooklands for 200 students in modern study bedrooms. The accommodation is designed to give privacy and the opportunity for social activity.

## Harper

Harper is the site where Physical Education, Dance and Sports Studies are based. It is on the west side of the town in a quiet district characterised by large Victorian houses. There are excellent facilities – three modern gymnasia, an indoor heated swimming pool and a dance studio. Close by are extensive playing fields and a fully equipped sports hall. The skill laboratory block is a recent addition and contains a range of sophisticated equipment to record and analyse movement skills. There are science laboratories, art/craft studios and a spacious modern library all set in mature gardens.

At Harper there are 150 residential places available in large comfortable rooms. Several common rooms are provided for general student use.

The Forrester Community Theatre at Harper is a focus for dance, drama and music in the town. There are plays and dance performances by touring professional groups and these alternate with student productions to give a varied programme of events.

## Wentworth

Wentworth is in the centre of the town and is traditionally the campus where adult and further education courses have been provided. It occupies a pleasant location by the river and is only a short walk from the town centre.

Apart from many lecture rooms Wentworth boasts modern engineering workshop blocks, a large computer centre, business studies, hairdressing and catering facilities. A recently opened technology centre consisting of laboratories for computer aided design, digital communications, fibre optics and robotics is a major new investment. Wentworth has a record of working with local industry and it is intended that its major contribution to the prosperity of the area will continue. There is also a sports hall, gymnasium and a spacious well-equipped library which add to the resources available for the thousands of students who undertake full-time and part-time study.

# Section 1

## Discovering quantitative methods

Section 1 consists of a number of Units that are related to Dale Institute, an educational establishment which provides the backdrop to the book. Each unit consists of a problem arising from the life and work of the people within the Institute; solving the problem will enable you to learn something of the principles and practice of quantitative methods. Every unit has associated Tasks and in order to help you deal with these there are 'helplines' to the appropriate part of the Information Bank in Section 2.

The topic(s) dealt with by each unit are specified at the beginning of the unit. So, the units can be:

    (i)  worked through in order

or  (ii)  dipped into according to your needs.

Each unit also has extended tasks which will normally require more time and make use of a computer to develop your spreadsheet skills and programming capabilities. These tasks also include investigations and practical activities that will further develop your understanding of quantitative methods.

The units cover the topics in the same sequence as Section 2. The table below shows the relation of units to topics.

| Information Bank topic (Section 2) | Section 1 Units |
|---|---|
| Mathematical models | 1 – 3 |
| Functions and graphs | 4 – 11 |
| Numerical methods (1) | 12 – 13 |
| Numercial methods (2) | 14 – 16 |
| Statistics | 17 – 24 |
| Descriptive statistics | 17 – 29 |
| Inferential statistics (1) | 30 – 36 |
| Inferential statistics (2) | 37 – 43 |
| Simulation | 44 – 48 |
| Linear programming | 49 – 52 |
| Transportation and assigment | 53 – 57 |
| Routing | 58 – 60 |
| Critical path analysis | 61 – 62 |

At the end of the appropriate units are the references to those consolidation tasks in Section 3 that you will be able to tackle at that point.

# Unit contents

# Unit 1: Paper models

*Variables; relationships; model types*

Some Computer Science students at the Institute undertake a short course concerned with mathematical modelling. In one session they are divided into groups, each group being given a different problem to investigate and model. Before trying to construct the mathematical model each group is given a large sheet of paper and asked to make a list of all the factors which they think have some part to play in the problem. They are also to make a brief note of any possible general relationships between the variables and parameters on the list. After some consideration, one group's piece of paper looks like this:

---

**Problem statement**

'How long will it take me to do the washing-up for myself and my flat-mates?'

| *Variables / Parameters* | *Relationships* |
|---|---|
| Number of plates ($n$) | $n$ is dependent on $p$ |
| Amount of washing-up liquid used ($l$) | $l$ is dependent on $f$ and $w$ |
| Type of food ($f$) | |
| Temperature of water ($t$) | if $t$ decreases, $d$ and $l$ increase |
| Size of plates ($s$) | |
| Amount of water used ($w$) | |
| Number of people ($p$) | |
| Time elapsed since meal eaten ($e$) | if $e$ increases, so does $d$ |
| Amount of use of dishcloth/scourer ($d$) | |

---

## ■ Tasks

1. Comment on this group's efforts:

   a) State which of the factors on the list are variables and which are parameters.

   b) Are there any important factors missing, or any relatively unimportant factors included?

   c) Are the stated relationships reasonable?

   d) Are there any likely missing relationships?

2. The problems given to the other groups were:

   ❏ How long will it take me to travel between the Wentworth and Brooklands campuses?

   ❏ Where is the best place for a new coin-operated telephone kiosk on the Brooklands campus?

   ❏ Will I be able to read the blackboard notes in the lecture theatre?

   ❏ How long will I have to wait for the lift in the 7-storey Wentworth Tower building?

   ❏ Will I find a parking space in the student car-park?

   ❏ How long will I be in the Brooklands cafeteria at lunch-time?

   ❏ Will I pass my end-of-year examinations?

In each case:

a) Write down the possible contents of the group's piece of paper.

b) Say whether the mathematical model will be mainly deterministic or stochastic.

 See Section 2: The Information Bank – *Mathematical models*  pages 95–99; 102–104

# Unit 2: Paint-pots

**Topic: Modelling**

*Formulation; solution; spreadsheet application*

The walls and ceiling of some of the lecture rooms on the Brooklands campus are to be given a fresh coat of paint. Each room is a similar size (9m long; 6m wide; 3.5m high) and overlooks the grounds on one side. This outer wall is all glass except for brickwork surrounding the window (0.5m above, 1m below, 1m each end). The campus site manager needs to calculate how many litres of paint are required for each room.

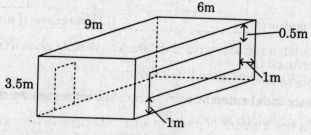

## ■ Tasks

1. Make a list of the relevant variables for this problem.

2. Write down any simplifying assumptions that can be made and use them to shorten the list, if possible.

3. Make a note of the sort of calculations that you need to make in order to solve this problem.

4. Assuming 1 litre of paint is sufficient to cover 10m², calculate the amount of paint required.

5. The site manager asks you to provide him with a mathematical model – a form of 'ready reckoner'. He wants to be able to use this to calculate the amount of paint needed for other rooms. You can assume that the rooms are similar in style but must allow for possible variations in length, width etc.

a) Start by writing down your model in words, something like this:

'Multiply the length by the width, ... divide by area covered by 1 litre of paint, ...'

b) Translate your model into mathematical terms, similar to

$$P = lw \dots$$

where:  $P$ is the amount of paint required, in litres
    $l$ is the length of the room, in metres
    $w$ is the width of the room, in metres,  etc ...

c) i)  Validate your model by using it to confirm the solution to Task 4.

   ii)  Use your model to find the amount of paint for a room which is 10m long by 7.5m wide by 4m high. Does the answer seem reasonable?

See Section 2: The Information Bank – *Mathematical models* pages 95–104

☐ **Extended tasks**

6. Implement your model on a spreadsheet. The layout might resemble the following, with the relevant data in columns A – E and result in column G (formulas are not shown):

| | A | B | C | D | E | F | G |
|---|---|---|---|---|---|---|---|
| 1 | | | 'Room | painting | calculator' | | |
| 2 | Length (m) | Width (m) | Height (m) | Window (m$^2$) | Rooms | | Paint (litres) |
| 3 | 9 | 6 | 3.5 | 14 | 1 | | 14.5 |
| 4 | 10 | 7.5 | 4 | 20 | 1 | | 19.5 |
| 5 | 7.5 | 4 | 3.5 | 11 | 4 | | 39.8 |
| .. | ... | | ... | ... | ... | | ... |
| .. | ... | ... | ... | ... | ... | | ... |
| .. | ... | ... | ... | ... | ... | | ... |

7. a) Validate your spreadsheet model with the data and results shown in the above layout.

b) Use your spreadsheet to investigate the following:

i) Which of length, width or height has the most effect on the amount of paint required?

ii) How sensitive is the amount of paint to small changes in the various measurements?

For example, if an error of 20 cm is made when measuring the length of a room, does this drastically affect the amount of paint required?

Similarly, what about small changes in the width/height/surrounding brickwork?

You will have to decide how to measure this sensitivity.

 See Section 3: Further Tasks and Investigations page 325 *Q 1 and 2*

# Unit 3: Travel expenses
**Topic: Modelling**

*Formulation; solution; spreadsheet application*

For students who are training to be teachers, part of their course is spent in a school where they practise the skills of being a teacher. If the school is too far away for daily travel, the student will be in lodgings for the period of the teaching experience. Other students who have their own transport travel to school daily. For this they are allowed to claim travelling expenses at the standard rate of 25p per mile. If they share transport the driver can claim an extra 0.5p per passenger per mile. However, they can claim only for the difference in mileage between the distance to the school and the distance they would normally cover if travelling to Dale. For instance, a student who normally undertakes a return journey of 17 miles daily, which rises to 24 miles daily whilst on teaching experience, can claim only for the extra 7 miles. For administrative purposes, students have to submit a claim form each week.

## ■ Tasks

1. Formulate a mathematical model which shows the relationship between:

    $W$ – the weekly amount which can be claimed
    $n$ – the number of passengers
    $d$ – the normal daily return mileage travelled to Dale
    $m$ – the daily return mileage travelled to the school
    $r$ – the rate per mile

    The model should be in the form: $W = ......$

2. Make a list of any assumptions that you are making in your model.

3. a) Use your model to calculate the weekly claim for a student who transports an extra three students for a return journey of 35 miles when the normal return mileage is 12 miles.

    b) The rate per mile is adjusted to 27.5p, the rate for passengers remaining unchanged. Recalculate the allowable claim in part (a).

 See Section 2: The Information Bank – *Mathematical models* pages 97–104

## ☐ Extended tasks

4. Develop a spreadsheet model (or write a computer program) to produce a ready-reckoner 'look-up' table for this situation. For instance:

    i) the number of passengers could be columns on the spreadsheet

    ii) the return excess mileage could be rows on the spreadsheet

    iii) the cells at the intersection of a row and column contain formulas which calculate and display the amount of claim payable. For example, the intersection of row 20 and column 3 represents the weekly amount payable for a student and 3 passengers travelling an extra 20 miles per day.

    You will also need to decide how best to incorporate the rate per mile, given that it varies occasionally.

5. Which of the variables have the most effect on the value of $W$?

    For example, is it more economical for the Institute to send

    i) a small number of students a long distance, or

    ii) a large number of students a small distance, for their teaching experience?

    (The spreadsheet of Task 4 would be useful for this investigation).

 See Section 3: Further Tasks and Investigations page 325 *Q 1 and 2*

# Unit 4: Sporting graphs

*Interpretation; sketching*

**Topic: Graphs**

As part of the B.Ed. course at the Institute, all students who are training to become Secondary School teachers of Physical Education also have to study a subsidiary subject. This is intended to enable them to gain experience in teaching a classroom-based subject, to broaden their outlook and to provide them with a second teaching strength. In the case of those students who choose

Mathematics as their subsidiary subject, part of the course involves a study of the mathematical aspects of a variety of sports. Since nearly all sports involve motion, either of people or of objects, the students are given the task of producing 'motion graphs' for selected sports. They are given a list of sports which they observe, discuss and then try to summarise in graphical terms. One group produced a selection of graphs, some of which are shown here:

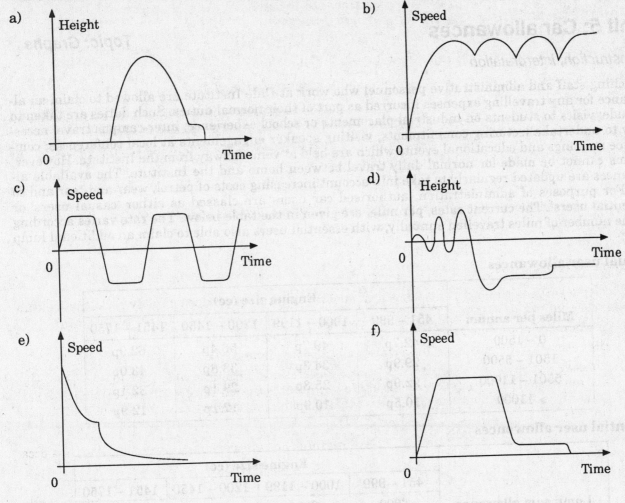

### ■ Tasks

The sports for which they had to produce motion graphs were:

| | | |
|---|---|---|
| 4 × 100m sprint relay | Swimming | Drag racing |
| 110m hurdles | Freefall parachuting | Hammer throwing |
| Springboard diving | Pole vault | Fishing |
| Clay pigeon shooting | Trampolining | |

1. a) Match a sport from the list with a graph from (a) – (f).
   b) Highlight and explain the main features of each graph.

2. Produce a possible motion graph for each of the remaining sports on the list.

See Section 2: The Information Bank – *Functions and Graphs* pages 108–111

See Section 3: Further Tasks and Investigations pages 326–327 *Q 4, 5, 6*

# Unit 5: Car allowances

**Topic: Graphs**

*Construction; interpretation*

Teaching staff and administrative personnel who work at Dale Institute are allowed to claim an allowance for any travelling expenses incurred as part of their normal duties. Such duties are taken to include: visits to students on industrial placements or school experience; inter-campus travel necessary to undertake lecturing commitments; visiting speaker engagements at local conferences; committee meetings and educational events which are held at venues away from the Institute. However, claims cannot be made for normal daily travel between home and the Institute. The available allowances are updated regularly to take into account increasing costs of petrol, wear-and-tear and so on. For purposes of administration, authorised car users are classed as either 'casual users' or 'essential users'. The current rates, per mile, are given in the table below. The rate varies according to the number of miles travelled annually, with essential users also able to claim an additional lump sum:

**Casual user allowances**

| Miles per annum | Engine size (cc) | | | |
|---|---|---|---|---|
| | 451 – 999 | 1000 – 1199 | 1200 – 1450 | 1451 – 1750 |
| 0 – 1500 | 42.7p | 49.7p | 56.4p | 62.9p |
| 1501 – 5500 | 29.9p | 34.3p | 38.8p | 43.0p |
| 5501 – 11000 | 22.9p | 25.8p | 29.1p | 32.1p |
| > 11000 | 10.5p | 10.9p | 12.1p | 12.9p |

**Essential user allowances**

| Lump sum allowance | Engine size (cc) | | | |
|---|---|---|---|---|
| | 451 – 999 | 1000 – 1199 | 1200 – 1450 | 1451 – 1750 |
| | £600 | £690 | £810 | £900 |
| 0 – 11000 miles | 22.9p | 25.8p | 29.1p | 32.1p |
| > 11000 miles | 10.5p | 10.9p | 12.1p | 12.9p |

## ■ Tasks

1. Consider those casual users who have 1300cc cars.

   Using the information given, complete this table of values and construct a graph which shows the total allowance payable ($t$) as a function of the annual mileage ($m$):

| $m$ ('000 miles) | 0 | 2 | 4 | 6 | 8 | 10 | 12 | 14 | 16 |
|---|---|---|---|---|---|---|---|---|---|
| $t$ (£) | | 1040 | | | 3125.50 | | | | |

   Also, take into account critical 'changeover' values e.g. 1500 miles).

2. a) Use the graph to estimate the amount of travel expenses that can be claimed for:

   i) 800 miles    ii) 3210 miles    iii) 7654 miles    iv) 12452 miles

   b) Check the accuracy of your estimates by calculation and calculate the relative error in each case.

See Section 2: The Information Bank – *Functions and Graphs* pages 105–107; 113
                                – *Numerical Methods* pages 136–137

☐ **Extended tasks**

3. a) Construct a spreadsheet model(s) which calculates travel expenses for the different type of users. The sophistication of the model will obviously depend on the facilities offered by the particular package, but the aim should be to produce a model which is as flexible as possible. That is, it should be possible to use the model to produce the travel expenses payable for any given user, car engine capacity and annual mileage.

   As an alternative, write a computer program to perform the same task.

   b) Validate your model with the results of Task 2.

4. Does an 'essential user' always get a larger annual travelling allowance than a 'casual user' with the same annual mileage?

   This problem could be tackled, for instance:

   i) by superimposing appropriate graphs on the same axes, or

   ii) using the spreadsheet of Task 3

See Section 3: Further Tasks and Investigations page 325 *Q 3*; page 328 *Q 7 and 8*

# Unit 6: Leaflets

*Topic: Graphs and functions*

*Construction; interpretation; linear functions*

A merger has been proposed between Dale Institute and a college of higher education. A prominent county councillor has been invited to speak to the students' union on the future development of the Institute if the merger goes ahead. Students' union events of this nature are not usually well attended, so the union's executive committee decide to look into the cost of printing leaflets to advertise the event. These would be distributed to students and around the Institute. After some discussion and information gathering, there seem to be two options:

☐ *Option 1* is to photocopy the leaflets using Dale's in-house photocopying facilities. This is available to students at a cost of 5p per A4 sheet.

☐ *Option 2* is to contract out the printing to a local printers. Their charge consists of £20 for making the plate from which the copies are made, plus an additional 0.5p per copy.

### ■ Tasks

1. Construct a mathematical model which gives the cost of printing (£c) as a function of the number of copies printed (n), for Option 1.

2. Construct a similar model for Option 2.

3. a. Construct a table of values for each of the options (0 ≤ n ≤ 500)

   b. On the same pair of axes draw two graphs, one for each option.

4. What do the graphs tell you about the relative merits of each printing option?

 See Section 2: The Information Bank – *Functions and Graphs* pages 105–107; 112–117

### ☐ Extended task

5. Construct a spreadsheet model and use it to investigate how the relative merits of the two options would be affected by changes in the various costs.

   Try to summarise your results.

 See Section 3: Further Tasks and Investigations pages 329–330 *Q 9–11*

## Unit 7: Pot-pourri (1)

*Topic: Graphs and functions*

*Construction; interpretation; linear and quadratic functions*

Several students form a small cooperative venture in order to raise money for a children's charity. After some initial research and discussion they decide to package and sell pot-pourri. One of the students makes contact with a local supplier who is willing to provide them with the raw materials free of charge. In return they will acknowledge the supplier's help on their packaging. Each student has been allocated a specific responsibility within the cooperative, for example: marketing, distribution, accounts etc. but each person will contribute to the work of packaging the goods.

After a series of meetings to discuss strategy, the students are convinced that the selling price will be the strongest influence on the number sold. Some of them are unhappy about wasting time producing quantities of packaged pot-pourri which may remain unsold if the selling price is fixed at a price which is too high. The marketing director therefore agrees to carry out a sample survey within the Institute in order to ascertain likely sales. Within a week she has carried out the survey and analysed the results. The following information is produced at the next meeting:

| Selling price per packet (pence) | Estimated sales (no. of packets) |
|---|---|
| 40 | 530 |
| 90 | 130 |

The marketing director also produces the following graphical model of the results:

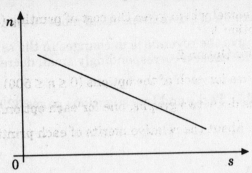

s represents the selling price of a packet, in pence;

n represents the estimated number of packets likely to be sold.

After some argument about the reliability of the survey, it was decided to determine the best selling price from this information and proceed with the next stage of the project.

## ■ Tasks

1. What does the result of the marketing director's analysis tell you about the relationship between the selling price and likely sales?

2. The marketing director believes that the relationship between the number of packets sold ($n$) and the selling price ($s$) is given by the mathematical model:

$$n = 850 - 8s$$

Complete the following table of values for the model, and draw an accurate graph.

| s (pence) | 0 | 10 | 20 | 30 | 40 | 50 | 60 | 70 | 80 | 90 | 100 | 110 |
|---|---|---|---|---|---|---|---|---|---|---|---|---|
| n | | | | | 530 | | | | | 130 | | |

3. Use your graphical model to answer these questions:

   a) What are the likely sales when the selling price is 66p?

   b) What selling price is likely to result in 250 being sold?

   c) When $s = 110$, $n = -30$. What does this mean?

   d) When $s = 0$, $n = 850$. What does this mean?

   e) Do the answers to (c) and (d) suggest anything about the limitations of the model?

 See Section 2: The Information Bank – *Functions and Graphs* pages 105–107; 112–117

4. a) Formulate a mathematical model which gives the relationship between the revenue ($r$) and the selling price ($s$). ('Revenue' is the amount of money received from sales).

   b) Construct a suitable table of values, draw a graph and use it to estimate the selling price which maximises the revenue.

 See Section 2: The Information Bank – *Functions and Graphs* pages 117–122

## Extended task

5. Construct a spreadsheet version of the mathematical model formulated in Task 4.

   Use it to find out how sensitive the revenue is to changes in the selling price. For instance, does a small increase in selling price cause a correspondingly small decrease in revenue?

See Section 3: Further Tasks and Investigations pages 329–333 *Q 9–16*

# Unit 8: Pot-pourri (2)

*Topic: Graphs and functions*

*Modelling; quadratic and cubic functions*

The packaging for the pot-pourri (see Unit 7 – 'Pot-pourri') is to be in the shape of an open rectangular box. This will be filled with pot-pourri and covered with clear plastic film. Each box is to be made from an A4 piece of card (measuring approximately 30 cm by 20 cm) by cutting a small square from each corner and then folding up the edges, as shown in this diagram:

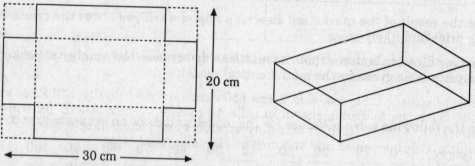

## ■ Tasks

1. a) Formulate a mathematical model which gives the volume of the box ($V$ cm³) as a function of the size of the square cut-out ($s$ cm).

   b) What assumptions are there in your model?

   c) Draw a graph of your model showing the relationship between $s$ and $V$, for $0 \leq s \leq 10$.

   d) Use the graph to estimate the maximum volume of pot-pourri that the box can hold.

   e) Estimate from the graph the size of the square cut-out which gives this maximum volume.

2. The clear plastic film is to cover the top and sides of the box.

   a) Formulate a mathematical model for the area of plastic film needed ($A$ cm²) as a function of the size of the square cut-out ($s$ cm). Again, state any assumptions present in your model.

   b) Use the model to calculate the area of plastic film needed for the box with the maximum volume

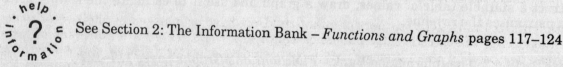

See Section 2: The Information Bank – *Functions and Graphs* pages 117–124

3. The size of A4 is more accurately given as 29.6 cm by 20.8 cm. How much of an error is there in the original solutions to Task 1 and Task 2?

See Section 2: The Information Bank – *Numerical methods* pages 135–139

☐ **Extended task**

4. Develop a spreadsheet model which can be used to calculate the size of the cut-out in Task 1(e). One possible layout is given below with most of the data and formula not shown.

|   | A | B | C | D | E | F | G |
|---|---|---|---|---|---|---|---|
| 1 | | | 'Maximum | volume | spreadsheet' | | |
| 2 | | | | Increment = | 1 | | |
| 3 | Cutout (cm) | | Length (cm) | Width (cm) | Height (cm) | | Volume (cm$^3$) |
| 4 | 0 | | ... | ... | ... | | ... |
| 5 | *a4+E2* | | ... | ... | ... | | ... |
| 6 | *a5+E2* | | ... | ... | ... | | ... |
| .. | ... | | ... | ... | ... | | ... |
| 14 | *a13+E2* | | ... | ... | ... | | ... |

Formulas are shown in italics. Upper case letters denote absolute cell references; lower case letters denote relative cell references.

An important feature of this model is the use of an increment. Initially, cell E2 is set to 1 and cell A4 set to 0. With the formulas shown in cells A5 to A14, column A will generate cut-out sizes with values: 0, 1, 2, 3, ... 10. If appropriate formulas are placed in columns C, D, E and G, the corresponding box dimensions and volumes will be calculated. Now:

i) scan column G for the maximum volume; for example, suppose this is in row 6.

ii) look at column A, row 6, for the corresponding cut-out size; in this case it would be 2.

iii) this means that the required cut-out size is between 1cm and 3cm; so, change the contents of cell A4 to 1 and the contents of cell to E2 to 0.2. The spreadsheet will now be updated to show volumes corresponding to cut-out sizes with values: 1, 1.2, 1.4, 1.6 ... 3.

iv) repeat steps similar to (i), (ii) and (iii), adjusting the values in cells A4 and E2 each time until the desired level of accuracy is achieved.

See Section 3: Further Tasks and Investigations pages 331–333 *Q 12–16*

# Unit 9: Reading difficulty

*Topic: Graphs and functions*

*Modelling; linear and non-linear functions*

A group of students, training to be teachers of infant children, have been asked by their tutor to determine the readability of some recently published children's books. There are hundreds of tests which have been designed for this purpose. They have been developed for different styles of writing and different age-groups. They are all aimed, however, at producing a figure which represents the difficulty level of the text. So, for instance, a book with a readability level of 12 is more difficult to read than one with a readability level of 8. The method of calculation varies, but is usually based on a sample passage of text selected from the book; it then involves counting the occurrence of such variables as: number of words per sentence, number of polysyllabic words (words with more than three syllables), proportion of 'familiar' and 'unfamiliar' words, and so on. After some research and consideration, one group of students decide to use one of the easier formulas to administer: Sticht's FORCAST formula. This measure of readability is given by the mathematical model:

$$R = 25 - \frac{n}{10}$$

where:   i)   $R$ is the readability level

ii)   $n$ is the number of one-syllable words in a passage of 150 words.

## ■ Tasks

1.  a)   Select a sample of text from a children's book and obtain a value for $n$. Use it to calculate a value of $R$ for the chosen sample.

b)   Use the same method to obtain a value of $R$ for *this* book.

c)   What conclusions can you draw from the results obtained in (a) and (b) ?

d)   Sketch a graph which shows $R$ as a function of $n$.

2.  Another group of students decide to use McLaughlin's SMOG formula. (SMOG is an acronym for 'Simple Measure Of Gobbledegook'). This is given by the mathematical model:

$$R = 8 + \sqrt{p}$$

where:   i)   $R$ is the readability level

ii)   $p$ is the number of polysyllabic words in 30 sentences of text

a)   Calculate SMOG readability levels for the same books as in Task 1.

b)   Do there seem to be any similarities between the two sets of results?

c)   Construct a graph which shows $R$ as a function of $p$.

 See Section 2: The Information Bank – *Functions and graphs* pages 114–117

## □ Extended Tasks

3.  A measure of readability level, which is more complex to calculate, is Gunning's FOG formula. (FOG is an acronym for 'Frequency Of Gobbledegook'). This is given by the mathematical model:

$$R = 0.4\left(\frac{w}{s} + \frac{100p}{w}\right) + 5$$

where:   i)   $R$ is the readability level

ii)   $s$ is the number of sentences in the selected sample passage

iii)   $w$ is the number of words in the selected sample passage

iv)   $p$ is the number of polysyllabic words

a)   Calculate FOG readability levels for the books in Task 1, compare them with the previous results and note any similarities.

b) Prepare a spreadsheet which models the FOG formula and use it to compare a variety of texts (different subject areas, different levels etc) in your institution's library.

4. Try to develop your own simple mathematical model for calculating readability and validate it using a suitable method.

 See Section 3: Further Tasks and Investigations page 334–335 *Q 17–20*; page 336 *Q 23*

# Unit 10: Minibus
## *Topic: Graphs and Functions*

### *Non-linear functions*

The Institute has a small fleet of three 15-seater minibuses which are used by staff and students for visits to other educational institutions, fieldwork, trips to outward bound centres, occasional inter-campus travel, and so on. The amount of useage by the different campuses varies, so the mileage covered by each minibus is not uniform. The finance department is keen to economise and asks members of staff in the Department of Mathematics and Technology to investigate the running costs for each minibus and to suggest a method of minimising them. It soon becomes clear that some of the costs are mileage dependent, (fuel, servicing and part of the depreciation), and some are independent of the mileage (road tax, insurance and the remainder of the depreciation). However, since the mileage is the major influence on running costs, the staff decide that the sensible approach is to concentrate on minimising the cost per mile. After some research and collection of information the following mathematical model is developed. The running cost per mile ($c$, measured in pence) is represented as a function of the annual mileage ($m$, measured in '000 miles):

$$c = \frac{250}{m} + \frac{m^2}{5} + 12.5$$

### ■ Tasks

1. Complete this table of values and construct a graph which shows cost / mile as a function of the mileage:

| m ('000 miles) | 0 | 1 | 2 | 3 | 4 | 5 | 6 | 7 | 8 | 9 | 10 | 11 | 12 |
|---|---|---|---|---|---|---|---|---|---|---|---|---|---|
| c (pence / mile) | | | | | | 67.5 | | | | | 57.5 | | |

2. Use the graph to estimate the annual mileage which minimises the running cost per mile.

3. What would be your recommendation?

 See Section 2: The Information Bank – *Functions and graphs* pages 105–107; 112–129

### ☐ Extended Task

4. a) Develop a spreadsheet which models this situation.

   b) Use your spreadsheet to:

   i) find an accurate solution to Task 2 (using a method similar to that outlined in Unit 8, Task 4)

   ii) investigate the sensitivity of the cost per mile to changes in the annual mileage.

See Section 3: Further Tasks and Investigations pages 334–335 *Q 17–20*; page 333 *Q 23*

# Unit 11: Bounciness

**Topic: Graphs and Functions**

*Modelling; exponential functions*

A group of Sports Science students are investigating the bounciness of the different types of balls used in various sports. A test rig, incorporating video units, is set up in the Harper campus sports hall to measure the rebound quality of the balls. In one experiment, a tennis ball is dropped from a height of 10m and its bounces recorded. Freeze-frame examination shows the tennis ball to have a bounciness of 0.56 since each bounce is about 56% as high as the previous one. The height of each bounce is a function of the bounce number.

■ **Tasks**

1. a) Complete the following table for the tennis ball experiment:

| Bounce number ($n$) | 0 | 1 | 2 | 3 | 4 | 5 | 6 | 7 | 8 |
|---|---|---|---|---|---|---|---|---|---|
| Height of bounce in metres ($h$) | 10 | 5.6 | | | | | | | |

b) Draw a graph showing the relationship between $n$ and $h$.

c) Use the graph to predict what the rebound height will be on the 10th bounce.

d) i) Formulate a mathematical model which represents $h$ as a function of $n$, for the tennis ball.

ii) Use the model to predict the height on the 10th bounce.

iii) How many bounces before the rebound height is less than 1 cm?

2. a) Refine your model to give $h$ as a function of $n$ for a ball with a bounciness of $b$, where $0 < b < 1$.

b) Use your refined model to test the validity of the following statement:

' A ball with a bounciness of 0.8 takes twice as many bounces as a ball with a bounciness of 0.4 to rebound less than 1cm.'

c) Tennis balls are supposed to have a bounciness of between 0.53 and 0.58. How would variations in the bounciness in this range affect the answer to Task 1(d) (iii)?

 See Section 2: The Information Bank – *Functions and graphs* pages 105–107; 128–129

☐ **Extended Task**

3. a) The students discover from a textbook that the time taken for a ball to stop bouncing is given by the mathematical model:

$$T = \sqrt{\frac{2h}{981}} \frac{(1+\sqrt{b})}{(1-\sqrt{b})}$$

where $T$ is the total bouncing time (in seconds), h is the original height (in centimetres) and b is the bounciness ($0 < b < 1$). How long is it before the tennis ball stops bouncing?

b) Some of the students are experimenting with a variety of synthetic materials to try and improve their bounciness for use in a range of sports. This research project is being sponsored by a local sports equipment manufacturer who is interested in the marketing potential. Increasing the rebound quality of the material increases the total bouncing time (*and the more exciting it becomes for spectators);* however, such improvements also affects production costs. The manufacturer, therefore, wants an analysis undertaken to assess the effect of increases in bounciness on total bouncing time. Construct an appropriate spreadsheet model, carry out the analysis and try to summarise your findings.

 See Section 3: Further Tasks and Investigations pages 336 *Q 21, 22*

# Unit 12: Calculating $\pi$

*Topic: Numerical Methods*

*Approximation; errors*

The irrational number $\pi$ is approximately 3.14159 (5D). One method of calculating its value is to use a series such as:

$$\frac{\pi}{4} = 1 - \frac{1}{3} + \frac{1}{5} - \frac{1}{7} + \frac{1}{9} - \frac{1}{11} + \frac{1}{13} - \ldots\ldots$$

The accuracy of the calculation depends on how many terms of the series are added together; that is:

| | | |
|---|---|---|
| One term: | $\frac{\pi}{4} \approx 1$ | $\Rightarrow \pi \approx 4 \times 1 \approx 4$ |
| Two terms: | $\frac{\pi}{4} \approx 1 - \frac{1}{3}$ | $\Rightarrow \pi \approx 4 \times 0.67 \approx 2.7(1D)$ |
| Three terms: | $\frac{\pi}{4} \approx 1 - \frac{1}{3} + \frac{1}{5}$ | $\Rightarrow \pi \approx 4 \times 0.87 \approx 3.5(1D)$ |
| Four terms: | $\frac{\pi}{4} \approx 1 - \frac{1}{3} + \frac{1}{5} - \frac{1}{7}$ | $\Rightarrow \pi \approx 4 \times 0.72 \approx 2.9(1D)$ |

and so on.

Note:

i) The more terms used in the calculation, the closer the answer becomes to the true value of $\pi$.

ii) In this particular case, successive answers *oscillate* about the value of $\pi$; that is, the calculated values are alternately above and below the true value i.e. 4, 2.7, 3.5, 2.9 . . . .

Calculating the value of $\pi$, using various series similar to the one above is a common programming exercise used on various computing courses at Dale Institute. This particular exercise is designed to:

i) introduce students to the idea of a 'loop'

ii) identify various methods of controlling loops

iii) encourage efficiency in programming techniques

iv) highlight the need for care when dealing with errors in calculations

The number of terms needed to approximate the value of p is also dependent on the particular method; some series converge to the correct solution quicker than others. The students are asked to compare different series for their speed of convergence; that is, the number of terms needed before a specified level of accuracy is achieved.

## ■ Tasks

1. Use a calculator, with the different series below, to work out the value of π obtained when 5 terms are used. In each case:

   i)   round the answer to a sensible number of decimal places

   ii)  calculate the absolute and relative errors in the value

   a)  $\dfrac{\pi}{2} = \dfrac{2}{1} \times \dfrac{2}{3} \times \dfrac{4}{3} \times \dfrac{4}{5} \times \dfrac{6}{5} \times \dfrac{6}{7} \times \dfrac{8}{7} \times \dfrac{8}{9} \times \cdots$

   b)  $\dfrac{\pi}{8} = \dfrac{1}{2^2 - 1} + \dfrac{1}{6^2 - 1} - \dfrac{1}{10^2 - 1} + \dfrac{1}{14^2 - 1} - \dfrac{1}{18^2 - 1} + \cdots$

   c)  $\dfrac{\pi^2}{6} = \dfrac{1}{1^2} + \dfrac{1}{2^2} + \dfrac{1}{3^2} + \dfrac{1}{4^2} + \dfrac{1}{5^2} + \cdots$

   d)  $\dfrac{\pi^2}{8} = \dfrac{1}{1^2} + \dfrac{1}{3^2} + \dfrac{1}{5^2} + \dfrac{1}{7^2} + \dfrac{1}{9^2} + \cdots$

   e)  $\pi = 3 + \dfrac{4}{3^3 - 3} - \dfrac{4}{5^3 - 5} + \dfrac{4}{7^3 - 7} - \dfrac{4}{9^3 - 9} + \cdots$

**help ? information** See Section 2: The Information Bank – *Numerical methods* pages 134–137

## □ Extended Tasks

2. Write computer programs and use them to compare the different series by finding out in each case:

   i)   the value obtained by taking 100 terms of the series

   ii)  the number of terms needed before 2D accuracy is achieved

   The programs could have either of the following general structures:

   (1)  Initialise total = 0
   ┌→ FOR term = 1 TO 100
   │     Calculate term
   │     Add to total
   └─ NEXT term
        Calculate value of p

   (2)  Initialise total = 0
   ┌→ WHILE term < 0.001
   │     Calculate term
   │     Add to total
   └─ ENDWHILE
        Calculate value of p

3. If you are familiar with recursion, repeat Task 2 for this series:

$$\pi = \cfrac{4}{1 + \cfrac{1^2}{2 + \cfrac{3^2}{2 + \cfrac{5^2}{2 + \cfrac{7^2}{2 + \cdots \text{etc}}}}}}$$

See Section 3: Further Tasks and Investigations pages 337–338 *Q 1–3*

# Unit 13: Calculating Device

*Topic: Numerical Methods*

*Errors; error propagation*

As part of her assessed project work, an Electronic Engineering student constructs a working proto-type of a simple calculating device which stores numbers in floating-point binary form. Constraints on equipment and time mean that she has to limit the accuracy of the device by using only one byte to represent each number.

**Within each byte:**

i)   the first 4 bits are used to represent the mantissa ($m$)

ii)  the last 4 bits are used to represent the exponent ($p$)

So, a number $N$ is stored in the form:

$$N = m \times 2^p$$

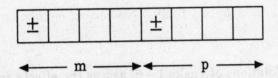

In each half, the first bit is used as a sign bit.

## ■ Tasks

1.  Draw diagrams which show how the following floating-point binary numbers would be represented in the device:

    a) 1.110   b) 0.0101  c) 11.011 d) 0.001101   e) −101.11

2.  Represent the following decimal numbers stored as floating-point binary numbers in the device:

    a) 0.25    b) 3.5 c) −0.625 d) 4.125 e) −1.375

3.  Calculate

    i)   the absolute error

    ii)  the relative error in the stored value of each of these numbers:

    a) 5.5 b) 8.5 c) 3.25   d) 9.125   e) −13.25

4.  Calculate the relative error in the results of these calculations as performed by the device:

    a) 2.5 + 5   b) 3.5 + 9.25   c) 7.5 + 0.25   d) 0.125 + 6.5 e) 2.5 − 0.25

5.  a) Calculate the values of the following, as performed by the device:

    i)   2.5 + 0.375 + 0.75

    ii)  0.375 + 0.75 + 2.5

    b)  Why does ii) give a more accurate answer?

6. The student is aware of the device's limited accuracy in representing single numbers. However, she wishes to assess how these inaccuracies affect the result of repetitive operations. To measure the effect, she programs the device to perform loops which are supposed to give an exact total of 6. The general structures of each of the loops are outlined below:

(1)    REP 6
       total = total + 1

(2)    REP 5
       total = total + 1.2

(3)    REP 12
       total = total + 0.5

(4)    REP 10
       total = total + 0.6

(5)    REP 48
       total = total + 0.125

REP $n$ means: 'Repeat the following instruction, $n$ times'.

The variable 'total' is initialised to zero prior to each program run.

Calculate:

a)  the total that each program actually produces

b)  the relative error, where appropriate

 See Section 2: The Information Bank – *Numerical methods* pages 139–143

□ **Extended task**

7.  By reconsidering the calculations of Tasks 1 – 6, assess the effects on accuracy of redesigning the device so that the value of $m$ is represented in 5 bits and the value of $p$ is represented in 3 bits

See Section 3: Further Tasks and Investigations pages 338–339 Q 4–7

# Unit 14: ComputaCare
**Topic: Numerical Methods**

*Numerical integration; errors*

The Institute is examining its current maintenance contracts with regard to its stock of microcomputers. The Computer Centre receives information from 'ComputaCare', a leading independent micro-based maintenance company which provides a wide-ranging service for different makes of micros. In its literature, ComputaCare offers a 9.00 a.m. – 5.30 p.m. service with an eight-hour maximum response time and bases the cost of maintenance on i) the type and ii) the age of the equipment. The annual charge for one particular type of microcomputer is calculated according to the following mathematical model :

$$C = 210t - 10t^2$$

where:  i)  $C$ is the annual cost, in £

ii)  $t$ is the age of the micro, in years

The useful life of a microcomputer at the Institute is four years.

■ **Tasks**

1.  a) Construct a table of values and draw a graph which shows $C$ as a function of $t$ ($0 \le t \le 4$).

    b) Calculate the total maintenance cost during a four-year period by using:

       i) the Trapezium Rule

       ii) Simpson's Rule

    c) Calculate

       i) the absolute error

       ii) the relative error in the answer given by the Trapezium Rule.

2.  Another maintenance company, MaintEase, uses the mathematical model:

$$C = 20 + 170t + t^2$$

Carry out similar procedures to those in Task 1 and find out whether MaintEase provides a cheaper service over a four-year period.

See Section 2: The Information Bank – *Numerical Methods*
pages 134 – 137; 145 – 148

☐ **Extended task**

3.  How would the solutions to Tasks 1 & 2 change if, because of the level of maintenance provided, the useful life of a microcomputer were eventually extended to six years ?

Assume that the models used by the maintenance companies are still appropriate for this period.

See Section 3: Further Tasks and Investigations
pages 339 – 341; Q8 – 11

# Unit 15: The Golden Ratio                    *Topic: Numerical Methods*

*Iteration; graphical representation*

As part of their course, students of mathematics look at its links with man-made and natural environments; this study encompasses areas such as music, genetics, nature, art and architecture. students usually encounter the *Golden Ratio* early on in the course since it features in areas as diverse as astronomy, biological growth and architectural design.

A line is said to be divided in Golden Ratio if the two pieces are such that:

$$\frac{\text{Smaller piece}}{\text{Larger piece}} = \frac{\text{Larger piece}}{\text{Whole line}}$$

A             C        B

$x$          1

So, in the diagram, point C will divide the line AB in Golden Ratio if:

$$\frac{CB}{AC} = \frac{AC}{AB}$$

If AC = $x$ and CB = 1:

$$\frac{1}{x} = \frac{x}{(1+x)}$$

which can be rewritten as:

$$(1+x) = x^2$$

This gives the equation:

$$x^2 - x - 1 = 0.$$

The positive root of this equation is the Golden Ratio; it is given the symbol $\phi$ (pronounced 'Phi'). The value of $\phi$ is a little more than 1.5.

The Golden Ratio is also important in the study of aesthetics. An example of this is the Golden Rectangle; this is a rectangle with a length and width which are in Golden Ratio. For instance, if the width is 1 unit, the length is $\phi$ units. Its proportions are supposed to make it the most pleasing rectangle to look at; that is, its length and width appear balanced.

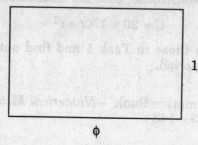

## ■ Tasks

1.  a)  Construct a table of values for the quadratic function: $y = x^2 - x - 1 \ (0 \le x \le 4)$.

    b)  Observe where the sign changes and confirm that the value of $\phi$ lies between 1 and 2.

2.  a)  Use the 'Decimal Search' technique to calculate $\phi$ correct to 3D.

    b)  Verify your solution to a) by using the 'Interval Bisection' technique.

> **?** help information
> See  Section 2: The Information Bank  – *Numerical methods*
> pages 148 – 150

3.  The equation $x^2 - x - 1 = 0$ can be rearranged to give the following iterative processes:

$$x_{n+1} = 1 + \frac{1}{x_n}; \qquad x_{n+1} = x_n^2 - 1$$

$$x_{n+1} = \sqrt{1 + x_n}; \qquad x_{n+1} = \frac{1}{x_n - 1}$$

For each process:

a)  Use an initial starting value of $x_0 = 1.5$ to calculate $\phi$, (if possible), correct to 3D.

b)  Draw a diagram which shows its convergence or divergence.

> **?** help information
> See  Section 2: The Information Bank  – *Numerical methods*
> pages 150 – 158

☐ **Extended Tasks**

4. a) Develop the Newton-Raphson process which can be used to solve the equation $x^2 - x - 1 = 0$.

   b) Use the process with an initial value of $x_0 = 1.5$ to calculate $\phi$ correct to 3D.

5. Develop spreadsheet models to implement the processes used in Tasks 3 & 4.

See Section 3: Further Tasks and Investigations pages 342–343 *Q 12–18*

# Unit 16: The Fish Pond (1)           *Topic: Numerical methods*

*Iteration; graphical representation*

At any given time, the Institute's Environmental Studies Unit has a variety of on-going experimental projects which are concerned with current environmental issues such as global warming, pollution, waste disposal, industrial development, wildlife conservation, rain forest destruction, consumerism and over-population.

A particular concern is in the area of population dynamics; that is, how populations fluctuate over a period of time. Some populations are subject to regular variations, others are not; for instance, the sudden growth in rabbit populations which can lay waste to farmland; unexpected plagues of locusts which can devastate crops; annual variations in the bacteria or viruses which cause epidemics.

One long-term project is attempting to gain some insight into this complex area by carrying out a detailed study of the population dynamics of a small fish-pond located in the grounds of the Brooklands campus; it is primarily concerned with how the population growth and decline of the fish is affected by available food and space. The project director is aware that the fish population could also be drastically affected by such things as temperature, humidity, acidity, predators etc. and has therefore set up a controlled environment which maintains these factors at a reasonably constant level. The information which has already been collected about the fish population suggests the following general cycle of behaviour:

1. fish numbers increase
2. available food and space diminishes
3. fish numbers decrease
4. more food and space becomes available
5. fish start to breed again

The population ($x$) at any given time can be represented by a fraction between 0 and 1. A value of $x = 0$ means that fish numbers have decreased to the point of extinction; a value of $x = 1$ means that fish numbers have reached saturation level. For example, $x = 0.8$ means that the fish population is 80% of that which the pond is capable of accommodating.

The population data already collected suggest the following iterative model of its behaviour:

$$x_{n+1} = rx_n(1 - x_n)$$

where: $n$ is the number of the year under consideration

   $x_n$ is the fish population in year $n$ (e.g. $x_6$ represents the population in year 6)

   $r$ is a growth rate (e.g. a value of $r = 3$ means that the population in any year is 3 times as big as the population in the previous year).

For instance, with a growth rate of 2.5 and an initial population of 0.05:

23

| $n$ | $x_n$ |
|---|---|
| 0 | 0.050 |
| 1 | $2.5 \times 0.050 \times (1 - 0.050) = 0.119$ |
| 2 | $2.5 \times 0.119 \times (1 - 0.119) = 0.262$ |
| 3 | $2.5 \times 0.262 \times (1 - 0.262) = 0.483$ |
| 4 | $2.5 \times 0.483 \times (1 - 0.483) = 0.624$ |
| 5 | $2.5 \times 0.624 \times (1 - 0.624) = 0.587$ |
| 6 | $2.5 \times 0.587 \times (1 - 0.587) = 0.606$ |
| 7 | $2.5 \times 0.606 \times (1 - 0.606) = 0.597$ |
| 8 | $2.5 \times 0.597 \times (1 - 0.597) = 0.601$ |
| 9 | $2.5 \times 0.601 \times (1 - 0.601) = 0.599$ |
| 10 | $2.5 \times 0.599 \times (1 - 0.599) = 0.600$ |
| 11 | $2.5 \times 0.600 \times (1 - 0.600) = 0.600$  etc ... |

In this case, the population fluctuates but eventually (after 10 years) reaches a 'steady state' of 0.600. That is, the fish population stabilises at 60% of the capacity of the pond:

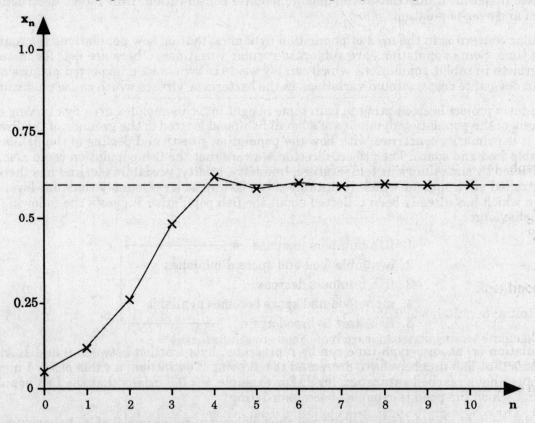

Notice that the population oscillates above and below its eventual steady state.

## ■ Tasks

1. If the initial population is 0.05:

   a)  Calculate what happens for each of these growth rates

      i)  $r = 0.5$   ii)  $r = 0.8$  iii)  $r = 1$   iv)  $r = 1.5$  v)  $r = 2$   vi)  $r = 2.6$  vii)  $r = 2.8$

   b)  Draw a graph of the population's behaviour in each case

2. Does the initial population affect what happens eventually ? e.g. try $x_0 = 0.3$

3. Try to summarise and interpret your findings.

4. Another way to show the behaviour of the population is a diagram of its iterative process. For instance, the iterative process for a growth rate of 2.5 is: $x_{n+1} = 2.5x_n(1 - x_n)$.

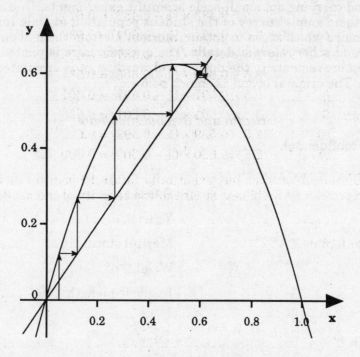

Draw graphs to show the iterative processes when    i) $r = 0.5$    ii) $r = 1.5$    iii) $r = 2.5$

  See Section 2: The Information Bank – *Numerical methods* pages 150–158

☐ **Extended task**

5. If the initial population is 0.05:

   a)  Calculate what happens for each of these growth factors:

       i) $r = 3$    ii) $r = 3.2$    iii) $r = 3.4$    iv) $r = 3.6$    v) $r = 3.8$    vi) $r = 4$

   b)  In each case:

       i)  Draw a graph to show the population's behaviour (as in Task 1)

       ii) Draw a graph to show the iterative process (as in Task 4)

   c)  How are these growth factors different from those of Task 1 in their effect on the population ?

  See Section 3: Further Tasks and Investigations pages 343–348 *Q 19–21*

# Unit 17: Health and diet questionnaire

**Topic: Statistics**

*Sampling; questionnaire design; data analysis and interpretation*

Students working towards a certificate in Food Science are required to write a report on a detailed study of the relationship between health and diet. Much of this work is concerned with studying available literature and carrying out small-scale scientific experiments. One student decides to supplement his report with a sample survey of the student population at Dale Institute. As a first step, he designs a questionnaire which seeks to obtain information from them about their general state of health, eating habits and other relevant details. The questionnaire is piloted with a small group of students, then, after improvements to the design and wording, it is circulated to a larger sample of one hundred students. The original layout is shown below:

---

*Health and diet questionnaire*

This survey is confidential.

Name: . . . . . . . . . . . . . . . . . . . . . . . .

Age: . . . . . . . . . .   D.O.B.: . . . . . . . . . .

Course: . . . . . . . . . . . . . . . . . . . . . .  Year: . . . . . . . . . .

Are you male or female ? . . . . . . . . . . .  Marital status: . . . . . . . . . . . . .

Height: . . . . . . . . . . . . .  Weight: . . . . . . . . . . . .

Arm length: . . . . . . . . . . . . .  Inside leg length: . . . . . . . . . . . . .

Do you smoke ? . . . . . . . . . . . . .

If so, how much ? . . . . . . . . . . . . . . . . . . . . . . . . . . . . . . . . . . . . . . . . . . . . . . . . . . . . . .

Do you play much sport or not ? . . . . . . . . . . . . .

If so, which? . . . . . . . . . . . . . . . . . . . . . . . . . . . . . . . . . . . . . . . . . . . . . . . . . . . . . . . . . . .

How long do you exercise for? (please tick):  Less than 1 hour . . . . . . . .

               1 – 2 hrs . . . . . . . .

               2 – 3 hrs . . . . . . . .

               3 – 4 hrs . . . . . . . .

               4 – 5 hrs . . . . . . . .

               over 5 hrs . . . . . . . .

How healthy are you? . . . . . . . . . . . . . . . . . . . . . . . . . . . . . . . . . . . . . . . . . . . . . . . . . . . . .

Typical day's intake of food, including breakfast, lunch, dinner and snacks:

1. Tea . . . .  2. Coffee . . . .  3. Cereal . . . .  4. Beans . . . .  5. Spaghetti . . . .

6. Soup . . . .  7. Pie . . . .  8. Bread . . . .  9. Rice . . . .  10. Chicken . . . .

11. Beef . . . .  12. Lamb . . . .  13. Fish . . . .  14. Pork . . . .  15. Chips . . . .

16. Carrots . . . .  17. Peas . . . .  18. Crisps . . . .  19. Cake . . . .  20. Yoghurt . . . .

21. Fruit . . . .  22. Other . . . .

---

## ■ Task

1. a) Comment on the wording/layout of the questionnaire and suggest improvements .

 b) Describe a sampling method that would be suitable for the student to use in choosing his sample of 100. (Dale Institute caters for approximately 10000 full-time and part-time students).

 c) List the likely practical difficulties of implementing the survey and make suggestions as to how they might be overcome.

2. Sixty questionnaires are returned; some of the data is summarised below:

| Student number | Sex | Year group | Ht. (m) | Wt. (kg) | Student number | Sex | Year group | Ht. (m) | Wt. (kg) |
|---|---|---|---|---|---|---|---|---|---|
| 1 | F | 1 | 1.58 | 54 | 31 | F | 1 | 1.74 | 54 |
| 2 | M | 3 | 1.83 | 86 | 32 | F | 1 | 1.55 | 47 |
| 3 | F | 1 | 1.58 | 54 | 33 | F | 3 | 1.70 | 60 |
| 4 | F | 4 | 1.60 | 62 | 34 | M | 1 | 1.74 | 74 |
| 5 | F | 1 | 1.64 | 53 | 35 | F | 1 | 1.60 | 65 |
| 6 | F | 1 | 1.50 | 48 | 36 | F | 2 | 1.67 | 60 |
| 7 | M | 1 | 1.79 | 98 | 37 | F | 4 | 1.70 | 64 |
| 8 | F | 1 | 1.57 | 51 | 38 | M | 1 | 1.78 | 76 |
| 9 | F | 1 | 1.60 | 66 | 39 | F | 1 | 1.71 | 67 |
| 10 | F | 1 | 1.64 | 57 | 40 | F | 4 | 1.67 | 76 |
| 11 | M | 1 | 1.80 | 80 | 41 | F | 1 | 1.74 | 75 |
| 12 | F | 1 | 1.67 | 58 | 42 | M | 1 | 1.75 | 70 |
| 13 | F | 4 | 1.70 | 59 | 43 | M | 1 | 1.80 | 70 |
| 14 | F | 1 | 1.69 | 57 | 44 | M | 1 | 1.74 | 69 |
| 15 | F | 1 | 1.70 | 64 | 45 | F | 4 | 1.60 | 60 |
| 16 | F | 1 | 1.64 | 53 | 46 | F | 2 | 1.68 | 60 |
| 17 | F | 1 | 1.71 | 65 | 47 | M | 1 | 1.78 | 76 |
| 18 | F | 1 | 1.50 | 63 | 48 | F | 1 | 1.65 | 63 |
| 19 | F | 1 | 1.62 | 59 | 49 | F | 2 | 1.57 | 53 |
| 20 | M | 1 | 1.78 | 62 | 50 | F | 2 | 1.73 | 49 |
| 21 | F | 2 | 1.65 | 58 | 51 | M | 2 | 1.70 | 72 |
| 22 | F | 4 | 1.60 | 60 | 52 | F | 2 | 1.62 | 53 |
| 23 | F | 1 | 1.53 | 54 | 53 | F | 2 | 1.65 | 53 |
| 24 | F | 2 | 1.86 | 87 | 54 | F | 2 | 1.65 | 63 |
| 25 | F | 1 | 1.65 | 65 | 55 | M | 2 | 1.85 | 81 |
| 26 | F | 1 | 1.59 | 49 | 56 | M | 2 | 1.85 | 72 |
| 27 | F | 1 | 1.66 | 57 | 57 | M | 2 | 1.73 | 78 |
| 28 | F | 1 | 1.76 | 65 | 58 | M | 2 | 1.75 | 76 |
| 29 | F | 1 | 1.61 | 50 | 59 | F | 2 | 1.60 | 52 |
| 30 | F | 1 | 1.51 | 50 | 60 | F | 2 | 1.58 | 51 |

The student wishes to know the group's mean weight but is put off by the amount of calculation involved. So, he decides to select a sample of 10 and use their mean weight as an approximation.

a) Select 10 students from the list by using:

 i) random sampling

 ii) systematic sampling

 iii) stratified sampling

b) Calculate the mean weight in each case.

c) i) Compare your answers in b) to the actual mean weight of the whole group

   ii) Comment on the accuracy of each sample.

 See Section 2: The Information Bank – *Statistics* pages 160–167; 184–185

 See Section 3: Further Tasks and Investigations pages 349–351 *Q 1–7*

# Unit 18: Cars                                           *Topic: Statistics*

*Sampling; frequency; distributions; data display; analysis and interpretation*

As part of an 'Introductory Statistics' course, students are required to identify a topic of interest to them and undertake a sample survey. One particular group showed an interest in comparing the ages of cars belonging to staff and students. At the Harper campus, staff and students park their vehicles in a single shared car park; however, it is a fairly straightforward matter to distinguish between them. Anyone intending to use the Institute's car park is required to notify administrative staff at the beginning of the academic year. They are then issued with a windscreen ticket (green for students, blue for staff) which must be displayed when parking on institute property. There are almost twice as many green tickets as blue tickets issued. The group decide to select a stratified sample and carry out the survey at 11 a.m. on a Thursday morning; they note the colour of each ticket and the vehicle's year of registration. The results of the survey are shown below:

*Green*

| C | E | # | # | Y | F | F | C | A | # |
|---|---|---|---|---|---|---|---|---|---|
| E | Y | # | E | C | A | E | Y | F | A |
| C | X | E | C | F | F | D | # | # | F |
| # | E | # | Y | # | H | D | A | X | J |
| D | E | C | # | Y | Y | A | F | H | C |
| Y | A | G | D | D | # | F | A | G | E |
| A | Y | B | # | J | E | B | H | A | D |
| H | A | E | F | G | D | E | D | F | A |
| # | # | Y | X | C | X | G | X | # | F |
| D | E | # | # | # | X | D | D | # | # |

*Blue*

| J | G | F | A | F | E | F | H | J | C |
|---|---|---|---|---|---|---|---|---|---|
| F | F | F | H | F | E | # | F | # | E |
| H | B | H | # | C | G | # | E | D | B |
| F | X | # | H | H | G | H | D | H | X |
| # | Y | J | C | Y | E | E | E | Y | E |

Note:  a) X ≡ 1981, Y ≡ 1982, A ≡ 1983 etc.

b) # ≡ prior to X (assume 1980)

**■ Tasks**

1. Comment on the suitability of the sampling method.

2. a) Construct a frequency distribution of registration letters for each group of users.

   b) Display the two distributions as:

      i)  percentage bar charts

      ii) comparative pie charts

3. a) For each group of users, calculate:

      i)  the mean age in years

      ii) the standard deviation of the ages

   b) By comparing the graphs and calculated figures, try to describe any differences between them.

 See Section 2: The Information Bank – *Descriptive Statistics* pages 170–187; 193–202

 See Section 3: Further Tasks and Investigations pages 351–358 *Q 8–12*

# Unit 19: Salary negotiations　　　　*Topic: Statistics*

*Measures of central tendency; measures of dispersion*

The governors of Dale Institute are negotiating with teaching unions concerning a forthcoming pay rise. Current annual salaries for teaching staff range from £13000 to £28000. The various members of the negotiating team want to determine the effect on salaries of different forms of a settlement. At present, they are considering the relative benefits of two alternative pay rise formulas:

   i)  a flat rise of £1100

   ii) a 6% rise

**■ Tasks**

Use this sample of staff salaries to check your ideas about the answers to the following questions:

   £18610　　£15940　　£13250　　£21980　　£15670　　£23540　　£18920　　£13630

1. If every member of staff is given a flat rise of £1100, calculate the effect on:

      i)   the mean salary

      ii)  the median salary

      iii) the quartiles

      iv)  the standard deviation

2.  If every member of staff is given a 6% rise, calculate the effect on:

    i)   the mean salary

    ii)  the median salary

    iii) the quartiles

    iv)  the standard deviation

3.  Considering your answers to Tasks 1 and 2:

    a)  Which is the best pay formula for those members of staff who have a salary which is near:

        i)   the lower end of the pay scale

        ii)  the centre of the pay scale

        iii) the upper end of the pay scale

    b)  Which pay formula is likely to be the cheaper option in terms of funding the pay rise ?

   See Section 2: The Information Bank – *Descriptive Statistics* pages 184–202

☐ **Extended Task**

4.  What would be the effect of combining a flat rise of £500 *and* a 5% increase on:

    i)   the mean salary

    ii)  the median salary

    iii) the quartiles

    iv)  the standard deviation ?

   See Section 3: Further Tasks and Investigations pages 353–361 *Q 13–27*

# Unit 20: Crossing                                        *Topic: Statistics*

*Data collection by observation; data display; analysis and interpretation*

The Brooklands campus is sited on Brooklands Avenue, a wide main road which runs in an approximately north – south direction. There are two schools (Lower School, 5-9 years; Middle School, 9-13 years) sited near the same road, on opposite sides. This involves children who attend these schools having to cross the road in both directions, invariably at peak traffic times. Currently, there is no 'lollipop' provision at the start or finish of the school day. Also, i) elderly residents living in sheltered housing units situated on the eastern side have to cross the road to visit shops on the western side ii) many Dale Institute students rent flats or houses in the extensive western housing area and so have to cross the road several times during the day. The road is a busy route for traffic at all times of day and concern has been mounting for some time about the safety of children, elderly people, students and other members of the public.

A group of students decide to prepare a case for the provision of a pedestrian crossing and present it to the local council, for consideration. However, they discover that the need for a crossing is governed by certain levels of traffic flow and pedestrian movement. So, it is necessary to undertake a formal statistical study of the situation in order to support their case. Initial investigation shows that the most suitable place for such a crossing is that shown by the line AB on the diagram below:

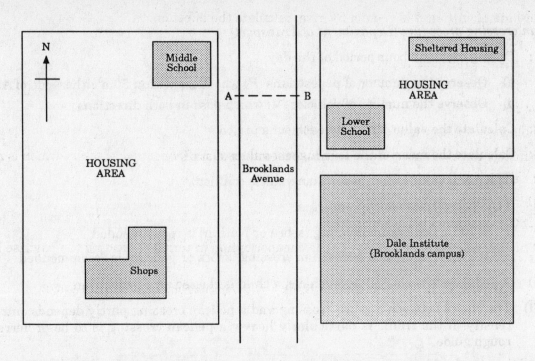

The group refer to Department of Transport guidelines for determining whether a pedestrian crossing is required. Briefly, the guidelines suggest that they should:

i)   observe traffic flow and pedestrian movement in the vicinity of the crossing site

ii)  use the collected data to calculate a value called the 'pedestrian-vehicle conflict'

The students organise themselves into teams, each team being responsible for a specified time period. They survey traffic and pedestrian movement during one Monday between 6 a.m. and 10 p.m. according to the DoT's procedure (see below); the recording is done on a specially designed data collection sheet. Later, the raw data are organised and transferred to a separate summary sheet; this is shown here, partly completed:

| Time period | Time of day | Pedestrians (P) | Vehicles (V) | Conflict ($PV^2$) |
|:-----------:|:-----------:|:---------------:|:------------:|:-----------------:|
| 1  | 0600 – 0700 | 130 | 380 | $0.19 \times 10^8$ |
| 2  | 0700 – 0800 | 252 | 504 | |
| 3  | 0800 – 0900 | 495 | 980 | |
| 4  | 0900 – 1000 | 281 | 962 | |
| 5  | 1000 – 1100 | 167 | 850 | $1.21 \times 10^8$ |
| 6  | 1100 – 1200 | 183 | 712 | |
| 7  | 1200 – 1300 | 391 | 820 | $2.63 \times 10^8$ |
| 8  | 1300 – 1400 | 328 | 806 | |
| 9  | 1400 – 1500 | 185 | 813 | |
| 10 | 1500 – 1600 | 290 | 809 | |
| 11 | 1600 – 1700 | 493 | 823 | $3.34 \times 10^8$ |
| 12 | 1700 – 1800 | 297 | 961 | |
| 13 | 1800 – 1900 | 181 | 843 | |
| 14 | 1900 – 2000 | 150 | 562 | $0.47 \times 10^8$ |
| 15 | 2000 – 2100 | 124 | 320 | |
| 16 | 2100 – 2200 | 50  | 116 | |

*Pedestrian crossing procedure (Department of Transport)*

Step 1: During each one-hour period of the day:

    a) Observe the number of pedestrians ($P$) who cross within 50m either side of $AB$

    b) Observe the number of vehicles ($V$) which pass in both directions

Step 2: Calculate the value of $PV^2$ for each time period

Step 3: Calculate the mean of the four highest values of $PV^2$

    (The mean value is the 'pedestrian-vehicle conflict').

Step 4: If the pedestrian-vehicle conflict is:

    i) $> 10^8$, a pedestrian crossing (zebra or pelican) is recommended

    ii) $> 2 \times 10^8$, a divided pedestrian crossing (zebra or pelican) is recommended

Notes: i) A pedal cycle is classed as a vehicle; a child is classed as a pedestrian

    ii) The choice between a zebra crossing and a pelican crossing partly depends ontraffic intensity. If the traffic is particularly heavy, a pelican crossing is to be preferred. As a rough guide:

| Conflict | Mean V | Crossing type |
|---|---|---|
| $> 10^8$ | $< 300$ | Zebra |
| $> 10^8$ | $> 300$ | Pelican |
| $> 2 \times 10^8$ | $< 700$ | Divided zebra |
| $> 2 \times 10^8$ | $> 700$ | Divided pelican |

## ■ Tasks

1. a) Comment on the reliability of the students' data and how it might be improved.

    b) i) Display the hourly pedestrian and vehicle data with the aid of a suitable graph.

       ii) Describe any interesting features of the graph.

    c) Calculate suitable summary figures (e.g. mean, S.D.) for the pedestrian and vehicle data.

    d) Complete the table of results, writing each value in the 'conflict' column in the form $N \times 10^8$, where $N$ is rounded to 2D; e.g. $130 \times 380^2 = 18772000 \approx 0.19 \times 10^8$.

    e) Carry out the remainder of the DoT procedure and verify that:

       i) the pedestrian-vehicle conflict has a value of $3.37 \times 10^8$

       ii) the type of crossing recommended is a 'divided pelican'

2. Identify a similar situation in your own area and undertake the same sort of study:

    a) Decide on the organisation and timing of the survey

    b) Design suitable sheets for the collection and summary of the data

    c) Carry out the DoT procedure to determine the type of crossing recommended

    d) Write a report which gives details of your methods, results and conclusions

See Section 2: The Information Bank
- *Statistics* pages 160 – 167
- *Descriptive Statistics* pages 173 – 202

☐ **Extended task**

3. It is possible to display the same information in graphical form. The following diagram shows:

   i) the graph of: $PV^2 = 2 \times 10^8$

   ii) a point representing the Brooklands Avenue situation (mean $P$, mean $V$)

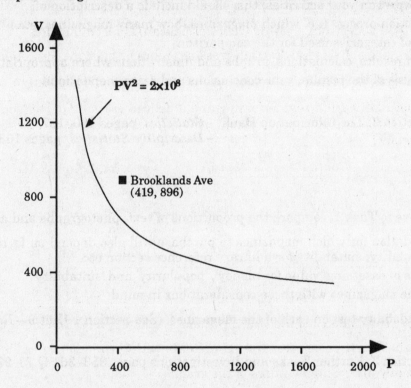

Construct an accurate graph and show on it a point representing your situation. (You may need to draw the graph of $PV^2 = 10^8$, depending on your values).

See Section 3: Further Tasks and Investigations
pages 353 – 361; Q 13 – 27

# Unit 21: Magazines                                    *Topic: Statistics*

*Data collection by experiment; data display; analysis and interpretation*

For some time, the Library and Resources Centre at Dale Institute has been considering extending its range of reference magazines. A recent small increase in its budget means that extra finance is now available to buy more monthly and quarterly magazines. Computing is one area that will benefit from this increased provision, but unfortunately the limited budget will not stretch to the purchase of every magazine currently on the market. An analysis and comparison of the various publications is necessary before recommendations can be made.

## ■ Tasks

1.  Choose a selection of computing magazines and compare the proportion of space allocated to different categories, for example:

    Regular items, such as:

    Editorial (News; Readers' letters; Technical queries; Personal ads)

    Features                    Hardware and software reviews

    Games                       Programming

    Education

    (This list is only a suggestion; you may wish to modify it).

2.  Write a short report on your activities; this should include a description of:
    - i)  the selection process (i.e. which magazines, how many magazines, etc.)
    - ii) the list of categories used for the comparison
    - iii) tables of results, calculations, graphs and illustrations where appropriate
    - iv) an analysis of the results, your conclusions and recommendations

 See Section 2: The Information Bank – *Statistics*  pages 160–167

– *Descriptive Statistics*  pages 168–201

## ☐ Extended task

3.  As an alternative to Task 1, compare the proportions of text, photographs and advertisements.

4.  The recommendation for which magazines to purchase will also depend on factors such as: value for money, popularity, suitability for a library reference section etc.
    - a)  Devise ways of assessing 'value for money', 'popularity' and 'suitability'.
    - b)  Compare the magazines with these considerations in mind.

5.  Carry out a readability test on each of the magazines. (See Section 1 Unit 9 – *Reading difficulty*.)

 See Section 3: Further Tasks and Investigations pages 353–361 *Q 13–27*

# Unit 22: I.T. experience

*Topic: Statistics*

*Data collection by questionnaire; data display and interpretation*

At the beginning of each academic year, a questionnaire is circulated to all new students on full-time and part-time courses based at the Brooklands campus. The purpose of the exercise is to determine the extent of the students' previous experience of information technology, and to monitor their progress during the year. So, the questionnaire is circulated to the same students at the end of the academic year to see what changes have taken place. The number surveyed in June is normally smaller than that in September due to student withdrawals, transfers to other institutions etc.

Some students are enrolled on computing degree courses; however, most are non-specialists who need basic I.T. skills to support their studies. For instance, a word processor or a DTP package is very important to all students in the preparation and presentation of coursework; books and magazine articles can be referenced with a database; interactive video can provide an alternative means of learning. The information collected, therefore, is vital in ensuring that all students continue to receive adequate support. A part of the current year's survey results is as follows:

| Time of Survey: September | | Number of Students: 220 | | | |
|---|---|---|---|---|---|
| Question 1: Have you heard of the following? | | | | | |
| Question 2: Do you know what they are used for? | | | | | |
| | Responses to Q1 | | | Responses to Q2 | |
| Word processor | Yes: 216 | No: 4 | Yes: 196 | No: 24 | |
| Database | Yes: 180 | No: 40 | Yes: 79 | No: 141 | |
| Spreadsheet | Yes: 96 | No: 124 | Yes: 55 | No: 165 | |
| Desk-top publishing | Yes: 98 | No: 122 | Yes: 43 | No: 177 | |
| Electronic mail | Yes: 71 | No: 149 | Yes: 48 | No: 172 | |
| Interactive video | Yes: 28 | No: 192 | Yes: 19 | No: 201 | |

| Time of Survey: June | | Number of Students: 203 | | | |
|---|---|---|---|---|---|
| Question 1: Have you heard of the following? | | | | | |
| Question 2: Do you know what they are used for? | | | | | |
| | Responses to Q1 | | | Responses to Q2 | |
| Word processor | Yes: 203 | No: 0 | Yes: 203 | No: 0 | |
| Database | Yes: 191 | No: 12 | Yes: 97 | No: 106 | |
| Spreadsheet | Yes: 128 | No: 75 | Yes: 87 | No: 116 | |
| Desk-top publishing | Yes: 133 | No: 70 | Yes: 83 | No: 120 | |
| Electronic mail | Yes: 95 | No: 108 | Yes: 71 | No: 132 | |
| Interactive video | Yes: 49 | No: 154 | Yes: 41 | No: 162 | |

## ■ Task

1.  a) Display the assembled data in the form of appropriate graphs.

    b) Describe any interesting features of the graphs.

See Section 2: The Information Bank
      – *Statistics* pages 160–167
      – *Descriptive Statistics* pages 173–181

## □ Extended Task

2.  A supplementary survey is to be organised in order to obtain more detailed information from the same students about any computing equipment that they have access to at home. The Institute is considering purchasing similar equipment so that students can do more follow-up work out of class contact time; this may possibly reduce the time needed to familiarise students with essential hardware and software.

    a) Devise a set of questions that could form the basis for a survey of the makes and uses of the personal computers and other hardware/software in students' homes. (You need to give some thought to what is meant by the term 'personal computer').

b) It is proposed to send a copy of your questionnaire to a sample of the students. Describe *three* possible ways of selecting the sample.

c) List the likely practical difficulties of implementing the survey and make suggestions as to how they might be overcome.

d) Pilot the questionnaire in your own institution and modify it in the light of experience.

e) Carry out the survey and write a report describing your methods, results and conclusions; the report should be illustrated with suitable graphs.

 See Section 3: Further Tasks and Investigations pages 353–361 *Q 13–27*

# Unit 23: Printers
*Topic: Statistics*

*Use of secondary data; data display; analysis and interpretation*

A catalogue of computer equipment, at educational discount prices, is circulated direct to students by a mail order company. A special financial package is available, arranged through the Students' Union, for students who wish to purchase equipment. Repayments start when the student's course of study has been completed. One section of the catalogue gives specifications for a number of dot-matrix printers as shown in the table below. The president of the Students' Union considers that this section of the catalogue, with the information presented in this form, is too baffling for the great majority of students. As someone who is considered knowledgeable in these matters, you have been asked to write a short supplementary report that summarises and illustrates the data.

| Manufacturer | Number of pins | Draft speed | NLQ speed | Buffer size | Number of fonts | Price (£) |
|---|---|---|---|---|---|---|
| Seikosha | 9 | 200 | 40 | 21K | 2 | 170 |
| Seikosha | 9 | 300 | 50 | 10K | 2 | 365 |
| Citizen | 9 | 120 | 25 | 4K | 2 | 130 |
| Citizen | 9 | 160 | 40 | 8K | 4 | 220 |
| Star | 9 | 44 | 36 | 4K | 8 | 160 |
| Star | 9 | 180 | 45 | 16K | 4 | 225 |
| Epson | 9 | 200 | 30 | 4K | 2 | 255 |
| Epson | 9 | 265 | 55 | 4K | 4 | 420 |
| Epson | 9 | 300 | 60 | 8K | 4 | 580 |
| Seikosha | 9 | 280 | 96 | 5K | 9 | 575 |
| Seikosha | 24 | 240 | 80 | 44K | 9 | 280 |
| Seikosha | 24 | 324 | 108 | 10K | 9 | 495 |
| Citizen | 24 | 120 | 40 | 8K | 3 | 220 |
| Citizen | 24 | 160 | 53 | 8K | 5 | 305 |
| Star | 24 | 200 | 67 | 7K | 5 | 265 |
| Star | 24 | 200 | 67 | 30K | 5 | 305 |
| Star | 24 | 240 | 80 | 41K | 25 | 485 |
| Epson | 24 | 180 | 60 | 8K | 2 | 370 |
| Epson | 24 | 300 | 88 | 6K | 2 | 605 |
| Epson | 24 | 300 | 88 | 6K | 2 | 705 |

■ **Task**

1. Write the report, which should:

    i) be illustrated with appropriate and accurate graphs

    ii) contain calculated summary figures e.g. mean, standard deviation

 See Section 2: The Information Bank – *Statistics*  pages 160–167

– *Descriptive Statistics*  pages 168–202

 See Section 3: Further Tasks and Investigations pages 353–361 *Q 13–27*

# Unit 24: Snacks                          *Topic: Statistics*

*Data analysis and interpretation; Normal distribution*

The Student's Union provide snacks on the Brooklands campus when the cafeteria is closed by setting up mobile trolleys sited in that area. The trolleys provide a much needed source of extra income but need careful management in order to maximise profit. There are two factors that need to be considered when the group of students responsible for maintaining the trolleys decide how many of each particular item to order from the wholesalers; these are:

    i) a lack of available secure storage space

    ii) the loss of potential sales by ordering insufficient stock

Consequently, careful records are kept of sales for each of the different snacks so that the right amount of stock is ordered to satisfy demand from students while not exceeding available storage space. For instance, these records show that for one particular snack, (*Snackeroo*), the daily sales figures are normally distributed with a mean of 32 and a standard deviation of 6.

■ **Tasks**

1. Use tables to calculate the proportion of days that demand for *Snackeroo* is likely to be:

    i) less than 25

    ii) more than 40

    iii) between 20 and 30

2. How many days each month can the students expect to have a demand for *Snackeroo* of:

    i) less than 20

    ii) more than 45

    (Assume there are 30 days in a month).

3. What range of demand can be expected 95% of the time ?

 See Section 2: The Information Bank – *Descriptive Statistics* pages 201–212

☐ **Extended Task**

4. The Harper campus students record the following daily sales of *Snackeroo* over a one-month period:

| 6 | 11 | 27 | 23 | 17 | 9 | 4 | 30 | 17 | 25 |
|---|----|----|----|----|---|---|----|----|----|
| 13 | 20 | 8 | 21 | 42 | 22 | 27 | 31 | 22 | 19 |
| 37 | 22 | 26 | 18 | 20 | 33 | 35 | 28 | 15 | 23 |

a) Calculate the mean and standard distribution for this data.

b) Assuming that daily sales are normally distributed, use tables to calculate the proportion of days that the Harper campus demand for *Snackeroo* is likely to:

i) exceed 40

ii) fall below 5

 See Section 3: Further Tasks and Investigations pages 361–363 *Q 28–33*

# Unit 25: Repairs

*Data analysis and interpretation; Normal distribution*

**Topic: Statistics**

The heavy student usage of the microcomputer equipment at Dale Institute results in quite a high failure rate of monitors, keyboards, disc drives, mice, printers etc. Although most minor repairs can be dealt with in-house by Computer Services staff, items with serious faults are often packaged and sent to a contract repair firm. The Institute has not the finance or space for large quantities of replacement hardware to be kept on standby in case faults develop. However, it is vital that repairs are carried out as soon as possible in order that teaching staff and students have adequate access to sufficient equipment.

A technician in Computer Services is asked by his supervisor to keep a record of the turn-round repair time for a selection of computer equipment. This information is readily available from records; the following are the number of days between the despatch of each of 80 faulty items and their return to the Institute:

| 14 | 11 | 12 | 3 | 9 | 12 | 18 | 3 | 12 | 6 |
|----|----|----|---|---|----|----|---|----|---|
| 11 | 7 | 11 | 7 | 9 | 13 | 15 | 9 | 7 | 19 |
| 10 | 14 | 9 | 14 | 9 | 12 | 8 | 4 | 11 | 13 |
| 10 | 10 | 5 | 13 | 10 | 11 | 12 | 6 | 12 | 13 |
| 13 | 9 | 7 | 9 | 13 | 17 | 8 | 12 | 10 | 12 |
| 15 | 11 | 6 | 10 | 4 | 7 | 10 | 10 | 7 | 8 |
| 10 | 8 | 9 | 7 | 10 | 13 | 18 | 6 | 13 | 4 |
| 11 | 8 | 8 | 9 | 13 | 7 | 19 | 11 | 2 | 16 |

■ **Tasks**

1. Calculate the mean and standard deviation of the data.

2.  a) Assuming that the data is approximately normally distributed, use tables to calculate the proportion of repair times which should be:

    i)   longer than 15 days

    ii)  shorter than 6 days

    iii) between 7 and 13 days

    b) Compare the calculated values in a) with the actual proportions of repairs taking these times.

    c) What conclusions can you draw ?

 See Section 2: The Information Bank – *Descriptive Statistics* pages 201–212

## ☐ Extended Task

3.  A rival firm, EasiFix, is anxious to gain the Institute's contract for computer equipment repairs. So, it decides to give a guarantee that all repairs will be carried out within 10 days. From past experience, the management at EasiFix know that their repair times are normally distributed with a mean of 9 days and a standard deviation of 1.8 days.

    a) What proportion of the time is the Institute likely to receive repaired items later than promised ?

    b) EasiFix supplement their guarantee with a £25 cash-back offer if the repair takes longer than 14 days. What is the likely cost to them over a series of 500 repair jobs ?

    c) To what time should EasiFix amend their guarantee if they want only 20% of repairs to be late ?

    d) What proportion of repairs will be carried out within 7 days if EasiFix can reduce the standard deviation to 1.5 days, keeping the mean repair time the same ?

 See Section 3: Further Tasks and Investigations pages 361–363 *Q 28–33*

# Unit 26: Printer test                                  *Topic: Statistics*

*Correlation*

The Computer Services Unit is considering the bulk purchase of 24-pin dot-matrix printers for distribution around the various campuses; they are to be located in study areas, libraries and computer centres. Prior to purchase it is decided to obtain the opinions of a selection of users as to the printers' general performances. The results are to determine the make of printer which will eventually be purchased as standard.

Ten printers are obtained on a trial basis from various suppliers and situated in key places in the Institute. It is decided to assess the printers according to three criteria:

- speed
- print quality
- cost

The data for speed and cost are easily available from the suppliers. The print quality is assessed by asking the selected users to give each printer a mark out of ten; all the marks are then averaged to give a single mark out of ten for each printer.

The assembled data at the end of the trial period is shown below:

| Manufacturer | Speed (cps) | Price (£) | Print quality (/10) |
|---|---|---|---|
| Seikosha | 80 | 280 | 6 |
| Seikosha | 108 | 495 | 2 |
| Citizen | 40 | 220 | 9 |
| Citizen | 53 | 305 | 8 |
| Star | 67 | 265 | 6 |
| Star | 67 | 305 | 7 |
| Star | 80 | 485 | 8 |
| Epson | 60 | 370 | 6 |
| Epson | 88 | 605 | 5 |
| Epson | 88 | 705 | 5 |

### ■ Tasks

1. a) Rank the printers in order of 'Print quality' and 'Price'.

   b) Calculate Spearman's correlation coefficient for the two variables.

2. Repeat Task 1 for the two variables 'Print quality' and 'Speed'.

3. Interpret the results obtained in Tasks 1 & 2 and comment on their reliability.

4. What recommendations would you make regarding purchase of a suitable printer ?

 See Section 2: The Information Bank – *Descriptive Statistics* pages 212–218

 See Section 3: Further Tasks and Investigations pages 363–364 *Q 34–37*

# Unit 27: Wheat

*Topic: Statistics*

*Correlation and regression*

Dale Institute has, for some years, developed and organised agricultural courses for those students wishing to enter farming and related industries. The institute's annexe, where the courses are based, is several miles to the south of Chelford in fertile surroundings. Apart from course offerings, there are several research projects active at any one time; some are funded by grants from central government, others by sponsorship from businesses and industries that have an interest in the outcome of the research.

As part of one such project, experiments are being undertaken to determine the extent to which the quantity of a certain fertiliser used on a crop affects the yield. It is hoped that information gathered from this project will help to maximise the potential of land that is treated with the fertiliser.

The experiments concern several hectares of land, sown with wheat, and treated with a nitrogen-based fertiliser. The fertiliser level for each hectare is measured in kilograms of nitrogen; the yield is measured in tonnes of wheat. The following experimental data have been gathered over a period of time:

| Fertiliser level (kg of N/ha) | Crop yield (t of wheat/ha) |
|---|---|
| 6 | 3.4 |
| 17 | 3.6 |
| 17 | 3.9 |
| 19 | 4.4 |
| 31 | 4.1 |
| 33 | 4.5 |
| 39 | 4.7 |
| 46 | 4.3 |
| 65 | 4.7 |
| 70 | 5.2 |
| 75 | 5.1 |

## ■ Tasks

1.  a) Construct a scatter diagram to show the relationship between 'Crop yield' and 'Fertiliser level'.

    b) Describe the relationship that seems to exist between the two variables.

2.  a) Calculate Pearson's correlation coefficient for the data.

    b) Interpret the result.

3.  a) Use the method of least-squares to determine the equation of the line-of-best-fit for the data.

    b) Draw the regression line on the scatter diagram.

    c) Use the regression equation to estimate the crop yield when treated with a fertiliser level of:

    i)   12 kg N/ha

    ii)  55 kg N/ha

    iii) 87 kg N/ha

    iv) 125 kg N/ha

    d) How reliable are the values obtained in c)?

See Section 2: The Information Bank – *Descriptive Statistics* pages 212–215; 218–223

☐ **Extended Tasks**

4. Extra data becomes available from further experiments:

| Fertiliser level (kg of N/ha) | Crop yield (t of wheat/ha) |
| --- | --- |
| 115 | 6.4 |
| 127 | 5.8 |
| 130 | 6.0 |
| 133 | 5.5 |
| 138 | 5.8 |
| 146 | 4.8 |
| 149 | 5.1 |
| 156 | 4.2 |
| 158 | 5.1 |
| 164 | 4.4 |
| 168 | 4.9 |
| 170 | 3.6 |
| 178 | 4.0 |
| 180 | 3.3 |

a) Construct a scatter diagram to show the relationship between the two variables.

b) Describe the relationship.

c) Calculate Pearson's correlation coefficient for the data and interpret the result.

5. a) Determine the line-of-best-fit for the data.

b) Use it to calculate the expected yield for a fertiliser level of 152 kg N/ha.

c) Assess the reliability of the answer to b).

6. Taking into account the scatter diagrams and various calculations in Tasks 1–5, try to summarise and explain the relationship between fertiliser level and crop yield.

See Section 3: Further Tasks and Investigations pages 363–366 Q 34–40

# Unit 28: Jumpers

*Topic: Statistics*

*Correlation and regression*

In order to develop an effective training programme, some of the Institute's athletics team are studying the effect of body parameters on the ability to undertake certain sports. For instance, the high jump and long jump specialists are investigating the factors which could affect the ability to jump. These include:

| | | |
| --- | --- | --- |
| Height | Weight | Leg length |
| Foot size | Pulse rate | Arm length |
| Shoulder width | Age | Gender |

They set up a simple experiment whereby individuals are invited to stand on a pressure-sensitive mat and jump vertically from a standing start, the object being to stay in the air for as long as possible. The mat is linked to a microcomputer which is running a piece of software designed to measure the time difference between leaving and landing on the mat. The time is measured correct to the nearest 0.01 seconds and displayed on the screen. Each person is allowed three jumps and their time is obtained by choosing the maximum of the three measurements. Prior to undertaking a full-scale experiment at the Institute, the students decide to carry out a trial run at a local secondary school using a sample of fourteen-year old children. The students supervise the jumps on the pressure mats; the children split into small groups and measure their own heights, weights etc.

The jump times and selected personal data for a class of 25 children are as follows:

| Gender (M / F) | Height (cm) | Weight (kg) | Foot size (cm) | Pulse rate (beats/min) | Leg length (cm) | Arm length (cm) | Jump time (secs) |
|---|---|---|---|---|---|---|---|
| M | 160 | 40 | 27 | 96 | 95 | 69 | 0.53 |
| M | 166 | 43 | 26 | 84 | 103 | 70 | 0.49 |
| M | 180 | 96 | 29 | 60 | 109 | 76 | 0.44 |
| F | 168 | 50 | 21 | 84 | 98 | 62 | 0.44 |
| M | 167 | 51 | 27 | 84 | 106 | 71 | 0.56 |
| F | 170 | 50 | 27 | 50 | 107 | 75 | 0.53 |
| M | 163 | 50 | 26 | 84 | 99 | 74 | 0.53 |
| M | 163 | 54 | 27 | 66 | 100 | 65 | 0.53 |
| F | 174 | 58 | 29 | 54 | 108 | 75 | 0.45 |
| F | 161 | 50 | 25 | 73 | 97 | 69 | 0.44 |
| M | 170 | 60 | 31 | 54 | 98 | 68 | 0.52 |
| F | 178 | 56 | 34 | 66 | 110 | 77 | 0.48 |
| F | 179 | 55 | 34 | 60 | 110 | 70 | 0.42 |
| F | 164 | 60 | 30 | 72 | 101 | 70 | 0.47 |
| F | 170 | 65 | 30 | 81 | 102 | 72 | 0.44 |
| F | 165 | 48 | 24 | 59 | 100 | 70 | 0.45 |
| F | 164 | 48 | 24 | 49 | 99 | 70 | 0.46 |
| F | 161 | 58 | 25 | 55 | 94 | 70 | 0.44 |
| F | 158 | 50 | 25 | 50 | 97 | 64 | 0.47 |
| F | 155 | 62 | 28 | 51 | 108 | 77 | 0.47 |
| M | 168 | 51 | 28 | 66 | 110 | 74 | 0.64 |
| M | 160 | 47 | 28 | 72 | 101 | 68 | 0.48 |
| M | 157 | 39 | 31 | 62 | 100 | 68 | 0.60 |
| M | 171 | 58 | 26 | 84 | 110 | 77 | 0.64 |
| M | 171 | 47 | 25 | 78 | 105 | 74 | 0.62 |

### ■ Tasks

1.  Investigate possible relationships between body parameters and ability to jump:

    a)  Construct scatter diagrams to show the relationship between, for instance, *Height* and *Jump time*.

    b)  Calculate, and interpret, suitable correlation coefficients.

2. By constructing separate scatter diagrams, investigate whether certain correlations seem to be different for males and females.

3. Describe possible sources of errors in this experiment.

 See Section 2: The Information Bank – *Descriptive Statistics* pages 212–223

 See Section 3: Further Tasks and Investigations pages 363–366 *Q 34–40*

# Unit 29: Snack foods
*Topic: Statistics*

*Correlation; measures of central tendency; measures of dispersion*

A discussion, concerning value-for-money of various foods, takes place in a Food Science lecture. As a result, the lecturer sets the students the task of investigating the situation. One group decide to undertake a small-scale statistical experiment in order to compare several different brands of snack food. Twenty-four packets, representing a cross-section of the different varieties on sale, are selected at random from the shelves of a local supermarket. Back at the institute, measurements are taken and tests carried out on the packet contents. The factors considered are:

| | |
|---|---|
| Stated weight | as quoted on the packet, in gms |
| Actual weight | measured to the nearest 0.1 gm |
| Price | per packet, in pence |
| Freshness | number of days to 'eat by' date |
| Fat content | as quoted on the packet, in gms per 100 gm |
| Appearance | a mark allocated out of 6; 1 is 'excellent', 6 is 'poor' |
| Tastiness | a mark allocated out of 6; 1 is ' excellent, 6 is 'poor' |

Four other students are used for the 'appearance' and 'tasting' parts of the experiment. They are asked, as a group, to discuss their results and agree on a mark out of 6 for each packet. After the experiments, the results are tabulated (see table on following page).

■ **Task**

1. Construct scatter diagrams and calculate appropriate correlation coefficients to investigate the relationships between various pairs of variables; for instance:

   i) 'Stated weight' and 'Price'

   ii) 'Freshness' and 'Appearance'

   iii) 'Appearance' and 'Taste'

   iv) 'Price' and 'Taste'

   v) 'Fat content' and 'Taste'

   vi) 'Fat content' and 'Appearance'

 See Section 2: The Information Bank – *Descriptive Statistics* pages 212–223

| Packet | Stated weight | Actual weight | Price | Freshness | Fat content | Appearance | Taste |
|--------|---------------|---------------|-------|-----------|-------------|------------|-------|
| A | 26 | 26.9 | 19 | 28 | 36.8 | 6 | 6 |
| B | 26 | 25.1 | 19 | 34 | 36.8 | 5 | 5 |
| C | 26 | 26.2 | 19 | 14 | 36.8 | 6 | 5 |
| D | 26 | 26.8 | 19 | 14 | 36.8 | 5 | 6 |
| E | 28 | 29.0 | 19 | 0 | 34.3 | 2 | 4 |
| F | 30 | 29.7 | 19 | 42 | 35.0 | 2 | 1 |
| G | 30 | 31.0 | 19 | 41 | 35.0 | 4 | 3 |
| H | 30 | 31.9 | 19 | 49 | 35.0 | 5 | 5 |
| I | 30 | 31.3 | 19 | 49 | 36.7 | 3 | 5 |
| J | 25 | 25.5 | 19 | 42 | 36.8 | 4 | 3 |
| K | 25 | 25.2 | 19 | 28 | 36.8 | 4 | 4 |
| L | 25 | 24.8 | 19 | 28 | 36.8 | 1 | 4 |
| M | 25 | 25.8 | 19 | 34 | 36.8 | 6 | 6 |
| N | 25 | 25.6 | 16 | 27 | 38.0 | 3 | 1 |
| O | 25 | 25.7 | 19 | 14 | 36.8 | 5 | 6 |
| P | 40 | 35.3 | 23 | 49 | 36.0 | 4 | 1 |
| Q | 27 | 27.7 | 16 | 91 | 36.0 | 2 | 2 |
| R | 75 | 74.7 | 39 | 42 | 38.0 | 2 | 2 |
| S | 40 | 41.0 | 24 | 21 | 37.5 | 1 | 1 |
| T | 40 | 40.8 | 23 | 42 | 36.0 | 2 | 4 |
| U | 75 | 75.8 | 39 | 35 | 38.0 | 3 | 3 |
| V | 27 | 28.4 | 16 | 86 | 36.0 | 1 | 2 |
| W | 27 | 28.9 | 16 | 91 | 36.0 | 6 | 3 |
| X | 75 | 76.5 | 39 | 49 | 36.0 | 1 | 1 |

☐ **Extended Task**

2.  Write a short report which summarises the findings and recommends a 'best buy'.

    The report might include:
    i)  Graphs and appropriate summary measures (e.g. mean, standard deviation).
    ii) Calculation of values which measure value-for-money (e.g. cost / gm).

See Section 3: Further Tasks and Investigations pages 363–366 *Q 34–40*

# Unit 30: Computer delivery                    *Topic: Statistics*

*Multiplication law of probability*

The Computer Services Unit at Dale Institute deal with various suppliers for a wide range of computing products; these range from complete microcomputer systems to consumable items such as printer paper. Some suppliers are more reliable than others and it is sometimes the case that incorrect or faulty equipment is delivered. Detailed records have been kept over 10 years and from this experience it appears that the firm which is the main supplier of microcomputer systems:

i) delivers the wrong model of microcomputer about 4% of the time

ii) includes a faulty keyboard about 6% of the time

iii) omits an accessory (e.g. power cable, mouse) about 10% of the time

iv) includes a faulty monitor about 2% of the time

It can be assumed that all events are independent of one another.

### ■ Tasks

1. Calculate the probability that when a single microcomputer system is delivered it is:

   i) the correct model

   ii) complete with all accessories

   iii) the wrong model with a faulty keyboard

   iv) the correct model with a faulty monitor

   v) the wrong model with a power cable missing; the keyboard and monitor also both faulty.

2. a) The same firm later supplies 5 complete systems; calculate the probability that:

   i) they are all the correct model

   ii) all monitors are functioning properly

   iii) all systems have a complete set of accessories

   b) What extra assumptions have you made in answering this question ?

3. There is a 5% chance that a delivery will be late; what is the probability that the firm will be able to deliver a set of 20 correct models, which are complete and fully functional in all respects, by a specified date ?

See Section 2: The Information Bank – *Inferential Statistics* pages 224–230

See Section 3: Further Tasks and Investigations pages 367–369 *Q 1–10*

# Unit 31: One-armed Bandit

*Topic: Statistics*

*Addition and multiplication laws of probability; expectation*

The students' common room and bar on the Harper campus has the usual collection of recreational and social features. These include: snooker and pool tables, pinball machines, snacks and soft drinks dispenser, music centre and a one-armed bandit. All profits from the various items are donated to the Students' Union.

In order to eliminate the exorbitant rental charges charged by commercial enterprises, two Engineering students construct a one-armed bandit as part of a design project. The prototype model has been constructed with some assistance in the underlying probability theory from friends studying Mathematics. The amateur nature of the project convinces the other students that it should be possible to beat the system. So, it is a common sight to see small groups gathered round the machine attempting to judge the best time either

a) to quit after a long run of losses or

b) to start playing after observing others losing heavily.

The machine has 4 revolving drums containing pictures of squares, diamonds, hexagons and circles. It costs 15p for each turn on the machine and prizes are paid out according to certain winning combinations.

The drums are designed as follows:

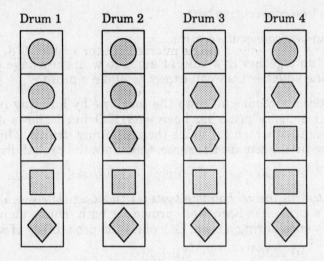

The winning combinations are:

|  | *Combination* |  |  |  | *Prize* |
|---|---|---|---|---|---|
| (i) | ◇ | ◇ | ◇ | ◇ | £20 |
| (ii) | ◇ | ◇ | ▢ | ▢ | £10 |
| (iii) | ○ | ○ | ○ | ○ | £5 |
| (iv) | ○ | ○ | ⬡ | ⬡ | £1 |

■ **Tasks**

1. Assuming that the drums operate independently, calculate the probability of:

    i)   Drum 1 showing a diamond

    ii)  Drums 1 and 2 both showing squares

    iii) No drum showing a circle

2. Calculate the probability of winning:

    i)  £20 in one turn

    ii)  £10 in one turn

    iii) £5 in one turn

    iv) £1 in one turn

    v)  A total of £6 in two consecutive turns

    vi) A total of £20 in two consecutive turns

3. A group of students club together in a vain attempt to win; they have 625 consecutive turns on the machine. Determine whether they can expect to make a profit.

4. The designers later make a modification to the machine by building in a 'freeze' bonus. At the end of a turn, whether or not a prize has been won, if Drum 1 shows a diamond it stays frozen and the user has a free turn which activates the remaining drums. This bonus is only available once during a turn; the prizes remain the same. Calculate the probability of winning in one turn:

    i)  £40        ii)  £30

5. A further refinement to the 'freeze' bonus allows for the user to freeze Drums 1& 2 after the first turn, whether or not a prize has been won. providing both drums show the same picture. This bonus is only available once during a turn. Calculate the probability of winning in one turn:

    i)  £40        ii)  £30        iii) £10

See Section 2: The Information Bank – *Inferential statistics* pages 224–231

☐ **Extended Task**

6. a)  The machine later develops a fault; Drums 2 & 3 get stuck when they both show a diamond. They remain in this state for the following turn and then free themselves. What effect does this have on the probabilities of winning the different prizes ?

   b)  The designers are unable to rectify the fault, so decide to alter the prize amounts instead. Suggest possible changes in the amounts that will ensure the machine still operates at a profit.

See Section 3: Further Tasks and Investigations pages 367–369 *Q 1–10*

# Unit 32: Hardware components

*Topic: Statistics*

*Addition and multiplication laws of probability*

The linking of electronic hardware components into functional systems is a feature of many Electrical Engineering courses at Dale Institute. The components are of different types and vary in cost according to their complexity. The Institute purchases them in bulk from a single supplier who carries out reliability tests in order to assess the likelihood that a component will fail when incorporated in a system.

The components are of four different types: A, B, C and D. From previous reliability tests it is known that:

i)   component A has a probability of failure of 0.1

ii)  component B has a probability of failure of 0.08

iii) component C has a probability of failure of 0.04

iv)  component D has a probability of failure of 0.02

■ **Task**

1.  The following test systems are constructed from the components. In each case calculate the probability that the system will function properly; that is, an output is received at Y when an input is applied at X:

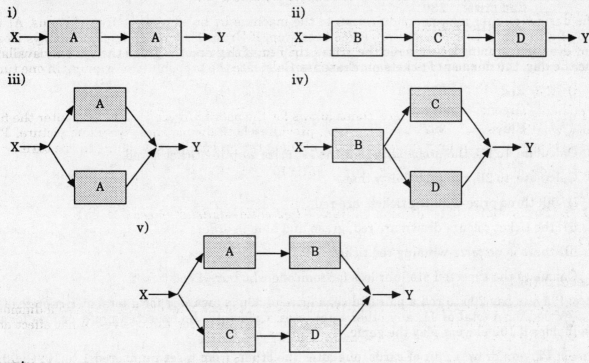

i)
ii)
iii)
iv)
v)

See Section 2: The Information Bank – *Inferential statistics* pages 224–230

See Section 3: Further Tasks and Investigations pages 367–369 *Q 1–10*

# Unit 33: Games
*Topic: Statistics*

*Addition and multiplication laws of probability; expectation*

A summer fair is held annually at the Institute, usually in June. The event is extremely popular, attracting hundreds of people from all parts of the county. The purpose is to raise money which is then donated to various charities nominated by the Students' Union. There are many attractions run by the students who are responsible for the design, organisation and financial aspects of their sideshow or stall. One of the most profitable features of the event is the 'Lady Luck' arena which is an area of the fair set aside for games of chance; these include The Wheel of Fortune, Roll-a-Coin, Bingo, and Lucky Dip.

The design of these games is crucial; past experience has shown that miscalculating the prize money or the chance of winning can drastically affect the profits from the event. Consequently, all such games are analysed beforehand to check whether they are likely to make a profit or a loss.

### ■ Tasks

1. *Raffle*: Coloured numbered tickets (red, green, blue) costing 40p, 20p and 10p each respectively are sold. At the end of the afternoon, three ticket numbers are drawn from a barrel; the prize money is:

   1st prize: £50
   2nd prize: £30
   3rd prize: £15

   However, if a winning ticket is red the prize is tripled; if the ticket is green the prize is doubled. On the day, the number of tickets purchased is:

   Red:    575
   Green:  464
   Blue:   392

   a) Calculate, to 2D, the probability that the 1st prize winning ticket is red.

   b) Calculate, to 2D, the probability that

   i)   all three prize-winning tickets are red

   ii)  the ticket colours drawn are red, green and blue in order

   iii) there is no prize-winning red ticket

   c) Calculate the expected profit or loss for someone who buys 1 red ticket.

2. *Dice*: Players pay 20p to roll a pair of dice; a prize of 50p is awarded for a total of 7, a prize of £1 is awarded for a total of 11; any other total loses. Calculate the expected profit or loss for the stallholder if 100 players play the game.

3. *Cards*: Players draw a pair of cards, one after the other, from a set numbered 1 to 10; the first card is not replaced before drawing the second card. If the sum of the two numbers on the card is even, the player wins £1; if the sum of the two numbers is odd the player pays a penalty of £1.

   a) Calculate the player's expected profit or loss in this game.

   b) What is the effect on the expected profit or loss if the '10' card is removed ?

4. *Wheel of Fortune*: This is a 10-sided spinner divided into equally-sized sections, as shown on the following page.

   A player pays 20p to spin the wheel; when it stops the pointer identifies the winning (or losing) section; two sections are marked 'Money back'. So, the player either wins the amount shown, loses the 20p entry fee, or gets the entry fee back.

   a) Calculate the probability that a player will, in a single spin:

   i)   get their money back

   ii)  win £1

   iii) win something

   iv)  lose

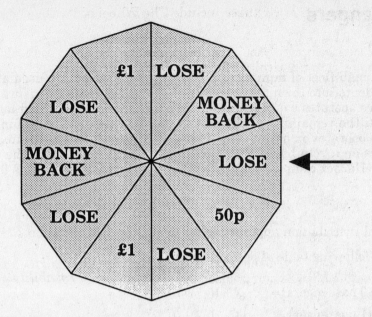

b) Calculate the player's expected profit.

5. *Roll-a-coin*: A grid of squares, consisting of lines 4cm apart, is drawn on a large board. Players roll 10p coins down a ramp; if a coin lands completely inside one of the squares it wins a prize, otherwise it is lost.

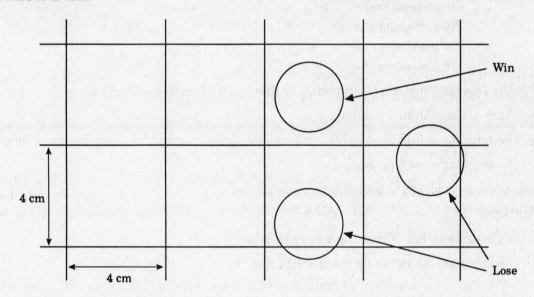

By considering where the centre of a coin must land for a player to win, calculate the probability of winning at this game, given that a 10p coin has a diameter of 2.4cm.

See Section 2: The Information Bank – *Inferential statistics* pages 224–231

See Section 3: Further Tasks and Investigations pages 367–369 *Q 1–10*

# Unit 34: Passengers

*Topic: Statistics*

*Binomial distribution*

The Institute has a small fleet of minibuses of varying sizes which are used at weekends for transporting resident students into town for purposes of shopping, visits to leisure centres, places of interest etc. The service operates every hour, on the hour, and is partly paid for by charging passengers a small amount; the remainder of the cost is met by Student Union funds. No bookings take place and the service operates on a first-come-first-served principle. The driving is shared by a group of volunteer students on a rota basis. From previous records kept about the usage of the 8-seater minibus based at the Harper campus, the probability that a passenger seat is filled is 0.7.

## ■ Tasks

1. Why is a Binomial Distribution appropriate for modelling this situation ?

2. a) Complete the following table of probabilities:

   *Probability*

   $P(0 \text{ passengers}) = {}_8C_0 (0.7)^0 (0.3)^8 =$

   $P(1 \text{ passenger}) = {}_8C_1 (0.7)^1 (0.3)^7 =$

   $P(2 \text{ passengers}) = $

   $P(3 \text{ passengers}) = $

   $P(4 \text{ passengers}) = $

   $P(5 \text{ passengers}) = $

   $P(6 \text{ passengers}) = $

   $P(7 \text{ passengers}) = $

   $P(8 \text{ passengers}) = $

   b) Use the table to calculate the probability that, on a normal weekend run:

   i) there are less than 3 passengers

   ii) the minibus is full

   iii) there are at least 5 passengers

3. a) Construct a graph of the probability distribution.

   b) Calculate:

   i) the mean number of passengers per journey

   ii) the standard deviation for the distribution

See Section 2: The Information Bank – *Inferential statistics* pages 231–233

## ☐ Extended tasks

4. On the Brooklands campus, the following frequency distribution is produced from the records for the previous 100 journeys of its 10-seater minibus:

| No. of passengers | 0 | 1 | 2 | 3 | 4 | 5 | 6 | 7 | 8 | 9 | 10 |
|---|---|---|---|---|---|---|---|---|---|---|---|
| No. of journeys | 0 | 1 | 1 | 5 | 11 | 19 | 24 | 20 | 13 | 5 | 1 |

a) Calculate the mean number of passengers per journey.

b) i) Assuming that a Binomial Distribution is appropriate to model this situation, use your answer to part a) to calculate a value for $p$, the probability that a passenger seat is filled.

   ii) Complete the following table of Binomial Distribution probabilities using the value of $p$:

|  |  |  | Probability | Expected Frequency | Observed Frequency |
|---|---|---|---|---|---|
| P(0 passengers) | = | $_{10}C_0\,(\quad)^0\,(\quad)^{10}$ = |  |  | 0 |
| P(1 passenger) | = | = |  |  | 1 |
| P(2 passengers) | = | = |  |  | 1 |
| P(3 passengers) | = | = |  |  | 5 |
| P(4 passengers) | = | = |  |  | 11 |
| etc |  |  |  |  |  |

(The 'Expected Frequency' column represents how many of the 100 minibus journeys are expected to carry that number of passengers; it is obtained by multiplying each value in the 'Probability' column by 100).

By comparing the last two columns, can you say whether the Binomial Distribution appears to be a good model of this situation; that is, does the distribution of the passengers *expected* on the minibus seem to match the distribution of the passengers actually *observed* using it ?

5. a) Carry out a similar comparison of 'Expected Frequency' and 'Observed Frequency' for the Harper campus 8-seater minibus.

   b) Do these results seem to confirm the suitability of a Binomial Distribution model ?

6. Calculating probabilities for the Binomial Distribution can be tedious when using a calculator. So, write a computer program that will produce, for any given input value of p (the probability of a 'success'), an output of the binomial probabilities for different values of $n$ and $r$. The output is best arranged in table form and might resemble:

| $p = 0.7$ | | | | | | | $n$ | | | | | |
|---|---|---|---|---|---|---|---|---|---|---|---|---|
|  | 1 | 2 | 3 | 4 | 5 | 6 | 7 | 8 | 9 | 10 | 11 | etc |
| 0 | . | . | . | . | . | . | . | . | . | . | . | . |
| 1 | . | . | . | 0.0756 | . | . | . | . | . | . | . | . |
| $r$    2 | * | . | . | . | . | . | . | . | . | 0.0014 | . | . |
| 3 | * | * | . | . | . | 0.1852 | . | . | . | . | . | . |
| 4 | * | * | * | . | . | . | . | 0.1361 | . | . | . | . |
| etc | * | * | * | * | . | . | . | . | . | . | . | . |

See Section 3: Further Tasks and Investigations pages 370–371 *Q 11–15*

# Unit 35: Goals

*Topic: Statistics*

*Poisson distribution*

Every Wednesday afternoon, the Institute fields a number of teams against other colleges and universities in a range of sports, including football. The 'A' teams takes part in a league competition, each league consisting of 21 teams who play each other only once during a season. The nature of the academic year means that no more games are possible

During the year there is also a knockout competition for an annually awarded trophy; this competition involves the same teams and the final takes place after all league games have been completed. The final takes place at a neutral ground.

This year, Dale Institute's 'A' team have reached the final of the knockout competition and are due to play against a rival team who have averaged 1.9 goals per match. Dale's results for the season are shown below (Dale's goals are shown first):

| | | | | |
|---|---|---|---|---|
| 1 – 2 | 2 – 1 | 2 – 1 | 1 – 3 | 0 – 1 |
| 1 – 1 | 1 – 3 | 2 – 0 | 3 – 2 | 0 – 1 |
| 2 – 1 | 2 – 0 | 4 – 1 | 3 – 3 | 2 – 2 |
| 3 – 1 | 3 – 2 | 0 – 2 | 0 – 1 | 2 – 2 |

## ■ Tasks

1.  a)  Calculate the mean number of goals ($m$) that Dale have scored in the season's games.

    b)  Use your answer to part a) to calculate the probabilities that Dale score:

    i)  0 goals      ii) 1 goal      iii) 2 goals      iv) 3 goals

    v)  4 goals      vi) 5 goals      vii) more than 5 goals

2.  Calculate the probability that the opposition score:

    i)  0 goals      ii) 1 goal      iii) 2 goals      iv) 3 goals

    v)  4 goals      vi) 5 goals      vii) more than 5 goals

3.  a)  Calculate, to 2D, the probability that:

    i)   Dale win the match 3 – 1

    ii)  there are less than 3 goals scored in the match

    iii) the match is a draw

    b)  What is the most likely score in the match ?

    c)  What assumptions have you made in the answers to parts a) & b) ?

 See Section 2: The Information Bank – *Inferential statistics* pages 233–234

## ☐ Extended task

4.  As is the case with the Binomial Distribution, the calculation of Poisson probabilities can be time-consuming. So, write a computer program that will calculate these probabilities for a range of values of $\mu$ and $r$. The output is best arranged in table form and might resemble:

| | μ 1 | 1.5 | 2 | 2.5 | 3 | 3.5 | 4 | 4.5 | 5 | 5.5 | 6 | etc |
|---|---|---|---|---|---|---|---|---|---|---|---|---|
| 0 | | | | · | · | | · | | · | | | · |
| 1 | | | · | 0.2052 | · | | · | | · | | | · |
| r  2 | * | * | · | · | · | · | · | · | · | 0.0618 | · | · |
| 3 | * | * | * | * | · | 0.2158 | · | · | · | · | | · |
| 4 | * | * | * | * | * | * | · | 0.1898 | · | · | | · |
| etc | * | * | * | * | * | * | * | * | · | · | | · |

 See Section 3: Further Tasks and Investigations pages 370–372 *Q 12, 16–20*

# Unit 36: Administration

*Topic: Statistics*

*Binomial distribution; Poisson distribution; Normal distribution*

The Brooklands campus has an administration block that houses a reception area, general offices, campus managers and student services personnel. The receptionist is responsible for welcoming visitors and directing incoming telephone calls through the main switchboard. Secretarial staff in the general office undertake a variety of tasks such as record-keeping, finance and dealing with enquiries about courses. Campus managers are responsible for such things as upkeep of buildings, ground maintenance, security and car parking facilities. The student services office handles matters relating to student accommodation, loans, travel expenses etc.

## ■ Tasks

In the following tasks, choose the appropriate probability distribution to model each situation. State the assumptions, if any, that you make in each case.

1. a) Telephone calls come into the switchboard at a mean rate of 3 per minute. Calculate the probability that there are:

   i) 2 calls during a one-minute period

   ii) more than 5 calls during a one-minute period

   iii) 50 calls in a fifteen-minute period

   b) The receptionist leaves the switchboard for two minutes to pass an urgent message to the campus manager who is based in a nearby office. What is the probability that there are no incoming calls during this time ?

   c) There is a maximum of 8 calls that can be connected at any one time. Assuming that each call lasts for three minutes, what is the probability that the switchboard will be fully loaded ?

2. There are four electronic typewriters in the general office. Past records show that such typewriters are out of action for about 8% of the time because of malfunction. Calculate the probability that, on any given day, none of the typewriters are working.

3. The campus manager is interrupted, on average, twice during his lunch-hour. What is the probability that he manages to get an uninterrupted lunch ?

4. One of the secretaries produces typed text that, on average, contains two misprints per page. She has to type a document which consists of 5 pages. Calculate the probability that the document is free of misprints.

5. Office staff are supposed to arrive for work at 8.30 a.m. Some arrive early, but traffic conditions in Chelford often cause late arrivals. The mean amount of time that staff arrive late is 2.5 minutes with a standard deviation of 5 minutes. Calculate the proportion of the staff who, on any given day, arrive:

    i)   after 8.45 a.m

    ii)  before 8.30 a.m.

6. There are 5 telephones in the general office that teaching staff can use for making external calls. There is a 70% chance that a telephone is in use at any given time. Calculate the probability that, if a member of staff wants to make a call, there are no telephones free.

7. The campus manager has to deal with interruptions to the power supply on average once a month. Assuming that a month is 4 weeks, calculate the probability that there will be at least 1 interruption in any given week.

8. The administration block is lit by fluorescent lighting, there being some 500 tubes in total. The manufacturers claim that each tube should last for a mean time of 2500 hours with a standard deviation of 240 hours. Each light is switched on for 2000 hours each year and if a tube develops a fault, the campus manager replaces it at a cost of £5 per tube. Calculate the likely total annual cost for tube replacement.

9. Students arrive at the student services office with a mean arrival rate of 1 student per 15-minute period. The student services officer cannot deal with more than six students per hour. Calculate the proportion of time that students will have to wait to speak to him.

10. Boxes of envelopes are delivered each month to the general office. Each box contains 250 envelopes and, from past experience, about 10% of them do not have enough gum on them. So, the person who normally receives the mail decides to adopt a procedure of selecting a sample of 20 envelopes from a box chosen at random. If the sample contains five or more envelopes which do not have enough gum the delivery is not accepted, otherwise the delivery is accepted and the envelopes put into stock.

Calculate the probability that a delivery is accepted.

See Section 2: The Information Bank – *Inferential statistics* pages 202–212; 231–234

See Section 3: Further Tasks and Investigations pages 370–372 *Q 11–20*

# Unit 37: Health and diet

*Topic: Statistics*

*Confidence limits (population mean)*

The data following was collected as part of a survey into health and diet (see: Section 1 Unit 17– *Health and diet questionnaire*).

| Student number | Sex | Year group | Ht. (m) | Wt. (kg) | Student number | Sex | Year group | Ht. (m) | Wt. (kg) |
|---|---|---|---|---|---|---|---|---|---|
| 1 | F | 1 | 1.58 | 54 | 31 | F | 1 | 1.74 | 54 |
| 2 | M | 3 | 1.83 | 86 | 32 | F | 1 | 1.55 | 47 |
| 3 | F | 1 | 1.58 | 54 | 33 | F | 3 | 1.70 | 60 |
| 4 | F | 4 | 1.60 | 62 | 34 | M | 1 | 1.74 | 74 |
| 5 | F | 1 | 1.64 | 53 | 35 | F | 1 | 1.60 | 65 |
| 6 | F | 1 | 1.50 | 48 | 36 | F | 2 | 1.67 | 60 |
| 7 | M | 1 | 1.79 | 98 | 37 | F | 4 | 1.70 | 64 |
| 8 | F | 1 | 1.57 | 51 | 38 | M | 1 | 1.78 | 76 |
| 9 | F | 1 | 1.60 | 66 | 39 | F | 1 | 1.71 | 67 |
| 10 | F | 1 | 1.64 | 57 | 40 | F | 4 | 1.67 | 76 |
| 11 | M | 1 | 1.80 | 80 | 41 | F | 1 | 1.74 | 75 |
| 12 | F | 1 | 1.67 | 58 | 42 | M | 1 | 1.75 | 70 |
| 13 | F | 4 | 1.70 | 59 | 43 | M | 1 | 1.80 | 70 |
| 14 | F | 1 | 1.69 | 57 | 44 | M | 1 | 1.74 | 69 |
| 15 | F | 1 | 1.70 | 64 | 45 | F | 4 | 1.60 | 60 |
| 16 | F | 1 | 1.64 | 53 | 46 | F | 2 | 1.68 | 60 |
| 17 | F | 1 | 1.71 | 65 | 47 | M | 1 | 1.78 | 76 |
| 18 | F | 1 | 1.50 | 63 | 48 | F | 1 | 1.65 | 63 |
| 19 | F | 1 | 1.62 | 59 | 49 | F | 2 | 1.57 | 53 |
| 20 | M | 1 | 1.78 | 62 | 50 | F | 2 | 1.73 | 49 |
| 21 | F | 2 | 1.65 | 58 | 51 | M | 2 | 1.70 | 72 |
| 22 | F | 4 | 1.60 | 60 | 52 | F | 2 | 1.62 | 53 |
| 23 | F | 1 | 1.53 | 54 | 53 | F | 2 | 1.65 | 53 |
| 24 | F | 2 | 1.86 | 87 | 54 | F | 2 | 1.65 | 63 |
| 25 | F | 1 | 1.65 | 65 | 55 | M | 2 | 1.85 | 81 |
| 26 | F | 1 | 1.59 | 49 | 56 | M | 2 | 1.85 | 72 |
| 27 | F | 1 | 1.66 | 57 | 57 | M | 2 | 1.73 | 78 |
| 28 | F | 1 | 1.76 | 65 | 58 | M | 2 | 1.75 | 76 |
| 29 | F | 1 | 1.61 | 50 | 59 | F | 2 | 1.60 | 52 |
| 30 | F | 1 | 1.51 | 50 | 60 | F | 2 | 1.58 | 51 |

## ■ Tasks

1. a) Select 10 students from the list by using a suitable sampling method.

   b) Considering the weights of these students, calculate the mean and standard deviation.

   c) Determine a 95% confidence interval for the mean weight of all the students.

2. Determine a 99% confidence interval for the mean height of all the students.

See Section 2: The Information Bank – *Inferential statisticss* pages 235–239

□ **Extended Task**

3. Is the mean height of the male students significantly different to that of the female students ?

 See Section 3: Further Tasks and Investigations pages 373–375 *Q 21, 23–25, 28, 29*

# Unit 38: The Fish Pond (2)                    *Topic: Statistics*

*Confidence limits (population proportion)*

A small fish-pond is located in the grounds of the Brooklands campus; it is primarily concerned with a project on how the population level of the fish is affected by available food and space (see: Section 1 Unit 16 – *The Fish Pond*). In order to monitor the effects on the population of the various environmental factors it is necessary to determine, as accurately as possible, the fish population in the pond at any given time.

Obviously it is impossible to catch all of the fish for counting purposes. So, when it is required to estimate the number of fish in the pond a sample of fish is caught, tagged and released back into the pond. After a suitable time interval, another sample is caught and the proportion of these which are tagged is noted. The number of fish in the pond is then estimated by calculating:

$$\frac{\text{Size of first sample}}{\text{Proportion of tagged fish in second sample}}$$

For instance, suppose the first sample consists of 20 fish; when a second sample of 50 fish are caught, 10 of these are observed to be tagged. The proportion of fish in the pond that are tagged is deduced to be $\frac{10}{50} = 0.2$; so, an estimate for the number of fish in the pond is, therefore, $\frac{20}{0.2} = 100$:

■ **Tasks**

1. A first sample of 50 fish are caught and tagged; when a second sample of 40 fish are caught it is noted that 23 are tagged.

   a) By considering the proportion of tagged fish in the second sample, determine a 95% confidence interval for the proportion of fish in the pond that are tagged.

   b) Use the answer to a) to determine a 95% confidence interval for the number of fish in the pond.

2. Using similar methods to Q.1, determine a 99% confidence interval for the number of fish in the pond.

3. The project director wishes to estimate the number of carp in the pond. A sample of 44 carp are caught and tagged; a second sample of 32 carp contain 26 that are tagged. Determine 95% and 99% confidence intervals for the number of carp in the pond.

 See Section 2: The Information Bank – *Inferential statistics* page 240

 See Section 3: Further Tasks and Investigations pages 373–375 *Q 22, 26–30*

# Unit 39: Crisps                                    *Topic: Statistics*

*Significance testing (single mean)*

As an exercise in small-scale data collection and analysis, a group of Mathematics students decide to consider the weights of packets of crisps. They are concerned to find out whether the bags contain the correct weight. They think that, even though there is usually some variation between the stated weight on the bags and the actual weight of crisps, the variation is quite acceptable. So, to test out this hypothesis they purchased thirty 30g packets of crisps, over a period of several days, from the Brooklands campus snack bar. The crisps are manufactured by the same company. The actual weight of each bag of crisps is measured to the nearest 0.1 gm and the results are tabulated as follows:

| Packet | Actual weight | Packet | Actual weight |
|--------|---------------|--------|---------------|
| 1 | 29.6 | 16 | 29.3 |
| 2 | 29.5 | 17 | 29.1 |
| 3 | 28.7 | 18 | 28.7 |
| 4 | 29.3 | 19 | 30.2 |
| 5 | 29.0 | 20 | 30.1 |
| 6 | 28.6 | 21 | 29.8 |
| 7 | 31.0 | 22 | 28.8 |
| 8 | 29.6 | 23 | 29.4 |
| 9 | 30.2 | 24 | 32.0 |
| 10 | 28.9 | 25 | 27.6 |
| 11 | 29.2 | 26 | 27.8 |
| 12 | 27.8 | 27 | 28.0 |
| 13 | 28.7 | 28 | 29.5 |
| 14 | 28.9 | 29 | 30.1 |
| 15 | 29.4 | 30 | 29.9 |

■ **Tasks**

1. a)  Calculate the mean and standard deviation of the weight of the crisps.

   b)  Test the hypotheses:

   $H_0$: the mean weight of a packet of crisps is 30g

   $H_1$: the mean weight of a packet of crisps is not 30g

   c)  Test the hypotheses:

   $H_0$: the mean weight of a packet of crisps is 30g

   $H_1$: the mean weight of a packet of crisps is less than 30g

 See Section 2: The Information Bank – *Inferential statistics* page 240

See Section 3: Further Tasks and Investigations pages 375–377 *Q 31, 32, 36*

# Unit 40: Chinese proverb
*Topic: Statistics*

*Significance testing (difference between two means)*

There is an ancient Chinese proverb which says:

> *'I hear, and I forget*
>
> *I see, and I remember*
>
> *I do, and I understand'*

In order to test out the validity of some of the proverb, a lecturer in Educational Psychology devises an experiment for two groups of his students who are at the same stage of a course.

During a lecture session with group A, he reads out a list of twenty random items (e.g. elephant, football, motorway etc); the students are not allowed to make notes but have to memorise as many of the items as possible. Once the list has been read out, the students have two minutes to write down as many of the items as they can recall. The lecturer then re-reads the list and the students mark as correct any items that they have successfully recalled; this becomes their score for that part of the experiment.

In a different lecture session with group B, the lecturer produces twenty different items, one at a time, from a large box. He shows the students the items, replacing each one in the box before drawing out the next. Afterwards, the students have two minutes to write down as many items as they can recall. The number correctly recalled is their score for this part of the experiment.

The lecturer notes the results for each group; these are shown below:

*Group A*

| Student | 'Hear' score | Student | 'Hear' score |
|:---:|:---:|:---:|:---:|
| 1 | 8 | 16 | 9 |
| 2 | 6 | 17 | 12 |
| 3 | 9 | 18 | 15 |
| 4 | 3 | 19 | 10 |
| 5 | 12 | 20 | 11 |
| 6 | 11 | 21 | 16 |
| 7 | 7 | 22 | 10 |
| 8 | 10 | 23 | 5 |
| 9 | 15 | 24 | 8 |
| 10 | 7 | 25 | 14 |
| 11 | 5 | 26 | 17 |
| 12 | 9 | 27 | 11 |
| 13 | 14 | 28 | 13 |
| 14 | 4 | 29 | 16 |
| 15 | 12 | 30 | 7 |

*Group B*

| Student | 'See' score | Student | 'See' score |
|---|---|---|---|
| 1 | 12 | 16 | 10 |
| 2 | 11 | 17 | 14 |
| 3 | 15 | 18 | 18 |
| 4 | 6 | 19 | 8 |
| 5 | 13 | 20 | 12 |
| 6 | 14 | 21 | 19 |
| 7 | 7 | 22 | 15 |
| 8 | 16 | 23 | 7 |
| 9 | 17 | 24 | 10 |
| 10 | 10 | 25 | 16 |
| 11 | 10 | 26 | 17 |
| 12 | 9 | 27 | 14 |
| 13 | 15 | 28 | 16 |
| 14 | 9 | 29 | 16 |
| 15 | 17 | 30 | 7 |

## ■ Tasks

1.  a)  Calculate the mean and standard deviation for:

    i)  the 'Hear' scores

    ii) the 'See' scores

    b)  Calculate the standard error of the difference between the two means

2.  Assume that the null hypothesis and alternative hypothesis are:

    $H_0$: there is no difference between the mean scores of the two sets of data

    $H_1$: there is a difference between the mean scores of the two sets of data

    Carry out a significance test at:

    i)  the 5% level

    ii) the 1% level

3.  Do you think the results show that there is some truth in the proverb ?

See Section 2: The Information Bank – *Inferential statistics* pages 241–244

See Section 3: Further Tasks and Investigations pages 375–378 *Q 34, 37–39*

# Unit 41: Newspapers

*Topic: Statistics*

*Confidence limits; significance testing*

As part of a media study project, you have been asked to compare two newspapers in terms of their text and other features. You decide to investigate whether there are any significant differences between items such as sentence length etc.

## ■ Tasks

Choose two newspapers (for instance, 'The Sun' and 'The Independent'):

1. For each newspaper:

   a) Select a random sample of about 50 sentences, count the number of words in each sentence and construct a frequency table of the results.

   b) Calculate the mean and standard deviation of the number of words per sentence.

   c) Calculate the standard error of the difference between the two means.

   d) Carry out a test to see if there is any significant difference between the two means.

2. In a similar manner to Task 1, consider the mean word length of the two newspapers.

3. Investigate whether there is any significant difference between the two newspapers in respect of:

   i) the mean length of words used in the crosswords

   ii) the mean cost per page

4. a) For each newspaper, choose one page and calculate the proportion of space allocated to advertisements.

   b) Determine 95% and 99% confidence intervals for the proportion of the whole newspaper that is allocated to advertisements. Check your answer.

5. a) For each newspaper, choose one page and calculate the proportion of space allocated to photographs.

   b) Determine 95% and 99% confidence intervals for the proportion of the whole newspaper that is allocated to photographs. Check your answer.

6. What conclusions can you draw from these investigations?

See Section 2: The Information Bank – *Inferential statistics* pages 238–244

See Section 3: Further Tasks and Investigations pages 375–378 *Q 34, 35, 37–39*

# Unit 42: Pitches

*Topic: Statistics*

*Goodness-of-fit (Chi-squared test)*

The Dale Institute 1st XV rugby team usually achieve a reasonable degree of success during a season. A newly appointed coach, however, has recently taken over responsibility for team training and he is not too impressed with the team's results for the previous two seasons. He has obtained information regarding the state of the pitch during the games and constructed a table of the results (see below). During his first team talk he uses the information to convince players that they need to improve the standard of play on poor pitches. He feels that their play is affected by the quality of the pitch.

|  |  | Match result | | |
| --- | --- | --- | --- | --- |
|  |  | Win | Draw | Loss |
| | Good | 9 | 5 | 3 |
| State of pitch | Medium | 10 | 6 | 6 |
| | Bad | 6 | 6 | 11 |

■ **Tasks**

1. Formulate an appropriate null hypothesis and carry out a $\chi^2$ test on the above data to determine if the team coach is correct in his belief that the state of the pitch affects the team's performance.

2. Inspired by the coach's example, other members of the Sports Science teaching staff investigate connections between factors that might affect sporting performance.

   a) The following data relates to the smoking habits of regular male and female team members taken from a variety of sports:

|  |  | Sex of student | |
| --- | --- | --- | --- |
|  |  | Male | Female |
| | Non-smokers | 9 | 14 |
| Type of smoker | Light smokers | 11 | 6 |
| | Heavy smokers | 7 | 3 |

   Formulate an appropriate null hypothesis and determine whether there is a significant difference in smoking habits between male and female students.

   b) The following data relates the observed aggressiveness of various sports team members to the colour of their hair:

|  |  | Hair colour | | | |
| --- | --- | --- | --- | --- | --- |
|  |  | Brown | Black | Blonde | Red |
| | Easy-going | 9 | 4 | 4 | 3 |
| Temperament | Lively | 7 | 3 | 6 | 4 |
| | Fiery | 6 | 3 | 5 | 6 |

   Formulate an appropriate null hypothesis and determine whether there is any connection between hair colour and temperament.

 See Section 2: The Information Bank – *Inferential statistics* pages 244–247

□ **Extended tasks**

3. Collect data, set up contingency tables and carry out $\chi^2$ tests to investigate the validity of the following hypotheses (or think of one of your own):

❏ More women than men are left-handed

❏ More women than men are vegetarians

❏ More women than men fail their driving test at the first attempt

❏ More women than men buy small cars

❏ More men than women study technology-based courses

❏ Women read more than men

❏ More men than women watch sport

❏ More men than women play sport

❏ Ability in Mathematics is related to nationality

❏ Smoking habits are related to drinking habits

See Section 3: Further Tasks and Investigations pages 380–381 *Q 45–49*

# Unit 43: Students

*Topic: Statistics*

*Significance testing*

With the decrease in the number of 18-year olds it is suggested that the standard of entry to higher education at Dale Institute is being allowed to fall in order to fill available places. In 1983 the mean 'A'-level points score of the intake of 125 students to the four-year full-time B.Ed. course (a course for prospective teachers) was 3.98 with a standard deviation of 1.51. For the 1988 entry of 136 students the mean points score was 3.71 with a standard deviation of 1.95. (Note that the 'points' score for a student is based on 5 points for each grade A, 4 for each grade B, 3 for each grade C, 2 for each grade D and 1 for each grade E).

Dale's Student Registry Office keeps careful records of, amongst other information, the destination of those students who graduate. Current records reveal that 110 of the 116 students graduating in 1987 took up a teaching appointment, whilst 19 of the 125 students graduating in 1992 did not take up a teaching appointment. Some staff commented that this showed that teaching had declined as a career both in status and relative pay, consequently accounting for the lower proportion of students entering the profession.

■ Tasks

1. Carry out a suitable significance test on the difference between the mean 'A'-level points scores for the 1983 and 1988 intakes to the B.Ed. course to determine whether the figures support the idea that the entry standard is being allowed to fall.

2. Carry out a suitable significance test on the difference between the proportions of the 1987 and 1992 B.Ed. graduates that enter teaching to determine whether the figures support the staff's concerns about the decline of teaching as a career.

3. Many students on the B.Ed. course at Dale undertake part-time work in order to supplement their grant. This is of some concern to teaching staff who suspect that this may have adverse effects on those students' academic performances. As part of a related research project, one lecturer has obtained figures connected with the 'A'-level examinations performances of 120 students currently on the B.Ed. course. He also circulates a questionnaire to these students requesting information about any part-time paid work done during their 'A'-level study years. The tables below give details of this information:

*Table A*

| No. of 'A'-level passes | | Sex of student | |
| --- | --- | --- | --- |
| | | Male | Female |
| | 0 | 3 | 6 |
| | 1 | 6 | 11 |
| | 2 | 12 | 15 |
| | 3 | 24 | 27 |
| | 4 | 7 | 9 |

*Table B (Students with paid employment for 5 hours or less per week)*

| No. of 'A'-level points | No. of students |
| --- | --- |
| 0 – 2 | 3 |
| 3 – 5 | 8 |
| 6 – 8 | 16 |
| 9 – 11 | 7 |
| 12 – 14 | 5 |
| 15 – 17 | 3 |
| 18 – 20 | 2 |

*Table C (Students with paid employment for more than 5 hours per week)*

| No. of 'A'-level points | No. of students |
| --- | --- |
| 0 – 2 | 16 |
| 3 – 5 | 18 |
| 6 – 8 | 23 |
| 9 – 11 | 10 |
| 12 – 14 | 5 |
| 15 – 17 | 3 |
| 18 – 20 | 11 |

a) With reference to Table A:

i) determine if there is any significant difference between the mean number of 'A'-level passes obtained by male students and female students

ii) use a $\chi^2$ test to determine if there is any significant difference between male and female students in respect of the number of 'A'-level passes obtained

b) With reference to Tables B & C:

i) construct a histogram for each table

ii) calculate the mean and standard deviation of the 'A'-level points scores in each case

iii) determine if there is any significant difference between the mean 'A'-level points scores for those students who worked for 5 hours or less per week and those students who worked for more than 5 hours per week

c) Any observations or conclusions ?

See Section 2: The Information Bank – *Inferential statistics* pages 240–247

 See Section 3: Further Tasks and Investigations pages 375–381 *Q 31–49*

# Unit 44: Cafeteria

*Topic: Simulation*

*Monte Carlo techniques*

A Computer Science student at the institute has been requested by her course tutor to undertake a study of the rather congested situation that arises in the cafeteria due to the large number of staff and students queueing for lunch. After some initial investigation she decides to study the system by means of a simulation with a view to alleviating the situation.

## ■ Tasks

1.  a)  What sort of considerations will have influenced the student in her decision to opt for the simulation approach to the problem?

    b)  Identify the main variables that are likely to figure in the student's model of the system.

    c)  Prior to modelling the system on a computer by writing a program, she decides to perform a manual 'run' of her model. Explain the value of doing this.

2.  The distribution of arrivals and services (per minute) at the cafeteria service-point as follows:

| No. of arrivals | Frequency | Probability | Random numbers | No. of services | Frequency | Probability | Random numbers |
|---|---|---|---|---|---|---|---|
| 8  | 8%  | 0.08 | 00–07 | 7  | 9%  | 0.09 | 00–08 |
| 9  | 22% |      |       | 8  | 19% |      |       |
| 10 | 38% |      |       | 9  | 42% |      |       |
| 11 | 26% |      |       | 10 | 25% |      |       |
| 12 | 6%  | 0.06 | 94–99 | 11 | 5%  | 0.05 | 95–99 |

    a)  Complete the table, assigning a probability and a range of random numbers to each event.

    b)  Considering these two variables only, perform a manual simulation of a 30-minute time period tabulating the results in an appropriate form.

    c)  Calculate the average queue length.

 See Section 2: The Information Bank – *Problem-solving techniques* pages 248–254

## ☐ Extended Tasks

3.  a)  Either develop a spreadsheet or write a computer program to simulate the situation. For instance, a program might have the following general structure:

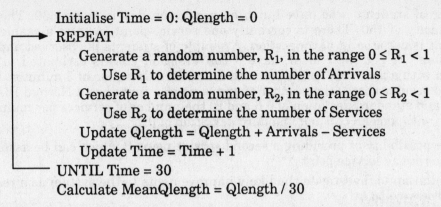

```
Initialise Time = 0: Qlength = 0
REPEAT
      Generate a random number, R₁, in the range 0 ≤ R₁ < 1
            Use R₁ to determine the number of Arrivals
      Generate a random number, R₂, in the range 0 ≤ R₂ < 1
            Use R₂ to determine the number of Services
      Update Qlength = Qlength + Arrivals – Services
      Update Time = Time + 1
UNTIL Time = 30
Calculate MeanQlength = Qlength / 30
```

b)  Use the spreadsheet / program to investigate the sensitivity of the congestion to variations in the service rate. For instance, what happens if an improvement can be made, as follows:

| No. of services | Frequency |
|---|---|
| 7 | 2% |
| 8 | 10% |
| 9 | 26% |
| 10 | 40% |
| 11 | 22% |

Assume that the arrivals rate stays the same.

c)  Similarly, investigate the sensitivity of the congestion to variations in the arrival rate.

d)  Any conclusions?

4.  A more detailed study of the cafeteria congestion is to be undertaken. A diagram of the cafeteria and the lunchtime queueing situation is shown below:

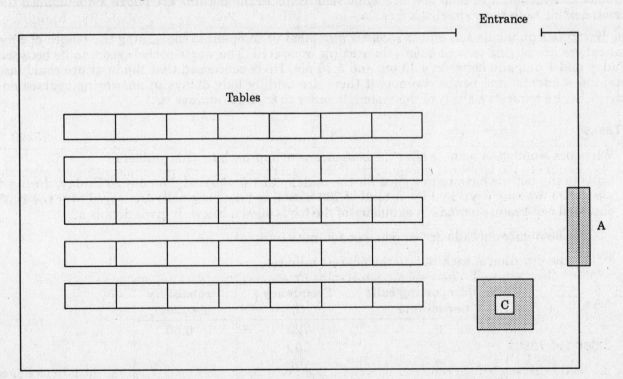

The number of students who have lunch on any given day is about 600. The cafeteria has a seating capacity of 150. There is currently one service-point (A) and a cashier-point (C). The cashier-point is not a point of congestion. A sample of students is observed and the 'table time' taken by them (to eat their meal, have a conversation etc.) is estimated to have a Normal Distribution with a mean of 18 minutes with a standard deviation of 3 minutes. For simplicity, it is decided to assume that i) the number of arrivals per minute has a Normal Distribution with a mean of 10 and standard deviation of 0.6 and ii) the number of services per minute has a Normal Distribution with a mean of 9 and standard deviation of 0.7

There is the possibility of providing a second service-point B which can be assumed to have the same service rate as service-point A.

a)  Use simulation to investigate the likely improvements to the system as a result of providing an extra service-point.

b)  What recommendations would you make?

c)  Any suggestions for further improvements to the model?

5.  Identify a congested queuing system in your own situation. Use simulation to investigate the problem and suggest possible solutions.

See Section 3: Further Tasks and Investigations pages 382–387 *Q 1–10*

# Unit 45: Telephone hotline                     *Topic: Simulation*

*Monte Carlo techniques*

Dale Institute has a special telephone hot-line dedicated to dealing with the many calls from prospective students concerning requests for prospectuses, general enquiries about courses, re-registration for further study, course fees and so on. This line is particularly busy during the late Summer months, prior to each new academic year. Calls to the hot-line are put in a queue until the person dealing with the enquiries is free.

The Institute's public liaison officer receives a number of complaints concerning the length of time that callers are having to wait before their call is answered. The worst periods seem to be between midday and 1 pm, and between 4.30 pm and 5.30 pm. He is concerned that the institute could lose potential students, and hence revenue, if there are unduly long delays in answering courses enquiries. So, he requests a study of the system in order to try and improve it.

## ■ Tasks

1.  Why does simulation seem to offer the best means of approaching this problem ?

2.  Calls to the hotline have been logged for the midday to 1 pm period, Monday to Friday, during 4 weeks (20 working days) in July. A total of 720 incoming telephone calls are logged over the 1200 observed one-minute periods. A summary of the log is shown below. It gives details of:

    i)   the number of calls arriving in a one-minute interval

    ii)  the duration of each call (to the nearest minute)

| No. of incoming calls per minute | Frequency (f) | Probability (f ÷ 1200) |
|---|---|---|
| 0 | 720 | 0.60 |
| 1 | 300 | |
| 2 | 120 | |
| 3 | 60 | |

| Duration of call (minutes) | Frequency (f) | Probability (f ÷ 720) |
|---|---|---|
| 1 | 216 | 0.30 |
| 2 | 130 | |
| 3 | 108 | |
| 4 | 72 | |
| 5 | 65 | |
| 6 | 50 | |
| 7 | 36 | |
| 8 | 29 | |
| 9 | 14 | |

a) Complete the tables, giving the associated probabilities correct to 2D.

b) Assign a range of two-digit random numbers to each event.

c) Perform several manual simulations of the midday to 1 pm period, tabulating the results in an appropriate form. One possible format is outlined below (the random numbers are taken from the first column of Appendix A):

| Incoming calls | | | Call timings | | | Call durations | | |
|---|---|---|---|---|---|---|---|---|
| Time | Random number | Number of calls | Put in queue | Answered | Waiting time (mins) | Random number | Duration of call (mins) | End of call |
| 12:00 | 53 | 0 | | | | | | |
| 12:01 | 63 | 1 → | 12:01 | 12:01 | 0 | 35 | 2 | 12:03 |
| 12:02 | 63 | 1 → | 12:02 | 12:03 | 1 | 98 | 9 | 12:12 |
| 12:03 | 02 | 0 | | | | | | |
| 12:04 | 64 | 1 → | 12:04 | 12:12 | 8 | 85 | 6 | 12:18 |
| 12:05 | 58 | 0 | | | | | | |
| 12:06 | 34 | 0 | | | | | | |
| 12:07 | 03 | 0 | | | | | | |
| 12:08 | 62 | 1 → | 12:08 | 12:18 | 10 | 08 | 1 | 12:19 |
| 12:09 | 07 | 0 | | | | | | |
| 12:10 | 01 | 0 | | | | | | |
| 12:11 | 72 | 1 → | 12:11 | 12:19 | 8 | 88 | 6 | 12:25 |
| 12:12 | 45 | 0 | | | | | | |
| 12:13 | 96 | 3 → | 12:13 | 12:25 | 12 | 43 | 2 | 12:27 |
| | | | 12:13 | 12:27 | 14 | 50 | 3 | 12:30 |
| | | | 12:13 | 12:30 | 17 | 22 | 1 | 12:31 |
| 12:14 etc | 96 | 3 | 12:14 | 12:31 | 17 | 31 | 2 | 12:33 |

d) What assumption has been made in this model?

e) Calculate the average time that callers are kept waiting.

f) Calculate the proportion of time that the receptionist is idle.

3. One suggestion put forward is that a second hotline facility be provided during the busy periods. The calls would still be placed in a queue but dealt with by whichever receptionist happens to be available. Repeat the manual simulations assuming that there are now two hotlines:
   a) Is it better to use the same, or a different, collection of random numbers as in Task 2 ?
   b) Calculate the average time that callers are likely to be kept waiting.
   c) Calculate the likely proportion of idle time for each receptionist.

4. What recommendations would you make as a result of the simulations in Task 2 and Task 3?

5. Make suggestions as to how the simulation could be improved.

 See Section 2: The Information Bank – *Problem-Solving Techniques* pages 249–254

□ **Extended Task**

6. Either develop a spreadsheet model or write a computer program to simulate the situation:
   a) Use the manual simulation results to validate the computer model.
   b) Do the results of the computer simulation seem to confirm the recommendations of Task 4 ?

 See Section 3: Further Tasks and Investigations pages 382–387 *Q 1–10*

# Unit 46: Brand-switching
*Topic: Simulation*

*Monte Carlo techniques*

As part of a Business Studies course, students are examining the phenomenon of 'brand-switching' (customers changing from one product brand to another). The course tutor divides the class members into groups and asks each to undertake a small-scale study of this phenomenon, the particular topic under study to be chosen by the group members. The time allowed for the study is one term.

One group decides to observe student behaviour in their smoking habits. Over a period of 10 weeks they observe one student who has very indecisive tendencies and regularly changes his brand of cigarettes. He is currently hovering between three different brands and changes every week. Which brand he is likely to change to depends on which brand he is using at the moment and if he decides to change at all. The diagram on the page following shows the probabilities of various transitions, based on the Business Studies group's observations. (For example, if he is currently smoking brand B, there is a probability of 0.2 that he will change to brand A, a probability of 0.1 that he will change to brand C and a probability of 0.7 that he will not change brands that week).

The group wishes to know which brand of cigarette the student is most likely to be smoking at any given time. One member suggests that a simulation of the student's smoking habits may reveal trends that are not apparent from their assembled information.

■ **Task**

1. Complete these tables (or similar) of transition probabilities and assign random numbers:

| Event | Probability | Random numbers | Event | Probability | Random numbers | Event | Probability | Random numbers |
|-------|-------------|----------------|-------|-------------|----------------|-------|-------------|----------------|
| A to A | 0.5 | 0 – 4 | B to A | | | C to A | | |
| A to B | 0.3 | 5 – 7 | B to B | | | C to B | | |
| A to C | 0.2 | 8 – 9 | B to C | | | C to C | | |

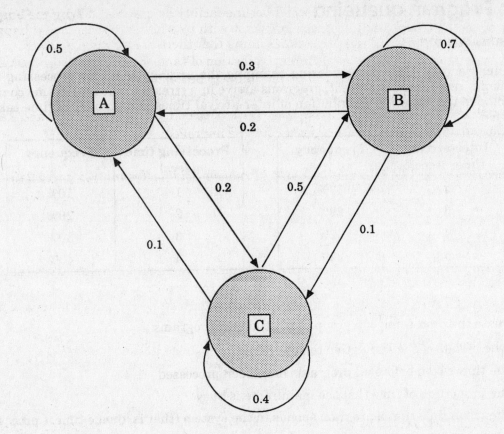

a) Carry out a manual simulation of a 50-week period of this student's smoking habit, assuming that he is currently smoking brand B, tabulating the results in an appropriate form.

b) Which brand of cigarette is he most likely to be smoking at any given time?

c) How reliable is the result obtained in b), and how may it be improved?

 See Section 2: The Information Bank – *Problem-Solving Techniques* pages 249–254

☐ **Extended Tasks**

2. a) Either develop a spreadsheet model or write a computer program to simulate the situation.

   b) Run the spreadsheet / program over a variety of simulated time periods.

   c) What seems to happen to the likelihood of the student smoking each brand of cigarette ?

3. a) Investigate the sensitivity of the results to variations in the transition probabilities. For instance, what are the resulting effects if the transition probabilities from brand B to brands A, B and C are 0.2, 0.6 and 0.2 respectively ?

   b) Any conclusions?

 See Section 3: Further Tasks and Investigations pages 382–387 *Q 1–10*

# Unit 47: Program queueing

*Topic: Simulation*

*Event-based simulation*

The Computer Services Unit is considering changing the arrangements for processing Computer Science students' programs. At present, programs arrive in a stream to the mainframe computer and are found to have the following distribution of inter-arrival times and amount of time taken to process programs:

| Inter-arrival times (secs) | Frequency |
| --- | --- |
| 2 | 17% |
| 3 | 29% |
| 4 | 32% |
| 5 | 22% |

| Processing time (secs) | Frequency |
| --- | --- |
| 1 | 10% |
| 2 | 20% |
| 3 | 30% |
| 4 | 40% |

## ■ Task

1. a) Simulate the processing of a group of 20 students' programs.

   b) Use the results of the simulation to determine:

   i) the time taken before all programs have been processed

   ii) the proportion of time that the mainframe is busy

   iii) the mean time that a program spends in the system (that is, queue time + process time)

   c) The Computer Services Unit is considering the possibility of dividing the programs into two equal independent streams. Each of the streams would be processed by a minicomputer which is capable of processing programs at half the rate of the mainframe. That is, each of the two minicomputers has a program processing time distribution as follows:

| Processing time (secs) | Frequency |
| --- | --- |
| 2 | 10% |
| 4 | 20% |
| 6 | 30% |
| 8 | 40% |

   i) Simulate the processing of the same 20 programs by the two minicomputers

   ii) Are the two minicomputers a better proposition than the mainframe in terms of the mean time that a program spends in the system ?

See Section 2: The Information Bank – *Problem-Solving Techniques* pages 260–262

See Section 3: Further Tasks and Investigations pages 389–390 *Q 13, 14*

# Unit 48: Pseudo-random numbers

*Topic: Simulation*

*Pseudo-random number generation*

This unit is concerned with investigating ways of producing pseudo-random numbers.

a) *Mid-square method*

A very simple and crude method introduced by Von Neumann.

> Step 1:  Choose a two-digit number (the *seed*) and square it
> Step 2:  Use the middle two digits as the next number in the sequence
> Step 3:  Repeat from step 1

For example:  $23^2 = 0529$

$52^2 = 2704$

$70^2 = 4900$

etc. producing the sequence: 23, 52, 70, 90 . . . . . . . . . .

The *cycle length* (the number of random numbers obtained before the sequence starts to repeat) of a sequence of random numbers produced by this method can be very short. For example: 35, 22, 48, 30, 90, 10, 10, 10 . . . . . . . . . . . This sequence degenerates very rapidly.

A further problem is that not all numbers produced by this method have the same probability of occurring; that is, it tends to favour certain numbers. The choice of the initial seed is critical in this respect. An interesting method from a historical point-of-view but useless for practical purposes.

b) *Mid-product method*

This variation on the mid-square method was introduced to overcome some of its deficiencies.

> Step 1:  Choose *two* initial seeds and multiply them together
> Step 2:  Use the middle two digits as a new second seed
> Step 3:  Repeat from step 1

For example:  71 33  ➡  $71 \times 33 = 2343$

33 34  ➡  $33 \times 34 = 1122$

34 12  ➡  $34 \times 12 = 0408$

12 40  ➡  $12 \times 40 = 0480$

40 48  ➡  $40 \times 48 = 1920$

etc.

producing the sequence: 71, 33, 34, 12, 40, 48 . . . . . . . . . .

The cycle length is longer than that produced by the mid-square method as it requires both seeds to repeat before the sequence can repeat; however, it is still too short for practical purposes.

■ **Tasks**

1. For the mid-square method:

   a) Investigate the cycle lengths for different seeds. Any conclusions ?

   b) Does the method favours lower numbers ?

   c) Write a computer program to produce random numbers by this method, for any given seed.

   d) Modify the method / program to produce i) three-digit ii) four-digit numbers.

2. For the mid-product method:

   a) Investigate cycle lengths of various sequences produced by this method.

   b) Write a computer program to produce random numbers by this method, for any given seeds.

   c) Modify the method / program for i) three-digit ii) four-digit numbers.

   d) How uniform is the distribution of the numbers produced by this method?

 See Section 2: The Information Bank – *Problem-Solving Techniques* pages 250–251

☐ **Extended tasks**

3. *Additive congruential methods*

   The Fibonacci sequence is a well-known example of this sort of generator:

   $$1, 1, 2, 3, 5, 8, 13, 21, 34 \ldots\ldots\ldots\ldots$$

   Each number in the sequence is produced by adding together the two previous numbers and so needs two seeds. The process for generating the Fibonacci sequence can be written:

   $$n_i = n_{i-1} + n_{i-2}$$

   In general, additive congruential sequences are of the form:

   $$n_i = n_{i-1} + n_{i-k} \ (\text{mod } m)$$

   ($k$ can be any integer, but the sequence obviously assumes $k$ seeds).

   For instance, consider the process:

   $$n_i = n_{i-1} + n_{i-3} \ (\text{mod } 10)$$

   Using the three seeds 3, 4, 6 this process generates the sequence:

   $$3, 4, 6, 9, 3, 9, 8, 1, 0, 8, 9, 9, 7, 6, 5, 2, 8, 3, 5 \ldots\ldots\ldots$$

   Investigate additive congruential methods for various seeds and values of $k$ and $m$.

4. *Multiplicative congruential methods*

   These methods use the process:

   $$n_i = an_{i-1} \ (\text{mod } m)$$

   For instance, consider the process: $n_i = 2n_{i-1} \ (\text{mod } 5)$

   Using an initial seed of 1, the process generates the sequence:

   $$1, 2, 4, 3, 1, 2, 4, 3 \ldots\ldots\ldots\ldots \text{ (extremely short cycle length)}$$

   Investigate multiplicative congruential methods for various seeds and values of $a$ and $m$.

5. Multiplicative congruential methods produce pseudo-random numbers which stand up well to statistical tests for randomness. Consequently, these methods are widely used to produce pseudo-random sequences. Research the method used by a computer of your choice.

 See Section 3: Further Tasks and Investigations pages 388–389 *Q 11, 12*

# Unit 49: Tables

*Topic: Linear programming*

## Graphical method

Seating arrangements in the Wentworth campus cafeteria are proving to be inadequate. The institute have, therefore, made a commitment to the purchase of additional furniture to cope with demand and have earmarked money for this purpose.

Flexibility in layout is an important consideration; so, it is decided to buy tables that can be interlocked in different arrangements. There are two types of tables, the Octo and the Quattro, that are suitable. Each Octo seats 8 people and occupies $7m^2$ of floor space; each Quattro seats 4 people and occupies $3m^2$ of floor space. Seating for at least 480 people is required. Allowing for chairs and movement of people, the amount of floor space available for tables is $600m^2$.

Since the units may need to be rearranged for functions such as conferences, there must be at least as many Quattros as Octos to allow for variations in layout. For similar reasons there must be at least 30 Octos.

The Institute also wishes to purchase the smallest total number of tables to meet its requirements; this is for reasons of maintenance, storage, movement and cleaning.

## ■ Tasks

1. Assuming that *x* Octos and *y* Quattros are purchased:

   a) Explain why the amount of seating required means that:

   $$2x + y \geq 120$$

   b) Formulate three more constraints.

   c) Write down the objective function.

2. a) Show the constraints on a graph.

   b) Highlight the feasible region.

3. a) Use the graph to determine the number of Quattros and Octos that should be bought.

   b) Calculate:

   i) the number of people that can be accommodated

   ii) the amount of floor space occupied

4. An Octo costs £140 and a Quattro costs £60. The management decides to spend as little as possible on the seating units:

   a) Write down the new objective function.

   b) What is the cheapest combination of Quattros and Octos ?

   c) What is the number of people accommodated ?

   d) If the price of a Quattro increases to £100, how does this affect the solutions to (b) and (c) ?

 See Section 2: The Information Bank – *Problem-Solving Techniques* pages 263–270

 See Section 3: Further Tasks and Investigations pages 391–392 *Q 15–17*

# Unit 50: Car park

**Topic: Linear programming**

*Simplex algorithm; maximisation; ≤ constraints*

Car parking on the Brooklands campus is a major problem. On busy days, students are forced to park their cars in nearby side-streets; this usually results in complaints from residents. A questionnaire circulated by the Students' Union reveals that some students are willing to pay a small charge for a guaranteed parking space. It is decided to assess the viability of this scheme since the amount of income generated by this facility is likely to determine whether it proceeds at all.

The space that could be used for this facility has an area of no more than 360m². Each motorbike is allowed 2m² and each car allowed 6m²; however, regulations limit parking to no more than 80 vehicles. The charge is to be £1 per day for each motorbike and £2 per day for each car. It is the aim to maximise the amount of income generated.

## ■ Tasks

1. Assuming that $x$ motorbikes and $y$ cars use the parking facility:

   a) Formulate (and simplify where possible) two constraints in terms of $x$ and $y$.

   b) Write down the objective function.

2. Use the simplex algorithm to determine:

   i) the number of spaces that should be allocated to motorbikes and cars

   ii) the maximum possible daily income

3. Confirm your solution by using the graphical method.

 See Section 2: The Information Bank – *Problem-Solving Techniques* pages 270–274

## ☐ Extended Task

4. Since some cars occupy much more space than others, it is decided to charge £1 for motorbikes, £2 for cars and £3 for large cars (these are allowed 8m² for parking).

   Assuming that $z$ large cars use the parking facility:

   a) Reformulate the linear programming problem in terms of $x$, $y$ and $z$.

   b) Use the simplex algorithm to determine:

   i) the number of spaces that should be allocated to motorbikes, cars and large cars

   ii) the maximum possible daily income

 See Section 3: Further Tasks and Investigations pages 392–393 *Q 19–21*

# Unit 51: Accommodation

**Topic: Linear programming**

*Simplex algorithm; maximisation; ≤ and ≥ constraints*

The increase in the number of students enrolling on full-time higher education courses means that the Institute needs to consider the provision of extra residential accommodation. Within the campus there is a large area of the grounds, some $18000m^2$, on which it is proposed to build a mixture of houses and flats. The anticipated building cost for a house is £50000 and for each flat is £40000; there is a financial ceiling of £2800000 for the development. The amount of space taken up by each house is $500m^2$; each flat takes up $150m^2$. To achieve a balance of accommodation it is also desired to build at least 10 houses and 20 flats.

The average number of students that can be accommodated by each house is 4, each flat accommodating an average of 2 students. The intention is to provide residence for as many students as possible.

### ■ Tasks

1. Assuming that $x$ houses and $y$ flats are built:

   a) Formulate (and simplify where possible) four constraints in terms of $x$ and $y$.

   b) Write down the objective function.

2. a) Use the simplex algorithm to determine how many houses and flats should be built.

   b) Calculate:

   i) the maximum number of students that can be accommodated

   ii) the cost of building the development

3. Confirm your solution by using the graphical method.

See Section 2: The Information Bank – *Problem-Solving Techniques* pages 270–278

See Section 3: Further Tasks and Investigations pages 392–394 *Q 17–21*

# Unit 52: River pollution

**Topic: Linear programming**

*Simplex algorithm; minimisation*

There are three industrial concerns (BigCo, MidCo and LilCo) on the upper reaches of the River Dale that regularly discharge pollutants into the river. They have been informed by environmental officers that they must take immediate steps to reduce the levels of these pollutants. Each factory produces two types of pollutant, P and Q; the pollutant levels in the river need to be reduced by at least 45 tons of P and at least 80 tons of Q. This can be achieved by processing the waste from each factory, but at a cost.

Processing each ton of waste from BigCo reduces the amount of P by 0.3 ton and of Q by 0.5 ton.

Processing each ton of waste from MidCo reduces the amount of P by 0.15 ton and of Q by 0.9 ton.

Processing each ton of waste from LilCo reduces the amount of P by 0.6 ton and of Q by 0.6 ton.

The costs of processing waste at BigCo, MidCo and LilCo are respectively £6, £9 and £12 per ton. The companies agree to reduce pollution levels by the required amounts but wish to minimise the total cost.

### ■ Tasks

1. Assuming that the number of tons of waste processed at BigCo, MidCo and LilCo are $x$, $y$ and $z$ respectively:

   a) Explain why the desired reduction in the level of pollutant P means that:
   $$2x + y + 4z \geq 300$$
   b) Formulate, and simplify, another constraint in terms of $x$, $y$ and $z$.
   c) Write down the objective function.

2. a) Formulate the dual problem.
   b) Use the simplex algorithm to determine:
   i)   the quantity of waste that each factory should process
   ii)  the total cost of reducing the pollution level

3. Confirm your solution to Task 2 by using the graphical method.

 See Section 2: The Information Bank – *Problem-Solving Techniques* pages 274–277

 See Section 3: Further Tasks and Investigations pages 395 *Q 22*

# Unit 53: File storage

**Topic: Transportation**

*North-west corner rule; least cost rule; unequal supply and demand*

A Computer Science student with her own microcomputer has built up a considerable collection of software and associated files during her time at Dale. These consist mainly of written assignments produced on a desk-top publishing package, spreadsheet templates and database files. The amount of use that she makes of the different packages and files varies, as does the device on which they are stored. The computer has a hard disc drive, twin floppy disc drives and a tape streamer.

She decides to reorganise her files according to the amount of usage each gets and the retrieval times of the various storage devices. Each term, on average, she accesses a DTP file four times, a spreadsheet file twice and a database file once. Estimates of the number of files that she needs to store are: DTP – 140; spreadsheet – 100; database – 60. She estimates that with her present facilities there is sufficient storage space for 100 files on hard disc, 50 files on floppy disc and 150 files on tape.
When the files are accessed she reckons that the retrieval time (in seconds) depends on the file type and the storage device, as follows:

|           |           | Storage device |              |
|           | Hard disc | Floppy disc | Tape streamer |
|-----------|-----------|-------------|---------------|
| DTP       | 4         | 10          | 17            |
| Spreadsheet | 2       | 6           | 9             |
| Database  | 3         | 8           | 15            |

*File type* labels the rows DTP, Spreadsheet, Database.

The student wishes to store the files so that the total time spent on retrieval is a minimum.

■ **Tasks**

The student formulates the information as a transportation problem and starts to construct a tableau:

| File type | Storage device | | | Storage requirements |
|---|---|---|---|---|
| | Hard disc | Floppy disc | Tape | |
| DTP | 16 | 40 | 68 | 140 |
| Spreadsheet | | | | |
| Database | | | | |
| *Storage capabilities* | | | | |

1. a) Explain why the information concerning DTP files gives the first row of the tableau.

   b) Complete the tableau.

2. a) Use the North-West corner rule to obtain an initial allocation.

   b) Use the transportation algorithm to determine:
      i)  the optimum allocation of files
      ii) the minimum total time spent on file retrieval in a term

 See Section 2: The Information Bank – *Problem-Solving Techniques* pages 279–289

☐ **Extended task**

3. She later realises that she has overestimated the number of files that need to be stored. The revised estimates are:

   DTP 130;    spreadsheet 80;    database 40

   a) Construct an initial tableau.

   b) Use the 'least cost' rule to obtain an initial allocation.

   c) Use the transportation algorithm to determine:

      i)  the optimum allocation of files

      ii) the minimum total time spent on file retrieval in a term

 See Section 3: Further Tasks and Investigations pages 396–397 *Q 23–26*

# Unit 54: Activity day

*Topic: Transportation*

*North-west corner rule; degeneracy; unequal supply and demand*

Each month, groups of local school children are invited to the institute to take part in a variety of indoor activities organised by students. The locations used for the activities vary each month according to the types of activity on offer; the schools involved also change from month to month.

Student volunteers provide transport for the children between their schools and the institute's three campuses. In one particular month, groups of children from four different schools (A, B, C, D) are invited for activity day. Activities have been organised at the Brooklands, Harper and Wentworth campuses.

The number of children from each school, the numbers which can be catered for at the different campuses and the distances (in miles) between schools and campuses are as follows:

| *Campus* | *School* | | | | *Campus provision* |
|---|---|---|---|---|---|
| | A | B | C | D | |
| Brooklands | 2 | 2 | 4 | 5 | 35 |
| Harper | 7 | 4 | 5 | 3 | 25 |
| Wentworth | 4 | 3 | 5 | 6 | 5 |
| *No. of children involved* | 30 | 20 | 10 | 5 | 65 |

There is sufficient transport for the number of children involved; however, since students use their own cars, they obviously wish to minimise the total distance travelled.

## ■ Tasks

1.  a)  Use the North-West corner rule to obtain an initial allocation.

    b)  Use the transportation algorithm to determine:

    i)  the optimum allocation of children to activities

    ii)  the minimum total distance travelled

2.  School B are having a school photograph taken on activity day, so are unable to send their children. How should the remaining children be reallocated in order to keep the total travelling distance to a minimum ?

See Section 2: The Information Bank – *Problem-Solving Techniques* pages 279–296

See Section 3: Further Tasks and Investigations pages 396–397 *Q 23–26*

# Unit 55: Examinations

*Topic: Transportation*

*Vogel's rule; unequal supply and demand; inadmissable routes*

Examinations are an important feature of the annual calendar at Dale Institute, particularly during the Summer Term when most students are involved. The arrangements can cause a lot of disruption to the timetable since it is necessary to use the larger teaching spaces for examination purposes.

There are strict regulations governing the seating arrangement and invigilation in examination rooms; so, a major consideration is the provision of adequate numbers of tables and chairs in each of the designated locations. The Institute maintains a stock of furniture for just such occasions; for practical reasons, these are kept in several storage areas on each campus.

On the Brooklands campus the areas designated as examination locations are the Conference Centre, Main Hall and Sports Hall. The furniture is kept in four storage areas which can be called A, B, C and D. The following information shows the situation with respect to tables:

| Available | | Required | |
|---|---|---|---|
| Store A: | 90 | Conference Centre: | 20 |
| Store B: | 50 | Main Hall: | 50 |
| Store C: | 40 | Sports Hall: | 130 |
| Store D: | 20 | | |

■ **Task**

1. The distances, in metres, between the various storage areas and examination locations are:

| | A | B | C | D |
|---|---|---|---|---|
| Conference Centre | 70 | 30 | 50 | 40 |
| Main Hall | 30 | 60 | 50 | 40 |
| Sports Hall | 40 | 50 | 60 | 80 |

The tables have to be moved by the caretaking staff; they naturally wish to minimise the total distance that the tables move.

a) Construct a suitable tableau from the available information.

b) Obtain an initial allocation using Vogel's rule.

c) Use the transportation algorithm to determine:

   i) the optimum allocation of tables

   ii) the minimum total distance moved by the tables

2. On closer inspection, it is discovered that there may be only 100 tables required in the Sports Hall.

   What effect might this have on the table allocation ?

3. Before the movement of tables is due to begin, important building work takes place in certain corridors. In particular, the route between Store B and the Main Hall cannot be used, nor can the route between Store C and the Sports Hall. What effect does this have on the solution to the original problem ?

See Section 2: The Information Bank – *Problem-Solving Techniques* pages 279–297

 See Section 3: Further Tasks and Investigations pages 396–397 *Q 23–26*

# Unit 56: Swimmers                    *Topic: Assignment*

*Hungarian method; mismatched rows and columns*

Dale students are about to take part in a national swimming competition with teams arriving from all over Britain. The usual range of events are being staged at the Olympic-sized swimming pool on the Harper campus.

One event in which the team manager has high hopes of success is the $4 \times 100$m medley relay. In this event there are four different swimmers who, in turn, swim 100m of backstroke, breaststroke, butterfly and freestyle. He has a squad of six swimmers from which to choose the four who will make up the relay team. In practice he has timed each of the six swimmers for each stroke over 100m; their times, in seconds, are:

|  |  | Swimmer | | | | | |
|---|---|---|---|---|---|---|---|
|  |  | A | B | C | D | E | F |
|  | Backstroke | 71 | 69 | 73 | 69 | 70 | 66 |
| *Event* | Breaststroke | 73 | 77 | 71 | 72 | 74 | 75 |
|  | Butterfly | 68 | 72 | 77 | 67 | 71 | 65 |
|  | Freestyle | 61 | 61 | 59 | 60 | 57 | 59 |

The team manager wishes to assign four members of the squad in order to minimise their total time.

## ■ Tasks

1.  a)  Use the Hungarian method to determine the assignments.

    b)  Calculate the team's total time.

2.  A week before the competition, Swimmer E injures himself in training and is unable to take part.

    a)  Determine how the team manager can assign four of the remaining squad members.

    b)  How much slower than the original medley team are this new team ?

3.  An intensive training programme means that swimmer B manages to reduce his time for the breaststroke to 72 secs. How does this affect the new assignment and the team's time ?

 See Section 2: The Information Bank – *Problem-Solving Techniques* pages 297–300

 See Section 3: Further Tasks and Investigations pages 398–399 *Q 27–30*

# Unit 57: Compatibility

*Topic: Assignment*

*Hungarian method; maximisation; mismatched rows and columns*

A group of male and female students at Dale decide to enliven their existence by seeking compatible partners. As a first step they design, photocopy and circulate a questionnaire to other students requesting personal details such as height, hair colour, likes/dislikes, interests etc. The questionnaires returned from eighteen students (nine males, nine females) are selected for the initial experiment. Marks are awarded for areas of similarity between the two sets and an overall measure of compatibility (25 = extremely compatible; 0 = not at all compatible) is obtained for each possible student pairing. The compatibility measures for the eighteen students are:

|  |  | A | B | C | D | E | F | G | H | I |
|---|---|---|---|---|---|---|---|---|---|---|
|  | a | 19 | 22 | 20 | 16 | 17 | 12 | 17 | 18 | 19 |
|  | b | 16 | 21 | 17 | 18 | 15 | 17 | 15 | 17 | 18 |
|  | c | 10 | 16 | 20 | 14 | 16 | 14 | 13 | 12 | 15 |
|  | d | 20 | 13 | 15 | 17 | 19 | 21 | 18 | 20 | 20 |
| *Males* | e | 22 | 16 | 17 | 19 | 14 | 22 | 17 | 18 | 15 |
|  | f | 16 | 14 | 13 | 13 | 19 | 22 | 16 | 12 | 11 |
|  | g | 15 | 18 | 19 | 17 | 17 | 20 | 18 | 17 | 18 |
|  | h | 18 | 19 | 12 | 16 | 16 | 16 | 18 | 18 | 19 |
|  | i | 20 | 15 | 16 | 19 | 15 | 19 | 15 | 20 | 21 |

*Females* (column group header above A–I)

## ■ Task

It is decided to pair male and female students so as to maximise the total overall group compatibility.

1. a) Use the Hungarian method to determine the optimum student pairings.

   b) Calculate:
   i) the group's overall measure of compatibility
   ii) the mean compatibility of each student pair

2. Before the pairings are made, student F decides not to take part after all.

   a) Reassign the remaining students.

   b) How does this affect the mean compatibility ?

3. Not wishing that one of the male students should be left out, a replacement for F is found. The new student, J, has the following compatibility measures with the male students:

   16  17  13  18  20  15  17  19  16

   Reassign the students.

See Section 2: The Information Bank – *Problem-Solving Techniques* pages 297–300

See Section 3: Further Tasks and Investigations pages 398–399 *Q 27–30*

# Unit 58: Inter-campus travel

***Topic: Routing***

*Shortest path*

The map shows the relative positions of the Brooklands campus and the Harper campus. On many occasions students have to travel between campuses for lectures and other sessions. There are a variety of routes that can be taken, whether the students walk or travel by bike. However, since there is little time between lecture sessions, students are keen to minimise the travelling distance.

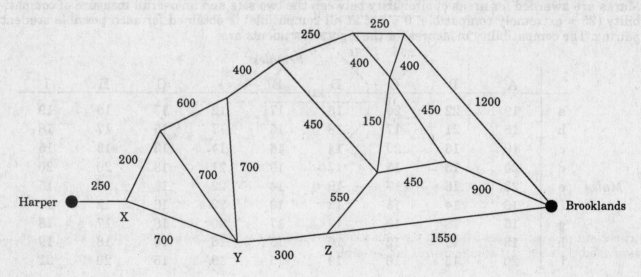

## ■ Tasks

1.  Use the shortest path algorithm to determine the shortest route between the two campuses (distances shown are in metres).

2.  If a student travels by bike the speed along main roads (the route HXYZB shown on the diagram) is only 10 km/h, compared with 20 km/h along minor roads, because of traffic lights, extra vehicles etc. Use the shortest path algorithm to determine the route that minimises total travel time.

**?** *help information*  See Section 2: The Information Bank – *Problem-Solving Techniques* pages 303–305

⇨ *further tasks*  See Section 3: Further Tasks and Investigations page 402 *Q 33*

# Unit 59: Telephone extensions

***Topic: Routing;***

*Minimum connector*

The diagram below shows the relative positions of eight staff areas (labelled A–H) of the Wentworth campus that are to be supplied with additional internal telephone extensions. The main switchboard is also shown on the diagram, labelled S.

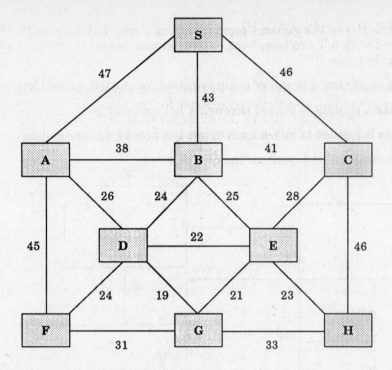

The distances in metres between the various areas are shown; if no distance is given, then it can be assumed that a direct connection is not possible.

■ **Tasks**

1. a) Use Prim's algorithm to determine the minimum amount of cable needed for all the extensions.

   b) Draw the minimum connector showing how the cable should be linked between areas.

2. Later, before the work is carried out, a request is made for a further extension in area I which is 35m from F, 38m from G and 36m from H. No other direct connections to I are possible.

   a) Determine how much more cable is required.

   b) Draw the new minimum connector.

 See Section 2: The Information Bank – *Problem-Solving Techniques* pages 305–309

☐ **Extended Tasks**

3. Write a computer program that implements Prim's algorithm for network data input in matrix form.

   The program output should give:

   i) the minimum connector length

   ii) node labels denoting the connections

   (Note that, normally, inadmissible connections are shown by an X in the matrix; for computer purposes, it is appropriate instead to insert a relatively high numerical value for each such connection. By this means, the algorithm is extremely unlikely to choose the connection).

4. The diagram below shows the general **room** layout of a new building on the Brooklands campus. The points marked with a T are telephone extension points and P marks the point of entry to the building of the main cable.

a) Calculate the minimum amount of **cable** required for the job, given that:

i) the extension cabling is ducted **through** a hollow ceiling

ii) 2m of cable is needed to reach **each** extension point from the ceiling

b) Show the minimum cable layout **on the** diagram.

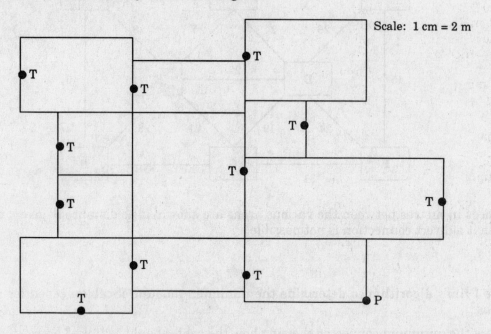

Scale: 1 cm = 2 m

See Section 3: Further Tasks and Investigations pages 400–401 *Q 31, 32*

# Unit 60: The Grand Tour

*Topic: Routing*

*Travelling salesman*

At several points in the year there are interviews for applicants who are seeking entry onto the 4-year degree courses. These are normally held at the Brooklands campus. On the day of the interview, applicants are given a brief outline of the programme for the day, a talk by the registrar who explains entry procedures, matters relating to grants etc. and an informal session with existing students. A small group of applicants is placed with a student who deals with any further queries and who generally assumes responsibility for them for the time prior to individual interviews with members of staff. Part of this informal session is a tour of the key facilities of the campus and takes in the library, computer centre, dining hall etc. It is obviously better if a student can visit each point on the campus tour once and once only before returning to the starting-point (which is usually the dining hall).

A diagram of the relative positions of these key features is shown below:

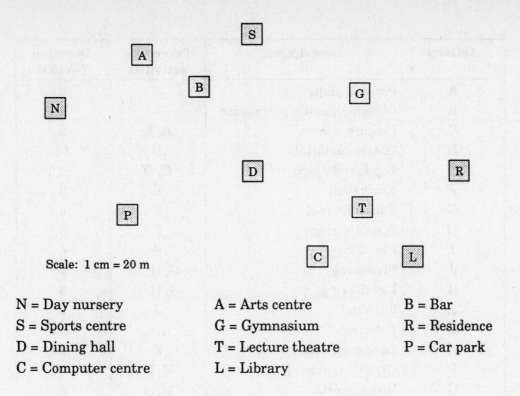

Scale: 1 cm = 20 m

N = Day nursery      A = Arts centre      B = Bar
S = Sports centre      G = Gymnasium      R = Residence
D = Dining hall      T = Lecture theatre      P = Car park
C = Computer centre      L = Library

## ■ Task

1. Assuming that direct routes are possible between all of the key features, obtain an upper bound and a lower bound for the distance travelled on the tour.

See Section 2: The Information Bank – *Problem-Solving Techniques* pages 309–311

See Section 3: Further Tasks and Investigations page 403 *Q 34, 35*

# Unit 61: Sports complex      *Topic: Critical path analysis*

*Network construction; critical path*

An extensive new complex is to be built on the Harper campus to increase the institute's provision for sport and recreation activities. It is also intended to provide social and changing areas so that the whole complex can be used, on a hire basis, by individuals and groups within the local community. On the following page is a list of the activities, their durations and other dependent activities, that have been identified as comprising the overall project. These include all the construction aspects and matters relating to the opening ceremony.

## ■ Tasks

1. Construct a network diagram showing the given information.

| Activity | Description | Preceding activities | Duration (weeks) |
|----------|-------------|----------------------|------------------|
| A | Prepare plans | --- | 3 |
| B | Obtain planning permission | --- | 8 |
| C | Prepare site | A, B | 2 |
| D | Obtain materials | B | 10 |
| E | Lay foundations | C, D | 4 |
| F | Erect shell | E | 9 |
| G | Construct roof | F | 4 |
| H | Install wiring | F | 5 |
| I | Plumbing | F | 6 |
| J | Plastering | G, H, I | 4 |
| K | Lay flooring | G, H, I | 5 |
| L | Fittings | J | 3 |
| M | Painting | K, L | 2 |
| N | Landscape site | F | 2 |
| P | Organise catering | M, N | 2 |
| Q | Invite guests | M, N | 6 |

2. Use the diagram to determine:

   i)   the EST for each activity

   ii)  the LFT for each activity

   iii) the minimum possible completion time for the sports complex

   iv)  the critical path

3. For each activity, calculate its:

   i)   total float

   ii)  free float

 See Section 2: The Information Bank – *Problem-Solving Techniques* pages 312–322

## ☐ Extended Tasks

4. The project coordinator is reluctant to specify an exact completion time for the sports complex since the activities are likely to be subject to some variation in duration. After some research she obtains the most optimistic and the most pessimistic completion times for each activity. These are given, in weeks, in the table on the following page.

   a) Use PERT principles to complete the table by calculating, for each activity time:

      i)  the mean

      ii) the standard deviation

| Activity | Optimistic duration | Most likely duration | Pessimistic duration | Mean | Standard deviation |
|---|---|---|---|---|---|
| A | 2 | 3 | 5 | $\dfrac{2+12+5}{6}=3.17$ | $\dfrac{5-2}{6}=0.5$ |
| B | 6 | 8 | 10 | | |
| C | 1.5 | 2 | 3 | | |
| D | 8 | 10 | 13 | | |
| E | 3 | 4 | 5 | | |
| F | 8 | 9 | 11 | | |
| G | 3 | 4 | 6 | $\dfrac{3+16+6}{6}=4.17$ | $\dfrac{6-3}{6}=0.5$ |
| H | 3.5 | 5 | 7 | | |
| I | 5 | 6 | 7 | | |
| J | 2.5 | 4 | 6 | | |
| K | 4 | 5 | 6.5 | | |
| L | 2 | 3 | 4 | | |
| M | 1.5 | 2 | 3 | $\dfrac{1.5+8+3}{6}=2.08$ | $\dfrac{3-1.5}{6}=0.25$ |
| N | 1.5 | 2 | 3 | | |
| P | 1.5 | 2 | 2.5 | | |
| Q | 5 | 6 | 8 | | |

b) Determine:

   i)   the mean time and standard deviation for completion of the overall project

   ii)  95% confidence intervals for completion of the overall project

c) If the project coordinator wants a 99% chance that the facilities are available for the start of the new academic year (September 1), when should work begin ?

5. Develop a spreadsheet model that, given the optimistic duration, most likely duration and pessimistic duration for each activity in a project network, calculates the mean time and standard deviation for:

   i)   each activity

   ii)  the overall project

 See Section 3: Further Tasks and Investigations pages 404–408 *Q 36–39*

# Unit 62: Concert            *Topic: Critical path analysis*

*Network construction; critical path; PERT*

The Students' Union is to take responsibility, with the assistance of a local entertainments agency, for organising a Midsummer's Day open-air rock concert at the Brooklands campus. The following is a list of activities that have been identified, together with their respective durations:

| Activity | Description | Duration (weeks) |
|---|---|---|
| A | Obtain permission | 8 |
| B | Prepare site | 6 |
| C | Hire engineers | 4 |
| D | Hire hands | 6 |
| E | Organise local radio publicity | 4 |
| F | Organise local press publicity | 4 |
| G | Print posters | 3 |
| H | Print tickets | 4 |
| I | Organise refreshments | 2 |
| J | Prepare electronics | 6 |
| K | Rehearsals | 2 |
| L | Display posters | 4 |
| M | Sell tickets | 4 |

## ■ Tasks

1. a)  Determine the likely precedence relationships for the activities.

   b)  Construct a network diagram for the project.

2.  Use the diagram to determine:

    i)   the EST for each activity

    ii)  the LFT for each activity

    iii) the minimum possible completion time for the project

    iv)  the critical path

3.  For each activity, calculate its :

    i)   total float

    ii)  free float

 See Section 2: The Information Bank – *Problem-Solving Techniques* pages 312–322

## □ Extended Task

4.  The Students' Union obtains rough estimates for how much each activity is likely to vary from its most likely duration. These are given, in days, in the following table. So, for instance, (–4, +6) means that the activity has an optimistic completion time that is 4 days ahead of the most likely time and a pessimistic completion time that overruns the most likely time by 6 days:

    a)  Use PERT principles to complete the table by calculating, for each activity's time:

    i)   the mean

    ii)  the standard deviation

| Activity | Most likely duration (weeks) | Possible variation (days) | Mean (weeks) | Standard deviation (weeks) |
|---|---|---|---|---|
| A | 8 | (−7, +14) | $\dfrac{7+32+10}{6}=8.17$ | $\dfrac{10-7}{6}=0.5$ |
| B | 6 | (−5, +10) | $\dfrac{5.29+24+7.43}{6}=6.12$ | $\dfrac{7.43-5.29}{6}=0.36$ |
| C | 4 | (−5, +7) | | |
| D | 6 | (−7, +7) | | |
| E | 4 | (−3, +4) | | |
| F | 4 | (−3, +4) | | |
| G | 3 | (−2, +4) | | |
| H | 4 | (−3, +4) | | |
| I | 2 | (−2, +3) | | |
| J | 6 | (−5, +10) | | |
| K | 2 | (−1, +4) | | |
| L | 4 | (−3, +5) | | |
| M | 4 | (−3, +5) | | |

b) Determine:

   i)   the mean time and standard deviation for completion of the overall project

   ii)  95% confidence intervals for completion of the overall project

c) When should the project be started if the Students' Union wants a 99% chance that the concert arrangements will be completed by the scheduled date ?

 See Section 3: Further Tasks and Investigations pages 404–408 *Q 36–39*

# Section 2

## The information bank

This section is made up of 13 topics (units) and provides the background information and principles that are necessary to undertake the Tasks in Sections 1 and 3. It is cross-referenced from Section 1 and 3 so that you only need use it when directed to a particular topic from that section. Further references are also given to other parts of the Information Bank that may prove helpful in understanding the material, as well as to wider reading.

*Contents:*

# Unit 1: Mathematical models

> This section aims to help you to:
>
> 1. identify the different types of models
> 2. understand what is meant by a 'mathematical model'
> 3. appreciate the value of mathematical models
> 4. identify and apply the stages in the modelling process
> 5. appreciate the use of a spreadsheet as a modelling tool

## What is a model?

To model something is to create another, simpler, form of the original which possesses all its important features. So, for example, the following could all be considered to be models:

| | | |
|---|---|---|
| Train set | Doll's house | Architect's plan |
| Opinion poll | Military manoeuvres | Crime reconstruction |
| Crash-test rig | Flight simulator | War games |
| Business decision games | Map | Diagram |
| Cartoon | | |

The items on the list are all representations of reality; some are closer to reality than others; some need to be closer to reality than others. They have also been constructed for a variety of different purposes. For instance, train sets and dolls' houses are scaled-down versions of the real things; war games are used to represent actual war scenarios; cartoons mimic life and so on. However, the underlying reasons for constructing war games are obviously different from those which prompt the production of cartoons.

## Why build a model?

The purpose of building a model is usually to try and learn something about the behaviour of the original. By experimenting with the model, lessons can be learned about the real thing. So, for example, the results of opinion polls provide pointers for a real election; using a flight simulator gives invaluable practice and guidance for trainee pilots; reconstructing a crime may assist the police in apprehending the villains.

There are several advantages in using a model. For instance, suppose that a new design of chemical plant is proposed. It is possible to construct a 'computer model' which can be programmed with all the necessary information about the features of the proposed design. When the program is run the computer model mimics the real thing; that is, it behaves like an actual chemical plant. The model can then be used for experiments in order to discover whether certain temperatures are likely to be exceeded and what the resulting effects might be. If these prove disastrous, modifications can then be made to the design before the real plant is built. Without the model, the outcome may prove extremely costly in terms of time, money and lives.

Obviously the quality of information and feedback received by manipulating a model will only be as good as the quality of the model itself. In other words, the model must be as accurate a representation of the original as possible. If the model is badly constructed and not representative of the original, any conclusions based on observations of the model are likely to be inaccurate.

# Mathematical models (1)

Models can be broadly classified as follows:

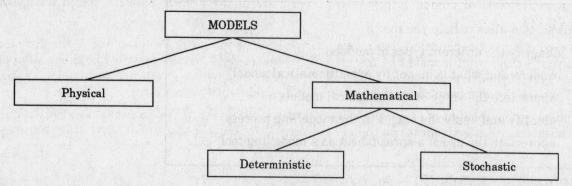

The type and quality of the model constructed depends not only on the situation that it is meant to represent but also the purpose for which it is required. Dolls' houses and crash-test rigs, although both examples of *physical models*, have entirely different purposes; the degree of accuracy required in the models varies accordingly. The behaviour of vehicles and dummies when subjected to crash-tests is something that needs to be as close as possible to the real thing. The results of such tests influence vehicle safety design and so accuracy is vital. Whilst accuracy and attention to detail is also desirable for a doll's house, it cannot be said to be a matter of life and death.

A *mathematical model* is a representation of a real situation in abstract, rather than physical, terms. The terms 'deterministic' and 'stochastic' refer respectively to the absence or presence of random elements in the model. For instance, the familiar formula:

$$A = \pi r^2$$

is simply a mathematical model which represents the area of a circle (A) in terms of its radius (r). If the radius of the circle is known, the area can be calculated. It is also a *deterministic* model since the effect of changing the value of *r* can be determined precisely. On the other hand, a mathematical model of the build-up of traffic at a busy road junction must somehow incorporate those elements which are subject to unpredictable behaviour; for instance, the arrival pattern of cars, weather / road conditions and accidents. Such a model would therefore be termed a *stochastic* (or *probabilistic*) model since its behaviour is partly governed by chance events.

Now, the same situation can often be modelled in several different ways. For instance, the following are all representations of the area of a circle:

1)                                      2)                                      3)

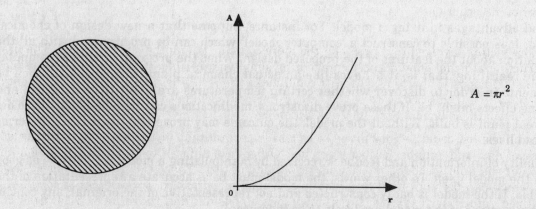

$A = \pi r^2$

(1)  is a diagrammatic model. It shows what is meant by the area of a circle.

(2)  is a graphical model. It shows how the area of a circle changes as its radius changes.

(3)  is a mathematical model. It provides an estimate of the area of a circle, based on its radius. ($\pi \approx 3.14$)

Which model is used depends on the purpose for which it is intended. For instance, if the purpose is to show a young child what is meant by the area of a circle, model #1 would probably be the most appropriate. However, if the purpose is to calculate the area of a circle with a given radius, model #3 is the most useful; (model #2 could be used for this purpose, but would not be as accurate).

So, a model can be thought of as a representation with a definite purpose. Once the purpose of building a model is known, its effectiveness can then be considered in terms of how well it serves that purpose.

## Mathematical models (2) – An example

The structure of this book can be modelled diagrammatically, as follows:

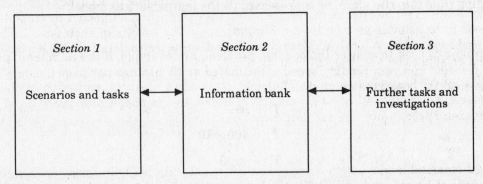

Now consider the following problem: 'How long will it take to read this book'?

Although a diagrammatic model such as the one above is suitable for *its* purpose (i.e. showing the book's structure) it is not suitable to calculate the answer to this problem. A different type of model is needed.

There are several factors which could influence the amount of time taken to read the book, and these need to be given some thought before the model is constructed. For instance:

    the number of pages
    the reading speed
    the readability of the text
    the time of day
    the number of interruptions
    the reader's mood

Generally, the more factors involved in a problem, the more complex the mathematical model. The first attempt at constructing a model should aim to make it as simple as possible, so it is sensible to reduce the length of the list. Obviously, shortening the list could make the resulting model not very representative of the actual situation. If this proves to be the case, refinements will need to be made and this might include bringing some of these factors back into the reckoning.

Some of the items on the list could be considered to be less important than others and can be discarded; for example, 'time of day' and 'number of interruptions'. Others are difficult to *quantify* (i.e. give a numerical value to); for example, 'reader's mood' and 'readability of text'. These can also be removed from the list. Factors which can be quantified are usually classified as *variables*, *parameters* or *constants*. Constants have fixed values; for example, the number p is a constant and its value ($\approx 3.14$) does not change under any circumstances. Variables and parameters have values which can change; these are described later.

Once the list has been made more manageable, some *relationships* (ways that the variables are linked) need to be found. Now, one way the total time can be calculated is:

i)   count the number of pages altogether

ii)  estimate the time to read one page

iii) multiply the answers to (i) and (ii)

Thinking about the type of calculations involved helps to state a relationship in a verbal form such as:

Total reading time = number of pages × time to read one page

It is normal practice to use letters to represent the variables which feature in the mathematical model; the letters chosen should remind you of the variable that they represent. So, the main variables involved in this example could be represented as:

$T$   -   the total reading time

$p$   -   the number of pages

$m$   -   the number of minutes needed to read each page

The total reading time can, therefore, be represented as the mathematical model:

$$T = pm \tag{1}$$

The model can now be used to answer the original problem. For example, if the number of pages is taken to be 400 (i.e. $p = 400$) and your reading speed is estimated at 10 minutes per page (i.e. $m = 10$), the total time needed to read the book is calculated as follows:

$$T = pm$$
$$\therefore \ T = 400 \times 10$$
$$\therefore \ T = 4000$$

$\therefore$ Using model (1), the total reading time for the book is 4000 minutes.

As a first attempt at formulating a model, (1) seems adequate. However, in any mathematical model there are *assumptions* which underlie the thinking; initially, assumptions are chosen which make the model as simple as possible. Model (1) assumes that every page in the book takes the same amount of time to read. This is not a reasonable assumption and could affect the accuracy of the calculation.

Each section is of a different nature; Sections 1 & 3 are activity-based whilst Section 2 is for reference purposes. So, the amount of time needed for each page in the different sections is likely to vary.

So, if:   $p_1$ represents the number of pages in Section 1

$m_1$ represents the number of minutes needed to read one page of Section 1

$p_2$ represents the number of pages in Section 2

$m_2$ represents the number of minutes needed to read one page of Section 2

$p_3$ represents the number of pages in Section 3

$m_3$ represents the number of minutes needed to read one page of Section 3

a better model is:

$$T = p_1 m_1 + p_2 m_2 + p_3 m_3 \tag{2}$$

Time for section 1        Time for section 3
Time for section 2

Model (2) is likely to be more accurate than model (1) since it now takes into account the difference in length of each section and the different reading times for each page.

If $p_1 = 100$, $p_2 = 150$, $p_3 = 150$, $m_1 = 12$, $m_2 = 10$ and $m_3 = 20$:

then: $$T = 100 \times 12 + 150 \times 10 + 150 \times 20$$

$\therefore$ $$T = 5700$$

So, a better estimate of time needed to read the whole book is 5700 minutes.

## Mathematical models (3) - Variables and parameters

The mathematical model:

$$T = p_1m_1 + p_2m_2 + p_3m_3$$

is not only more accurate but also flexible since it can be used to estimate your reading time for other books with the same structure, not just this particular book. In that case:

i)   $p_1$, $p_2$ and $p_3$ are called *variables* since the number of pages is likely to change from book to book

ii)   $m_1$, $m_2$ and $m_3$ are *parameters* since your reading speed is unlikely to change for books of this type.

Distinguishing between variables and parameters is not always straightforward. It depends on how the model is to be used. For example, suppose that the model were being used to investigate the reading speeds of a variety of different people using this same book. In that case $p_1$, $p_2$ and $p_3$ would be considered to be the parameters of the model (since the number of pages remains the same during the course of the investigation) and $m_1$, $m_2$ and $m_3$ the variables (since different people are likely to have different reading speeds). On the other hand, if the model were being used to investigate the reading times for different people with a variety of books, all of $p_1$, $p_2$, $p_3$, $m_1$, $m_2$, and $m_3$ would be classed as variables.

The mathematical model (2) could be further refined in order to try to make it even more accurate e.g. within one particular section, the time for each page may still vary; for instance, pages with diagrams / graphs might not take as long as pages of text. This factor could be catered for by incorporating more variables into the model. Obviously, if more is built into the model the more accurate and realistic it becomes, though at the same time more complicated to use.

A mathematical model should, therefore:

i)   contain all the essential features in order that it is as accurate a representation as possible

ii)   not be too complex to manipulate

## Mathematical models (4) – Use of spreadsheets

Because of the amount of calculation required, it is sensible to implement the mathematical model (2) on a computer package called a *spreadsheet*. A spreadsheet consists of a number of *cells* arranged in rows and columns and can be thought of as a two-dimensional calculator. (See diagram on following page)

The size of a spreadsheet will vary from package to package but typically can have hundreds or thousands of rows and columns. The on-screen page will probably show just a portion of the full sheet.

A cell is identified by the intersection of the row and column where the cell is located. For example, the highlighted cells in the diagram are F2, D3 and E5. Each cell can contain:

      either  (i)   a piece of text

      or      (ii)  a number

      or      (iii) a formula

| | A | B | C | D | E | F | G |
|---|---|---|---|---|---|---|---|
| 1 | | | | | | | |
| 2 | | | | | | | |
| 3 | | | | | | | |
| 4 | | | | | | | |
| 5 | | | | | | | |
| .. | | | | | | | |
| .. | | | | | | | |

Cell

*Text* is entered to provide information about the entries in the spreadsheet. For example, a typical piece of text would be an overall title (e.g. 'Household Expenditure') or a column heading (e.g. 'Food').

*Numbers*, once they have been entered into the cells, can be manipulated in a variety of different ways. A spreadsheet is a number-cruncher in the same sort of way that a word processor is a text-cruncher. It can, for instance, add up the contents of a column of cells and arrive at a total.

*Formulas* are used to inform the spreadsheet what to do with the numbers in the different cells. For instance, it may be required to multiply the contents of two cells (e.g. A3 and A4) and put the result in a third cell (e.g. A10). The formula: A3*A4 would be entered into cell A10; however, it is the result which is displayed in that cell, *not* the formula itself. The formula stays hidden in the background. If changes are made to the numbers in A3 or A4, the result shown in A10 is automatically recalculated.

There are certain operations that a spreadsheet is required to perform so regularly e.g. totals, averages, counts etc., that they are provided as *standard functions*. It is then simply a matter of entering the function rather than a user-defined formula. For example, a function such as: SUM(A1:A20) would total the contents of all the cells A1, A2, ..........A20 and is more efficient than entering the formula: A1+A2+..........+A20. The range of standard functions available depends on the particular spreadsheet package.

Most packages also provide a range of other built-in facilities which include:

i) Cell-level manipulation e.g. moving / copying blocks of cells, formatting, sorting

ii) Sheet-level manipulation e.g. insertion / deletion of rows and columns, global formatting, windows

iii) Graph-plotting e.g. histograms, pie-charts, line graphs, scatter diagrams

iv) Other options e.g. printing, saving / retrieving, protection, macros

The sophisticated facilities afforded by the spreadsheet make it probably the best all-purpose mathematical tool currently available. It can support any application where numerical calculations are involved. Some of its many uses will be highlighted during the course of this text and include not only modelling but also data organisation / manipulation, problem-solving and numerical analysis. The reader should, therefore, take the earliest opportunity to become familiar with any readily available spreadsheet package.

There are plenty of spreadsheet packages to choose from, including: Lotus 1-2-3, Multiplan, SuperCalc, 2020, Schema, ASEASYAS etc. All provide similar facilities; however, the most important feature of a spreadsheet is the way that it can release the user from number-crunching activities and provide an excellent medium for experimentation. As an example of this, consider the mathematical model constructed earlier:

$$T = p_1 m_1 + p_2 m_2 + p_3 m_3$$

In this case, the spreadsheet layout might resemble the one shown below:

| | A | B | C | D | E | F | G |
|---|---|---|---|---|---|---|---|
| 1 | | | 'Book Reading Time' Model | | | | |
| 2 | $p_1$ | $p_2$ | $p_3$ | $m_1$ | $m_2$ | $m_3$ | Total time needed |
| 3 | 100 | 150 | 150 | 12 | 10 | 20 | 5700 |
| 4 | 100 | 150 | 150 | 12 | 8 | 20 | 5400 |
| 5 | ... | ... | ... | ... | ... | ... | ... |
| 6 | ... | ... | ... | ... | ... | ... | ... |
| .. | ... | ... | ... | ... | ... | ... | ... |
| .. | 100 | 150 | 200 | 10 | 4.5 | 20 | 5675 |

Formula: A3*D3 + B3*E3 + C3*F3

i) Rows 1 & 2 contain the title and various column headings

ii) Values of $p_1$, $p_2$, $p_3$, $m_1$, $m_2$ and $m_3$ are placed in columns A – F.

iii) The formula: A3*D3 + B3*E3 + C3*F3 is placed in cell G3.

This would calculate the total time needed and display the result there.

iv) The formula is *replicated* (reproduced) in the other cells of column G. So:

cell G4 contains the formula: A4*D4 + B4*E4 + C4*F4,

cell G5 contains the formula: A5*D5 + B5*E5 + C5*F5, etc.

(Note that the formulas in G4, G5 etc. are not identical copies of the formula in G3. When the formula is copied, the spreadsheet automatically adjusts the row reference; without this adjustment, all the cells from G4 onwards would display the same result as that shown in G3. This type of cell referencing is known as *relative* referencing. When formulas are copied exactly, *absolute* referencing is used. The reader should refer to their spreadsheet manual to find out how to implement the different modes of referencing).

Once the model has been set up, it is a simple matter to change the contents of cells in columns A - F and observe the effect in column G. If the value of a cell is altered, then any other cells which contain formulas referring to it are recalculated and the new results displayed. For instance, cell G3 would be updated if changes were made to any of the other values in Row 3.

The spreadsheet model gives much scope for experimentation with the values of the different variables and parameters, so that their relative importance and interrelationship can be investigated. For instance, questions such as: (i) 'What effect would adding a further 50 pages to Section 3 have on the total time to read the book?' or: (ii) 'How would it affect the total reading time if I could improve my reading speed for Section 2 to 8 minutes per page?' or: 'Which is more important to the total reading time, number of pages or reading speed?' can be investigated. The real power of the spreadsheet lies in giving the user the freedom to experiment with the model rather than having to concentrate on the mechanical aspects of calculation.

# The stages of mathematical modelling

From the example it can be seen that mathematical modelling is concerned with using abstract mathematical models in order to solve 'real' problems. It is a process of moving between the 'real world' and the 'mathematical world' which involves well-defined stages:

i)    formulating the real problem

ii)   translating the real problem into an abstract mathematical problem

iii)  applying techniques to solve the mathematical problem

iv)   making sense of the answers obtained

v)    comparing the results with the real problem

The various stages are shown in the following diagram:

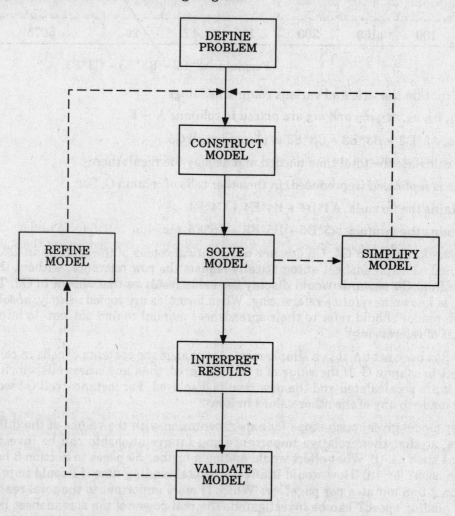

*Fig. 1*

### 1.  *Define Problem*

This is the stage at which you ask yourself what it is that you wish to know. The nature of the model that you construct depends very much on what you want it to do.

*e.g. How long will it take to read this book?*

2. *Construct Model*

   Translate the problem into mathematical terms. This is probably the most difficult stage since it involves being able to identify the important variables and finding enough connecting relationships between them so that you can produce some results. Tasks that might be carried out at this stage include:

   i)   drawing diagrams

   ii)  listing any factors relevant to the problem

   iii) writing down any assumptions that you have made

   iv)  giving each variable an appropriate symbol

   v)   constructing equations which relate the variables

   *e.g. The main factors which affect the total time (T) are the number of pages (p) and the number of minutes needed to read each page (m). This assumes that each page takes the same time to read. Now:*

   $$\text{Total reading time} = \text{number of pages} \times \text{time to read one page}$$

   *This relationship can be translated into the mathematical model: $T = pm$*

3. *Solve Model*

   At this stage you need to make sure that you have sufficient information (data, techniques, skill) to use the model to give the sort of results that you want. If not, it may be necessary to simplify the model (right-hand dotted line in Fig. 1) and construct a simpler version which you can handle.

   *e.g. If $p = 400$ and $m = 10$, $\therefore T = 400 \times 10 = 4000$.*

4. *Interpret Results*

   This stage is usually straightforward. It is simply a question of trying to understand the practical consequences of the solution obtained in Stage 3. This involves translating the mathematical solution back into the context of the original problem.

   *e.g. $T = 4000$ means that the total amount of time needed to read the book is 4000 minutes.*

5. *Validate Model*

   This is a crucial stage in the modelling process. At this stage you should ask yourself whether the model is representative enough and if the results obtained seem reasonable. If they are not acceptable, it is a question of trying to understand why and refining the model accordingly (left-hand dotted line in Fig. 1).

   *e.g. The solution of 4000 minutes seems reasonable, although it is difficult to say how accurate it is. A better model might be: $T = p_1m_1 + p_2m_2 + p_3m_3$ (as described earlier). This model gives an estimate of 5700 minutes. The accuracy of this result is also difficult to assess, but, since it has been calculated by using a more sophisticated model, it is likely to be more reliable.*

## Modelling skills

In order to become a competent modeller, the reader needs to become proficient in a whole range of skills and techniques. These are many and varied and are of great importance when dealing with applications. It is not possible to write down a list of *all* the skills and techniques that may be required in mathematical modelling. Some are based on practice and experience, others on intuition and common sense. Those encountered throughout this text are the ones most commonly involved in modelling and which can be developed by practice.

These include:

1. Handling information (collecting / recording / processing / presenting)
2. Interpreting information (in the form of: words / tables / formulas / diagrams / graphs)
3. Number (approximation, calculation)
4. Algebra (translation, manipulation)
5. Graphs (plotting, sketching, interpretation)

It should also be noted that mathematical modelling is concerned with *applying* mathematics. The difficulty lies not with learning and understanding the mathematics itself, but with knowing *where* and *how* to apply it. For instance, the skills on the above list are all useful ones to possess; however, the more important skill is being able to recognise problems where they might be helpful and how they can be applied to produce satisfactory solutions.

# Unit 2: Functions and graphs

This section aims to help you to:

1. understand the nature of graphs and functions
2. recognise standard graphs and functions
3. recognise the situations to which these standard models apply
4. construct tables of values for functions and to use them to plot graphs
5. put graphs to some useful purpose
6. sketch graphs

## What is a function?

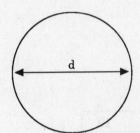

Consider the familiar mathematical model: $C = \pi d$.

This model provides helpful information in two ways:

i) the exact way that the circumference and diameter of a circle are related

ii) a means of calculating the circumference of any circle, if its diameter is known

There are various points to note in this example:

❏ Since the values of $C$ and $d$ can change, they are both called *variables*.

❏ The value of $\pi$ is given as approximately 3.14. As its value cannot change it is called a *constant*.

❏ d is called the *independent* variable (since it can take any value).

❏ C is called the *dependent* variable (since its value depends on the value of $d$).

For instance, when $d = 10$, $C = \pi \times 10 \approx 31.4$

So, a circle with a diameter of 10cm has a circumference of approximately 31.4cm.

❏ Two variables are often related in such a way that the value of one depends on the value of the other. The dependent variable is then said to be a *function* of the independent variable.

In this example, the circumference of a circle is a function of its diameter.

This can be stated:

i) more concisely as: $C = f(d)$ [read – '$C$ is a function of $d$'].

ii) more precisely as: $C = \pi d$ [the exact form of the functional relationship]

## What is a graph?

A graph is a means of showing a relationship in diagrammatic form.

The graph in Fig. 2 shows how the circumference of a circle is related to its diameter.

It depicts exactly the same relationship as before ($C = \pi d$), but in a different way.

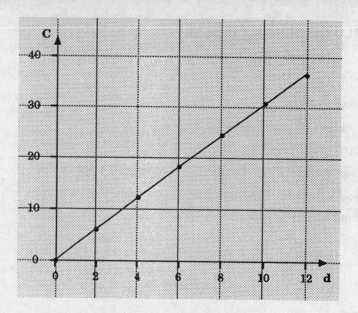

*Fig. 2*

There are various steps in drawing the graph of a function:

1. Construct a table of values
2. Draw axes with suitable scales
3. Plot and join points

Step 1    In the case of the function $C = \pi d$, the table of values looks like:

| $d$ (cms) | 0 | 2 | 4 | 6 | 8 | 10 | 12 |
|-----------|---|------|-------|-------|-------|------|-------|
| $C$ (cms) | 0 | 6.28 | 12.56 | 18.84 | 25.12 | 31.4 | 35.68 |

The circumference is calculated for each diameter. e.g. when $d = 4$, $C = \pi \times 4 \approx 12.56$.

Step 2    Drawing and scaling axes depends on the range of values to plotted. In this case:

i)    the diameters lie between 0 and 12. That is, $d$ is in the range $0 \le d \le 12$.

ii)    the circumferences lie between 0 and 36. That is, $C$ is in the range $0 \le C \le 36$.

So, the horizontal axis ($d$)  is scaled from 0 to 12, the vertical axis ($C$) from 0 to 36.

If a graph is to be used for estimation purposes, the scales should be chosen to ensure that the required accuracy is obtained. This usually means making the best use of the graph paper available, and constructing the largest graph possible.

Step 3    The information in the table can now be displayed on graph paper. (The usual way is to locate and plot the pairs of values as points on a grid called a *cartesian graph* – see Fig. 3).

The values in the table are treated as coordinate pairs and plotted on the axes:

   (0, 0), (2, 6.28), (4, 12.56), (6, 18.84), (8, 25.12), (10, 31.4), (12, 35.68)

After plotting, the points are joined to form a straight line (in this case) as shown in Fig. 2.

Once the graph is drawn, it is a simple matter to use it as an approximate calculator. That is, it can be used to estimate the circumference of a circle of known diameter, or vice-versa. Using graphs in this way is described in the section: 'Linear functions' (page 112).

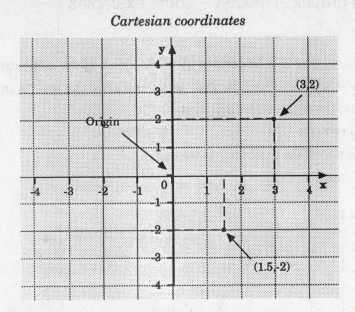

*Cartesian coordinates*

1.  The two lines which form the points of reference:

    a)  are at right angles to one another

    b)  cross at a point called the *origin*

    c)  are numbered with:

        i)   positive numbers above and to the right of the origin

        ii)  negative numbers below and to the left of the origin

2.  The horizontal *axis* (usually called the *x*-axis) represents the independent variable.

    The vertical axis (*y*-axis) represents the dependent variable.

3.  The position of any point is then described by two *coordinates*, one referring to the *x*-axis and the other to the *y*-axis. The *x*-coordinate and *y*-coordinate are used to represent the point, written as (*x,y*).

*Cartesian coordinates. Fig. 3*

If the exact form of a functional relationship is known (e.g. $C = \pi d$) then points can be calculated, plotted and joined to produce a graph of the relationship. There are many different possible functions and graph types, and these are described in the section: 'Standard Functions and Graphs' (pages 112–129).

Often, however, a graph may still be the clearest way of representing a relationship which cannot easily be described in mathematical terms. For instance, the visual display from a cardiograph gives a lot of information about the condition of a patient's heart, if interpreted correctly. On the other hand, constructing a mathematical model to describe the behaviour of the heart would be much more difficult, or even impossible. It is very important, therefore, not only to develop skills in constructing graphs but also in analysing and interpreting information presented in graphical form. The examples which follow show a variety of situations in graph form with the emphasis on those aspects.

# The interpretation of graphical models – some examples

### Example 1

In a talent competition, the winner is to be decided by the loudness of the audience's response.

Engineers monitor the audience sound level for each artist and show the results on a 'clapometer'.

The graph below represents the response for a pianist.

It shows the relationship between:

    i)    the time after the end of the performance ($t$) and

    ii)   the score on the clapometer ($s$).

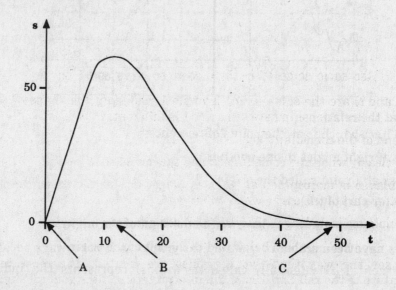

$t$ is measured in seconds; $s$ is a score between 0 and 100.

Various observations can be made about the graph:

    A – this is the point at which the artist finishes playing and the applause begins ($t = 0$)

    B – the applause builds up to reach a peak about here ($t = 15$), then starts to subside

    C – the applause gradually dies down to silence at this point ($t = 48$)

The graph also shows quite clearly that the score on the clapometer depends on how long the audience has been monitored. So:

a)    $t$ is the independent variable (since it can take any value).

    i)    $t < 0$ is the time period before the applause begins

    ii)   $0 \leq t \leq 48$ corresponds to the time that the applause lasts

    iii)  $t > 48$ corresponds to the time period after the applause has finished

b)    $s$ is the dependent variable (since its value depends on the value of $t$).

    i)    when $t < 0$, $s = 0$

    ii)   when $0 \leq t \leq 48$, $0 \leq s \leq 100$

    iii)  when $t > 48$, $s = 0$

c)    $s$ is a function of $t$.

    The value of $s$ is dependent on the value of $t$.

*Example 2*

This is a comedian's graph:

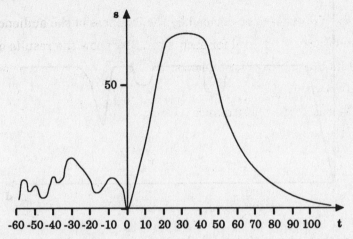

The two variables (*s* and *t*) are the same as in Example 1. However, the shape of the graph is not the same. This means that the relationship between *s* and *t* is different:

a)   *t* = 0 marks the end of the comedian's act

b)   the graph shows clearly when the comedian causes the audience to laugh.

c)   the audience applause is maintained at its peak longer for the comedian than the pianist; this is shown by the flatter part of the curve when 20 < *t* < 45.

d)   the comedian's applause lasts longer than the pianist's applause (*t* = 115).

Even though the axes have been scaled in the previous graphs, it is not always necessary to know exact values in order to see the way that two variables are related. The most important factor in understanding the nature of the relationship is the interpretation of the general shape and behaviour of the graph.

In the remaining examples, therefore, no scales or units are given for the two variables shown in each case. However, the main features are listed and the reader should be able to identify the corresponding parts of the graphs.

*Example 3*

This graph on the following page shows the speed of a racing car (on its first lap around a motor racing circuit) as a function of the distance it has travelled.

The two variables are:

i)    *d* – distance travelled from the starting point  and

ii)   *s* – speed of the car

Main features:

a)   the rapid acceleration at the start of the race

b)   the straight parts of the circuit

c)   the two fairly gentle bends, followed by one tight bend

d)   the deceleration into, and the acceleration out of, bends

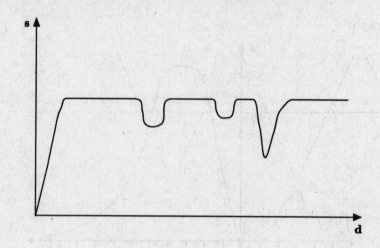

## Example 4

This graph shows the way that a person's bank balance varies over a 6-month period:

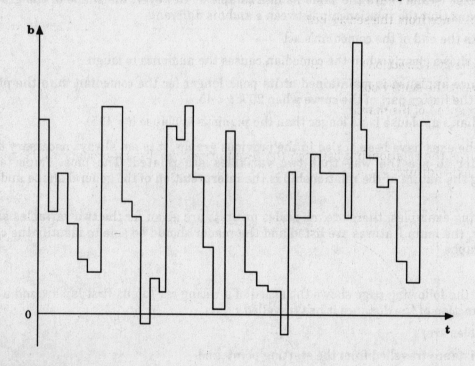

The two variables are:

    i)    $t$ – time elapsed  and

    ii)   $b$ – balance of the account

Main features:

a)   payments into the account

b)   withdrawals

c)   when the account is overdrawn

## Example 5

This graph shows the way that a guard on duty marches up and down outside his sentry box:

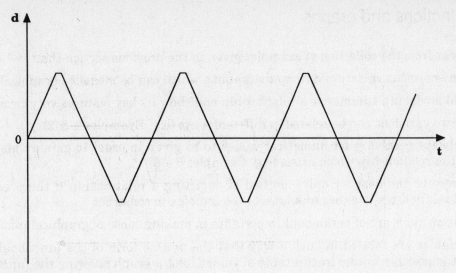

The two variables are:

 i)  $t$ – time elapsed  and

 ii)  $d$ – distance from the sentry box

Main features:

a)  when he changes direction

b)  when he is at the sentry box

c)  the steady speed of his march

*Example 6*

This graph shows the relationship between the revenue received from a product's sales and the amount of advertising expenditure:

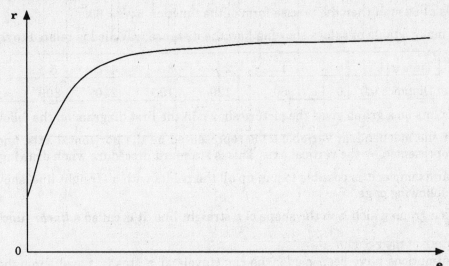

The two variables are:

 i)  $e$ – advertising expenditure  and

 ii)  $r$ – revenue from sales

Main features:

a)  some sales revenue is obtained without the need to advertise

b)  initial advertising significantly increases product sales

c)  increasing advertising expenditure has an ever-decreasing impact on sales

# Standard functions and graphs

It should be clear from the collection of examples given in the previous section that:

❏ there is an enormous variety of different situations which can be modelled graphically

❏ a graphical model can summarise a relationship and show its key features very clearly

❏ the same two variables can be related in different ways (e.g. Examples 1 & 2)

❏ it is not always necessary for numerical values to be given in order to gain an idea of the general nature of the relationship which exists (e.g. Examples 3 – 6)

❏ a graph may be the best (or only) method of depicting a relationship if the precise form of the functional relationship is either unknown or too complex to construct

❏ interpretation skills are of paramount importance in making sense of graphical information

When two variables are related in such a way that the precise form of the functional relationship is known, then it is possible to construct a table of values, plot a graph showing the function and then to use the graph in some way. However, there are a great many different variables and variety of possible functions. So, it is extremely useful to be familiar with the general features and graphs of the most common types of functions and to become able to recognise the sort of situation to which they apply.

In the following section, which is a kind of graph-spotter's guide, some standard functions will be detailed and their properties and uses highlighted.

## Linear functions (1)

Consider the relationship between:

i) the amount of time spent by a car on a motorway journey ($t$ – hours)

ii) the distance it travels ($d$ – miles)

The distance travelled is a function of the time. So, $d = f(t)$.

If the car travels at 60 mph then the precise form of the function is: $d = 60t$

It is possible to make a table of values showing how the distance travelled is related to the time:

| Time ($t$) | 0 | 1 | 2 | 3 | 4 | 5 |
|---|---|---|---|---|---|---|
| Distance ($d$) | 0 | 60 | 120 | 180 | 240 | 300 |

Plotting these points on a graph gives the picture shown in the first diagram on the following page.

Note again that the independent variable ($t$) is represented by the horizontal axis, and the dependent variable ($d$) is represented by the vertical axis. This is standard procedure when drawing graphs.

In this particular example, it is possible to join up all the points with a straight line, shown in the second diagram on the following page.

If a function has a graph which is in the shape of a straight line, it is called a *linear* function.

Note that:

a) certain assumptions have been made: the car travels at a steady speed throughout the journey; there are no hold-ups due to roadworks or weather conditions; the driver does not stop at service stations; etc

b) it is only possible to join up all the points with a straight line because the same number of miles is travelled in each hour

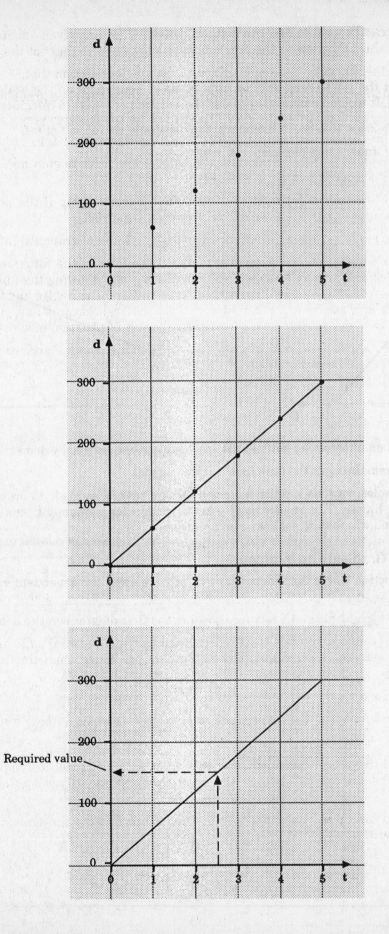

Once drawn, the graph can be used to find the distance travelled for any given amount of time, up to 5 hours. For instance, the third diagram on the previous page shows how to find out the distance travelled in 2.5 hours.

The value read off from the graph may only be approximate, depending on the scales chosen and the accuracy of the drawing. It would be necessary to use the function ($d = 60t$) to calculate the exact value.

i.e. when $t = 2.5$, $d = 60 \times 2.5 = 150$. So, in 2.5 hours, the car would travel 150 miles.

Two further examples of linear functions are:

a)

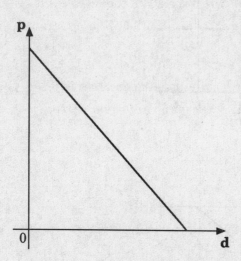

b)

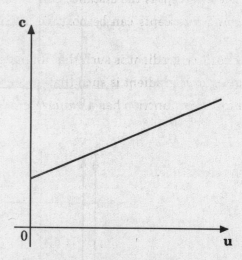

i)   distance travelled on a motorway journey ($d$)
ii)  amount of petrol remaining in the tank ($p$)

i)   telephone useage by domestic subscriber ($u$)
ii)  cost ($c$)

As in the previous examples, various simplifying assumptions have been made in order that the graphs of these functions are linear. The reader may like to pause for a moment, consider what these assumptions might be and whether or not they seem reasonable.

## Linear functions (2) – Gradient and Intercept

Fig. 4 shows a linear function where the independent variable is $x$ and the dependent variable is $y$.

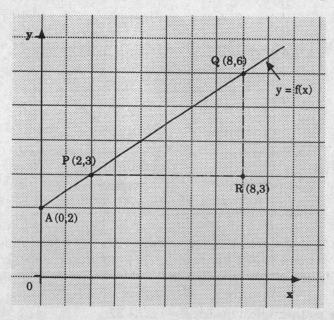

*Fig.4*

114

The *gradient* of the line is a measure of how steeply it rises. Since $y$ is a function of $x$, the gradient therefore measures how much $y$ increases compared to how much $x$ increases.

To find the gradient of the line in Fig. 4:

   i)    choose any two convenient points on the graph e.g. P (3, 2) and Q (8, 5)

   ii)   calculate the gradient by: $\dfrac{\text{vertical increase}}{\text{horizontal increase}} = \dfrac{QR}{PR} = \dfrac{6-3}{8-2} = \dfrac{3}{6} = \dfrac{1}{2}$

Another feature of interest is the *intercept*. This is where the graph cuts the $y$-axis.

In Fig. 4, the intercept is the distance OA. In this case, since A is the point (0, 2), the intercept is 2.

Gradients and intercepts can be positive, negative or zero, as shown in the following diagrams. Note that:

   i)    a *positive* gradient is such that an *increase* in $x$ causes a corresponding *increase* in $y$

   ii)   a *negative* gradient is such that an *increase* in $x$ causes a corresponding *decrease* in $y$

   iii)  any linear function has a *uniform gradient* i.e. all parts of the graph are equally steep

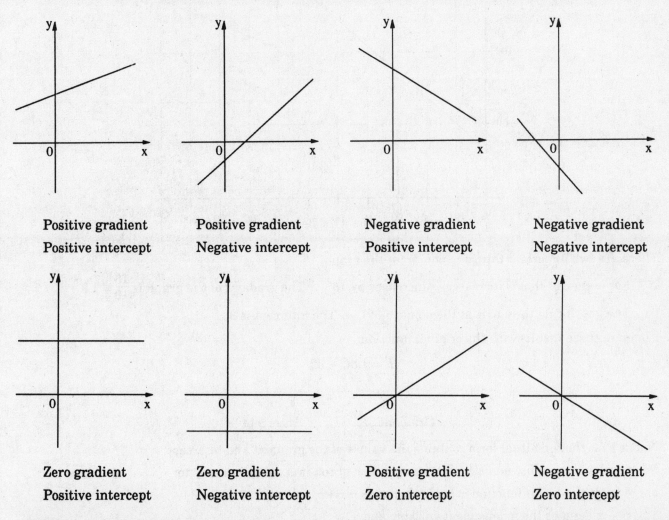

| Positive gradient | Positive gradient | Negative gradient | Negative gradient |
| Positive intercept | Negative intercept | Positive intercept | Negative intercept |

| Zero gradient | Zero gradient | Positive gradient | Negative gradient |
| Positive intercept | Negative intercept | Zero intercept | Zero intercept |

The diagrams also show that the gradient and intercept precisely determine the position of a graph relative to the axes. If these two values are known, the graph can be quickly visualised and sketched without the need to plot points accurately. This is possible if the precise form of the linear function is known.

For instance, consider the mathematical model: $F = 1.8C + 32$.

This gives:    i)    Fahrenheit temperatures as a function of Celsius temperatures

            ii)    a method of calculating Fahrenheit temperatures for any given Celsius temperature

Constructing a table of values for temperatures between 0° C and 100° C gives:

| C | 0 | 10 | 20 | 30 | 40 | 50 | 60 | 70 | 80 | 90 | 100 |
|---|---|----|----|----|----|----|----|----|----|----|-----|
| F | 32 | 50 | 68 | 86 | 104 | 122 | 140 | 158 | 176 | 194 | 212 |

The graph of the function looks like:

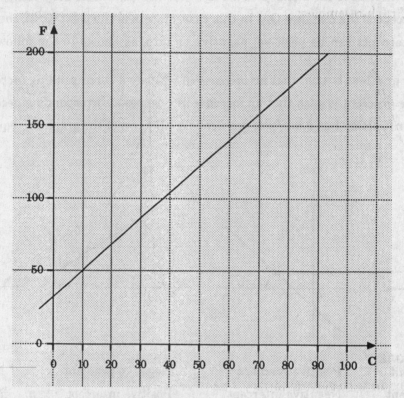

There are two important things to note from the graph:

i)    For every 10° that $C$ increases, $F$ increases by 18°. $\therefore$ The gradient of the graph is $\dfrac{18}{10} = 1.8$

ii)    The graph cuts the $y$-axis at the point (0,32). $\therefore$ The intercept is 32.

Compare these results with the original function:

$$F = 1.8C + 32$$

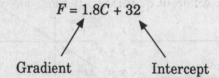

Gradient            Intercept

Notice that the functional form contains the values of the gradient and intercept.

So, in order to visualise and sketch a straight-line graph it is only necessary to:

a)    ensure the linear function is in the form: $y = mx + c$,   where

     i)    $x$ denotes the independent variable and

     ii)    $y$ denotes the dependent variable

b)    examine the function and note the value of:

     i)    $m$, the coefficient of $x$; this is the gradient of the straight line

     ii)    $c$, the constant; this is the intercept on the $y$-axis

*Examples*

a)

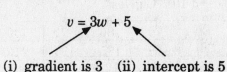

(i) gradient is 3    (ii) intercept is 5

∴ Graph resembles:

b)

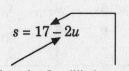

(i) gradient is -2    (ii) intercept is 17

∴ Graph resembles:

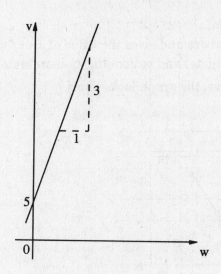

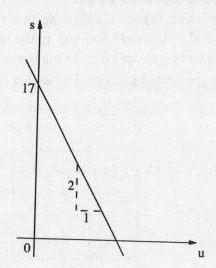

## Quadratic functions

A quadratic function has the general form: $y = ax^2 + bx + c$

i)   $x$ denotes the independent variable

ii)  $y$ denotes the dependent variable

iii) $a$, $b$ and $c$ are constants ($a>0$, else the function is linear)

By altering the values of $a$, $b$ and $c$ different quadratic functions are obtained. Some examples are:

$$y = x^2$$
$$y = x^2 + 5x$$
$$y = 3x^2 + 4x - 5$$
$$y = 5 - x^2$$

$$y = x^2 + 7$$
$$y = x^2 + 4x - 7$$
$$y = -2x^2$$
$$y = 12 + 7x - 0.5x^2$$

The coordinate calculations involved in graphs of this type of function tend to be more involved than for linear functions so it is advantageous, in most cases, to construct an expanded version of the table of values. Whereas in the case of a linear function only two points are required to fix the position of a straight line, more points are required in order to draw an accurate curve.

For example, consider the quadratic function: $y = x^2 + 2x - 3$ for values of $x$ in the range $-4 \le x \le 4$. The function is broken down into its component parts to construct the table of values. This helps to minimise mistakes and to notice them more easily if they do occur. The table of values looks like:

| $x$ | −4 | −3 | −2 | −1 | 0 | 1 | 2 | 3 | 4 |
|-----|-----|-----|-----|-----|-----|-----|-----|-----|-----|
| $x^2$ | 16 | 9 | 4 | 1 | 0 | 1 | 4 | 9 | 16 |
| $+2x$ | −8 | −6 | −4 | −2 | 0 | 2 | 4 | 6 | 8 |
| $-3$ | −3 | −3 | −3 | −3 | −3 | −3 | −3 | −3 | −3 |
| $y$ | 5 | 0 | −3 | −4 | −3 | 0 | 5 | 12 | 21 |

In this table, note that:

i)    the top line sets out the values of $x$

ii)   the next three lines lay out the three parts of the function: $x^2 + 2x - 3$

iii)  the bottom line is obtained by adding up the three lines above and gives the value of $y$, or $f(x)$

iv)  the points to be plotted are given by the top line ($x$-coordinate) and bottom line ($y$-coordinate)

When the points are plotted and joined up with a smooth curve, the graph looks like:

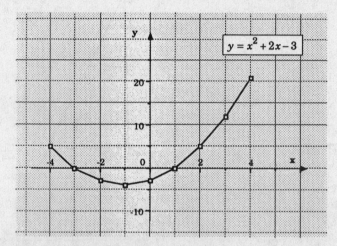

If necessary, extra points can be plotted by using intermediate values e.g. $x = 3.5$. This enables a more accurate curve to be hand-drawn and is particularly useful

i)    in the region of the curve's turning point and

ii)   where plotted points are quite far apart.

As the values of $a$, $b$ and $c$ change, so does the graph of the function $y = ax^2 + bx + c$

When $a = 1$, $b = 0$ and $c = 0$, the simplest quadratic function is obtained. That is: $y = x^2$

Constructing a table of values for this function in the range $-4 \leq x \leq 4$ gives:

| $x$ | -4 | -3 | -2 | -1 | 0 | 1 | 2 | 3 | 4 |
|-----|-----|-----|-----|-----|-----|-----|-----|-----|-----|
| $y$ | 16 | 9 | 4 | 1 | 0 | 1 | 4 | 9 | 16 |

and plotting the points produces the graph on the following page. Notice that:

i)    the points lie on a curve (called a *parabola*)

ii)   the gradient is not uniform i.e. some parts of the curve are steeper than others

iii)  the graph is symmetrical about the $y$-axis

iv)  the curve intercepts the $y$-axis at the origin (0, 0)

v)   the curve has one *turning-point*, at the origin. i.e. as the value of $x$ increases from -4 to 4, the value of $y$ decreases and then begins to increase again once past the origin (the table of values confirms this).

vi) as a result of ii) and (v), the left-hand half of the graph has a continually changing negative gradient while the right-hand half has a continually changing positive gradient. The gradient at the turning-point is zero.

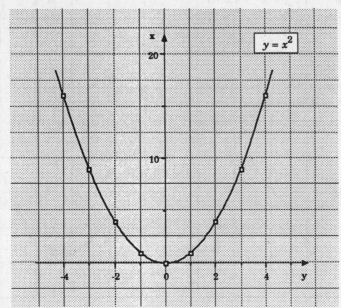

Now consider the following examples of functions which are related to $y = x^2$:

i)                                                          ii)

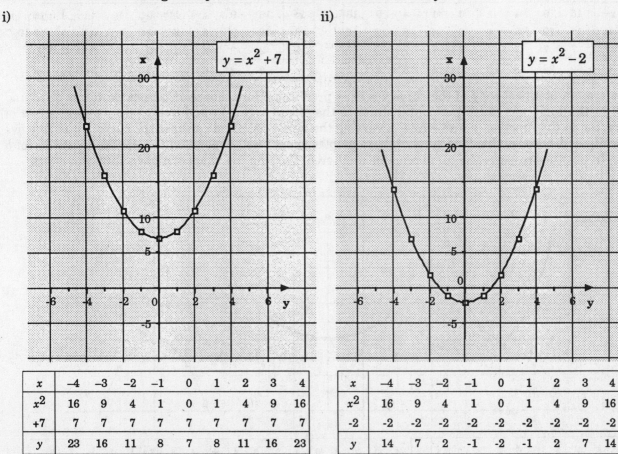

| $x$ | −4 | −3 | −2 | −1 | 0 | 1 | 2 | 3 | 4 |
|---|---|---|---|---|---|---|---|---|---|
| $x^2$ | 16 | 9 | 4 | 1 | 0 | 1 | 4 | 9 | 16 |
| +7 | 7 | 7 | 7 | 7 | 7 | 7 | 7 | 7 | 7 |
| $y$ | 23 | 16 | 11 | 8 | 7 | 8 | 11 | 16 | 23 |

| $x$ | −4 | −3 | −2 | −1 | 0 | 1 | 2 | 3 | 4 |
|---|---|---|---|---|---|---|---|---|---|
| $x^2$ | 16 | 9 | 4 | 1 | 0 | 1 | 4 | 9 | 16 |
| -2 | -2 | -2 | -2 | -2 | -2 | -2 | -2 | -2 | -2 |
| $y$ | 14 | 7 | 2 | -1 | -2 | -1 | 2 | 7 | 14 |

In each case an identical copy of the curve $y = x^2$ is produced. However, the effect of the '+7' and the '-2' is to shift the curve vertically upwards or downwards by that number of units.

The following two functions are also related to $y = x^2$:

iii)                                              iv)

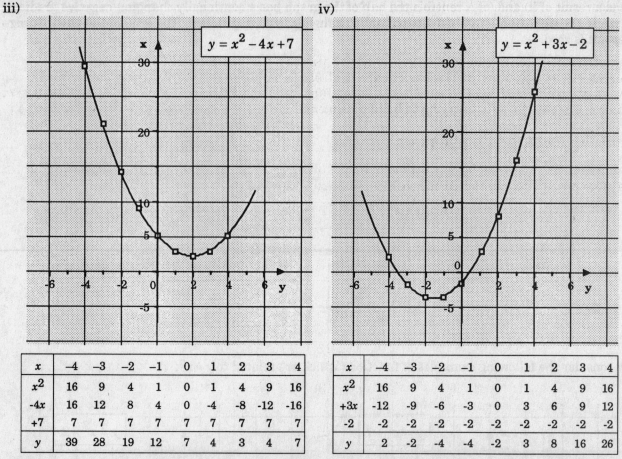

| $x$ | –4 | –3 | –2 | –1 | 0 | 1 | 2 | 3 | 4 |
|------|-----|-----|-----|-----|-----|-----|-----|-----|-----|
| $x^2$ | 16 | 9 | 4 | 1 | 0 | 1 | 4 | 9 | 16 |
| -4x | 16 | 12 | 8 | 4 | 0 | -4 | -8 | -12 | -16 |
| +7 | 7 | 7 | 7 | 7 | 7 | 7 | 7 | 7 | 7 |
| $y$ | 39 | 28 | 19 | 12 | 7 | 4 | 3 | 4 | 7 |

| $x$ | –4 | –3 | –2 | –1 | 0 | 1 | 2 | 3 | 4 |
|------|-----|-----|-----|-----|-----|-----|-----|-----|-----|
| $x^2$ | 16 | 9 | 4 | 1 | 0 | 1 | 4 | 9 | 16 |
| +3x | -12 | -9 | -6 | -3 | 0 | 3 | 6 | 9 | 12 |
| -2 | -2 | -2 | -2 | -2 | -2 | -2 | -2 | -2 | -2 |
| $y$ | 2 | -2 | -4 | -4 | -2 | 3 | 8 | 16 | 26 |

As before, an identical copy of the curve $y = x^2$ is produced. Here, however, the extra terms ('-4x' and '+3x') in the functions cause horizontal shifts to the left or right, in addition to the vertical shifts of before. So, in the function: $y = x^2 + bx + c$, varying the values of $b$ and $c$ causes the curve $y = x^2$ to move vertically and horizontally. The sizes of these displacements will depend on the particular values of $b$ and $c$. In all other respects the curve remains unaltered. Varying the value of $a$ has a different effect:

v)                      vi)                      vii)

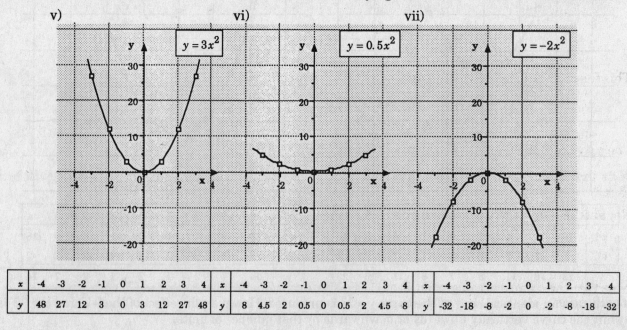

| $x$ | -4 | -3 | -2 | -1 | 0 | 1 | 2 | 3 | 4 |
|------|-----|-----|-----|-----|-----|-----|-----|-----|-----|
| $y$ | 48 | 27 | 12 | 3 | 0 | 3 | 12 | 27 | 48 |

| $x$ | -4 | -3 | -2 | -1 | 0 | 1 | 2 | 3 | 4 |
|------|-----|-----|-----|-----|-----|-----|-----|-----|-----|
| $y$ | 8 | 4.5 | 2 | 0.5 | 0 | 0.5 | 2 | 4.5 | 8 |

| $x$ | -4 | -3 | -2 | -1 | 0 | 1 | 2 | 3 | 4 |
|------|-----|-----|-----|-----|-----|-----|-----|-----|-----|
| $y$ | -32 | -18 | -8 | -2 | 0 | -2 | -8 | -18 | -32 |

It is clear that the value of $a$ controls the curvature of the graph. Making $|a|>1$ ($|a|$ means 'the size of $a$') has a narrowing effect on the graph whilst values of $|a| < 1$ widens it. If $a < 0$, the curve is also inverted.

The curves shown in the diagrams i) - (vii) are all variations on the general form: $y = ax^2 + bx + c$ with different values of $a$, $b$ and $c$. The basic shape is always a parabola but altering these values causes the curve to change its position and curvature. Understanding the overall effects of changing the values of $a$, $b$ and $c$ is extremely useful in trying to build up a mental picture of a graph before drawing it accurately.

## Alternative forms for: $y = x^2 + bx + c$

Quadratic functions of the form: $y = x^2 + bx + c$ (i.e. when $a=1$) can be written in alternative ways which give more precise information about position, location of turning-point etc.

For instance, consider the function: $y = x^2 - 2x - 3$. The table of values and graph for this function are:

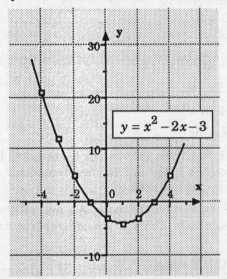

| $x$ | –4 | –3 | –2 | –1 | 0 | 1 | 2 | 3 | 4 |
|-----|----|----|----|----|----|----|----|----|----|
| $x^2$ | 16 | 9 | 4 | 1 | 0 | 1 | 4 | 9 | 16 |
| $-2x$ | 8 | 6 | 4 | 2 | 0 | -2 | -4 | -6 | -8 |
| $-3$ | -3 | -3 | -3 | -3 | -3 | -3 | -3 | -3 | -3 |
| $y$ | 21 | 12 | 5 | 0 | -3 | -4 | -3 | 0 | 5 |

This function can also be written as:

$$y = (x - 3)(x + 1) \qquad\qquad (1)$$

The curve cuts the x-axis at the points (3,0) and (-1,0).

Note that the $x$-coordinates have the same value as the numbers in (1) but with a sign change in each case.

Yet another way of writing the function is:

$$y = (x - 1)^2 - 4 \qquad\qquad (2)$$

Note that the curve's turning point is at (1,-4). These coordinates also appear in (2) with slight modification.

Rewriting this particular function in the forms (1) and (2) obviously helps to give a much clearer idea of the curve's main features and confirms the earlier drawing. Quadratic equations of this type can be rewritten in at least one of these forms. So, in general:

i) the function: $y = (x - p)(x - q)$ cuts the $x$-axis at $(p, 0)$ and $(q, 0)$

ii) the function: $y = (x - h)^2 + j$ has a turning-point at $(h, j)$.

See Section 3 Unit 1: *Modelling, graphs and functions*, Q 14.

## Cubic functions

The cubic function has a general form: $y = ax^3 + bx^2 + cx + d$

This is a natural extension to the quadratic function in that the highest power of $x$ is now 3 instead of 2.

Some examples of cubic functions are:

$$y = x^3$$
$$y = x^3 + 5$$
$$y = 2x^3 + 4x^2 - 3x - 11$$
$$y = x^3 + 7x - 4$$
$$y = 12 - 2x + x^3$$
$$y = 7 + 4x - 3x^3$$

There is an infinite number of cubic functions that can be constructed by varying the values of $a, b, c$ and $d$. The construction of tables of values is similar to the method for quadratic functions although the calculations are more involved, as might be expected.

The values of $a, b, c$ and $d$ change the features of the graph and although the various combinations give rise to an endless number of possibilities, there are some general principles which can help with the visualisation of such graphs.

i) The basic graph of $y = x^3$ has this S-shape:

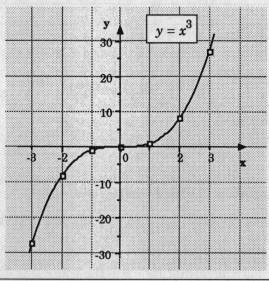

| $x$ | -3 | -2 | -1 | 0 | 1 | 2 | 3 |
|---|---|---|---|---|---|---|---|
| $y$ | -27 | -8 | -1 | 0 | 1 | 8 | 27 |

ii) adding extra $x$ or $x^2$ terms to the function increases or decreases the S-shape, as can be seen in this graph of: $y = x^3 + 4x^2 + x - 6$.

iii) a cubic function generally has 2 turning-points (but cannot have more than 2)

iv) a turning-point is either a *maximum point* (a 'hill') or a *minimum point* (a 'valley').

Note: A point where the gradient of the curve is zero, is termed a *stationary point*. Some stationary points are neither maximums nor minimums; these are called *points of inflexion*. For instance, the function $y = x^3$ has a point of inflexion at the origin.

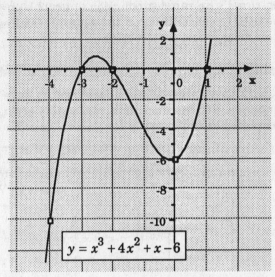

$$y = x^3 + 4x^2 + x - 6$$

*Fig 5*

v) positive and negative values of a have an effect similar to that for quadratic functions, as shown in the diagrams below:

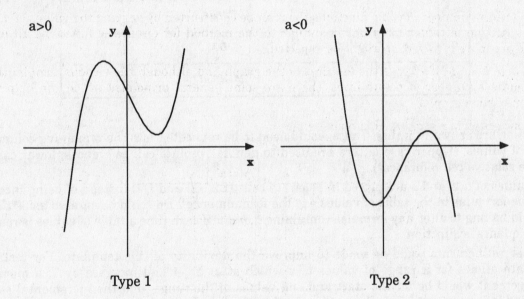

Type 1                    Type 2

As is the case with quadratic functions, there are other ways of writing some cubic functions which provide more helpful information about the likely shape and position of the graph. For instance, a cubic function which can be written as:

$$y = (x - f)(x - g)(x - h)$$

crosses the $x$-axis at the points $(f, 0)$, $(g, 0)$ and $(h, 0)$.

The function: $y = x^3 + 4x^2 + x - 6$ is equivalent to: $y = (x - 1)(x + 2)(x + 3)$. The points of intersection of the graph with the $x$-axis are, therefore: $(1, 0)$, $(-2, 0)$ and $(-3, 0)$. This can be seen in Fig 5.

It requires a good level of skill in algebraic manipulation to attempt this sort of rewriting process and it is worthwhile developing such skills. However, it should also be borne in mind that not all cubic functions can be written in alternative forms; more often than not, therefore, being able to plot graphs point by point is still the main requirement. Spreadsheet programs are most useful in this respect and their application to the creation of tables of values will be outlined next. Many spreadsheet packages also offer graph-drawing facilities. So, once the skill of drawing graphs with pencil and paper has been mastered, the rapid production of graphs on-screen provides much scope for investigation by allowing the user to concentrate on the general features and properties of different types of functions rather than their mechanical construction.

## Using spreadsheets to create tables of values

Generalised spreadsheet models can be developed which produce tables of values for cubic and other functions. For instance, it is reasonably straightforward to develop a template similar to this partially completed example set up for $y = x^2 + 4x + 3$ but which is easily modified for any quadratic function:

|   | A | B | C | D | E | F |
|---|---|---|---|---|---|---|
| 1 |   | Value of a | Value of b | Value of c |   |   |
| 2 |   | 1 | 4 | 3 |   |   |
| 3 |   |   |   |   |   |   |
| 4 | x | -4 | -3 | -2 | -1 | 0 |
| 5 | ax² |   |   | *B2\*d4\*d4* |   |   |
| 6 | bx |   |   | *C2\*d4* |   |   |
| 7 | c |   |   | *D2* |   |   |
| 8 | y |   |   | *d5+d6+d7* |   |   |

*Notes:*

1. Formulas are shown in italics. These would need to be replicated into the remaining columns of the table of values. (Upper case letters are used to denote absolute cell references; lower case letters denote relative cell references).

2. The values of $a$, $b$ and $c$ are placed in separate cells (B2, C2 and D2) instead of being incorporated into the formulas in the table of values e.g. the formula in cell D6 could be entered as: *4\*d4*. This is to avoid having to alter any formulas containing $a$, $b$ and $c$ each time a table of values is required for a new quadratic function.

3. Further refinements could be made to improve the flexibility of this template. For instance, the template allows for a range of values of $x$ which start at -4 and increase by 1; a more flexible arrangement would be for the start and end values of the range, and the incremental step, to be specified in separate cells (similar to the way that the values of $a$, $b$ and $c$ have been catered for) and appropriate formulas to contain them as absolute cell references. Whether this can be designed into the template depends on the facilities offered by the particular spreadsheet package being used.

4. Rows 4 and 8 are the most important since they provide the $x$-coordinates and $y$-coordinates of the points to be plotted. Rows 5, 6 and 7 could be considered unnecessary. However, the expanded version of the table of values provides opportunities for investigating the effect of changing the different component parts of the function on the position and shape of the graph.

## Other polynomial functions

Linear, quadratic and cubic functions are all examples of *polynomial* functions.

A polynomial function of $x$ consists of the sum of a collection of terms, each of which is either:

    i)   a number, or

or  ii)  a positive integer power of $x$ multiplied by a number

For instance: $4x$, $3x - 1$, $5x^2 + 6x - 3$ and $4x^3 - 0.5x + 17$ are all polynomials.

On the other hand: $x + \dfrac{1}{x}$, $\sqrt{x^2 - 16}$ and $\dfrac{2x^2 - 1}{x + 4}$ are not polynomials.

The multiplying number is called the *coefficient* and the highest power of the independent variable determines the *degree* of the polynomial. So, for example, $y = 3x^5 - 2x^2 + 7$ is a polynomial of degree 5.

Linear functions are polynomials of degree 1, quadratic functions are polynomials of degree 2 and cubic functions are polynomials of degree 3. There is obviously an endless collection of polynomial functions of higher degrees which can be constructed (e.g. quartic functions – which are polynomials of degree 4, and so on) and their graphs drawn in a similar fashion to that described in the previous sections. They are simply natural extensions to the progression of linear, quadratic and cubic functions, which are the most common. Clearly, all other polynomial functions cannot possibly be covered here. It is worth noting, however, that:

i)   the general form of a polynomial function of degree $n$ is:

$$y = a_0x^n + a_1x^{n-1} + a_2x^{n-2} + a_3x^{n-3} + \ldots\ldots + a_n,$$

where $a_0, a_1, a_2, \ldots a_n$ are coefficients, and $a_0 \neq 0$

ii)  the graph of a polynomial function generally gets more complex as the **number of terms increases**

iii) a polynomial function of degree $n$ has, at most, $n$-1 stationary points.

## Rational functions

Any function which can be represented as two polynomials in fractional form is called a *rational* function. So, for example: $y = \dfrac{2x^2 - 1}{x + 4}$ is a rational function (even though it is not a polynomial function).

The simplest rational function is $y = \dfrac{1}{x}$. Its graph looks like that shown below (table of values overleaf).

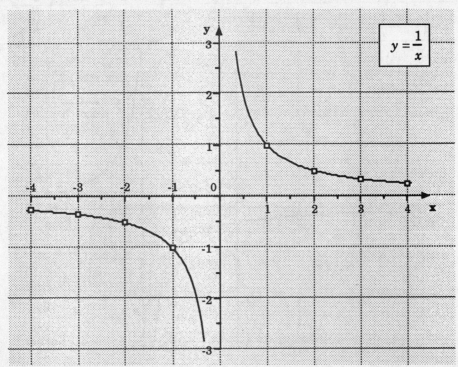

| $x$ | −4 | −3 | −2 | −1 | 0 | 1 | 2 | 3 | 4 |
|---|---|---|---|---|---|---|---|---|---|
| $y$ | $-\frac{1}{4}$ | $-\frac{1}{3}$ | $-\frac{1}{2}$ | −1 | ∞ | 1 | $\frac{1}{2}$ | $\frac{1}{3}$ | $\frac{1}{4}$ |

There are several things to note.

i)  The graph has a 'break' at $x = 0$, since the value of $\frac{1}{x}$ is not defined when $x = 0$.

   It is said to be *discontinuous* at $x = 0$.

ii)  The graph is in two parts, because of (i).

iii)  The shape of the graph is a *hyperbola*.

iv)  This type of rational function, where the numerator is 1, is also called a *reciprocal* function.

v)  In this graph, the $x$-axis and $y$-axis are asymptotes to the curve. An *asymptote* is a straight line which a curve approaches more and more closely, but never actually touches.

The general form of the reciprocal function is: $y = \dfrac{1}{ax + b}$

The main features of this type of function are:

i)  the graph is discontinuous at $x = \dfrac{b}{a}$, since the denominator is zero at this point.

ii)  asymptotes: the $x$-axis and the line $x = -\dfrac{b}{a}$.

As an example of a reciprocal function, consider the function: $y = \dfrac{1}{2x - 3}$

The table of values and graph are:

| $x$ | −3 | −2.5 | −2 | −1.5 | −1 | −0.5 | 0 | 0.5 | 1 | 1.5 | 2 | 2.5 | 3 |
|---|---|---|---|---|---|---|---|---|---|---|---|---|---|
| $y$ | $-\frac{1}{9}$ | $-\frac{1}{8}$ | $-\frac{1}{7}$ | $-\frac{1}{6}$ | $-\frac{1}{5}$ | $-\frac{1}{4}$ | $-\frac{1}{3}$ | $-\frac{1}{2}$ | −1 | ∞ | 1 | $\frac{1}{2}$ | $\frac{1}{3}$ |

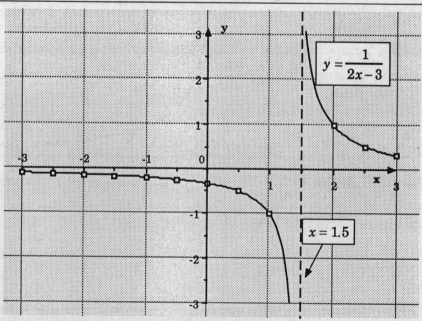

The horizontal asymptote is the $x$-axis; the vertical asymptote is the line $x = 1.5$

## Other rational functions

Many different types of rational functions exist; for instance, *linear* rational functions, where the numerator and denominator of the fraction are both linear. These functions have the form: $y = \dfrac{cx+d}{ax+b}$

As an example, consider the function: $y = \dfrac{5x+4}{2x-2}$

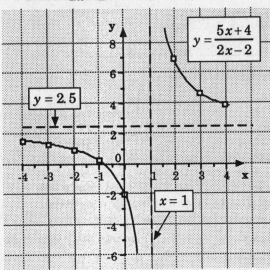

| $x$ | -3 | -2 | -1 | 0 | 1 | 2 | 3 |
|---|---|---|---|---|---|---|---|
| $y$ | $\dfrac{11}{8}$ | 1 | $\dfrac{1}{4}$ | -2 | $\infty$ | 7 | $\dfrac{19}{4}$ |

For this function:

i)   the *vertical* asymptote is where the value of the denominator is zero i.e. when $2x - 2 = 0 \Rightarrow x = 1$

ii)  the *horizontal* asymptote can be obtained by considering what happens as the value of $x$ increases.

e.g. when $x = 1000$, $y = \dfrac{5004}{2998} \approx \dfrac{5}{2}$

That is, when $x$ is a large number the '4' in the numerator and the '-5' in the denominator of the fraction are relatively unimportant. So, $y = \dfrac{5x+4}{2x-2} \approx \dfrac{5x}{2x} = \dfrac{5}{2}$

∴ The asymptotes are $x = 1$ and $y = 2.5$.

In general, the main features of the linear rational function $y = \dfrac{cx+d}{ax+b}$ are:

i)   the graph is discontinuous at $x = -\dfrac{b}{a}$

ii)  asymptotes: the line $x = -\dfrac{b}{a}$ and the line $y = \dfrac{c}{a}$

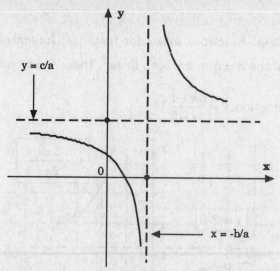

All linear rational functions have the same basic shape as the original function $y = \dfrac{1}{x}$. Varying the values of $a$, $b$, $c$ and $d$ has the effect of shifting the original curve left, right, up, down and stretching it in different ratios along the $y$-axis. The basic shape is still a hyperbola, however, so if a rough idea of the general position of the graph is required it is necessary only to find the positions of its asymptotes.

In the case of more complex functions, (for instance, rational functions where either the numerator, denominator or both are polynomials of a higher degree), the variety of possible shapes / stationary points / points of discontinuity etc is enormous. The use of spreadsheets to produce tables of values then becomes increasingly valuable if an accurately plotted graph is needed; however, so does the ability to identify the key features of a function e.g. asymptotes, if a general impression is all that is required. Some details of this can be found in the section - ' Elementary Curve Sketching'.

### Exponential functions

An exponential function has the general form $y = ka^x$ where $k$ and $a$ are constants and $x$ is the independent variable. Notice that the independent variable is in the power (or *exponent*), hence the name given to this type of function. $y = 2^x$ is an example of an exponential function.

The table of values and graph for this function are:

| $x$ | -4 | -3 | -2 | -1 | 0 | 1 | 2 | 3 | 4 |
|---|---|---|---|---|---|---|---|---|---|
| $y$ | $\dfrac{1}{16}$ | $\dfrac{1}{8}$ | $\dfrac{1}{4}$ | $\dfrac{1}{2}$ | 1 | 2 | 4 | 8 | 16 |

Graphs of $y = a^x$, for a variety of positive values of $a$, look like:

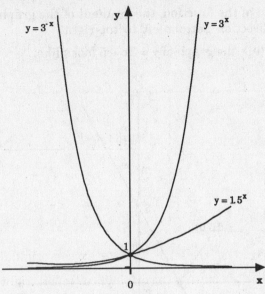

Note that:

i)    the whole of each graph lies entirely above the $x$-axis

ii)   the $x$-axis is an asymptote to the curve.

iii)  the intercept on the $y$-axis is 1.

iv)   the graph of $y = a^x$ is a mirror image of $y = a^{-x}$. The line of symmetry is the $y$-axis.

The graph of the function $y = ka^x$ is obtained by vertically scaling the graph of $y = a^x$ by a factor of $k$.

For instance, the point of intersection with the $y$-axis is $(k,0)$ instead of $(1,0)$.

## Elementary curve sketching

Using a computer to draw an accurate graph is not always convenient or appropriate. Sometimes it is sufficient, and quicker, to produce a sketch of the graph. A sketch shows the main features of the graph only and is not concerned with plotting every single point. Main features include:

i)    where the graph crosses the $x$-axis (i.e. where $y = 0$)

ii)   where the graph crosses the $y$-axis (i.e. where $x = 0$)

iii)  the graph's turning-points (if any)

iv)   the general shape and direction

### Sketching linear functions

A function with the general form: $y = mx + c$ is a straight line. Some aspects of linear functions which are helpful for sketching purposes are on pages 115–117.

Key features:

i)    where the graph cuts the $x$-axis

      e.g. the function $y = 2x + 5$ cuts the $x$-axis where $2x + 5 = 0 \Rightarrow y = -2.5$

      $\therefore$ the graph cuts the $y$-axis at the point (-2.5, 0)

ii)   where the graph cuts the $y$-axis

      e.g. inspecting the equation of the function, the graph cuts the $x$-axis at the point (0, 5)

iii)  the general direction of the line

e.g. inspecting the equation of the function, the gradient of the graph is 2; since this is positive, the line slopes in the general direction 'bottom-left' to 'top-right'

So, taking account of i), ii) and (iii), the graph of $y = 2x + 5$ looks like:

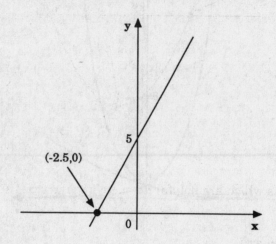

## Sketching quadratic functions

A function with the general form: $y = ax^2 + bx + c$ is a parabola. Some aspects of quadratic functions which are helpful for sketching purposes are on pages 118–122.

Key features:

i)  where the graph cuts the $x$-axis

e.g. the function: $y = x^2 - 2x - 8$ cuts the $x$-axis where $x^2 - 2x - 8 = 0 \Rightarrow (x-4)(x+2) = 0$

$$\Rightarrow x = 4 \text{ or } x = -2$$

∴ the graph cuts the $x$-axis at the points (4, 0) and (-2, 0)

ii)  where the graph cuts the $y$-axis

e.g. the function: $y = x^2 - 2x - 8$ cuts the $y$-axis where $y = 0^2 - 2 \times 0 - 8 \Rightarrow y = -8$

∴ the graph cuts the $y$-axis at the point (0, -8)

iii)  the turning-point of the graph; the function: $y = ax^2 + bx + c$ has a turning-point where $x = \dfrac{b}{2a}$

e.g. the function: $y = x^2 - 2x - 8$ has a turning-point where $x = \dfrac{2}{2} \Rightarrow x = 1$

∴ the graph has a turning-point at (1, -9)

iv)  the general direction of the graph

e.g. in the function: $y = x^2 - 2x - 8$, the coefficient of $x^2$ is positive

∴ the graph is not inverted

So, taking account of (i), (ii), iii) and (iv), the graph of $y = x^2 - 2x - 8$ looks like:

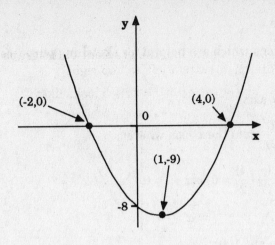

## Sketching cubic functions

Some aspects of cubic functions which are helpful for sketching purposes are on pages 122–123.

Key features:

i)   where the graph cuts the $y$-axis

e.g. the function: $y = x^3 - 4x^2 + 7$ cuts the $y$-axis where $y = 0^3 - 4 \times 0^2 + 7 \Rightarrow y = 7$

∴ the graph cuts the $x$-axis at the point $(0, 7)$

ii)  the general direction of the graph

e.g. in the function: $y = x^3 - 4x^2 + 7$, the coefficient of $x^3$ is positive

∴ the graph lies in a general direction from 'bottom-left' to 'top-right'

So, taking account of i) and ii) gives only limited possibilities for the graph, one of which is shown:

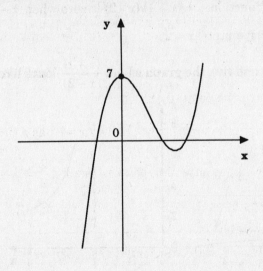

## Sketching rational functions

Some aspects of rational functions which are helpful for sketching purposes are on pages 125 – 128.
Key features:

i)   where the graph cuts the $x$-axis

e.g. the function: $y = \dfrac{(x+1)}{(x-2)}$ cuts the $x$-axis where:

$$\frac{(x+1)}{(x-2)} = 0 \Rightarrow x + 1 = 0$$

$$\Rightarrow x = -1$$

∴ the graph cuts the $x$-axis at (-1, 0)

ii)  where the graph cuts the $y$-axis

e.g. the function: $y = \dfrac{(x+1)}{(x-2)}$ cuts the $y$-axis where:

$$y = \frac{(0+1)}{(0-2)} \Rightarrow y = -0.5$$

∴ the graph cuts the $x$-axis at (0, -0.5)

iii) what happens as $x$ becomes large; that is, as $x \to \infty$ or $x \to -\infty$

e.g. for large values of $x$, the value of $y = \dfrac{(x+1)}{(x-2)} \approx \dfrac{x}{x} = 1$

∴ the graph has a horizontal asymptote: $y = 1$

iv) where the denominator is zero

e.g. the denominator of the function: $y = (x + 1)/(x - 2)$ is zero when $x - 2 = 0 \Rightarrow x = -2$

∴ the graph has a vertical asymptote: $x = 2$

So, taking account of (i), (ii), (iii) and (iv), the graph of $y = \dfrac{(x+1)}{(x-2)}$ looks like:

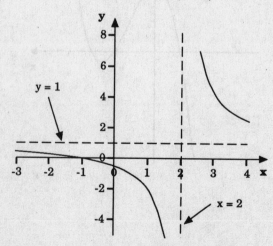

## Sketching exponential functions

All the aspects of exponential functions which are helpful for sketching purposes are on page 129.

In the case of all the above graphs, if additional information is required (for instance, locating the graph's turning-points), calculus techniques may be needed. (A detailed study of this topic is outside the scope of this text).However, depending on the skill of the individual, this may be counter-productive in terms of trying to save time by not plotting points. Spreadsheet models used to calculate tables of values can anyway be easily adapted to locate approximate turning-points by observing $x$- and $y$-coordinates calculated over a suitably small range. So, the choice between 'plot' and 'sketch' will depend on the preferences and skills of the individual, the time available and the accuracy required by the particular application.

# Unit 3: Numerical methods 1 – Numbers, approximations and errors

This section aims to help you to:

1. distinguish between different types of numbers
2. understand the meaning of *approximations* and *errors*
3. understand the difference between *absolute* errors and *relative* errors
4. analyse the effect of errors in calculations
5. appreciate how choice of method can reduce errors

## Types of numbers

It is possible to classify numbers as follows:

1. *Rational* numbers; these are made up of:

   i) Positive and negative *integers* (whole numbers): ...–5, –4, –3, –2, –1, 0, 1, 2, 3, 4, 5, ...

   ii) Fractions such as: $\frac{2}{3}, \frac{47}{8}, -\frac{17}{4}$, 0.37 and 6.2

   Rational numbers can be written in the form $\frac{m}{n}$ (where $m$ and $n$ are integers).

   Some rational numbers are also integers. For instance, $\frac{24}{6} = 4$.

2. *Irrational* numbers: these cannot be written in the form $m/n$. Examples include: p, +2, +5, and +7.

   Rational numbers and irrational numbers together make up the set of *real* numbers, as shown below:

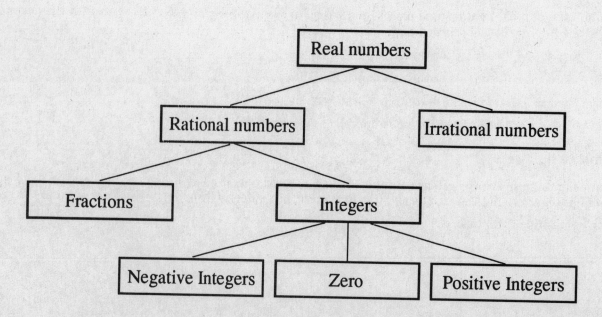

134

Rational numbers and irrational numbers can be distinguished from one another by their decimal representations. When written in such a form, rational numbers are always repeating decimals. For instance, the following are all rational numbers:

$$\frac{1}{2} = 0.5000 \ldots \ldots$$

$$\frac{1}{3} = 0.3333 \ldots \ldots$$

$$\frac{1}{6} = 0.1666 \ldots \ldots$$

$$\frac{2}{11} = 0.18\ 18\ 18\ 18\ 18 \ldots \ldots$$

$$\frac{1}{7} = 0.142857\ 142857\ 142857 \ldots \ldots$$

$$\frac{15}{13} = 1.153846\ 153846\ 153846 \ldots \ldots$$

Notice that, sooner or later, the decimal digits repeat themselves either singly or in groups.

The decimal representation of an irrational number also consists of an infinite sequence of digits. However, there is no repetition within the sequence. For example, the first 20 digits of the number p are:

$$p = 3.14159265358979323384 \ldots \ldots \ldots \ldots$$

## Approximations

Approximations to numbers contain fewer digits but still contain a sensible degree of accuracy. Two of the methods commonly used are:

i) *rounding* to a number of *decimal places*

ii) rounding to a number of *significant figures*

### Decimal places

To round off a number to $n$ decimal places, discard all digits to the right of the $n$th digit after the decimal point. If the first of these discarded digits is:

i) less than 5, do not alter the $n$th digit

ii) more than 5, add one to the $n$th digit

ii) exactly 5, round up or down to make the $n$th digit even

So, the value of p = 3.142 correct to 3 decimal places (written 3D).

### Significant figures

The rules for significant figures are similar; however, zeros i) at the beginning of a decimal or ii) at the end of an integer are not counted as significant figures, but must be included in the final number.

So, the value of p = 3.14 (3S).

*Examples:*

| Number | Rounded number (d.p.) | Rounded number (s.f.) |
|--------|----------------------|----------------------|
| 8.2371 | 8.24 (2D) | 8.2 (2S) |
| 193.85 | 193.8(1D) | 200(1S) |
| 0.43742 | 0.437(3D) | 0.437(3S) |
| 76.4068 | 76.407(3D) | 76.4(3S) |
| 0.666666... | 0.67(2D) | 0.67(2S) |
| 0.090909... | 0.1(1D) | 00.9(1S) |
| 8.10609 | 8.1061(4D) | 8.106(4S) |

# Errors

Whether working with pencil and paper, calculator or computer, there is a physical limit to the number of digits that can be retained in calculations. It is important, therefore, that numbers which are obtained as a result are written down along with some indication of their accuracy. This is usually stated in terms of the number of correct decimal places or significant figures. Also, whenever a number is rounded an error is introduced; if this number is then used in other calculations further errors may result.

For instance, consider this calculation:

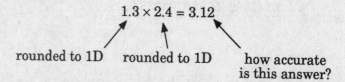

$$1.3 \times 2.4 = 3.12$$

rounded to 1D    rounded to 1D    how accurate is this answer?

1.3 could be any number between 1.25 and 1.35;  2.4 could be any number between 2.35 and 2.45.

Therefore, the answer could be anything from: $1.25 \times 2.35 = 2.9375$

up to : $1.35 \times 2.45 = 3.3075$

Rounding now gives an answer which could be anything between 2.9 and 3.3.

Such errors can accumulate during calculations involving addition, subtraction, multiplication and division. Assessing the error in solutions is an important feature of numerical methods and there are different ways that these errors can be measured.

## Absolute error

If $N$ is the exact value of a number, $n$ is the approximate value and e (pronounced 'epsilon') is the error in this approximation:

$$N = n + e$$

i.e. The accurate value is the approximate value plus the error.

Now, e could be positive or negative (depending whether $n$ is greater than or less than N). So, the *size* of the error is usually more important. This is denoted by $|e|$ and referred to as the *absolute error*.

Absolute error = |Accurate value – Approximate value|

For example, 37 may be taken as an approximation to 36.75. The error in this case is 36.75 - 37 = -0.25. ∴ The absolute error is 0.25.

## Relative error

This is the size of the error *compared* to the accurate value of the number.

$$\text{Relative error} = \frac{|\varepsilon|}{N} = \frac{\text{Absolute error}}{\text{Accurate value}}$$

($n$ is often used instead of N, since the accurate value is not usually known).

In the previous example, where $N = 37$ and $n = 36.75$, the relative error is: $\frac{0.25}{36.75} \approx 0.0068$

∴ The relative error is 0.007 (1S).

Note : The relative error usually gives a better indication of the accuracy than the absolute error.

For example,

i)   Suppose that a distance of 10m is measured as 9m.

In this case: absolute error = 1m; relative error $= \frac{1}{10} = 0.1$

ii)  Suppose that a distance of 1000m is measured as 1001m.

In this case: absolute error = 1m; relative error $= \frac{1}{1000} = 0.001$

Notice that the absolute error is the same in each case but the relative errors are vastly different. The second measurement is, therefore, much more accurate.

## Error bounds

An *error bound* is a limit set on the size of an error. It indicates the maximum possible size of the error.

Two examples follow.

i)   If the result of a calculation is 2.45 with an error bound of 0.002, this is the same as saying that the result is somewhere in the range 2.45 ± 0.002.

ii)  If a number is rounded to 3D at the end of a calculation, this is the same as saying that the maximum absolute error is $0.5 \times 10^{-3}$.

# Error propagation (accumulation)

If two numbers containing errors are used in calculations such as addition, subtraction, multiplication or division then the errors could either i) cancel out or ii) accumulate. Since the errors could accumulate, the error bound of the result must allow for this; that is, assume the worst possible case.

The degree to which errors accumulate depends on the type of operation being carried out. There are some simple rules which can be used to estimate the errors in the results of common arithmetic operations and these are given below:

## Addition (and subtraction)

If $e_1$ and $e_2$ are the error bounds in two numbers which are being added (or subtracted) then:

$$|\varepsilon| \leq e_1 + e_2$$

In other words, $e_1 + e_2$ is an error bound for the result.

## Multiplication (and division)

If $r_1$ and $r_2$ are the relative error bounds in two numbers which are being multiplied (or divided) then:

$$r \leq r_1 + r_2$$

In other words, $r_1 + r_2$ is a relative error bound for the result.

## An example of error estimation

Consider the numbers 5.23, 3.56 and 13.84 which have each been rounded to 2D and are to be used in further calculations.

a)  5.23 + 3.56:

The sum is 8.79

Absolute error in 5.23 = 0.005

Absolute error in 3.56 = 0.005

∴ Absolute error in sum ≤ 0.005 + 0.005 = 0.01

∴ 5.23 + 3.56 = 8.79 ± 0.01

∴ The sum lies between 8.78 and 8.80

The answer can be stated as either 8.8 (1D) or 8.79 ± 0.01

b)  5.23 × 3.56:

The product is 18.6188

Relative error in 5.23 = $\dfrac{0.005}{5.23} \approx 0.000957$

Relative error in 3.56 = $\dfrac{0.005}{3.56} \approx 0.001404$

∴ Relative error in product ≤ 0.000957 + 0.001404 ≤ 0.0024

∴ 5.23 × 3.56 = 18.6188 + 0.0024 × 18.6188

∴ The product lies between 18.5741 and 18.6635

The answer can be stated as either 19 (2S) or 18.619 ± 0.045

c)  5.23 × (13.84 − 3.56):

The result is 53.7644

Relative error in 5.23 = $\dfrac{0.005}{5.23} = 0.000957$

Absolute error in 13.84 − 3.56 ≤ 0.01

∴ Relative error in 13.84 − 3.56 = $\dfrac{0.01}{10.28} \approx 0.000973$

∴ Relative error in 5.23 × (13.84 − 3.56) ≤ 0.000957 + 0.000973 = 0.00193

∴ 5.23 × (13.84 − 3.56) = 53.7644 ± 0.00193 × 53.7644

∴ The result lies between 53.6607 and 53.8682

The answer can be stated as either 54 (2S) or 53.764 ± 0.105

Note that it is safer to over-estimate rather than under-estimate errors.

In general, when carrying out a calculation it is standard procedure to:

i)   work with at least one more digit than given in the original numbers

ii)  round answers *at the end* of the calculation

iii) state the accuracy achieved

iv) use a consistent number of *decimal places* when the calculation involves mainly additions and / or subtractions

v) use a consistent number of *significant figures* when the calculation involves mainly multiplications and / or divisions

## Errors in computer arithmetic

There are a variety of situations where computers can introduce errors which might not otherwise occur. For instance, the way that computers store and manipulate numbers can introduce additional errors. Possible sources of computer error include:

i) Number storage

ii) Number conversion

iii) Calculation

### Errors due to computer storage of numbers

A real number, N, is said to be in *floating-point decimal* if it is written in the form:

$$N = \pm m \times 10^p$$

where:   i)  *m* is called the *mantissa* and $0.1 \le m < 1$

ii) *p* is called the *exponent* and is an integer

For instance, the following numbers are all written in floating-point decimal form:

$$51.97 = 0.5197 \times 10^2$$
$$3256 = 0.3256 \times 10^2$$
$$175000000 = 0.175 \times 10^9$$
$$-241.69 = -0.24169 \times 10^3$$
$$0.06 = 0.6 \times 10^{-1}$$
$$0.000000025 = 0.25 \times 10^{-7}$$
$$-0.00064 = -0.64 \times 10^{-3}$$

Notice that:

a) the mantissa contains the significant figures

b) the exponent determines the position of the decimal point

c) both mantissa and exponent can be positive or negative:

i) the sign of the mantissa determines the sign of the number

ii) the sign of the exponent determines whether the point is shifted to left or right

In a similar way, numbers are usually stored in a computer in *floating-point binary* form. So, when a real number is stored it is first necessary for it to be converted into floating-point binary; that is, into the form:

$$N = \pm m \times 2^p \ (0.5 \le m < 1)$$

Consider these decimal numbers and their floating-point binary equivalents:

$$43.25 = 0.10101101 \times 2^6$$
$$-2.5 = 0.11 \times 2^1$$
$$0.0625 = 0.1 \times 2^{-3}$$
$$163.125 = 0.10100011001 \times 2^8$$

(For further information about the binary number system, the reader is directed to the text:'Computing' by P.M. Heathcote).

Now, if two bytes (16 bits) are used to store the above numbers, 10 bits (1 sign bit and 9 digits) might be allocated to the mantissa and 6 bits to the exponent:

| Number | Sign | Mantissa | Exponent |
|---|---|---|---|
| 43.25 | 0 | 1 0 1 0 1 1 0 1 0 | 0 0 0 1 1 0 |
| 163.125 | 0 | 1 0 1 0 0 0 1 1 0 | 0 0 1 0 0 0 |
| -2.5 | 1 | 1 1 0 0 0 0 0 0 0 | 0 0 0 0 0 1 |
| 0.0625 | 0 | 1 0 0 0 0 0 0 0 0 | 1 1 1 1 0 1 |

There are some general points to note:

i)   in the mantissa, the leftmost bit is always a 1; this makes the best use of the available bits and gives the maximum number of significant figures. This is known as *normalised form*.

ii)  the leftmost bit of the exponent represents its sign.

iii) the mantissa determines the precision and the exponent determines the range of numbers that can be represented in floating-point form.

iv)  the *relative error bound* for a floating-point form with $n$ bits allocated to the mantissa is $2^{-(n-2)}$

Notice that, in the case of 163.125 above, the rightmost two bits have been lost because there are only 9 bits available to store the significant figures. The actual number stored is, therefore, 163 with a relative error bound of $2^{-8}$. This means that the number, as represented, could be $163 \pm 2^{-8} \times 163 \approx 163 \pm 0.64$.

## Errors due to number conversion

Some fractions have exact binary equivalents. For example:

| Decimal number | Binary equivalent |
|---|---|
| $\frac{1}{2}$ | 0.1 |
| $\frac{1}{4}$ | 0.01 |
| $\frac{3}{4}$ | 0.11 |
| $\frac{5}{16}$ | 0.0011 |
| $\frac{29}{128}$ | 0.0011101 |

However, there is an infinite number of fractions which do not have exact binary equivalents. For example, converting the decimal fraction 0.2 into binary gives the recurring sequence:

$$0.0011\ 0011\ 0011\ 0011\ldots.$$

If 8 bits are used for the mantissa, this gives a representation of: 0.00110011. Converting this back to decimal gives 0.19921875. That is, there is a relative error of $\dfrac{0.00078125}{0.2} \approx 0.4\%$ in the representation. So, errors are introduced when numbers are converted into binary in order to be stored.

### Errors in calculation

It is important to realise that nearly all operations on a computer (apart from the addition, subtraction, multiplication and division of integers) give only approximate answers. Errors could be due to:

i)   a limit on the number of places available to store the result of a calculation

ii)  overflow

iii) rounding for normalising purposes (see below).

Errors can also be difficult to predict since software design (for instance, retaining more digits during a calculation than are required in the final answer) often reduces their effects.

## Other sources of error and their control

### Algorithmic errors

An *algorithm* is a step-by-step procedure used in the solution of a problem; examples of algorithms include: recipes, knitting patterns and self-assembly furniture instructions. A computer program is also an algorithm and the accuracy of the solution which it produces is dependent on the efficiency of the algorithm. Algorithms which take into account the operations involved and which reduce the number of calculations can often make considerable improvements in time as well as accuracy.

The order in which operations are carried out can often affect the accuracy of the result. For instance, in floating-point addition the steps are:

i)   make the exponents equal
ii)  add the mantissas
iii) normalise the result

As an example, consider the floating-point addition of the numbers X and Y where:

$$X = 0.10101101 \times 2^7$$

and

$$Y = 0.11011101 \times 2^2$$

Step 1:  Equalise the exponents.

   This is done by shifting the mantissa of the smaller number (Y) until its exponent is equal to the exponent of the larger number (X). In doing so, Y loses significant digits. So:

|   | Mantissa | Exponent |
|---|----------|----------|
| X | 0.10101101 | 00000111 |
| Y | 0.00000110 | 00000111 |

Step 2:  Add the mantissas. $\therefore X + Y = 0.10110011 \times 2^7$.

Step 3:  Normalise the result. This is not necessary in this example since the first significant digit is in the first position after the point.

141

Notice that, when adding (or subtracting) a large number and a relatively small number, significant figures are lost in the smaller. The effect of this is to introduce an error; in this case, the sum of X (86.5) and Y (3.453125) has been calculated as 89.5 whereas the exact answer is 89.953125. This represents a relative error of approximately 0.5%. As a consequence of this, when adding (or subtracting) three or more floating-point numbers, it is better to deal with them in *increasing* order of size. This then takes into account the accumulating effect of smaller numbers.

Errors can also cause distortion in the final result when large quantities of calculations are involved. The evaluation of polynomials is an example of this sort of situation and techniques such as *nesting* can help minimise such errors.

For instance, consider calculating the value of the function:

$$f(x) = 2x^3 + 7x^2 + 6x + 4$$

for different values of $x$..

One method is to calculate:

i)   $x^2$                    (1 multiplication)
ii)  $x^3$                    (1 multiplication)
iii) $2x^3$                   (1 multiplication)
iv)  $7x^2$                   (1 multiplication)
v)   $6x$                     (1 multiplication)
vi)  $2x^3 + 7x^2 + 6x + 4$   (3 additions)

So, a total of 5 multiplications and 3 additions is required to evaluate the polynomial for each value of $x$.

Nesting involves rewriting the polynomial in a different form, in this case:

$$f(x) = ((2x + 7)x + 6)x + 4$$

The calculations required are now:

i)   $2x + 7$                 (1 multiplication, 1 addition)
ii)  $(2x + 7)x$              (1 multiplication)
iii) $((2x + 7)x + 6)x$       (1 addition, 1 multiplication)
iv)  $((2x + 7)x + 6)x + 4$   (1 addition)

This method requires only 3 multiplications and 3 additions. When such calculations need to be repeated many times, the savings in errors and time can be considerable.

## Program loop statements

Consider a program loop statement such as:

```
FOR k =1 TO 100 STEP 0.2
    dosomething
NEXT k
```

This program segment should 'dosomething' when $k$ takes the values: 1, 1.2, 1.4, 1.6, . . . . . .100. However, 0.2 is a decimal quantity which does not have an exact binary equivalent. Since the step size is only approximated, any subsequent increments by this amount will just exaggerate the error. So, the loop may not be performed the expected number of times.

In this sort of situation it is better, therefore, to change the statement to something like:

```
FOR K=10 TO 1000 STEP 0.2
    k = K/10
    dosomething
NEXT K
```

This:

i) minimises the error in $k$ and

ii) ensures the loop is performed the expected number of times.

## Program conditional statements

Consider the statement:

IF X = Y THEN dosomething

The program segment should 'dosomething' if the values of the variables X and Y are equal. However, if the variables X and Y are the results of previous calculations, rounding may prevent them from *appearing* equal even if they *are* equal. In this sort of situation it is better to introduce a range or tolerance within which they can be considered as equal.

For example, a better version of the above statement is:

IF ABS(X – Y) < 10E - 8 THEN dosomething

$$|X - Y| \qquad 10^{-8}$$

When the difference between X and Y is less than 0.000 000 01 the program segment will 'dosomething'.

# Unit 4: Numerical methods 2 – Areas, iterations and solving equations

This section aims to help you to:

1.  understand what is meant by 'numerical methods'
2.  appreciate the need for numerical methods
3.  become familiar with numerical integration techniques
4.  become familiar with various iterative methods
5.  appreciate the relative merits of different iterative methods
6.  implement iterative processes on a computer

## What are numerical methods?

Once a mathematical model of a given situation has been constructed it is then necessary to try and obtain solutions to the equations which make up that model. In some cases there may exist standard analytical techniques (e.g. calculus) which can provide off-the-peg methods of solution. Sometimes, however, the complex nature of the model may prevnt the technique being applied. In other cases, there may be no standard technique which can be applied.

As a simple example, consider the solution of the equation: $3x - 7 = 0$.

*Analytical method*

If : $\qquad 3x - 7 = 0$

then : $\qquad\qquad 3x = 7$

$\qquad \therefore \quad x = \dfrac{7}{3}$

$\qquad \therefore \quad x = 2.3 \text{ (1D)}$

*Numerical method*

1)  Make an initial guess: since $3 \times 2 - 7 < 0$ and $3 \times 3 - 7 > 0$, solution lies between $x = 2$ and $x = 3$

2)  Try $x = 2.1$: $\quad 3 \times 2.1 - 7 < 0 \qquad \therefore x = 2.1$ is too small

    Try $x = 2.2$: $\quad 3 \times 2.2 - 7 < 0 \qquad \therefore x = 2.2$ is too small

    Try $x = 2.3$: $\quad 3 \times 2.3 - 7 < 0 \qquad \therefore x = 2.3$ is too small

    Try $x = 2.4$: $\quad 3 \times 2.4 - 7 > 0 \qquad \therefore x = 2.4$ is too big

    $\therefore$ Solution lies between $x = 2.3$ and $x = 2.4$

3)  Try $x = 2.31$: $\quad 3 \times 2.31 - 7 < 0 \qquad \therefore x = 2.31$ is too small

    Try $x = 2.32$: $\quad 3 \times 2.32 - 7 < 0 \qquad \therefore x = 2.32$ is too small

    Try $x = 2.33$: $\quad 3 \times 2.33 - 7 < 0 \qquad \therefore x = 2.33$ is too small

    Try $x = 2.34$: $\quad 3 \times 2.34 - 7 > 0 \qquad \therefore x = 2.34$ is too big

    $\therefore$ Solution lies between $x = 2.33$ and $x = 2.34$ $\therefore x = 2.3$ (1D)

In solving this linear equation, the analytical method is clearly superior to the numerical method.

144

However,

i) different types of equation need different analytical methods and

ii) no analytical method exists for solving equations of degree higher than 4. On the other hand, the numerical method outlined in the example (that is: make an initial guess and gradually improve it) can be applied equally well to linear and non-linear equations.

Numerical methods have been developed, therefore, to provide alternative approaches to the solution of problems, especially those which are not solvable by other methods. However, they should not just be thought of as a last resort but are

i) general techniques which can be applied to a whole range of different problems and

ii) extremely well suited to implementation on a computer.

An important aspect of numerical methods is deciding which is the most effective method in any given situation. There are many different methods to choose from and in order to judge the best method the following points will need to be considered:

1) speed (or efficiency) – this is directly related to the number of calculations involved, so a method which takes fewer calculations to reach the solution is to be preferred;

2) accuracy of solutions – this is dependent on the acceptable error in the calculated solution;

3) reliability – this is concerned with whether there are particular situations where the method does not work.

## Graphical area estimation

One way to find the area under a curve is to use algebraic integration. This can be quite involved and in some cases is impossible. An alternative approach is to use *numerical integration* which gives an approximate solution by using relatively simple techniques. Two techniques in common use are:

i) the Trapezium Rule and

ii) Simpson's Rule.

Consider the problem of finding the area shown in Fig. 1:

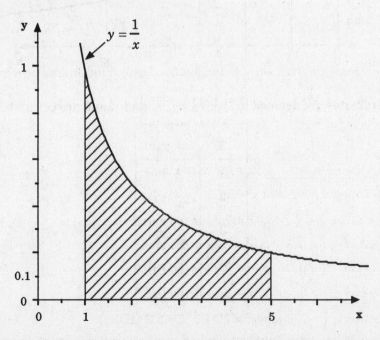

*Fig. 1*

*Note* : Standard notation for the area under the curve $y = f(x)$ between $x = a$ and $x = b$ is :

$$\int_a^b f(x)dx$$

In Fig. 1, therefore, the shaded area is denoted by:

$$\int_1^5 \left(\frac{1}{x}\right)dx$$

## The Trapezium Rule

The basis of this method is:

i)   divide the required area into any number of equally spaced strips (see Fig. 2)

ii)  join the tops of adjacent ordinates (*y*-values) to obtain a number of trapezia

iii) calculate and add together the areas of the trapezia

In words, the Trapezium Rule can be stated as:

Area under curve ≈ 0.5(width of a strip){(sum of first and last ordinates) + 2(sum of other ordinates)}

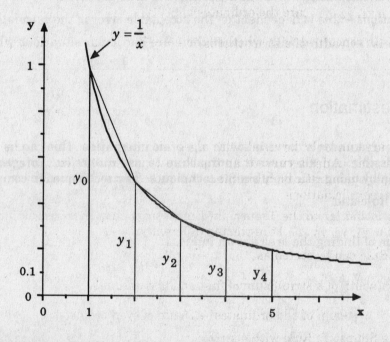

*Fig. 2*

In the example, the ordinates are denoted by: $y_0$, $y_1$, $y_2$, $y_3$ and $y_4$ and are calculated as follows:

| x | $y = \frac{1}{x}$ |
|---|---|
| 1 | 1 ($y_0$) |
| 2 | $\frac{1}{2}$ ($y_1$) |
| 3 | $\frac{1}{3}$ ($y_2$) |
| 4 | $\frac{1}{4}$ ($y_3$) |
| 5 | $\frac{1}{5}$ ($y_4$) |

There are 4 strips, so the width of each strip is: $\dfrac{(5-1)}{4} = 1$

Using the Trapezium Rule with 4 strips:

$$\int_1^5 \left(\dfrac{1}{x}\right)dx \approx 0.5 \times 1 \times \{y_0 + y_4 + 2(y_1 + y_2 + y_3)\}$$

$$= 0.5 \times 1 \times \{1 + \dfrac{1}{5} + 2(\dfrac{1}{2} + \dfrac{1}{3} + \dfrac{1}{4})\}$$

$$\approx 1.68 \ (2D)$$

The method is easily extended to any number of strips:

---

### The Trapezium rule

The area under the curve $y = f(x)$ between $x = a$ and $x = b$ using $n$ strips is given approximately by:

$$\int_a^b f(x)dx \approx 0.5h\Big[y_0 + y_n + 2\big(y_1 + y_2 + y_3 + \cdots y_{n-1}\big)\Big]$$

where   i)   $y_0, y_1, y_2 \ldots$ are the ordinates and

ii)   $h$ is the width of a strip; that is, $h = \dfrac{(b-a)}{n}$

---

## Simpson's Rule

Simpson's Rule (which can only be used with an even number of strips) generally gives a better approximation to the area under a curve than the Trapezium Rule. In fact, Simpson's Rule gives *exact* results when the graph is quadratic or cubic. Since it is so accurate, some scientific calculators use it as a built-in function for area calculations.

The use of ordinates is similar to the Trapezium Rule, except that 'even' ordinates (i.e. $y_2, y_4, y_6 \ldots$) and 'odd' ordinates (i.e. $y_1, y_3, y_5 \ldots$) are treated differently.

In words, Simpson's Rule can be stated as:

Area under curve $\approx \dfrac{1}{3}$ (width of a strip){(sum of first and last ordinates)

$+ 4$(sum of odd ordinates) $+ 2$(sum of even ordinates)}

In the example, using Simpson's Rule with 4 strips:

$$\int_1^5 \left(\dfrac{1}{x}\right)dx \approx \dfrac{h}{3}\{y_0 + y_4 + 4(y_1 + y_3) + 2y_2\}$$

$$= \dfrac{1}{3}\{1 + \dfrac{1}{5} + 4(\dfrac{1}{2} + \dfrac{1}{4}) + 2(\dfrac{1}{3})\}$$

$$\approx 1.62 \ (2D)$$

(Note that the method of algebraic integration gives a solution of 1.61 (2D). The relative error using the Trapezium Rule is 4.3%; using Simpson's Rule the relative error is only 0.6%).

Extending the method to any number of strips:

---

### Simpson's rule

The area under the curve $y = f(x)$ between $x = a$ and $x = b$ using n strips is given approximately by:

$$\int_a^b f(x)dx \approx \frac{h}{3}\left[y_0 + y_n + 4(y_1 + y_3 + y_5 + \cdots + y_{n-1}) + 2(y_2 + y_4 + y_6 + \cdots y_{n-2})\right]$$

where  i)  $y_0, y_1, y_2 \ldots$ are the ordinates and

ii)  $h$ is the width of a strip; that is, $h = \dfrac{(b-a)}{n}$ and

iii)  $n$ is even.

---

## The Solution of Equations

In order to solve the equation $f(x) = 0$, a good first step is to sketch its graph and see where it cuts the $x$-axis. This gives a good idea of i) how many roots (solutions) it has and ii) their approximate values.

For example, consider the solution of the equation: $x^3 - 4x^2 + 7 = 0$. The graph of $y = x^3 - 4x^2 + 7$ is:

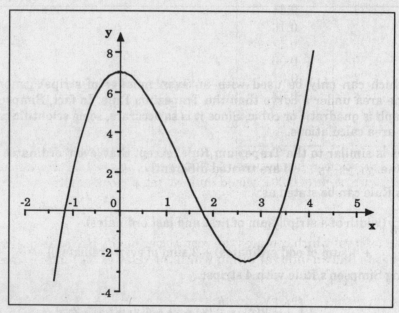

The graph cuts the $x$-axis at three points, so the equation has three roots:

i)   between $x = -2$ and $x = -1$

ii)  between $x = 1$ and $x = 2$ and

iii) between $x = 3$ and $x = 4$.

There are various methods which can be used to find the values of the roots more precisely. Two common techniques are: *decimal search* and *interval bisection*.

### Decimal Search

In the example, to find the root which lies between $x = 1$ and $x = 2$ values of the function are tabulated in steps of 0.1, as follows:

| $x$ | $x^3 - 4x^2 + 7$ |
|-----|-----------------|
| 1.0 | 4.00 |
| 1.1 | 3.49 |
| 1.2 | 2.97 |
| 1.3 | 2.44 |
| 1.4 | 1.90 |
| 1.5 | 1.38 |
| 1.6 | 0.86 |
| 1.7 | 0.35 |
| 1.8 | -0.13 |
| 1.9 | -0.58 |
| 2.0 | -1.00 |

The root must lie between $x=1.7$ and $x=1.8$ since the value of the function changes from positive to negative. i.e. it crosses the $x$-axis.

This search technique can be applied again for values between $x = 1.7$ and $x = 1.8$, with steps of 0.01:

| $x$ | $x^3 - 4x^2 + 7$ |
|-----|-----------------|
| 1.7 | 0.35 |
| 1.71 | 0.30 |
| 1.72 | 0.25 |
| 1.73 | 0.21 |
| 1.74 | 0.16 |
| 1.75 | 0.11 |
| 1.76 | 0.06 |
| 1.77 | 0.01 |
| 1.78 | -0.03 |
| . . . . | . . . . |
| . . . . | . . . . |

Solution is between 1.77 and 1.78

The table shows that the solution lies between 1.77 and 1.78, so $x = 1.8$ (1D). Repeating this process in the range 1.77 to 1.78, with steps of 0.001, would improve the accuracy by one more decimal place.

## Interval bisection

In this technique, the interval which contains the root is continually halved to narrow down the range of search. The first step is to find an interval within which the value of the function changes sign.

For the function $f(x) = x^3 - 4x^2 + 7$:

i)    $f(1) = 1^3 - 4(1^2) + 7 = 4$

ii)    $f(2) = 2^3 - 4(2^2) + 7 = -1$

Note that $f(1)$ means: 'the value of the function $y = f(x)$ when $x = 1$'.

So, the function $f(x) = x^3 - 4x^2 + 7$ has a root between $x = 1$ and $x = 2$.

This can be written as: $x = \{1, 2\}$, which means simply that '$x$ is a number between 1 and 2'.

The interval bisection process continues as follows:

Step 1:    $x = \{1, 2\}$; try interval midpoint: $x = 1.5$         $f(1.5) = 1.5^3 - 4 \times 1.5^2 + 7 = 1.375$

         Since $f(1.5) > 0, \therefore x = \{1.5, 2\}$

Step 2:    $x = \{1.5, 2\}$; try interval midpoint: $x = 1.75$        $f(1.75) = 1.75^3 - 4 \times 1.75^2 + 7 = 0.11$

         Since $f(1.75) > 0, \therefore x = \{1.75, 2\}$

Step 3:   $x = \{1.75, 2\}$; try $x = 1.875$                                  $f(1.875) = 1.875^3 - 4 \times 1.875^2 + 7 = -0.47$

Since $f(1.875) < 0$, $\backslash x = \{1.75, 1.875\}$

Step 4:   $x = \{1.75, 1.875\}$; try $x = 1.8125$                            $f(1.8125) = -0.19$

Since $f(1.8125) < 0$, $\backslash x = \{1.75, 1.8125\}$

Step 5:   $x = \{1.75, 1.8125\}$                                              $\therefore x = 1.8 \,(1D)$

If greater accuracy were required, the process would need to be repeated.

So, a general algorithm to find a root of the equation $f(x) = 0$ by interval bisection is:

i)   Find two points, $x = a$ and $x = b$, between which the graph of $y = f(x)$ crosses the $x$-axis.

That is, $f(a)$ and $f(b)$ have opposite signs.

ii)   Calculate $f(c)$ where $c$ is the midpoint of $\{a, b\}$.

iii)   If $f(c)$ has a different sign to $f(a)$, the root lies in $\{a, c\}$; repeat the algorithm on the interval $\{a, c\}$.

If not, then the root lies in $\{c, b\}$; repeat the algorithm on the interval $\{c, b\}$.


## What are Iterative Processes?

'Decimal search' and 'interval bisection' are particular examples of a collection of methods known as *iterative processes*. An iterative process is a rule or algorithm which obtains an approximation to a solution based on an earlier approximation. That is, make an initial estimate of the solution and then use the algorithm to gradually improve the estimate until the required accuracy is obtained.

This can be summarised as shown in Fig. 3 on the following page.

More formally, the features that an iterative process possesses are:

i)   an initial approximation, which we can call $x_0$

ii)   a rule for obtaining each new approximation $x_{n+1}$ from the previous approximation $x_n$

(The successive approximations can be called $x_1, x_2, x_3, x_4, \ldots$)

iii)   some way of deciding when to stop the process

The next sections look at ways that iterative processes are developed, in particular

i)   simple iterative methods and

ii)   the Newton-Raphson method.


## Iterative Processes (1) – Simple Iteration

Consider the methods which exist for solving quadratic equations such as: $x^2 - 6x + 7 = 0$. For instance:

Factorisation

Completing the square

Graph

Standard formula

These methods have differences in terms of the accuracy that is obtainable, the different sorts of mathematical skills needed and the failure of the method in certain cases.

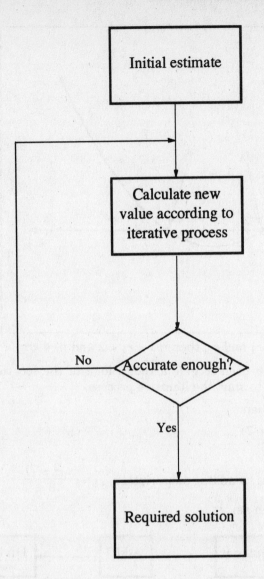

*Fig. 3*

It is also difficult (or sometimes impossible) to extend all of these methods to the solution of other more complex equations which may arise in mathematical modelling. For example, the standard formula which can be used to solve quadratic equations lacks the adaptability to solve other types of equations..

Iterative processes are much more flexible. So, although these processes will be illustrated by considering their application to the solution of a quadratic equation, it should be realised that the underlying principles can be applied to other types of equations.

Consider the quadratic equation: $x^2 - 6x + 7 = 0$.

A graph of the function is shown on the following page.

One root lies between 1 and 2. The other root lies between 4 and 5.

*Note*: To obtain estimates for the roots, construct a table of values for the function and observe where sign changes occur i.e.:

| x | -1 | 0 | 1 | 2 | 3 | 4 | 5 | 6 |
|---|----|---|---|---|---|---|---|---|
| y | 14 | 7 | 2 | -1 | -2 | -1 | 2 | 7 |

sign change     sign change

151

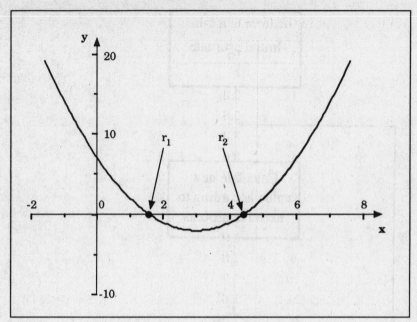

If the roots of the equation are denoted by $r_1$ and $r_2$, then i) $1 < r_1 < 2$ and ii) $4 < r_2 < 5$.

The graph and the table of values can be used to give a rough idea of the location of the roots and provide initial approximations with which to start the iterative process.

The quadratic equation $x^2 - 6x + 7 = 0$ is then:

i)   rearranged into the form: $x = \dfrac{(x^2 + 7)}{6}$

ii)  converted into an iterative process by adding subscripts: $x_{n+1} = \dfrac{(x_n{}^2 + 7)}{6}$

Diagrammatically the process can be shown as:

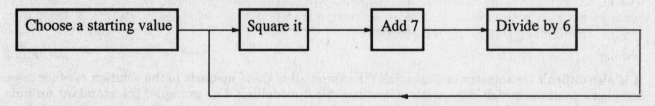

Of course, some means of deciding when this process should terminate needs incorporating. Usually this is when the difference between two successive iterated values is negligible. The definition of the word 'negligible' is dependent on the amount of acceptable error.

So, choosing $x_0 = 2$:

$$x_1 = \frac{(x_0{}^2 + 7)}{6} = \frac{(2^2 + 7)}{6} \approx 1.8$$

$$x_2 = \frac{(x_1{}^2 + 7)}{6} = \frac{(1.8^2 + 7)}{6} \approx 1.7$$

$$x_3 = \frac{(x_2{}^2 + 7)}{6} = \frac{(1.7^2 + 7)}{6} \approx 1.6$$

and so on.

Such calculations are better set out in the form of a table:

| n | $x_n$ | $x_{n+1}$ |
|---|---|---|
| 0 | 4 | 3.8 |
| 1 | 3.8 | 3.6 |
| 2 | 3.6 | 3.3 |
| 3 | 3.3 | 3.0 |
| 4 | 3.0 | 2.7 |
| 5 | 2.7 | 2.4 |
| 6 | 2.4 | 2.1 |
| 7 | 2.1 | 1.9 |
| 8 | 1.9 | 1.8 |
| 9 | 1.8 | 1.7 |
| 10 | 1.7 | 1.6 |
| 11 | 1.6 | 1.59 |
| 12 | 1.59 | 1.588 |
| 13 | 1.588 | 1.587 |
| 14 | 1.587 | 1.586 |
| 15 | 1.5859 | 1.5858 |
| 16 | 1.5858 | 1.58579 |
| 17 | 1.58579 | 1.585788 |
| etc. | etc. | etc. |

*Table A*

The table shows that the process *converges* (i.e. 'homes in') to the first root: $r_1 = 1.586$ (3D)

The number of iterations needed for convergence will be determined not only by the level of accuracy required but also by the initial value. For instance, if the initial value had been $x_0 = 1.5$, this would have reduced the number of iterations considerably.

Similarly, choosing $x_0 = 5$ gives:

| n | $x_n$ | $x_{n+1}$ |
|---|---|---|
| 0 | 5 | 5.3 |
| 1 | 5.3 | 5.8 |
| 2 | 5.8 | 6.8 |
| 3 | 6.8 | 8.9 |
| 4 | 8.9 | 14 |
| 5 | 14 | 34 |
| 6 | 34 | 194 |
| 7 | 194 | 6274 |
| etc. | etc. | etc. |

*Table B*

This shows that the process does not always converge; sometimes it *diverges*. That is, the values of successive iterations move further and further away from the root. (In fact, when this particular iterative process converges, it always converges to $r_1$ and never converges to $r_2$).

Other iterative processes can be obtained by different rearrangements of the original quadratic equation and these may give better results. For instance:

a)  $x_{n+1} = \sqrt{(6x_n - 7)}$     b)     $x_{n+1} = 6 - \dfrac{7}{x_n}$     c)     $x_{n+1} = \dfrac{7}{(6 - x_n)}$

Whether an iterative process converges or diverges to a solution depends on:

i)   the particular process being used

ii)  the value chosen as the initial approximation.

Simple iteration can be summarised as follows:

> ### Simple iteration
>
> i)     rearrange the equation to be solved into the form:
>
> $$x_{n+1} = F(x_n)$$
>
> ii)    obtain an initial approximation, $x_0$
>
> iii)   use i) to produce a sequence of successive approximations $x_1, x_2, x_3 \ldots$
>
> iv)    continue until the process converges to a solution, or diverges.

## Graphical representation of Simple Iteration

Consider again the iterative process: $x_{n+1} = \dfrac{(x_n^2 + 7)}{6}$                                                  (4.1)

It is possible to examine the behaviour of this process graphically.

Firstly, the graphs of $y = x$ and $y = \dfrac{(x^2 + 7)}{6}$ are drawn on the same pair of axes (see Fig. 4). These represent respectively the left-hand side and right-hand side of the equation (4.1). The roots of the original quadratic are the points of intersection of the two graphs.

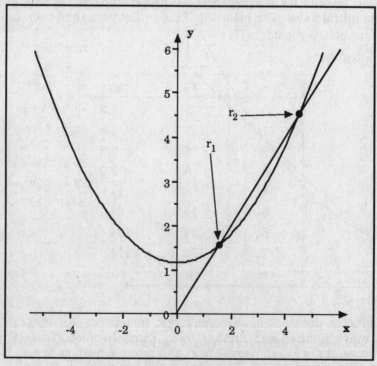

*Fig. 4*

154

Secondly, the path of the iterations is shown as an arrowed line (Fig. 5).

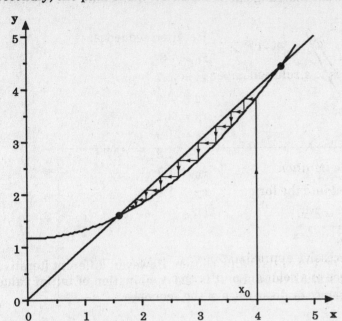

In this diagram, the initial value is $x_0 = 4$.

Each vertical arrowed line corresponds to a new iteration in the sequence:

$$x_0 = 4$$
$$x_1 = 3.8$$
$$x_2 = 3.6$$
$$x_3 = 3.3$$
$$x_4 = 3.0$$
$$x_5 = 2.7$$
$$x_6 = 2.4$$
$$x_7 = 2.1$$

etc.

*Fig. 5*

Notice the path of the iterations is 'up' to the curve, 'across' to the line, 'down' to the curve etc.

This general alternating pattern of curve-line-curve-line-curve etc. corresponds directly to the way the iterative process (4.1) is implemented. That is, repeated applications of:

i)   calculate value of $x_{n+1}$ (R.H.S. of equation 4.1)

ii)  set value of $x_n$ equal to value of $x_{n+1}$ (L.H.S. of equation 4.1)

Notice also that Fig. 5 confirms the convergent nature of the sequence of iterated values calculated previously (Table A).

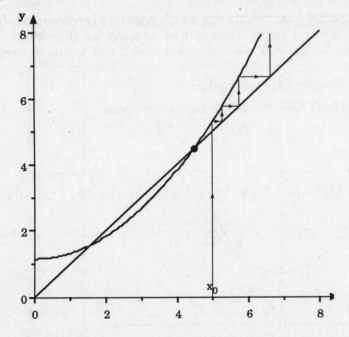

Iteration sequence:

$$x_0 = 5$$
$$x_1 = 5.3$$
$$x_2 = 5.8$$
$$x_3 = 6.8$$
$$x_4 = 8.9$$
$$x_5 = 14$$
$$x_6 = 34$$
$$x_7 = 194$$
$$x_8 = 6274$$

Different initial values will produce different iterative paths.

Illustrated above is the 'staircase' diagram for i) $x_0 = 5$ and below for ii) $x_0 = -3$.

155

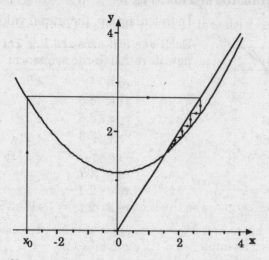

Iteration sequence:

$x_0 = -3$

$x_1 = 2.7$

$x_2 = 2.4$

$x_3 = 2.1$

$x_4 = 1.9$

$x_5 = 1.8$

$x_6 = 1.7$

$x_7 = 1.6$

etc.

The sequence will converge or diverge depending on the initial value chosen. However, different iterative processes behave in different ways for the same initial value. So, it is the combination of initial value *and* iterative process that determines the convergence or divergence of the sequence.

## Iterative Processes (2) – The Newton-Raphson method

Simple iteration is a straightforward method of developing iterative processes for the solution of equations. However, it has its limitations. For instance:

i)    such an iterative process may only converge to certain solutions

ii)   the success of using a process may depend entirely on the choice of initial value

iii)  the rate of convergence may be slow

The *Newton-Raphson* method is an important iterative process which is generally convergent, (providing the initial value is not poor), and which has a much faster rate of convergence than simple iterative processes. It does, however, assume a familiarity with calculus techniques. It can be summarised as:

---

Newton-Raphson method

To solve equations of the form $f(x) = 0$, use the iterative process:

$$x_{n+1} = x_n - \frac{f(x_n)}{f'(x_n)}$$

---

For example, consider again the equation: $x^2 - 6x + 7 = 0$.  Here, $f(x) = x^2 - 6x + 7 \Rightarrow f'(x) = 2x - 6$

The Newton-Raphson process is, therefore:   $x_{n+1} = x_n - \dfrac{(x_n^2 - 6x_n + 7)}{(2x_n - 6)}$ \hfill (4.2)

Choosing $x_0 = 2$:

$$x_1 = x_0 - \frac{(x_0^2 - 6x_0 + 7)}{2x_0 - 6} = 2 - \frac{(4 - 12 + 7)}{(4 - 6)} = 1.5$$

$$x_2 = x_1 - \frac{(x_1^2 - 6x_1 + 7)}{(2x_1 - 6)} = 1.5 - \frac{(2.25 - 9 + 7)}{(3 - 6)} \approx 1.58$$

and so on.

From the left-hand table below, it can be seen that the process converges to the first root: $r_1 = 1.586$ (3D)

Compare the rate of convergence of this method with that of simple iteration (Table A).

| n | $x_n$ | $x_{n+1}$ |
|---|---|---|
| 0 | 2 | 1.5 |
| 1 | 1.5 | 1.58 |
| 2 | 1.58 | 1.586 |
| 3 | 1.586 | 1.5858 |
| 4 | 1.5858 | 1.58579 |
| etc | etc | etc |

| n | $x_n$ | $x_{n+1}$ |
|---|---|---|
| 0 | 4 | 4.5 |
| 1 | 4.5 | 4.4 |
| 2 | 4.4 | 4.41 |
| 3 | 4.41 | 4.414 |
| 4 | 4.414 | 4.4142 |
| etc | etc | etc |

Choosing $x_0 = 4$ gives (second table above) a convergence to the second root: $r_2 = 4.414$ (3D)

Note: The amount of computation can often be reduced by simplifying the Newton-Raphson formula before using it for calculating the iterations. For example, eq'n 4.2 simplifies to:

$$x_{n+1} = \frac{x_n^2 - 7}{2x_n - 6}$$

## Computer Implementation of Iterative Processes

Iterative processes are, by definition, systematic and repetitive. This makes them ideally suited to realisation on a computer, either by writing a program or developing a spreadsheet model. This allows the user to:

i)  rapidly find solutions to problems which defeat standard methods

ii) investigate the behaviour of mathematical models under different initial conditions

The structures of typical program segments and spreadsheet models are outlined below.

### Program

(1)

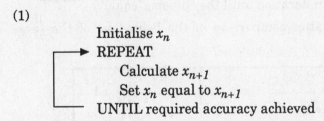

```
        Initialise x_n
        REPEAT
            Calculate x_{n+1}
            Set x_n equal to x_{n+1}
        UNTIL required accuracy achieved
```

After initialisation the process is repeated until such a time as the accuracy required in the solution is reached. This is usually tested by comparing the difference between $x_n$ and $x_{n+1}$ each time the loop is executed. If this difference is less than some acceptable tolerance e.g. 0.0000001, the process stops.

(2)

```
        Initialise x_n
        FOR iteration = 1 TO lots
            Calculate x_{n+1}
            Set x_n equal to x_{n+1}
        NEXT iteration
```

In this program segment, the process is repeated a predetermined number of times e.g. the variable 'lots' could be set to 1000. This might be wasteful in terms of time compared to the technique used in (1).

## Spreadsheet

By using 'circular referencing' (a method of specifying spreadsheet cell references which is similar in nature to the technique of recursion in programming), it is possible to develop spreadsheet templates which produce minimal output; for instance, the result of the last iteration only. However, for purposes of investigating the behaviour of iterative processes it is sensible to develop templates with structures similar to those illustrated below. The first template is for the iterative scheme given earlier (4.1) and produces results similar to those in Table A.

|   | A | B | C | D | E | F | G |
|---|---|---|---|---|---|---|---|
| 1 | | | | Simple Iteration Spreadsheet (1) | | | |
| 2 | | Iteration No | | $x_n$ | | $x_{n+1}$ | |
| 3 | | 0 | | 4 | | *(d3\*d3+7)/6* | |
| 4 | | *b3+1* | | *f3* | | *(d4\*d4+7)/6* | |
| 5 | | *b4+1* | | *f4* | | *(d5\*d5+7)/6* | |
| 6 | | *b5+1* | | *f5* | | *(d6\*d6+7)/6* | |
| .. | | ... | | ... | | ... | |

*Notes:*

1. Formulas are shown in italics. (Upper case letters are used to denote absolute cell references; lower case letters denote relative cell references).

2. Cell D3 has the initial value ($x_0$) for the iterative process. Cell F3 contains the formula representing the iterative process, based on cell D3. This formula is replicated in the other cells of column F.

3. The value in cell F3 ($x_1$) is copied across to cell D6, to become the next iterated value.

4. Some way of controlling the number of iterations is needed, for example:

   i)   fixed number of iterations

   ii)  values in columns D & F are compared at each iteration until they become 'equal'.

Alternatively, this template allows easier investigation/comparison of the behaviour of the same iterative process for different initial values:

|   | A | B | C | D | E | F |
|---|---|---|---|---|---|---|
| 1 | | | Simple Iteration Spreadsheet (2) | | | |
| 2 | Value of $x_0$ = | 1 | 2 | 3 | 4 | 5 |
| 3 | $x_1$ | *(b2\*b2+7)/6* | *(c2\*c2+7)/6* | *(d2\*d2+7)/6* | *(e2\*e2+7)/6* | *(f2\*f2+7)/6* |
| 4 | $x_2$ | *(b3\*b3+7)/6* | *(c3\*c3+7)/6* | *(d3\*d3+7)/6* | *(e3\*e3+7)/6* | *(f3\*f3+7)/6* |
| 5 | $x_3$ | *(b4\*b4+7)/6* | *(c4\*c4+7)/6* | *(d4\*d4+7)/6* | *(e4\*e4+7)/6* | *(f4\*f4+7)/6* |
| 6 | $x_4$ | ... | ... | ... | ... | ... |
| .. | ... | ... | ... | ... | ... | ... |

# Unit 5: Statistics

This section aims to help you to:

1. understand what is meant by the term 'statistics'
2. become familiar with the steps involved in a statistical study
3. appreciate the difference between *descriptive* statistics and *inferential* statistics
4. understand what is meant by 'sample' and 'population'
5. be able to use different sampling methods
6. become familiar with different methods of collecting data

## What is 'statistics' ?

The word 'statistics' can be used in several different ways. It can mean:

i) the whole area of subject study

   *e.g. The Faculty of Mathematics, Statistics and Computing at Dale Institute provides courses which include: 'Statistics for Economists', 'Engineering Statistical Techniques' and 'Applied Statistics for Geographers'.*

ii) an assortment of methods and techniques used to collect, describe and analyse data

   *e.g. a faculty lecturer uses statistics to analyse how her classes perform in skills tests, in order to gain information about their level of expertise.*

iii) a collection of data; that is, a set of values gathered by observation, experimentation or research

   *e.g. the institute's marketing unit collects statistics about the number and types of students who enrol on the faculty's courses in order to provide information for future marketing strategies.*

iv) specially calculated figures that summarises the data

   *e.g. the institute's examinations officer provides the faculty with statistics about their students' performances; for instance: i) the average number of examination passes gained per student ii) the distribution of grades.*

The description given in ii) is the most important. Statistics provides the means to study and model a whole variety of situations where observations or measurements are made. For instance, suppose there is a choice of two proposed by-pass routes for a large town. In order to make the best decision it would be necessary to collect as much data as possible regarding traffic flow, the likely environmental impact, the opinions of drivers and local residents etc. The resulting mass of data would then need to be summarised, displayed in a clear and concise form, and analysed to provide meaningful information on which to base the decision. In this case, therefore, a statistical study is the most appropriate way of making sense of a complex situation.

The stages involved in undertaking such a statistical study are:

   i) defining the problem
   ii) collecting appropriate data
   iii) analysing the data
   iv) interpreting the results

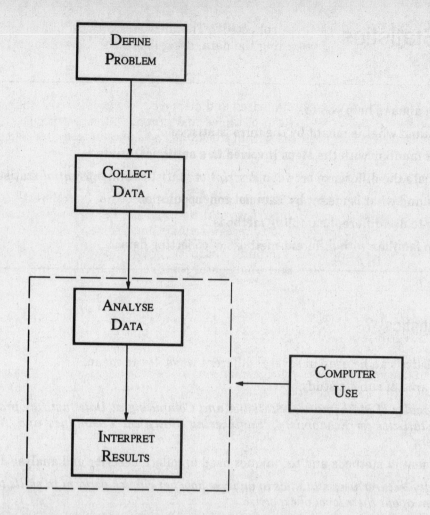

The diagram shows the different stages as being self-contained and in a definite sequence. In practice, this is unlikely to be the case; for instance, more data may need to be collected if the results prove inconclusive.

1.  *Define problem*

    A great deal of thought needs to be put into defining exactly what it is that the statistical study is trying to find out. Generally, the nature of the study is determined by one of two purposes:

    i)  Description  e.g. what is the age distribution of the student population at Dale Institute?

    > In this case, data concerning the ages of students within the institute could be summarised and presented in a suitable form (tables, graphs). The results might be helpful, for instance, in targeting advertising campaigns.

    ii) Inference  e.g. does VDU screen-glare affect the concentration of computer personnel?

    > In this case, data collected from a sample of staff working at Dale Institute Computer Centre might be used as a basis for making general statements about how it affects all U.K. computer industry personnel.

    At this stage it is necessary to be clear about what factors are involved, how they can be measured and what difficulties might occur at the data collection stage.

2.  *Collect data*

    Once the purpose of the study is clear, the collection of appropriate data can take place. At this stage it is also necessary to consider the methods of enquiry; for example: what data is to be collected / how much data is to be collected / how is the data to be collected / what is the source of the data / when is the data to be collected ? The answers to these questions may lead to other matters such as: methods of recording the data, designing a questionnaire and choosing a suitable sample.

3. *Analyse data*

   The collected data needs to be summarised and displayed to show its important features clearly and concisely; this is usually in the form of tables and graphs. Other available statistical techniques detect the existence of any patterns within the data. The choice of techniques used at this stage will depend on i) the sort of data collected and ii) the nature of the study.

4. *Interpret results*

   The function of this stage is to decide what conclusions can be drawn from the results of the analysis and how they relate to the original purpose of the study. It is also necessary to consider the accuracy and validity of these conclusions and to recognise their limitations.

It is at stages 3 & 4 where the use of computer database, graph-drawing and spreadsheet packages can help with the organisation, display and analysis of the data. This allows the user to concentrate on interpreting results and testing out ideas.

## Descriptive Statistics

The amount of data resulting from the collection stage of a statistical study is likely to be considerable. Descriptive statistics is concerned with the presentation of this sample data in a more manageable form. This involves a range of processes which include:

   i)   representing the information graphically

   ii)  calculating various statistics from the data

So, for instance, to gain some idea of the age profile of students at Dale Institute, *descriptive statistics* processes might include the following, all of which are described in more detail later:

a) rearranging and grouping the ages into *frequency distributions* in order to gain an at-a-glance overall impression of the data

b) constructing *graphs* in order that the age distribution can be presented in a visual form

c) calculating *averages*, in order to gain an impression about the typical age of the students

d) calculating *measures of dispersion*, in order to gain an impression of how the ages are distributed in relation to the average

e) investigating the way that the age of students may be related to another variable, such as performance in examinations. The interrelationship can be studied using *correlation* techniques.

Some examples of the sort of statement that can be made as a result of applying descriptive statistics processes are:

   'The average age of students undertaking computing courses is 28.5'

   'The proportion of male students attending Business Studies courses is 0.62'

   'The attendance at our Monday morning lecture varies between 25 and 30'

   'More women than men attend courses during daytime sessions'

   'Most students travel about 10 – 15 miles daily to get to the Institute'

   'There is a strong connection between Dale students' attendance rates and examination performances'

# Inferential Statistics

Descriptive statistics is concerned with organising and presenting collected data in a convenient, meaningful and usable form. Inferential statistics, however, is concerned with extending beyond the particular information available and attempting to make general predictions. As descriptive statistics is concerned with data that is available, so inferential statistics is concerned with data that is not available.

For instance, suppose that the Computer Centre manager at Dale Institute is concerned about the effect that VDU screen-glare might have on staff concentration. A simple experiment could be devised to investigate this problem; for example, the staff could be given a variety of similar screen-based tasks to perform. The screen-glare could be adjusted to a different level for each task and the task completion time recorded. If analysis of the collected data seems to indicate that the time taken to complete a task increases as screen-glare increases, then the following description of the results is quite reasonable:

'Screen-glare affects the concentration of Dale Institute computer personnel'

Several wider inferences (conclusions) could also be drawn, for instance:

1. 'Screen-glare affects the concentration of computer personnel in educational environments'

2. 'Screen-glare affects the concentration of all computer personnel'

3. 'Screen-glare affects the concentration of all computer users'

These are generalisations, based on results from the selection of people who *have* undergone the screen-glare experiment, about broader groups of people who *have not* undergone the experiment. As such, their validity needs to be treated cautiously. Statement #1 might not be unreasonable since it at least generalises to a similar group of people; statement #2 includes other computer personnel (e.g. business, industry) whose jobs may not involve the same sort of computer contact; statement #3 includes occasional users (e.g. home computer users) who are not really comparable to the original group.

Even though statement #1 may seem the most reasonable it should still be treated with a lot of caution. The experiment was carried out on the staff at Dale Institute Computer Centre, but are they typical of the sort of staff to be found in other educational computing environments ? That is, can Dale staff be considered to be representative of these people in terms of their abilities, experience, general health, proportion of males / females etc ? Clearly, the less typical that Dale staff are, the less likely the inference is to be valid.

Distinguishing between descriptive statistics and inferential statistics is important and is dependent on distinguishing between a *sample* (e.g. Dale computer personnel) and a *population* (e.g. all computer personnel).

# Populations and Samples

In statistical terms, the word *population* does not necessarily refer to a group of people. It refers to any group of things which share some common characteristic. So, examples of populations are: fluorescent tubes, packets of soap-powder, boxes of matches, garden gnomes, people living in England, people living in Great Britain, migraine sufferers, bottles of milk, students' I.Q. scores, road accidents occurring in Cornwall.

If information is required about fluorescent tubes (e.g. how long they last) or about people living in Great Britain (e.g. their eating habits), it is obviously impractical to study the entire population. A *sample* is a relatively small selection from the population (e.g. fluorescent tubes from a Chelford DIY store / Computer Science students at Dale Institute) which can be used as the basis for the study.

Inferences can be made about the population from the sample data (e.g. 'the average lifetime of fluorescent tubes is 1500 hours'). The size of the sample and the way that it is selected from the population determines the accuracy of the inferences. A sample is said to be *biased* if not all members of the population are equally likely to be selected. For instance, a survey about the quality of computing facilities which only seeks the opinions of Computer Science students, is based on a biased sample since they are not representative of the whole population.

The term *sampling frame* is taken to mean a list of all the members of a population. Example of this are:

1. People in the Chelford telephone directory
2. Books in Chelford town library
3. An enrolment list of students at Dale Institute

Often the method chosen to collect data may depend on the availability of a suitable sampling frame. For instance, there will not be a readily available sampling frame for people coming out of a football ground.

## Types of samples

Several different methods of selecting samples are outlined below; they are illustrated with reference to an enquiry into student opinion about the standard of food at the Harper campus cafeteria. In each case, assume that the population under consideration is 600 students and that a sample of 50 is required in each case.

1. *Census*

   This is the examining of every member of a population. So, all students would be asked for their opinions. This method is obviously only practical where the population is a manageable size.

2. *Random sample*

   This type of sample is chosen in such a way that every member of the population is equally likely to be selected. In order to select a random sample it must be possible to define a sampling frame; in this case, a list of all the students. The following procedure can be used in conjunction with the table of random numbers (Appendix A):

   Step 1: Assign each student on the list a three-digit number from 000 to 599
   Step 2: Start anywhere in the random numbers table (eg the first row)
   Step 3: Read three consecutive digits (eg 537)
   Step 4: Locate the student with the corresponding number on the list
   Step 5: Repeat from step 3 (eg 423) until 50 students have been chosen; if a random number has already been used, or is bigger than 599, ignore it.

   It should be noted that some sections of the population may be under-represented by this sampling method, since it is based on chance selections. For instance, by sheer chance, it may be that the chosen random numbers all correspond to female students on the list. For this reason, other methods exist which can be classified as either *pseudo-random* (i.e. not a truly random selection process but produces a sample which behaves like a random sample) or *non-random* (i.e. no randomness involved in the selection process).

3. *Systematic sample (pseudo-random)*

   Samples of this type are carried out by choosing a random starting-point and then systematically selecting members of a population at regular intervals. So, selection from a sampling frame is possible (e.g. a list of students' names) as is selection from a physical supply (e.g. a stream of students leaving a cafeteria). The method can be summarised as follows:

   Step 1: Select a student at random (eg the 35th student on a list)
   Step 2: Count down 600÷50 = 12 students (ie the 47th student)
   Step 3 Repeat from step 2 (ie the 59th, 71st, 83rd, ...students) until 50 students have been chosen; if the end of the list is reached, continue from the top of the list.

The *sampling interval* i.e. the gap between sampled items, depends on both the population size and the sample size. For example, if a sample of 50 students were required from a population of 1000 the sampling interval would be $\frac{1000}{50}$; that is, every 20th student.

4.    *Stratified sample (pseudo-random)*

Before a sample is selected the population is partitioned into groups (*strata*), the members of each group having some common feature. The proportion of members in each group then determines the proportion that is selected in the sample.

Step 1:    Partition the population into groups (e.g. male students / female students)

Step 2:    Calculate the proportion of each group in the population (e.g. 60% male / 40% female)

Step 3:    Calculate the numbers of students required within the sample so that the same proportions are maintained (i.e. 60% of 50 ∫ 30 male students, 40% of 50 ∫ 20 female students)

Step 4:    Select that number of students from each group by a random sampling method, as before (e.g. 30 males from the 360, 20 females from the 240)

The nature of the groups is determined by those features which are considered important to the enquiry. For instance, if it is considered that the age of a student is a factor that affects views about cafeteria food, the population might be split into age-bands e.g. 16-19, 20-25, 26-30 and 30-55. The proportions in each group then determine how many from each age-band are selected.

More than one stratification can take place at the same time. So, for instance, the population might be firstly partitioned into male / female groups; those groups may then each be further partitioned into four age-bands. The sample would then have to reflect the proportions within the eight groupings.

5.    *Multi-stage sample (pseudo-random)*

As the name implies, the sampling is carried out in a number of stages. The first stage reduces the population size by selecting subgroups from it; these subgroups together form the new population for the second stage.

First stage

Step 1:    Divide the population into a number of convenient groups (e.g. subject discipline areas such as: Computer Science, Business Studies, Languages, Humanities, Science, Catering, Engineering, Mathematics)

Step 2:    Select a random sample of those groups which will form the 'population' for the next stage (e.g. Business Studies, Humanities and Mathematics students)

Second stage

Step 3:    Select the required sample from the groups chosen at the first stage (e.g. randomly select 50 students from the three subject disciplines)

The number of groups chosen at the first stage is entirely arbitrary; however, this will affect how representative the final sample is of the overall population.

6.    *Quota sample (non-random)*

This firstly involves stratifying the population. The sample is then selected according to a quota based on the proportions in each of the strata.

Step 1:    Stratify the population (e.g. age-bands 16-19, 20-25, 26-30 and 30-55)

Step 2:    Calculate the proportion of each group in the population (e.g. 40%, 30%, 20%, 10%)

Step 3:    Calculate the numbers required for the sample (e.g. 40% of 50 ∫ 20 students aged 16-19, 30% of 50 ∫ 15 students aged 20-25, and so on).

Step 4:  Select the sample according to a quota system (e.g. someone is assigned to interview the 20 students aged 16-19. The first question asked of each student on leaving the cafeteria is concerned with age; if the student is in the 16-19 age-band, the interviewer asks the remaining questions; any student not in the 16-19 age-band is not interviewed. This process continues until the interviewer's quota of 20 students is reached).

Quota sampling leaves much of the sample selection to the discretion of the interviewer. This may lead to bias in the sample.

7.  *Cluster sample (non-random)*

This entails selecting sections of the population and sampling *all* the members of those sections.

Step 1:  Identify a section(s) of the population (e.g. Year 1 Computer Science students)

Step 2:  Select all the members of the section(s) as the sample (e.g. seek the views of all those students identified at Step 1).

If no sampling frame exists, this method provides a satisfactory alternative to multi-stage sampling.

| Method | Advantages | Disadvantages |
|---|---|---|
| Census | Complete and representative | Time-consuming |
| Random sampling | Unbiased | Sampling frame necessary Time-consuming |
| Systematic sampling | Easy to implement Sampling frame unnecessary | Possible bias if patterns exist in data |
| Stratified sampling | Unbiased | Sampling frame necessary Time-consuming |
| Multi-stage sampling | Quick and easy to implement | Possible bias due to first stage selection |
| Quota sampling | Quick and easy to implement | Possible bias due to interviewer |
| Cluster sampling | Relatively easy to implement | Possible bias due to selection process |

**Sampling methods: summary of advantages and disadvantages**

## Collecting data

There are 5 main ways that data can be collected:

❐ Observation
❐ Experiment
❐ Questionnaire
❐ Interview
❐ Secondary sources

### Observation

Data can be collected by direct observation of the subject under study; that is, by monitoring the situation and recording the required information in a suitable manner. For instance, an investigation into ways of easing queueing congestion in a supermarket would need some initial data collection to assess the current situation; that is, observation of customer flow-rates through the checkouts. An advantage of the observation method is that it does not interfere with normal events (contrast it, for instance, with street interviews) providing that the collection process is as unobtrusive as possible.

The use of a suitable recording form is most important; for instance, a form design for observing customer flow-rates might resemble:

| Supermarket check-out survey | | |
|---|---|---|
| Name . . . . . . . . . . . . . . . . . . . . . . . . . . . . . . . . . . . . . . . . . . Date . . . . . . . . . . . . . . . . | | |
| Supermarket . . . . . . . . . . . . . . . . . . . . . . . . . . . . . . . . . . Checkout number . . . . | | |
| Time period | Tally | No. of customers |
| 09.00 - 09.15 | | |
| 09.15 - 09.30 | | |
| 09.30 - 09.45 | | |
| 09.45 - 10.00 | | |
| 10.00 - 10.15 | | |
| 10.15 - 10.30 | | |

## Experiment

Quantities of data can be generated by experiments which are devised for specific purposes. For instance, suppose that the designer of a revolutionary computer keyboard wants to compare its performance to that of a conventional keyboard. Experiments could be devised to investigate the situation e.g. timing a variety of keyboarding tasks with both types of keyboard, then analysing the results for evidence of speed improvements. For this method of data collection to be valid, care is needed to ensure that experimental procedures are rigorous and consistent so that the data is not biased in any way.

## Questionnaire

A questionnaire is a set of questions designed to obtain facts and opinions and is normally delivered in person or by mail. For instance, a local council may use a questionnaire in seeking views about the quality of the services it provides. The design and administering of questionnaires is not an easy task; however, some brief guidelines are given below:

1.  Explain the purpose of the questionnaire and the likely benefits that will follow

2.  Keep the questionnaire as short as possible

3.  Use simple language; keep each question short and free of jargon

4.  Devise a simple form of response to each question e.g. Yes/No, multiple choice

5.  Ensure that the sequence of questions is logical

6.  Avoid personal questions

7.  Do not ask leading questions

8.  Avoid questions which require calculations or rely on the respondent's memory

9.  Give clear instructions regarding the return of the questionnaire

An example of a poorly designed questionnaire is shown below. The reader might like to consider which of the above guidelines are not followed:

Answer these:

Name . . . . . . . . . . . . . . . . . . . . . . . . . . . . . . . . . . . . . .

1.  Do you normally have toast and marmalade or cereal or bacon and eggs or nothing for breakfast ? . . . . . . . . . . . . . .

2.  Are you in favour of oligarchy ? . . . . . . . . . . . . . . . . . . . . . . . . . . . . . . . . . . . . . . . . .

3.  What do you think of the world today ? . . . . . . . . . . . . . . . . . . . . . . . . . . . . . . . . . .

4.  If none of the above, what do you have for breakfast ? . . . . . . . . . . . . . . . . . . . . . . . . .

5.  Do you have bad breath ? . . . . . . . . . . . . . . . . . . . . . . . . . . . . . . . . . . . . . . .

6.  Don't you agree that party political broadcasts are too long and tedious ? . . . . . . . . . . .

7.  How much television did you watch: a) last week b) last month c) last year ? . . . . . . . .

Please return this questionnaire when you have completed it.

The use of a pilot study is vital; small-scale testing of the questionnaire helps with the identification of any 'bugs' in the layout or wording. The design can then be modified before the questionnaire is put into full-scale operation.

## Interview

Interviews usually produce better response rates than questionnaires. For instance, a town planning department may seek opinions about the proposed route for a by-pass by door-to-door interviews of local residents. The quality of the information obtained will depend on several factors e.g. the quality of the interviewer, the use of a standard interviewing procedure in order to avoid bias, adequate time for the interview and so on. Telephone surveys are becoming more commonplace, although it is difficult to select a representative sample and avoid bias.

## Secondary sources

*Primary data* is data collected at first-hand as the result of a specific study; *secondary data* is data which is obtained second-hand from published sources or from the results of studies undertaken by other people for different reasons. For instance, a sociologist who is interested in comparing life-styles in the 18th & 20th centuries may make use of Government census material. A secondary data source can provide useful information but can also have its limitations e.g. it may not be entirely relevant or up-to-date. Many useful sources of secondary data exist, in particular: ' The Annual Abstract of Statistics' published by the Central Statistical Office; this publication, found in most libraries, provides much general Government information regarding population, education, business etc.

# Unit 6: Descriptive statistics

This section aims to help you to:

1. distinguish between different types of data
2. be able to organise, display and analyse data
3. be able to interpret the results of a statistical analysis
4. become familiar with the normal distribution

## Types of data

All items in a sample of data selected from a population share common characteristics. For instance, if the population is 'calculators' then the characteristics might include:

manufacturer
power source
number of digits displayed
number of built-in functions size
price
programmability
durability
weight
colour

The characteristics will vary from item to item e.g. some will display 10 digits, others 12; some will be blue, others grey; some will be battery-powered, others solar-powered and so on. This enables the items to be distinguished from one another. For this reason, the characteristics are usually called *variables*.

This table shows some sample data concerning a variety of calculators:

| Manufacturer | Power | Digits | Functions | Length (mm) | Width (mm) | Price (£) |
|---|---|---|---|---|---|---|
| Casio | Battery | 8 | 78 | 150 | 75 | 6.75 |
| Sharp | Battery | 10 | 147 | 145 | 75 | 7.75 |
| Texas | Solar | 10 | 164 | 130 | 70 | 9.99 |
| Casio | Solar | 8 | 129 | 140 | 70 | 9.99 |
| Casio | Battery | 10 | 167 | 140 | 70 | 9.99 |
| Sharp | Solar | 10 | 168 | 145 | 75 | 11.50 |
| Casio | Battery | 10 | 199 | 140 | 70 | 12.99 |
| Casio | Solar | 12 | 284 | 140 | 70 | 16.75 |
| Texas | Battery | 12 | 254 | 160 | 75 | 22.99 |
| Casio | Battery | 12 | 179 | 140 | 70 | 29.99 |

The variables which make up data are of two different types:

1. Category variables
2. Quantity variables

In the sample data:

i)   The variable 'manufacturer' is a *category variable* since it contains distinct categories: Casio, Sharp and Texas; each calculator can be placed in one of these categories.

   Similarly, 'power' is a category variable.

ii)  The remaining variables are *quantity variables* since they can be quantified (i.e. given a numerical value). Quantity variables can be either *discrete* or *continuous*.

   a)  Discrete variables are those which can take only certain values in a given range. So, for example, 'price' is a discrete variable since it can be £25.87 or £25.88 but not £25.872391.

      Similarly, 'digits', and 'functions' are discrete variables.

   b)  Continuous variables are those which can take any value in a given range. So, for instance, 'length' is a continuous variable since the accurate value could be 148.73258 mm, even though it is quoted as 150 mm.

      Similarly, 'width' is a continuous variable.

The different types of data can be summarised as follows:

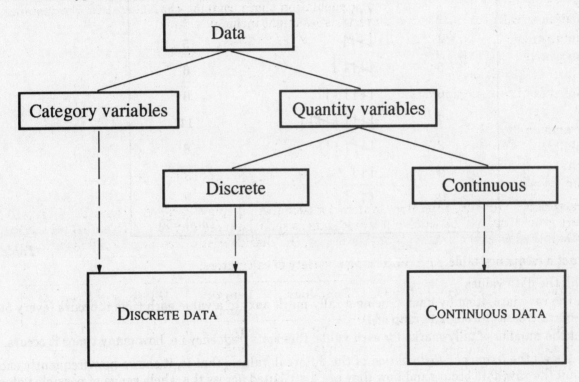

Note: Category variables are also considered to be discrete since there are only a certain number of possible categories for each variable. The important difference between types of data, therefore, is whether they are discrete or continuous. This difference determines, amongst other things, the sort of graph which is used to display the data.

## Organising data

When a large quantity of data has been collected, it needs organising so that some sense can be made of it. This *raw* data, as it is called, must be summarised in a systematic fashion.

## Frequency distributions (1) – Discrete data

The following data are the scores obtained by 50 students in a series of ten computer-based tasks designed to test their aptitude for computing. The students scored one point for each task success-fully completed:

| | | | | | | | | | |
|---|---|---|---|---|---|---|---|---|---|
| 8 | 4 | 7 | 6 | 8 | 9 | 3 | 6 | 8 | 7 |
| 10 | 7 | 5 | 6 | 3 | 8 | 7 | 7 | 7 | 2 |
| 9 | 1 | 8 | 5 | 7 | 4 | 8 | 6 | 7 | 10 |
| 6 | 8 | 4 | 7 | 3 | 5 | 6 | 4 | 5 | 6 |
| 3 | 8 | 5 | 4 | 9 | 7 | 5 | 7 | 2 | 6 |

A *frequency table* is a more convenient arrangement of the data, built up with the aid of tally-marks:

| Score | Tally | Frequency |
|:---:|:---:|:---:|
| 1 | I | 1 |
| 2 | I I | 2 |
| 3 | I I I I | 4 |
| 4 | ⊬⊬ | 5 |
| 5 | ⊬⊬ I | 6 |
| 6 | ⊬⊬ I I I | 8 |
| 7 | ⊬⊬ ⊬⊬ I | 11 |
| 8 | ⊬⊬ I I I | 8 |
| 9 | I I I | 3 |
| 10 | I I | 2 |
| | | Total = 50 |

*Table 1*

To construct a frequency table:

i) List all the data values
ii) Scan the raw data, item by item, placing a tally-mark next to a value each time it occurs (every 5th tally-mark crosses through a group of 4)
iii) Count the number of tally-marks for each value; this is its *frequency* i.e. how many times it occurs.

The table shows the *frequency distribution* of the different values; that is, it shows how frequently each value within the raw data occurs and how they are distributed across the whole range of possible values (in this case, 0 to 10). The frequency distribution is, therefore, the overall pattern of the data. It is also helpful in revealing underlying patterns which may not be obvious from the raw data; for instance, the majority of scores in this sample seem to be clustering around 6, 7 and 8.

If the raw data contains a wide range of discrete values, it is better to divide them into groups (*classes*). For example, the students gained the following scores in a longer I.Q. test, designed to assess their general intelligence:

| | | | | | | | | | |
|---|---|---|---|---|---|---|---|---|---|
| 113 | 106 | 100 | 91 | 100 | 96 | 112 | 107 | 125 | 98 |
| 105 | 101 | 121 | 101 | 104 | 92 | 101 | 98 | 97 | 110 |
| 103 | 127 | 94 | 120 | 101 | 93 | 98 | 93 | 93 | 109 |
| 100 | 91 | 108 | 111 | 95 | 103 | 95 | 118 | 106 | 123 |
| 102 | 98 | 117 | 98 | 117 | 104 | 98 | 102 | 93 | 105 |

To construct a grouped frequency table:

i) Scan the raw data for the maximum and minimum values

ii) Calculate the *range* of the values (range = maximum value – minimum value)

iii) Split the range into five to fifteen classes, each class covering the same amount (the *class interval*)

iv) Carry out the tally-mark procedure as before

In this case:

Minimum value = 91

Maximum value = 127

Range = 127 – 91 = 36

Since the range is about 40, the data can be split into eight classes each with a class interval of 5 i.e. each class covers five I.Q scores; for example, the class 90 – 94 includes 90, 91, 92, 93 and 94:

| I.Q. score | Tally | Frequency |
|---|---|---|
| 90 – 94 | ⊥⊥⊤ ||| | 8 |
| 95 – 99 | ⊥⊥⊤ ⊥⊥⊤ | 10 |
| 100 – 104 | ⊥⊥⊤ ⊥⊥⊤ ||| | 13 |
| 105 – 109 | ⊥⊥⊤ || | 7 |
| 110 – 114 | |||| | 4 |
| 115 – 119 | ||| | 3 |
| 120 – 124 | ||| | 3 |
| 125 – 129 | || | 2 |
| | | Total = 50 |

*Table 2*

*Note:*

i) There should be no overlap between classes; that is, each value should appear in only one class.

ii) There should be between five and fifteen classes. Too few classes and the variability within the data would lack sufficient detail; too many classes and the table would not really be a summary.

iii) Grouping data can lead to a loss of information. For example, the frequency table shows that there are eight I.Q. scores in the 90 – 94 class; however, it is not possible to identify individual scores from this information alone.

Category variables can be dealt with in a similar way. For example, the same 50 students were observed to be using the following types of calculators:

| Calculator | Tally | Frequency |
|---|---|---|
| Casio | ⊥⊥⊤ ⊥⊥⊤ ⊥⊥⊤ ⊥⊥⊤ | 20 |
| Texas | ⊥⊥⊤ ⊥⊥⊤ ⊥⊥⊤ | 15 |
| Sharp | ⊥⊥⊤ ⊥⊥⊤ | | 11 |
| Others | |||| | 4 |
| | | Total = 50 |

*Table 3*

## Frequency distributions (2) – Continuous data

Organising continuous data requires a little more care, but the same general principles used with discrete data still apply. As an example, consider the following data which represent the times (in seconds) that the sample of 50 students took to complete a keyboard task:

| | | | | |
|---|---|---|---|---|
| 24.3 | 23.5 | 25.7 | 24.4 | 24.3 |
| 24.2 | 24.3 | 23.6 | 25.1 | 23.1 |
| 25.1 | 24.5 | 24.2 | 23.9 | 22.6 |
| 26.0 | 25.2 | 21.1 | 23.3 | 22.4 |
| 24.6 | 22.9 | 26.2 | 23.2 | 23.6 |
| 22.7 | 23.2 | 24.7 | 25.4 | 24.1 |
| 24.7 | 25.8 | 22.6 | 23.1 | 23.6 |
| 24.1 | 24.5 | 23.7 | 22.9 | 23.7 |
| 21.8 | 26.9 | 23.1 | 23.5 | 22.4 |
| 25.6 | 23.9 | 25.2 | 24.1 | 23.6 |

In this case, the range of values is: $26.9 - 21.1 = 5.8$

So, the data can be split into twelve classes each with a class interval of 0.5 s:

| Time (secs) | Tally | Frequency |
|---|---|---|
| 21.0 – 21.4 | I | 1 |
| 21.5 – 21.9 | I | 1 |
| 22.0 – 22.4 | II | 2 |
| 22.5 – 22.9 | LHT | 5 |
| 23.0 – 23.4 | LHT I | 6 |
| 23.5 – 23.9 | LHT LHT | 10 |
| 24.0 – 24.4 | LHT IIII | 9 |
| 24.5 – 24.9 | LHT | 5 |
| 25.0 – 25.4 | LHT | 5 |
| 25.5 – 25.9 | III | 3 |
| 26.0 – 26.4 | II | 2 |
| 26.5 – 26.9 | I | 1 |
| | | Total = 50 |

*Table 4*

Note, for example, that the class $22.5 - 22.9$ actually includes any time in the range $22.45 \le$ time $< 22.95$; this is because the times have been recorded to the nearest 0.1 s.

# Displaying data

Another way to reveal the overall pattern of data is to represent its frequency distribution in graphical form.

The type of graph selected for display will depend on:

i)   the purpose (description or inference)

ii)  the data (discrete or continuous)

The examples which follow are some of the more common statistical graphs which can be used for descriptive purposes. General principles underlying their construction are given, as well as an outline of other variations which are provided by software packages. Some of the graphs are constructed with reference to the data and frequency distributions in the last section.

## Bar charts (discrete data)

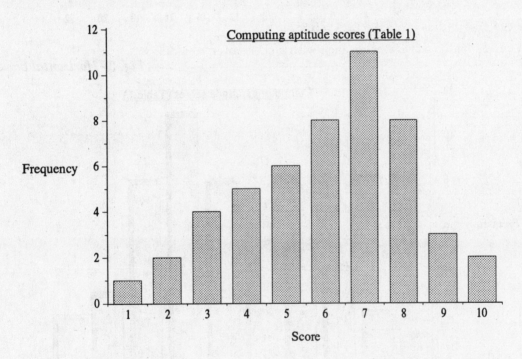

*Fig. 1 - Simple bar chart*

*Note:*

i)   All bars are of equal width.

ii)  The height of each bar usually represents frequency, although it can also represent e.g. a percentage.

iii) The bars are separated, to highlight the fact that the data is discrete.

iv)  Axes should be scaled / labelled and the bar chart suitably titled.

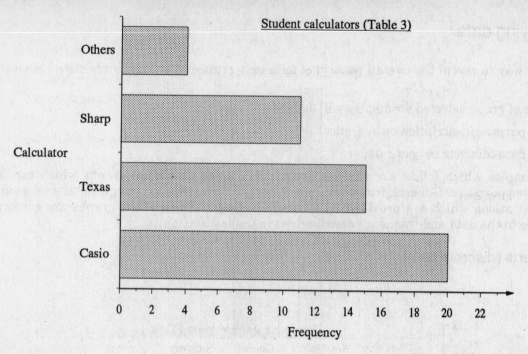

*Fig. 2 - Horizontal bar chart*

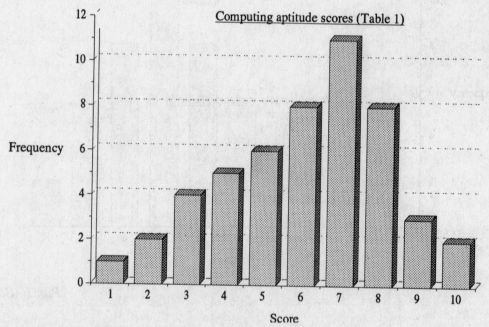

*Fig. 3 - 3D bar chart*

This data shows the number of male and female students on various types of courses at Dale Institute:

| Course | No. of males | No. of females |
|--------|--------------|----------------|
| Computing | 156 | 72 |
| Business Studies | 112 | 164 |
| Catering | 38 | 83 |
| Sociology | 28 | 52 |
| Economics | 64 | 56 |
| Humanities | 128 | 117 |

*Table 5*

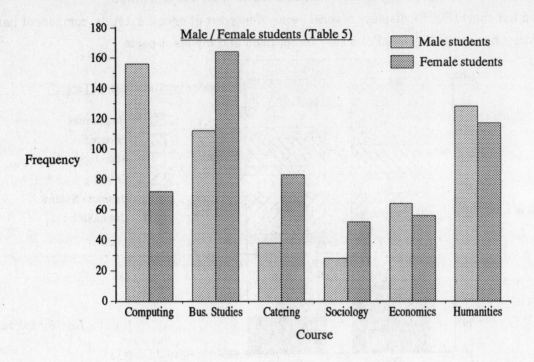

*Fig. 4 - Multiple Bar chart*

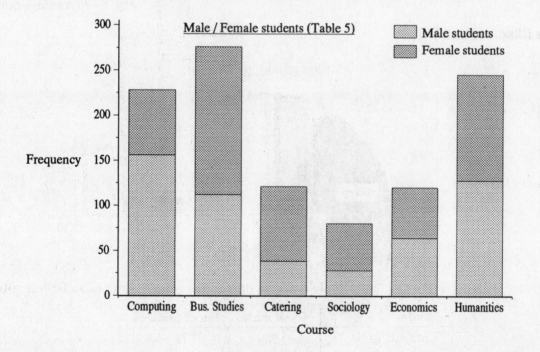

*Fig. 5 - Stacked bar chart*

*Note:*

i) Horizontal bar chart (Fig. 2): as effective as a vertical bar chart.

ii) 3D bar chart (Fig. 3): commonly provided in graph-drawing packages; graduation lines are provided to help with reading frequencies.

175

iii) Multiple bar chart (Fig. 4): displays several data features on a single graph.

iv) Stacked bar chart (Fig. 5): displays several items of interest at once e.g. totals, component parts.

v) Percentage bar chart (Fig. 6): allows easy comparison of component parts.

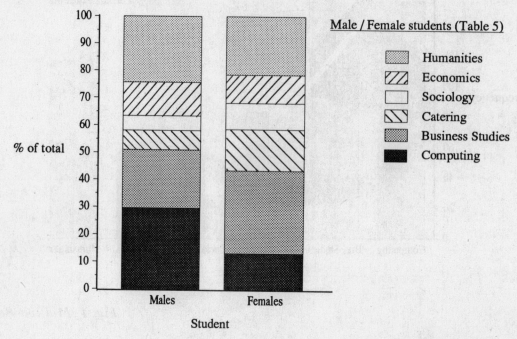

*Fig. 6 - Percentage bar chart*

## Pie charts (discrete data)

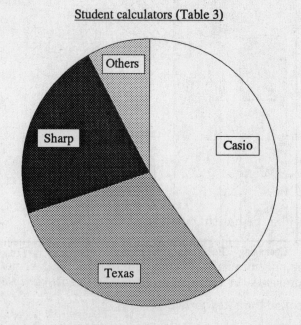

*Fig. 7 - Simple pie chart*

Student calculators (Table 3)

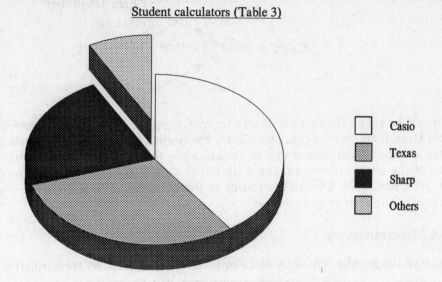

Casio

Texas

Sharp

Others

*Fig. 8 - 3D pie chart*

Male / Female students (Table 5)

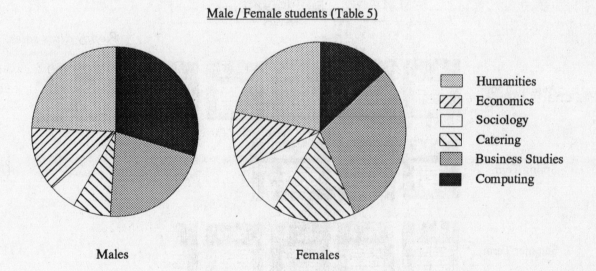

Humanities

Economics

Sociology

Catering

Business Studies

Computing

Males              Females

*Fig. 9 - Comparative pie charts*

*Note:*

i)   The pie chart is a circular, rather than a linear, representation.

ii)  Pie charts are used to show the size of constituent parts relative to the whole and to each other.

iii) A pie chart should be only used if the whole circle represents something meaningful; in Figs. 7 & 8,the whole circle represents the entire sample of 50 students observed.

iv)  Sectors should be labelled (or a key provided).

v)   Graph-drawing packages provide many options e.g. percentage pie charts, withdrawn sectors and 3D pie charts with user-defined viewing angle.

vi)  The angle of each sector is proportional to the corresponding frequency.

So, in Fig. 7, the calculations would be similar to:

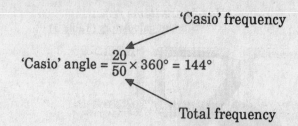

'Casio' frequency

$$\text{'Casio' angle} = \frac{20}{50} \times 360° = 144°$$

Total frequency

vii) Care should be taken if using pie charts for comparison (Fig. 9). In this example, there are less male students than females students overall; so, the *areas* of the two circles must be in proportion to the numbers involved. This means that if, for instance, there were 4 times as many females than males, the area of the female circle must be 4 times the area of the male circle. Therefore, the *radius* of the female circle should be 2 times the radius of the male circle. *In general, the radius proportion is the square root of the area proportion.*

## Pictograms (discrete data)

This table shows the number of floppy discs sold to students, term by term, during an academic year:

| Term | No. of discs sold |
|--------|-------------------|
| Autumn | 260 |
| Spring | 130 |
| Summer | 177 |

*Floppy discs sales.  Table 6*

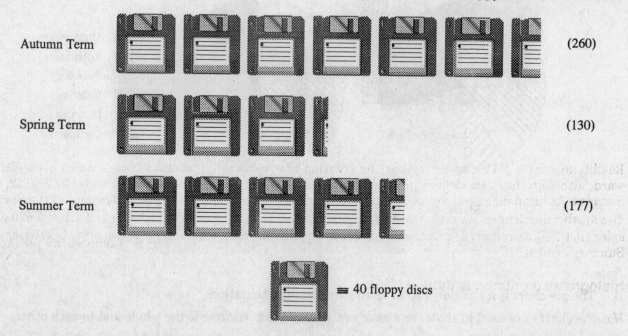

Autumn Term (260)

Spring Term (130)

Summer Term (177)

= 40 floppy discs

*Fig. 10 - Pictogram (1)*

*Note:*

i) The symbols used should be appropriate to the data.

ii) A pictogram is easier to understand if numbers are included on the diagram.

iii) A pictogram normally uses one of two conventions:

    a) a repeated symbol (Figs. 10 & 11)

    b) a variable-size symbol (Fig. 12)

*Hardware items requiring repair in 1 year.  Fig 11 – Pictogram (2)*

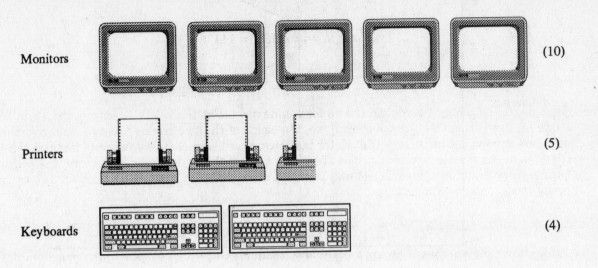

Monitors (10)

Printers (5)

Keyboards (4)

*Floppy disc sales (Table 6).  Fig. 12 – Pictogram (incorrect)*

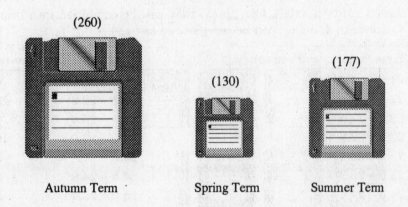

(260)

(130)

(177)

Autumn Term            Spring Term            Summer Term

Readily available DTP clip-art makes the creation of eye-catching pictograms reasonably straightforward, although they can be very imprecise and misleading if not constructed accurately. In Fig. 12, for instance, Autumn disc sales are double the Spring sales; however, doubling the dimensions of the Spring disc symbol quadruples its area. So the Autumn symbol, as shown, actually represents $4 \times 130 = 520$ disc sales (not 260 as required) and therefore needs scaling down by a considerable amount. Likewise, the Summer symbol.

## Histograms (continuous data)

*Note:*

i)   A histogram is a continuous diagram which resembles a bar chart without any gaps.

ii)  Unlike most bar charts, the bars of a histogram lie in a natural order according to the variable; so, it is meaningless to interchange them.

iii) Although normally used for continuous data, histograms can also be used to display discrete data organised as a grouped frequency distribution e.g. the student I.Q. data (Table 2).

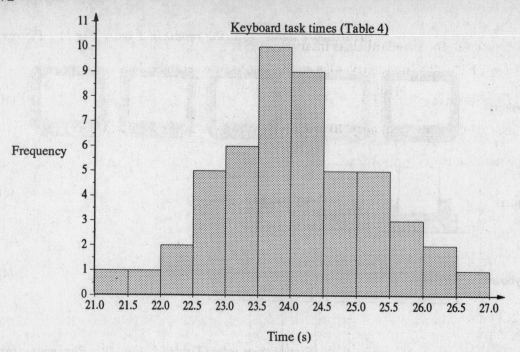

Fig. 13 - Histogram

iv) Where some classes contain only a few items, they can be combined into broader classes. So, the data of Table 4, shown in a) below, can be reorganised as in b):

| Time (secs) | Frequency |
|---|---|
| 21.0 – 21.4 | 1 |
| 21.5 – 21.9 | 1 |
| 22.0 – 22.4 | 2 |
| 22.5 – 22.9 | 5 |
| 23.0 – 23.4 | 6 |
| 23.5 – 23.9 | 10 |
| 24.0 – 24.4 | 9 |
| 24.5 – 24.9 | 5 |
| 25.0 – 25.4 | 5 |
| 25.5 – 25.9 | 3 |
| 26.0 – 26.4 | 2 |
| 26.5 – 26.9 | 1 |
| Total = | 50 |

| Time (secs) | Frequency |
|---|---|
| 21.0 – 22.4 | 4 |
| 22.5 – 22.9 | 5 |
| 23.0 – 23.4 | 6 |
| 23.5 – 23.9 | 10 |
| 24.0 – 24.4 | 9 |
| 24.5 – 24.9 | 5 |
| 25.0 – 25.4 | 5 |
| 25.5 – 25.9 | 3 |
| 26.0 – 26.9 | 3 |
| Total = | 50 |

a) Equal class intervals

b) Unequal class intervals

v) In a bar chart, the *height* of a bar represents the frequency; in a histogram, the *area* of a bar represents the frequency. Simply, this means that:

a) If the classes are of equal width, the height of each bar represents the frequency (Fig. 13).

b) If the classes are of unequal width, it is necessary to adjust the bar heights of the non-standard classes (Fig. 14). For instance, a class which has a width equivalent to two 'standard' classes needs to be half the height; so:

$$\text{Adjusted frequency} = \frac{\text{Actual frequency}}{\text{Number of standard classes included}}$$

In the example data, the standard class interval is 0.5 s:

a) the class 21.0 – 22.4 (frequency: 4) is equivalent to three standard classes

∴ adjusted frequency = $\frac{4}{3} \approx 1.3$

b) the class 26.0 – 26.9 (frequency: 3) is equivalent to two standard classes

∴ adjusted frequency = $\frac{3}{2} = 1.5$

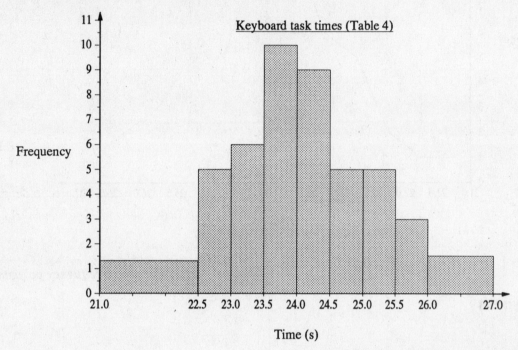

*Fig. 14 - Histogram (unequal class intervals)*

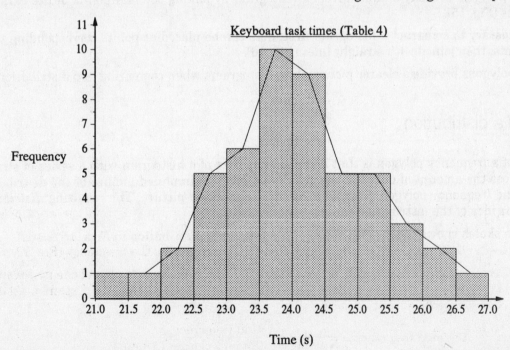

*Fig. 15 - Frequency polygon (1)*

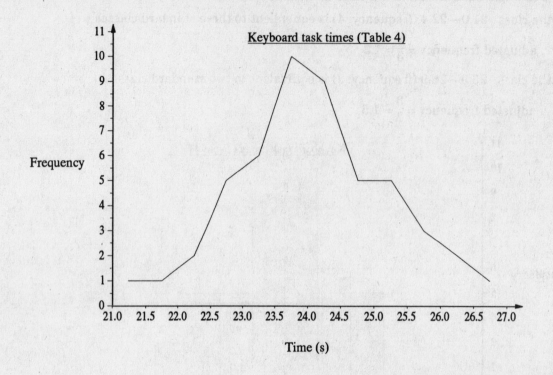

Keyboard task times (Table 4)

*Fig. 16 - Frequency polygon (2)*

## Frequency polygons

*Note:*

i) A *frequency polygon* is easily obtained from a histogram by joining the mid-points of the bars with straight lines (Fig. 15).

ii) It is not necessary to construct a histogram first; dots can be placed at points corresponding to the bar mid-points, then joined with straight lines (Fig. 16).

iii) Frequency polygons provide a clearer picture than histograms when comparing two distributions.

## The shape of a distribution

One advantage of a frequency polygon is that it replace the bars of a histogram with a series of straight lines. So, it reduces the amount of detail in the graph and gives a simplified picture of the distribution. Smoothing out the frequency polygon gives an even more simplified picture. The resulting *distribution curve* gives a clear idea of the distribution's underlying features.

For instance, this sketch shows the general shape of the frequency distribution in Figs. 15 & 16:

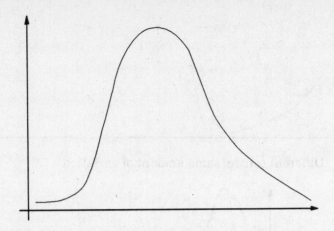

A distribution curve can have any one of several shapes, for example:

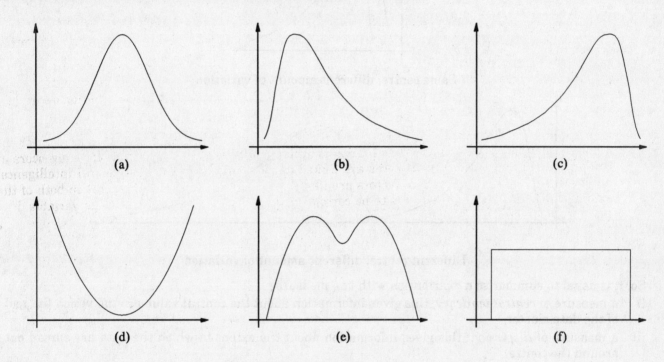

*Note:*

i)    Certain commonly occurring distributions have been given names; for example, in the diagrams above: a) is a *normal distribution*, d) is a *U-distribution* and (f) is a *rectangular distribution*.

ii)   Some distributions, such as a normal distribution, are symmetrical. If a distribution is not symmetrical it is said to be *skewed*; for example, b) and c) are skewed distributions.

Sets of data can be compared by looking at their distribution curves. Distributions with the same shape of distribution curve can still, though, be different in two respects:

i)    the location of the distribution's 'centre'

ii)   the amount of variation within the data

For instance:

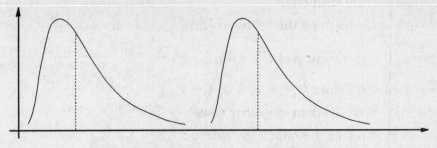

**Different centre, same amount of variation**

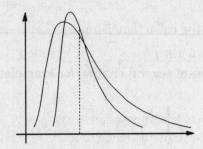

**Same centre, different amount of variation**

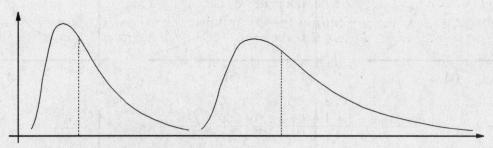

**Different centre, different amount of variation**

So, it is usual to summarise a distribution with two measures:

i) a measure of *central tendency*; this gives information about the central value around which the rest of the data cluster

ii) a measure of *dispersion*; this gives information about the extent to which the data are spread out around the centre

Skewed distributions can have an extra measure calculated which summarises the amount of skewness; for a symmetrical distribution this is obviously zero.

## Measures of central tendency (averages)

An *average* is a single value that is used to represent a distribution. It is supposed to be typical of the other values in the collection. Since it is usually near the centre of the distribution, it is also called a *measure of central tendency*.

There are several types of average; three of the more common are:

    i)   the mode

    ii)  the median

    iii) the mean

The *mode* is the value that occurs most often.

The *median* is the middle value when all the values are arranged in order of size.

The *mean* (also known as the *arithmetic mean*) is calculated from: $\dfrac{\text{The total of all the values}}{\text{The number of values}}$

For instance, consider the set of values: 3, 5, 8, 3, 6, 3, 4, 8, 2, 6

a)   the mode = 3 (there are more 3's than any other value)

b)   the median is found by choosing the middle value from: 2, 3, 3, 3, 4, 5, 6, 6, 8, 8

$$\uparrow$$
$$\text{median}$$

In this case, the middle value of the collection is halfway between the '4' and the '5'; $\therefore$ median = 4.5

c)   the mean is calculated from: $\dfrac{3+5+8+3+6+3+4+8+2+6}{10} = \dfrac{48}{10} = 4.8$

*Note:*

i)   for a category variable, the mode is the only sensible average to use

ii)   some distributions can have more than one mode; if it has two modes, it is said to be *bimodal*

ii)   for an *odd* number of values, the median is the middle value

    for an *even* number of values, the median is midway between the two middle values

iii)   if the distribution contains any *outliers* (non-typical extreme values), the mean is likely to be the most affected. For instance, suppose that the value '100' is included in the above collection; that is:

$$3, 5, 8, 3, 6, 3, 4, 8, 2, 6, 100$$

a)   Mode = 3

b)   Median of: 2, 3, 3, 3, 4, 5, 6, 6, 8, 8, 100 = 5

c)   Mean = $\dfrac{3+5+8+3+6+3+4+8+2+6+100}{11} = \dfrac{148}{11} \approx 13.45$ (2D)

The various computational methods that follow are written in the form of step-by-step procedures and in most cases are illustrated by example calculations using the earlier data of:

a)   Table 1, which shows the scores obtained by 50 students on a computing aptitude test

b)   Table 2, which gives the results of an I.Q. test taken by the same 50 students

The data is rewritten in slightly different forms according to the calculation being carried out; however, the data is the same and table names are similar e.g. Table 1a is a variation of Table 1 data etc.

## The mean of a frequency distribution

Considering the data of Table 1, suppose that it is required to calculate the mean score obtained by the students. The method can be summarised as follows (calculations – Table 1a):

Step 1:   Write, in columns:
      a)   the values of the variable (call these '$x$')
      b)   the frequencies with which each $x$-value occurs (call these '$f$')

Step 2:   Calculate an '$fx$' column (multiply each '$x$' by its corresponding '$f$')

Step 3:   Calculate $\Sigma f$, the sum of the '$f$' column
          (the symbol $\Sigma$, pronounced 'sigma', means 'the sum of')

Step 4:   Calculate $\Sigma fx$, the sum of the '$fx$' column

Step 5:   Calculate the mean using the formula:

$$\bar{x} = \frac{\sum fx}{\sum f}$$

($\bar{x}$, pronounced '*x* bar', is the symbol for the sample mean)

| Score | Frequency | |
| x | f | fx |
|---|---|---|
| 1 | 1 | 1 |
| 2 | 2 | 4 |
| 3 | 4 | 12 |
| 4 | 5 | 20 |
| 5 | 6 | 30 |
| 6 | 8 | 48 |
| 7 | 11 | 77 |
| 8 | 8 | 64 |
| 9 | 3 | 27 |
| 10 | 2 | 20 |
| | $\sum f = 50$ | $\sum fx = 303$ |

*Table 1a*

$$\therefore \bar{x} = \frac{\sum fx}{\sum f} = \frac{303}{50} \approx 6.06$$

This means that, on average, each student obtained a little over 6 marks. In other words, the mean is the number of marks that *each* student would have had to score in order for the whole group to achieve the same grand total of 303 marks. In practice, some students scored higher and some scored lower than the mean, hence the distribution of scores.

Each value of the variable is multiplied by its corresponding frequency in order to 'weight' it. For example, the 11 students who each scored 7 marks contributed 77 marks to the grand total of marks obtained by all the students; the other marks are similarly weighted.

*Note:*

i)   If the mean is calculated using the whole set of population data, it is called the *population mean*.

   The symbol for the population mean is the Greek letter $\mu$ (pronounced 'mew').

ii)  If the mean is calculated using a sample taken from the population data, it is called the *sample mean*.

   (In the example, the data are a sample; they don't represent the scores of *all* students who have taken the aptitude test, just this particular sample of 50).

iii) Invariably, the data involved is a sample collected by observation, questionnaire, experiment etc. from a wider population, so $\bar{x}$ is most often used.

## The mean of a grouped frequency distribution

Considering the data of Table 2, the method is similar to that for an ungrouped frequency distribution (calculations – Table 2a):

Step 1:   Write, in columns:
   a)   the classes
   b)   the class mid-points (these become the *x*-values)
   c)   the frequencies

Step 2: Proceed as for an ungrouped frequency distribution

| I.Q. score | Class mid-point x | Frequency f | fx |
|---|---|---|---|
| 90 – 94 | 92 | 8 | 736 |
| 95 – 99 | 97 | 10 | 970 |
| 100 – 104 | 102 | 13 | 1326 |
| 105 – 109 | 107 | 7 | 749 |
| 110 – 114 | 112 | 4 | 448 |
| 115 – 119 | 117 | 3 | 351 |
| 120 – 124 | 122 | 3 | 366 |
| 125 – 129 | 127 | 2 | 254 |
| | | $\Sigma f = 50$ | $\Sigma fx = 5200$ |

*Table 2a*

$$\therefore \; \bar{x} = \frac{\Sigma fx}{\Sigma f} = \frac{5200}{50} = 104$$

So, the mean I.Q. score of the group is 104.

Calculating the mean from a grouped distribution will probably introduce an error. This is because each value in a class is assumed to have the value of its mid-point. In the example, for instance, all 13 values in the 100 – 104 class are assumed to be 102; this is obviously not the case. However, some values in a class will be greater, and some smaller, than the class mid-point. So, these errors tend to cancel each other out and the overall error is likely to be relatively small.

Note that the procedure for calculating the mean is precisely the same when a continuous variable is involved, although a little more care is needed when calculating class mid-points.

## The median of a frequency distribution

The median is calculated using a *cumulative frequency distribution*. The method can be summarised as follows (calculations – Table 1b):

Step 1: Write, in columns:
    i)   the values of the variable     ii)   the frequencies

Step 2: Calculate a cumulative frequency column (a 'running total' of the frequencies)

Step 3: Locate the middle data item (for $n$ items, this is item number: $\frac{(n + 1)}{2}$

Step 4: The median is the value of the middle data item

| Score x | Frequency | Cumulative frequency f | |
|---|---|---|---|
| 1 | 1 | 1 | |
| 2 | 2 | 3 | (1 + 2 = 3) |
| 3 | 4 | 7 | (3 + 4 = 7) |
| 4 | 5 | 12 | (7 + 5 = 12) |
| 5 | 6 | 18 | (12 + 6 = 18) |
| 6 | 8 | 26 | etc. |
| 7 | 11 | 37 | |
| 8 | 8 | 45 | |
| 9 | 3 | 48 | |
| 10 | 2 | 50 | |

*Table 1b*

187

The cumulative frequency column shows that:

| | |
|---|---|
| 1 student has a score of 1 | (i.e. student #1 has a score of 1) |
| 2 students have a score of 2 or less | (i.e. students #2 to #3 have a score of 2) |
| 7 students have a score of 3 or less | (i.e. students #4 to #7 have a score of 3) |
| 12 students have a score of 4 or less | (i.e. students #8 to #12 have a score of 4) |
| 18 students have a score of 5 or less | (i.e. students #13 to #18 have a score of 5) |
| 26 students have a score of 6 or less | (i.e. students #19 to #26 have a score of 6) |
| and so on | and so on |

$$\therefore \text{Median} = 6$$

The middle student in a group of 50 students is student number: $\frac{(50 + 1)}{2} = 25.5$. There is no such student, so this can be interpreted as being halfway between the 25th & 26th students. So, the median score is halfway between the score obtained by the 25th student and the score obtained by the 26th student. Since both of these students scored 6, the median is also 6.

## The median of a grouped frequency distribution

When the data is grouped, it is possible to use a graph of the cumulative frequency distribution (called an *ogive*) to estimate the median. The method can be summarised as follows (calculations – Table 2b; graph – Fig. 17):

Step 1: Construct a cumulative frequency table, as for ungrouped data

Step 2: a) Construct graph axes showing:
  i) the values of the variable, horizontally
  ii) the cumulative frequency, vertically
 b) Plot each cumulative frequency against its corresponding class upper limit
 c) Join the plotted points:
  i) with a series of straight lines, if the variable is discrete
  ii) with a curve, if the variable is continuous

Step 3: a) Locate the middle item on the vertical axis (for $n$ items, this is item number: $\frac{n}{2}$)
 b) Read across to the ogive, down to the horizontal axis and note the median

Note that the location of the middle item is different for grouped data; that is, $\frac{n}{2}$ and not $\frac{(n + 1)}{2}$.

| I.Q. score | Frequency | Cumulative frequency |
|---|---|---|
| 90 – 94 | 8 | 8 |
| 95 – 99 | 10 | 18 |
| 100 – 104 | 13 | 31 |
| 105 – 109 | 7 | 38 |
| 110 – 114 | 4 | 42 |
| 115 – 119 | 3 | 45 |
| 120 – 124 | 3 | 48 |
| 125 – 129 | 2 | 50 |

*Table 2b*

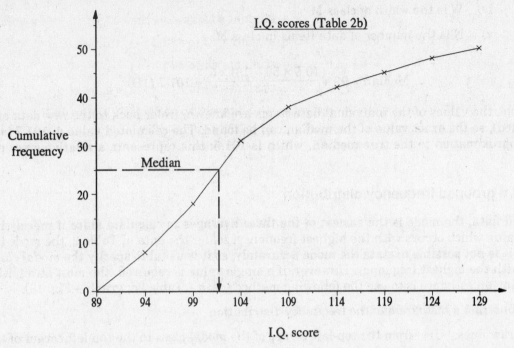

*Fig. 17 - Cumulative frequency distribution*

In Fig. 17:   i)   locate item number 25 on the vertical axis

ii)   read across to the graph, then down to the horizontal axis; ∴ median ≈ 102 (3S).

If a graphical method is not used, calculating the median for grouped data is rather more involved than for ungrouped data since the individual values within each class are not known. The method can be summarised as follows (calculations – Table 2c):

Step 1:   Construct a cumulative frequency table

| | I.Q. score | Frequency | Cumulative frequency |
|---|---|---|---|
| | 90 – 94 | 8 | 8 |
| | 95 – 99 | 10 | 18 |
| Class M → | 100 – 104 | 13 | 31 |
| | 105 – 109 | 7 | 38 |
| | 110 – 114 | 4 | 42 |
| | 115 – 119 | 3 | 45 |
| | 120 – 124 | 3 | 48 |
| | 125 – 129 | 2 | 50 |

*Table 2c*

Step 2:   Locate the class which contains the median item (call this class M)

Step 3:   Calculate the median using the formula:

$$\text{Median} = \frac{U + (0.5F - C)W}{N}$$

where:   i)   U is the upper limit of the class below class M

ii)   F is the total frequency

iii) C is the cumulative frequency up to, but not including, class M

iv) W is the width of class M

v) N is the number of data items in class M

$$\therefore \text{Median} = 99 + \frac{(0.5 \times 50 - 18) \times 5}{13} \approx 101.7 \text{ (1D)}$$

In this example, the values of the individual data items are known, (refer back to the raw data on which Table 2 is based), so the exact value of the median can be found. The calculated value of 101.7 is quite a reasonable approximation to the true median, which is 101.5; this represents a relative error of about 0.2%.

## The mode of a grouped frequency distribution

For ungrouped data, the mode is the easiest of the three averages to calculate since it merely involves locating the value which occurs with the highest frequency; so, for the data of Table 2, the mode is 7. For grouped data it is not possible to state the mode accurately, so it is usual to specify the *modal class*; that is, the class with the highest frequency. However, if a single value is required, the most straightforward way of obtaining an estimate is to use the following method (data – Table 2d; graph – Fig. 18):

Step 1:   Construct a histogram of the frequency distribution

Step 2:   Draw lines:   i)   from the top-left corner of the modal class to the top-left corner of the next class

ii)   from the top-right corner of the modal class to the top-right corner of the previous class

iii)   vertically down from the intersection of the two lines in i) and ii)

Step 3:   Note the mode on the horizontal axis.

|  | I.Q. score | Frequency |
|---|---|---|
|  | 90 – 94 | 8 |
|  | 95 – 99 | 10 |
| Modal class → | 100 – 104 | 13 |
|  | 105 – 109 | 7 |
|  | 110 – 114 | 4 |
|  | 115 – 119 | 3 |
|  | 120 – 124 | 3 |
|  | 125 – 129 | 2 |

*Table 2d*

In Table 2d, the modal class is 100 – 104; in Fig. 18 on the next page, the value of the mode is approximately 101. Note that the true mode, using the original raw data on which Table 2 is based, is 98.

## A relationship between mean, median and mode

As an alternative to a graphical method, and providing the frequency distribution has a single modal class, an approximate value for the mode can be calculated from the relationship:

$$\text{Mode} \approx \text{Mean} - 3(\text{Mean} - \text{Median})$$

Using the data of Table 2, and previous calculations for the mean and median, gives:

$$\text{Mode} \approx 104 - 3(104 - 101.7) = 97.1$$

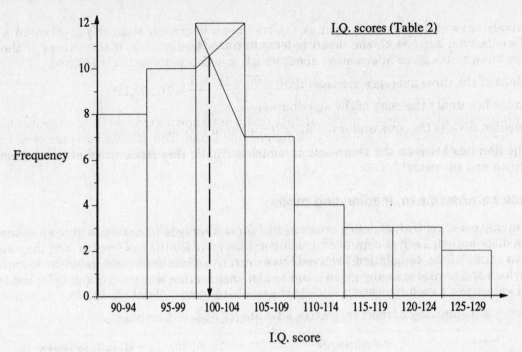

*Fig. 18 - Locating the mode*

## The effect of skewness on averages

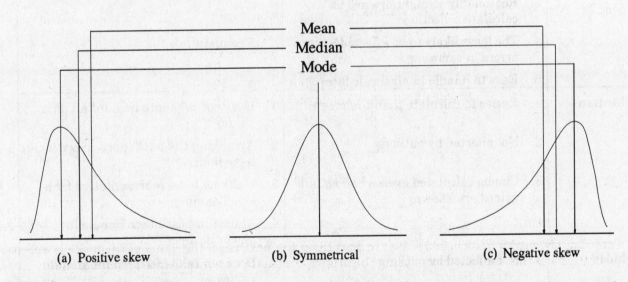

(a) Positive skew    (b) Symmetrical    (c) Negative skew

It has been mentioned earlier that any non-symmetrical distribution is said to be *skewed*; for example, a) and c) are skewed distributions. If the bulk of the data is offset towards the left of the distribution, as in (a), it is said to be *positively* skewed; if the bulk of the data is offset towards the right of the distribution, as in c), it is said to be *negatively* skewed.

In distribution a) the mean has been affected by the few extreme values in the tail and dragged to the right.

Distribution b) is a symmetrical distribution, with the mean, median and mode all having the same value.

191

In distribution c) the mean has been affected by the few extreme values in the tail and dragged to the left.

In a positively skewed distribution, such as (a), the mean is greater than the median; in a negatively skewed distribution, such as c), the mean is less than the median. So, if the values of the mean and median are known, this gives information about which way the distribution is skewed.

The positions of the three averages are such that:

i)   the mode lies under the peak of the distribution

ii)   the median divides the area under the distribution into two equal parts

iii)   the median lies between the mean and the mode (usually about one-third of the distance between the mean and the mode)

## The choice between mean, median and mode

All three measures of central tendency are designed for the same job; that is, to give an indication of the centre of a distribution. Each is obtained by using a different definition of 'centre' and they all have pros and cons in terms of the calculation involved. However, the most important question to consider when deciding which one to choose in any given situation is: 'Is it representative of the data?'; that is, 'Does the calculated value give a good indication of what the whole collection of data is like?'

The following is a summary of their respective advantages and disadvantages:

| | Advantages | Disadvantages |
|---|---|---|
| Mean | 1.  Takes into account all data values<br>2.  Most people understand it<br>3.  Reasonably straightforward to calculate collection<br>4.  The least likely to be affected by errors in sampling<br>5.  Easy to handle in algebraic form | 1.  Badly affected by outliers<br>2.  Rarely corresponds to an actual value in the data |
| Median | 1.  Easier to calculate than the mean<br>2.  Not affected by outliers<br>3.  Can be calculated even when not all values are known | 1.  Does not take into account all data values<br>2.  Arranging the data items in order can be tedious<br>3.  Unlikely to be representative for a small sample<br>4.  Almost impossible to handle in algebraic form |
| Mode | 1.  Not affected by outliers<br>2.  Is an important value of the variable | 1.  Does not take into account all data values<br>2.  Often impossible to determine accurately<br>3.  Unsuitable for handling in algebraic form |

The choice of an appropriate type of average in any given situation also depends on:

i)   the type of variable

ii)   the shape of the distribution

As a general guide:

| Variable type | Shape of distribution | Average |
|---|---|---|
| Discrete / Continuous | Symmetrical | Mean |
| Discrete / Continuous | Highly skewed | Median |
| Categorical | Single mode / modal class | Mode |

On balance, the mean is the preferred statistic to use since it possesses the most desirable properties and is the one that is commonly referred to as the 'average'.

## Measures of dispersion

The 'average' is a measure which gives some information about the centre of a distribution. Distributions differ, though, in ways other than their average values. For instance, consider these two collections of data:

$$\text{Set A:} \quad 1 \quad 2 \quad 3 \quad 4 \quad 5 \quad 6 \quad 7 \quad 8 \quad 9$$
$$\text{Set B:} \quad 3 \quad 4 \quad 4 \quad 5 \quad 5 \quad 5 \quad 6 \quad 6 \quad 7$$

The mean of set A is: $\dfrac{1 + 2 + 3 + 4 + 5 + 6 + 7 + 8 + 9}{9} = \dfrac{45}{9} = 5$

The mean of set B is: $\dfrac{3 + 4 + 4 + 5 + 5 + 5 + 6 + 6 + 7}{9} = \dfrac{45}{9} = 5$

So, if the average is used as the sole means of comparison, the two sets of data appear to be identical. This is obviously not the case. The data in set B has its values much closer to the average than set A. Graphs of the two distributions shows the difference more clearly:

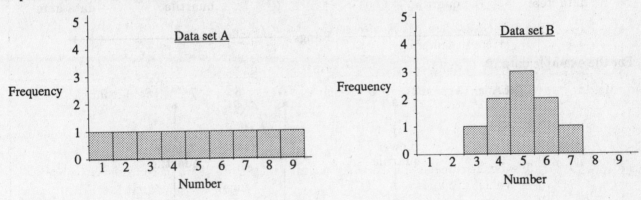

In order to measure such differences between distributions, the average is not suitable. There is a need for a different sort of measure to indicate whether the data items are closely clustered around the average or whether they are spread out over the range of the distribution. Such measures are called *measures of dispersion* (or *spread*).

There are several measures of dispersion, including:

i)  the range

ii)  the interquartile range

iii)  the standard deviation

## The range

The *range* is the difference between the lowest value and the highest value in the distribution.

So, for the example data:

    a)    set A: range = 9 − 1 = 8

    b)    set B: range = 7 − 3 = 4

This shows that the values in set A are spread out more than those in set B.

The range is simple to calculate but has its disadvantages, namely:

i)    it makes use of very little information; that is, it ignores all but two items of data

ii)    it is totally dependent on the two extreme values, so can be badly affected by any changes in these

iii)    it should be used with caution, particularly with data that contain outliers

iv)    it cannot identify the differences between two sets of data with the same extreme values e.g. the two sets of data: 2, 4, 6, 8, 10, 12, 14, 16, 18 and 2, 2, 2, 2, 2, 2, 2, 2, 18 both have range 16.

## The interquartile range

The *interquartile range* is one measure which deals with the problem of data containing outliers. In the same sort of way that the median divides a data set into two equal parts, the *quartiles* divide the data into four equal parts. The interquartile range is the difference between the *lower quartile* and the *upper quartile*. So, the interquartile range is the range of the middle 50% of the distribution:

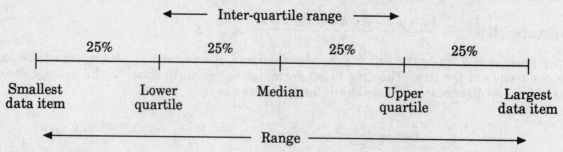

For the example data:

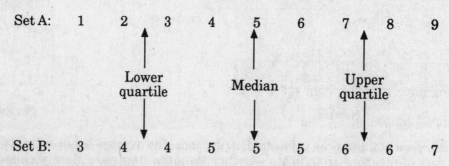

The following symbols are often used:

    $Q_1$ = Lower quartile

    $Q_2$ = Median

    $Q_3$ = Upper quartile

So,    i)    Set A: $Q_1$ = 2.5, $Q_2$ = 5, $Q_3$ = 7.5; interquartile range = 7.5 − 2.5 = 5

    ii)    Set B: $Q_1$ = 4, $Q_2$ = 5, $Q_3$ = 6; interquartile range = 6 − 4 = 2

(See note at top of next page for calculating location of quartiles).

Again, this shows that set A has the greater degree of spread within its data.

## The interquartile range of a frequency distribution

Using the computing aptitude task scores data of Table 1, the method can be summarised as follows (calculations – Table 1c):

Step 1:  Construct a cumulative frequency table

Step 2:  a)  Locate $Q_1$ (for n items, this is item number: $\dfrac{(n+1)}{4}$

   b)  Locate $Q_3$ (for n items, this is item number: $\dfrac{(3n+1)}{4}$

Step 3:  Calculate the interquartile range: $Q_3 - Q_1$

*Note:*

i)  the median of ungrouped data is located by calculating $\dfrac{(n+1)}{2}$ i.e. the halfway point; in a similar way the quartiles are located by calculating the one-quarter and three-quarter points

ii)  if the divisions at Step 2 leave any spare 'quarters' in the result, it is usual to round up or down to the nearest integer

| Score x | Frequency f | Cumulative frequency | |
|---|---|---|---|
| 1 | 1 | 1 | |
| 2 | 2 | 3 | |
| 3 | 4 | 7 | |
| 4 | 5 | 12 | |
| 5 | 6 | 18 | $Q_1 = 5$ (Lower quartile) |
| 6 | 8 | 26 | |
| 7 | 11 | 37 | |
| 8 | 8 | 45 | $Q_3 = 8$ (Upper quartile) |
| 9 | 3 | 48 | |
| 10 | 2 | 50 | |

*Table 1c*

∴  $Q_1$ is item number: $\dfrac{51}{4}$ i.e. item #13 = 5

   $Q_3$ is item number: $3 \times \dfrac{51}{4}$ i.e. item #38 = 8

∴  Interquartile range = 8 – 5 = 3

The interquartile range is a useful measure of spread. However, it is usually more helpful to know how much the data is spread *either side* of the centre of a distribution. So, the *semi-interquartile range* can be calculated; as its name implies, it is half of the interquartile range.

For this data, the semi-interquartile range = 1.5; from previous calculations, the median = 6.

The interpretation of these summary figures is that:

i)  the students obtained, on average, a score of 6

ii)  50% of the students have a score which is within 1.5 of the average i.e. between 4.5 and 7.5

## The interquartile range of a grouped frequency distribution

The most effective way of calculating the interquartile range in this case is to use a cumulative frequency curve. For instance, using the student I.Q. data of Table 2, the method can be summarised as follows (data – Table 2e, graph – Fig. 19):

Step 1:  Construct a cumulative frequency curve

Step 2:  a)  Locate $Q_1$ on the vertical axis (for $n$ items, this is item number: $\frac{n}{4}$)

         b)  Read across to the ogive, down to the horizontal axis and note the value of $Q_1$

Step 3:  Repeat Step 2 for $Q_3$ (for $n$ items, this is item number: $\frac{3n}{4}$ )

Step 4:  Calculate the interquartile range: $Q_3 - Q_1$

Recall that, for grouped data, the value of $Q_2$ is located by calculating $\frac{n}{2}$ rather than $\frac{(n+1)}{2}$. Similarly, $Q_1$ and $Q_3$ are located by calculating $\frac{n}{4}$ and $\frac{3n}{4}$ respectively, rather than $\frac{(n+1)}{4}$ and $\frac{3(n+1)}{4}$.

| I.Q. score | Frequency | Cumulative frequency |
|:---:|:---:|:---:|
| 90 – 94 | 8 | 8 |
| 95 – 99 | 10 | 18 |
| 100 – 104 | 13 | 31 |
| 105 – 109 | 7 | 38 |
| 110 – 114 | 4 | 42 |
| 115 – 119 | 3 | 45 |
| 120 – 124 | 3 | 48 |
| 125 – 129 | 2 | 50 |

$Q_1$ = item #12.5

$Q_3$ = item #37.5

*Table 2e*

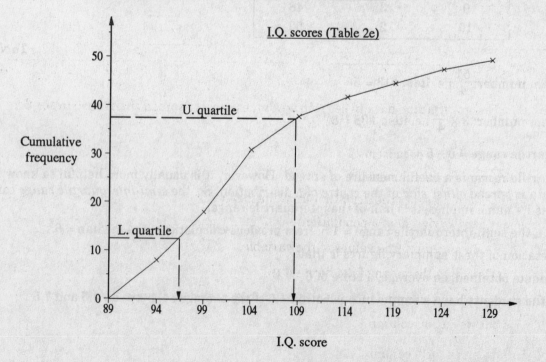

*Fig.19 - Finding the inter-quartile range*

$$\therefore \quad Q_1 \text{ is item number: } \frac{50}{4} \text{ i.e. item \#12.5} = 96.5$$

$$Q_3 \text{ is item number: } 3 \times \frac{50}{4} \text{ i.e. item \#37.5} = 108.5$$

$$\therefore \quad \text{Interquartile range} = 108.5 - 96.5 = 12$$

For this data, the semi-interquartile range = 6; from previous calculations, the median = 101.7.

The interpretation of these summary figures is that:

i)   the students have, on average, an I.Q. score of approximately 102

ii)  50% of the students have an I.Q. score which is within 6 of the average i.e. between 96 and 108

## The standard deviation

One disadvantage of the interquartile range is that, like the range, it takes account of only a few items of data. It is only influenced by whatever the lower quartile and upper quartile data items are, and ignores the rest. The *standard deviation* (S.D.) takes into account *every* data item by a) measuring the difference between each item and the mean and then b) calculating an overall deviation for the data set.

For instance, consider again the two data sets A and B. The following diagrams show by how much each data item is different from the mean (this difference is called the *deviation*). If the value of a data item is greater than the mean, it has a positive deviation; if it is less than the mean, it has a negative deviation:

Set A: 1 2 3 4 5 6 7 8 9

($\mu = 5$)

Set B: 3 4 4 5 5 5 6 6 7

($\mu = 5$)

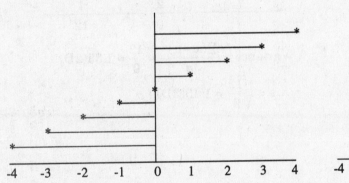 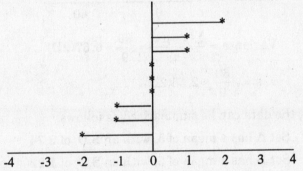

The diagrams clearly show that the data in set A have a much greater spread than those in set B.

In the diagrams:

i)   each asterisk represents a data item

ii)  the vertical line represents the mean

iii) the horizontal scale represents the deviation from the mean

To calculate the standard deviation of a population:

Step 1:  a)  Write, in a column, the values of the variable

        b)  Calculate the mean of the data set $\mu$

Step 2:  Calculate an $x - \mu$ column (subtract the mean from each data item in turn)

      This is the deviation column

Step 3:  Calculate an $(x - \mu)^2$ column

      This is the squared deviation column

197

Step 4: Calculate $\Sigma(x-\mu)^2$ the sum of the $(x-\mu)^2$ column

Step 5: Calculate the *variance* using the formula:

$$\text{Variance} = \frac{\Sigma(x-\mu)^2}{n} \quad (n \text{ is the number of data items})$$

Step 6: Calculate $\sqrt{\text{Variance}}$; this is the population S.D., $\sigma$ (pronounced sigma)

So, for the two example data sets:

| Set A ($\mu = 5$) | | | | Set B ($\mu = 5$) | | |
|---|---|---|---|---|---|---|
| **Number** | **Deviation from mean** | **Squared deviation** | | **Number** | **Deviation from mean** | **Squared deviation** |
| $x$ | $(x-\mu)$ | $(x-\mu)^2$ | | $x$ | $(x-\mu)$ | $(x-\mu)^2$ |
| 1 | -4 | 16 | | 3 | -2 | 4 |
| 2 | -3 | 9 | | 4 | -1 | 1 |
| 3 | -2 | 4 | | 4 | -1 | 1 |
| 4 | -1 | 1 | | 5 | 0 | 0 |
| 5 | 0 | 0 | | 5 | 0 | 0 |
| 6 | 1 | 1 | | 5 | 0 | 0 |
| 7 | 2 | 4 | | 6 | 1 | 1 |
| 8 | 3 | 9 | | 6 | 1 | 1 |
| 9 | 4 | 16 | | 7 | 2 | 4 |
| | 0 | 60 | | | 0 | 12 |

$$\text{Variance} = \frac{\Sigma(x-\mu)^2}{n} = \frac{60}{9} \approx 6.67 \text{(2D)} \qquad \text{Variance} = \frac{\Sigma(x-\mu)^2}{n} = \frac{12}{9} \approx 1.33 \text{(2D)}$$

$$\therefore s = \sqrt{\frac{60}{9}} \approx 2.58 \text{(2D)} \qquad\qquad \therefore s = \sqrt{\frac{12}{9}} \approx 1.15 \text{(2D)}$$

So, the data can be summarised as follows:

i) Set A has a mean of 5, with an S.D. of 2.74

ii) Set B has a mean of 5, with an S.D. of 1.22

In other words, the data in set A are more widely dispersed than the data in set B.

*Note:*

i) $\Sigma(x-\mu)$, the sum of the deviations, is *always* equal to 0; this is a useful way of checking that the deviation calculations are correct.

ii) Since adding the deviations always results in 0, they are squared, simply as a convenient way to remove the minus signs. For instance, it does not matter whether a data item is below the mean(negative deviation) or above the mean (positive deviation); all that really matters is that it is *different* to the mean.

iii) Because of ii), the result has to be 'unsquared' (i.e. square root) at some point to reverse the effects.

The value obtained before the square root is calculated is called the variance.

iv) The symbol for the population S.D. is $\sigma$; the symbol for the sample S.D. is $s$. (The data sets A and B in the example are assumed to be populations).

v) The formulas used to calculate $\sigma$ and $s$ are slightly different:

$$\text{Population S.D.:} \quad \sigma = \sqrt{\frac{\Sigma(x-\mu)^2}{n}} \qquad \text{Sample S.D.:} \quad s = \sqrt{\frac{\Sigma(x-\bar{x})^2}{n-1}}$$

vi) Computational versions of the formulas are:

$$\text{Population S.D.:} \quad \sigma = \sqrt{\frac{\Sigma x^2}{n} - \mu^2} \qquad \text{Sample S.D.:} \quad s = \sqrt{\frac{\Sigma x^2}{n} - \bar{x}^2} \times \sqrt{\frac{n}{n-1}}$$

(These look more cumbersome, but are quicker and more accurate for calculation purposes).

The following procedure makes use of a computational version of a formula given in (vi), which has been further adapted for use with frequency distributions.

## The standard deviation of a frequency distribution

The formulas used in the previous section can easily be modified to include frequencies. Considering the data of Table 1, the method for the sample S.D. is (calculations – Table 1d):

Step 1:  Write, in columns:

    a)  the values of the variable

    b)  the frequencies

Step 2:  Calculate columns for:  a) $fx$   b) $fx^2$

Step 3:  Calculate:   a) $\Sigma f$   b) $\Sigma fx$   c) $\Sigma fx^2$   d) $\bar{x}$

Step 4:  Calculate the sample S.D. using the formula:

$$s = \sqrt{\frac{\Sigma fx^2}{\Sigma f} - \bar{x}^2} \times \sqrt{\frac{\Sigma f}{\Sigma f - 1}}$$

| Score $x$ | Frequency $f$ | $fx$ | $fx^2$ |
|---|---|---|---|
| 1 | 1 | 1 | 1 |
| 2 | 2 | 4 | 8 |
| 3 | 4 | 12 | 36 |
| 4 | 5 | 20 | 80 |
| 5 | 6 | 30 | 150 |
| 6 | 8 | 48 | 288 |
| 7 | 11 | 77 | 539 |
| 8 | 8 | 64 | 512 |
| 9 | 3 | 27 | 243 |
| 10 | 2 | 20 | 200 |
| | $\Sigma f = 50$ | $\Sigma fx = 303$ | $\Sigma fx^2 = 2057$ |

*Table 1d*

$$\bar{x} = \frac{303}{50} = 6.06$$

199

$$\therefore s = \sqrt{\frac{\sum fx^2}{\sum f} - \bar{x}^2} \times \sqrt{\frac{\sum f}{\sum f - 1}}$$

$$= \sqrt{\frac{2057}{50} - 6.06^2} \times \sqrt{\frac{50}{49}}$$

$$= 2.12 \text{ (2D)}$$

Using the computational version of a formula reduces the errors substantially. This is because:

i)   the value of $\bar{x}$ may be inaccurate due to being rounded

ii)  if the non-computational version is used, subtracting this value of $\bar{x}$ from each corresponding $x$-value introduces an error into each value of $(x - \bar{x})$

iii) multiplying the results by a frequency would simply compound the errors

Note, however, that the computational version requires that $x$ is squared and subtracted only once. This minimises the introduction of rounding errors.

## The standard deviation of a grouped frequency distribution

The procedure for grouped data is similar to that for ungrouped data; the only difference is that the class mid-points are used as the $x$-values.

## Properties of the standard deviation

The standard deviation possesses a few properties that are very useful and which apply to any frequency distribution, whatever the shape:

i)   at least 56% of the data items fall within 1.5 standard deviations either side of the mean; that is, the values lie between $\mu - 1.5\sigma$ and $\mu + 1.5s$

ii)  at least 75% of the data items fall within 2 standard deviations either side of the mean; that is, the values lie between $\mu - 2\sigma$ and $\mu + 2\sigma$

iii) at least 89% of the data items fall within 3 standard deviations either side of the mean; that is, the values lie between $\mu - 3\sigma$ and $\mu + 3\sigma$

iv)  at least 94% of the data items fall within 4 standard deviations either side of the mean; that is, the values lie between $\mu - 4\sigma$ and $\mu + 4\sigma$

Knowing these facts is helpful in trying to summarise data in a meaningful way. For example, earlier calculations showed that student aptitude test scores are distributed with a mean of 6.06 and an S.D. of 2.12. This means, for instance, that at least 56% of the students have scores which lie between $6.06 - 1.5 \times 2.12$ and $6.06 + 1.5 \times 2.12$; that is, between 2.88 and 9.24. Or, more simply:

'about 60% of the students scored between 3 and 9'

## The choice between range, semi-interquartile range and standard deviation

These three measures are all designed to give an indication of the amount of spread within a distribution. All have advantages and disadvantages in terms of the complexity of calculations involved and how well they represent the variability of the data collection. As with the choice of 'average', the final choice of measure of dispersion is determined by a combination of these factors.

The advantages and disadvantages can be summarised as follows:

|  | **Advantages** | **Disadvantages** |
|---|---|---|
| Range | 1. Easily understood<br><br>2. Simple to calculate | 1. Only based on two extreme values<br><br>2. Badly affected by outliers<br><br>3. Unsuitable for handling in algebraic form |
| Semi-interquartile range | 1. Simple to find by using ogive<br><br>2. Not affected by outliers | 1. Only based on the middle half of data values<br><br>2. Unsuitable for handling in algebraic form |
| Standard deviation | 1. Takes into account all values<br><br>2. Quite straightforward to calculate<br><br>3. Suitable for handling in algebraic form | 1. Vital to nearly all further statistical work |

When deciding which is the most suitable measure of dispersion, similar considerations apply to those for choosing an average.

## Data display and analysis – a summary

The following is a general outline of the procedures to follow so that raw data can be processed and presented in a more meaningful form:

1. Organise it into a table to show up any patterns that might be present within it.

2. Illustrate the data with a suitable graph or diagram to provide a picture of the information.

3. Choose suitable measures to describe and summarise the data; these should normally include:

   a) a measure of central tendency (average): this is a figure which is representative of the data

   b) a measure of dispersion (spread): this indicates the amount of variation within the data

Decisions will have to be made regarding the choice of suitable graphs and measures; as a general guide:

| Variable type | Graphical form |
|---|---|
| Category | Bar chart / Pie chart |
| Discrete | Bar chart / Pie chart / Pictogram |
| Continuous | Histogram |

| Variable type | Shape of distribution | Average | Dispersion |
|---|---|---|---|
| Discrete / Continuous | Generally symmetrical | Mean | Standard deviation |
| Discrete / Continuous | Highly skewed | Median | Interquartile range |
| Category | Single mode / modal class | Mode | Not applicable |

## The use of spreadsheets

Calculating measures such as the mean and standard deviation is reasonably straightforward; if a calculator is being used, though, success is largely dependent on careful organisation of the data and systematic working. Also, the situation becomes more error-prone if there are large quantities of data to process. The tabulation of figures and the sort of calculations undertaken make a spreadsheet ideally suited to this task, particularly if the same sort of calculation is being repeated with different sets of data. The template shown below is an example of the type of arrangement needed for calculating the mean and S.D. of a grouped frequency distribution. The reader should be able to adapt the principles to meet their own requirements:

| | A | B | C | D | E | F | G |
|---|---|---|---|---|---|---|---|
| 1 | Grouped Frequency Distribution - Mean and SD for student IQ scores | | | | | | |
| 2 | Lower | Upper | Class midpt | Frequency | | | |
| 3 | class limit | class limit | x | f | fx | fx$^2$ | |
| 4 | 90 | 94 | *(b4+a4)/2* | 8 | *c4\*d4* | *c4\*e4* | |
| 5 | 95 | 99 | *(b5+a5)/2* | 10 | *c5\*d5* | *c5\*e5* | |
| .. | ... | ... | ... | ... | ... | ... | |
| .. | ... | ... | ... | ... | ... | ... | |
| 11 | 125 | 129 | *(b11+a11)/2* | 2 | *c11\*d11* | *c11\*e11* | |
| 12 | | | | *SUM(d4:d11)* | *SUM(e4:e11)* | *SUM(f4:f11)* | |
| 13 | | | | | | | |
| 14 | | Mean = | *e12/d12* | | S.D. = | | |
| 15 | | | | | | | |

*SQRT(f12/d12-c14\*c14)\*SQRT(d12/(d12-1))*

*Notes:*

1. Formulas are shown in italics. (Lower case letters denote relative cell references).

2. a) *SQRT (XX)* ≡ 'The square root of cell XX'

   b) *SUM(XX:YY)* ≡ 'The sum of all cells from XX to YY inclusive'

3. Various refinements could be made to this template. For example, at present the class limits are entered as data in columns A and B; this could be improved as follows: i) designate a cell to contain the class interval ii) enter the limits of the first class as data in cells A4 and B4 iii) enter appropriate formulas into the other cells in columns A and B to generate the remaining class limits. This makes the template easily adaptable to other sets of data. If the spreadsheet has the facilities, similar refinements could be made to allow entry of a variable number of classes (the example template is limited to 8).

## The Normal Distribution

This is probably the most important of all distributions since much data collected from observations of continuous variables fall approximately into this pattern. For instance:

Heights of people

Life-lengths of fluorescent tubes

Weights of packets of soap powder

Sizes of components produced by a machine

Ambulance response times to emergency calls

The normal distribution has a distinctive shape of distribution curve. The one below shows the approximate distribution of heights of 500 students at Dale Institute; it has been obtained by smoothing out a frequency polygon based on a histogram of observations:

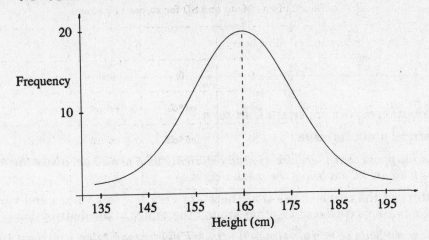

Most of the heights, as might be expected, are concentrated around the mean (in this case, 165 cm). The distribution tails off at either end since only a few students have heights which are very different from the mean. The resulting bell-shaped curve is characteristic of a normal distribution.

In the example above, the shape is only approximate since the underlying histogram of student heights does not have a set of values which conform exactly to this symmetrical shape. This is because it is based on the population of Dale Institute students, which is relatively small (a few hundred) compared to, for instance, the population of all British students (many thousands). A small number of observations may contain irregularities which tend to disappear when a larger number of observations are considered. The normal distribution is a theoretically ideal shape which applies to a population consisting of an infinite number of observations. The greater the number of observations, the closer the general shape becomes to the normal distribution. However, quite small samples of data can still produce distributions which resemble the normal distribution closely enough to be represented by it.

So, if a frequency distribution of the heights of all British students were drawn it would have a similar shape to the one shown for Dale students. The main difference would be the scaling of the frequency axis, modified to allow for thousands, rather than hundreds, of students. However, the overall shape would remain unaltered and it is this which is of importance. (The precise frequencies are relatively unimportant and will often be omitted from diagrams).

The normal distribution possesses well-defined and useful properties which make it suitable for modelling a wide variety of situations in such diverse areas as sociology, engineering, nuclear sciences, education, geography and market research. A thorough understanding of these properties is vital in order to use it in inferential statistics; that is, in making general statements about a population based on results obtained from a sample of data. For example, Dale Institute students can be considered as a sample selected from the population of all British students. *Their* mean height is 165 cm, so how sure can we be that *all* British students have a mean height of 165 cm ?

## Properties of the normal distribution

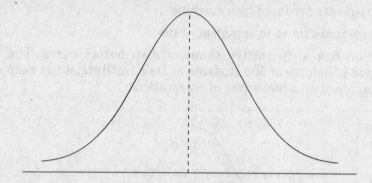

Some of the normal distribution curve's important features are:

i)   The curve is symmetrical about its mean.

*e.g. It is reasonable to suppose that there are as many students who are 20 cm above the mean height as there are students who are 20 cm below the mean height.*

ii)  The bell-shaped nature of the curve shows that there are very few low values and very few high values, with most observations clustered together around the centre of the distribution.

*e.g. There are very few students of minute size and very few students of huge size; most students will be about 'average' height.*

iii) The area under the curve represents the entire collection of observations. Like a histogram, its *area* is proportional to the number of observations.

*e.g. The area under the curve represents the student population at Dale Institute.*

iv)  The proportion of observations which lies within a certain interval decreases the further that the interval is from the mean.

*e.g. The proportion of students with heights between 185 cm and 195 cm is less than the proportion of students with heights between 165 cm and 175 cm, even though the interval size (10 cm) is the same.*

v)   In theory, the two 'tails' of the distribution never reach the horizontal axis (it is an asymptote). In other words, it is theoretically possible to have extreme values.

*e.g. It is theoretically possible that there are students with heights of 230 cm and 15cm; although in practice this is extremely unlikely, it is possible.*

vi)  The distribution's mean, median and mode all have the same value.

*e.g. The mean, median and mode of the student's heights is 165 cm.*

Now, for instance, consider the variable 'height' for the following three populations:

    i)   Students at Dale Institute

    ii)  Pupils at a 12-18 secondary school

    iii) Pupils at a 5-11 primary school

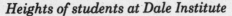

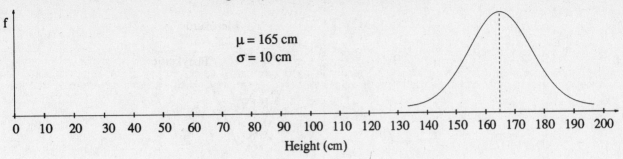

*Heights of students at Dale Institute*

$\mu = 165$ cm
$\sigma = 10$ cm

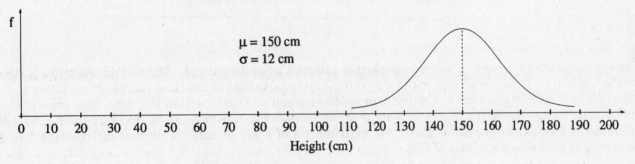

*Heights of pupils at a 12– 18 secondary school*

$\mu = 150$ cm
$\sigma = 12$ cm

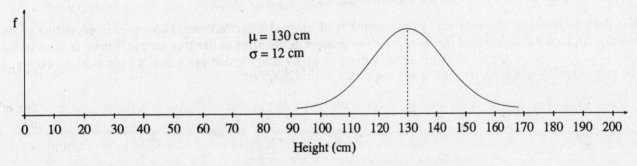

*Heights of pupils at a 5– 11 primary school*

$\mu = 130$ cm
$\sigma = 12$ cm

All of the populations are normally distributed; there are several points to note:

i)   The mean heights of the three populations increase as the overall age of the population increases; this is as expected.

ii)  The standard deviation of the student heights (10 cm) is smaller than the standard deviation of the school childrens' heights (12 cm). This is also as expected since the variation in height of people aged 18+ will clearly be less than the variation in height of children between the ages of 5 and 11, owing to the relatively slower rate of growth.

iii) The difference between the primary and secondary children is only in their mean heights (130 cm and 150 cm), the standard deviations being the same. That is, the variation in height within each age group is the same, both age groups having similar rates of growth.

The examples illustrate the fact that a normal distribution is characterised by its mean and its standard deviation. There is, therefore, an endless variety of normal distributions, each with its own mean and standard deviation. Some will be thin, some will be stocky and others will be shallow, as shown below:

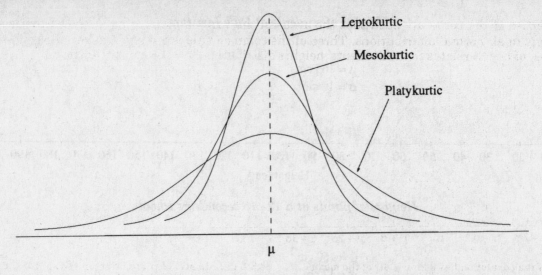

The extent to which a normal curve is peaked is referred to as its *kurtosis*. Normal distribution curves can be classed as *leptokurtic* (taller than usual) *mesokurtic* (usual shape) and *platykurtic* (flatter than usual). The kurtosis of a curve is dependent on the spread of values within the data. The greater the spread, the flatter the curve becomes. Note that, like skewness, kurtosis can be measured and provides valuable additional information about the distribution of a set of data. A normal distribution has a skewness of zero and a kurtosis of zero.

## Proportions under the normal distribution curve

It is easy to see that there is an infinite number of normal distributions. However, irrespective of its mean, standard deviation and kurtosis *the distribution of the area under any normal curve is always the same*. For example, suppose that the area is divided up by lines which are equally spaced at intervals of one standard deviation either side of the mean, as in this diagram:

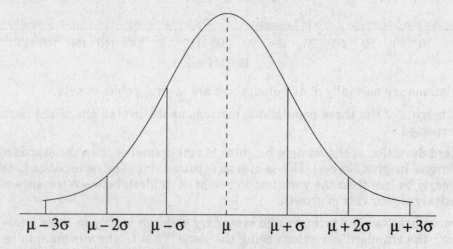

*Note:*

i)   the total area under the curve represents 100% of the population

ii)  $\mu + 2\sigma$ means: 'two standard deviations above the mean' etc.

iii) a normal distribution with mean $\mu$ and standard deviation s is referred to as $N(\mu, \sigma^2)$; notice that the second figure represents the *variance*. For example, the distribution of students' heights is $N(165,100)$.

The properties of the curve are such that the areas in the various portions have known precise values which apply to all normal distributions. Three of the common values are given below; alongside each is an example of how it relates to the students' heights distribution ($\mu = 165$ cm; $\sigma = 10$ cm):

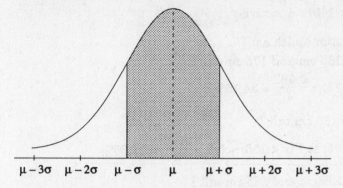

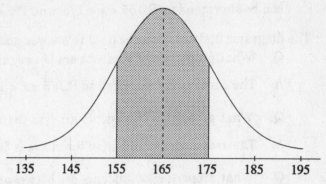

68.3% of the population lies within 1 SD of the mean

68.3% of Dale students are between $(165 - 10)$ cm and $(165 + 10)$ cm tall; that is, between 155 cm and 175 cm.

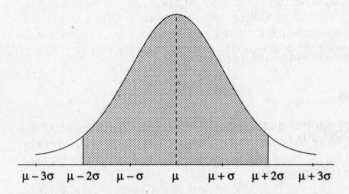

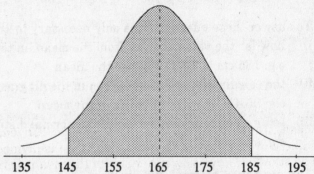

95.4% of the population lies within 2 SDs of the mean

95.4% of Dale students are between $(165 - 2\times10)$ cm and $(165 + 2\times10)$ cm tall; that is, between 145 cm and 185 cm.

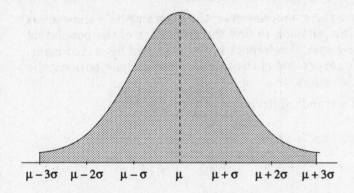

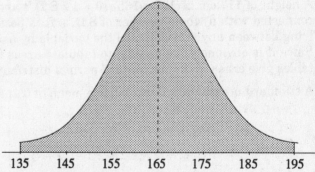

99.7% of the population lies within 3 SDs of the mean

99.7% of Dale students are between $(165 - 3\times10)$ cm and $(165 + 3\times10)$ cm tall; that is, between 135 cm and 195 cm.

*Note:*

i)   The proportions are often written as decimals, instead of percentages.

So: total area under curve = 100% = 1; 68.3% = 0.683; 95.4% = 0.954 and so on.

ii)  If $x$ represents the value of the variable under consideration (e.g. height), phrases such as:
'The proportion of observations that lie between 155 cm and 175 cm'
and      'The proportion of observations that are less than 145 cm'
can be shortened to: $P(155 < x < 175)$ and $P(x < 145)$ respectively.

The diagrams and areas can be used to answer questions such as:

Q.   'What proportion of students are between 165 cm and 175 cm tall ?

A.   The curve is symmetrical, so $P(165 < x < 175) = \dfrac{0.683}{2} = 34.15\%$

Q.   'What proportion of students are less than 155 cm tall ?

A.   The area under each half of the curve is 50%; so $P(x < 155) = 0.5 - \dfrac{0683}{2} = 15.85\%$

Q.   'What proportion of students are between 135 cm and 155 cm tall ?

A.   $P(x < 155) = 0.5 - \dfrac{0.683}{2} = 0.1585$; $P(x < 135) = 0.5 - \dfrac{0.997}{2} = 0.0015$

So, $P(135 < x < 155) = 0.1585 - 0.0015 = 15.7\%$

To answer these questions it is only necessary to know:
i)   how far the value is away from the mean, in terms of standard deviations
     e.g. 185 cm is 2 S.D.'s above the mean
ii)  the calculated proportions given in the diagrams
     e.g. 95.4% lie within 2 S.D.'s of the mean
iii) some elementary properties of the normal distribution
     e.g. symmetry, area under curve = 1

## The standard normal distribution

It is not possible to answer the following question by using the diagrams of the previous section:

'What proportion of students are taller than 177 cm ?'

A height of 177 cm is (177 − 165)/10 = 1.2 S.D.'s above the mean; however, the diagrams only show areas connected with a whole number of S.D.'s. It *is* possible, though, to find the proportion of the population lying between any two values of the variable by using special reference tables prepared by statisticians. Since it is obviously impractical to tabulate areas for every one of the infinite normal distributions, the tables give areas under a *standard* normal distribution curve.

A standard normal distribution has a mean of 0 and a standard deviation of 1; that is, N(0,1).

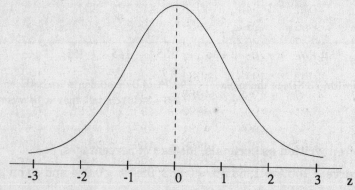

$z$ represents the number of standard deviations above or below the mean.

e.g. a value of $z = 2.4$ is 2.4 S.D.'s above the mean; a value of $z = -1.6$ is 1.6 S.D.'s below the mean.

This table gives the proportion of area under the standard normal curve, between $z = 0$ and any $z$-value:

z represents the number of standard deviations above or below the mean

| z | .00 | .01 | .02 | .03 | .04 | .05 | .06 | .07 | .08 | .09 |
|-----|------|------|------|------|------|------|------|------|------|------|
| 0.0 | .0000 | .0040 | .0080 | .0120 | .0160 | .0199 | .0239 | .0279 | .0319 | .0359 |
| 0.1 | .0398 | .0438 | .0478 | .0517 | .0557 | .0596 | .0636 | .0675 | .0714 | .0754 |
| 0.2 | .0793 | .0832 | .0871 | .0910 | .0948 | .0987 | .1026 | .1064 | .1103 | .1141 |
| 0.3 | .1179 | .1217 | .1255 | .1293 | .1331 | .1368 | .1406 | .1443 | .1480 | .1517 |
| 0.4 | .1554 | .1591 | .1628 | .1664 | .1700 | .1736 | .1772 | .1808 | .1844 | .1879 |
| 0.5 | .1915 | .1950 | .1985 | .2019 | .2054 | .2088 | .2123 | .2157 | .2190 | .2224 |
| 0.6 | .2258 | .2291 | .2324 | .2357 | .2389 | .2422 | .2454 | .2486 | .2518 | .2549 |
| 0.7 | .2580 | .2612 | .2642 | .2673 | .2704 | .2734 | .2764 | .2794 | .2823 | .2852 |
| 0.8 | .2881 | .2910 | .2939 | .2967 | .2996 | .3023 | .3051 | .3078 | .3106 | .3133 |
| 0.9 | .3159 | .3186 | .3212 | .3238 | .3264 | .3289 | .3315 | .3340 | .3365 | .3389 |
| 1.0 | .3413 | .3438 | .3461 | .3485 | .3508 | .3531 | .3554 | .3577 | .3599 | .3621 |
| 1.1 | .3643 | .3665 | .3686 | .3708 | .3729 | .3749 | .3770 | .3790 | .3810 | .3830 |
| 1.2 | .3849 | .3869 | .3888 | .3907 | .3925 | .3944 | .3962 | .3980 | .3997 | .4015 |
| 1.3 | .4032 | .4049 | .4066 | .4082 | .4099 | .4115 | .4131 | .4147 | .4162 | .4177 |
| 1.4 | .4192 | .4207 | .4222 | .4236 | .4251 | .4265 | .4279 | .4292 | .4306 | .4319 |
| 1.5 | .4332 | .4345 | .4357 | .4370 | .4382 | .4394 | .4406 | .4418 | .4429 | .4441 |
| 1.6 | .4452 | .4463 | .4474 | .4484 | .4495 | .4505 | .4515 | .4525 | .4535 | .4545 |
| 1.7 | .4554 | .4564 | .4573 | .4582 | .4591 | .4599 | .4608 | .4616 | .4625 | .4633 |
| 1.8 | .4641 | .4649 | .4656 | .4664 | .4671 | .4678 | .4686 | .4693 | .4699 | .4706 |
| 1.9 | .4713 | .4719 | .4726 | .4732 | .4738 | .4744 | .4750 | .4756 | .4761 | .4767 |
| 2.0 | .4772 | .4778 | .4783 | .4788 | .4793 | .4798 | .4803 | .4808 | .4812 | .4817 |
| 2.1 | .4821 | .4826 | .4830 | .4834 | .4838 | .4842 | .4846 | .4850 | .4854 | .4857 |
| 2.2 | .4861 | .4864 | .4868 | .4871 | .4875 | .4878 | .4881 | .4884 | .4887 | .4890 |
| 2.3 | .4893 | .4896 | .4898 | .4901 | .4904 | .4906 | .4909 | .4911 | .4913 | .4916 |
| 2.4 | .4918 | .4920 | .4922 | .4925 | .4927 | .4929 | .4931 | .4932 | .4934 | .4936 |
| 2.5 | .4938 | .4940 | .4941 | .4943 | .4945 | .4946 | .4948 | .4949 | .4951 | .4952 |
| 2.6 | .4953 | .4955 | .4956 | .4957 | .4959 | .4960 | .4961 | .4962 | .4963 | .4964 |
| 2.7 | .4965 | .4966 | .4967 | .4968 | .4969 | .4970 | .4971 | .4972 | .4973 | .4974 |
| 2.8 | .4974 | .4975 | .4976 | .4977 | .4977 | .4978 | .4979 | .4979 | .4980 | .4981 |
| 2.9 | .4981 | .4982 | .4982 | .4983 | .4984 | .4984 | .4985 | .4985 | .4986 | .4986 |
| 3.0 | .4987 | .4987 | .4987 | .4988 | .4988 | .4989 | .4989 | .4989 | .4990 | .4990 |
| 3.1 | .4990 | .4991 | .4991 | .4991 | .4992 | .4992 | .4992 | .4992 | .4993 | .4993 |
| 3.2 | .4993 | .4993 | .4994 | .4994 | .4994 | .4994 | .4994 | .4995 | .4995 | .4995 |
| 3.3 | .4995 | .4995 | .4995 | .4996 | .4996 | .4996 | .4996 | .4996 | .4996 | .4997 |
| 3.4 | .4997 | .4997 | .4997 | .4997 | .4997 | .4997 | .4997 | .4997 | .4997 | .4998 |

e.g. To find the area between $z = 0$ and $z = 1.74$:
   i)   find 1.7 in left-hand column
   ii)   move across row; read value in 0.04 column (0.4591)

## Use of standard normal distribution tables – some examples

The following examples show how the tables can be used to find the proportion of area under the standard normal distribution curve between any two $z$-values.

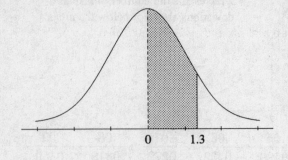

Area between $z=0$ and $z=1.3$ is 0.4032. ie 40.32%

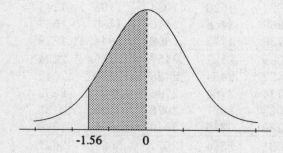

Area between $z=0$ and $z=-1.56$ is 0.4406. ie 44.06%

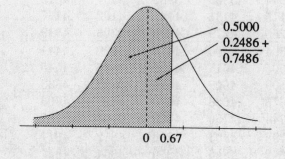

0.5000
$$\frac{0.2486 +}{0.7486}$$

Area below $z=0.67$ is 0.7486. ie 74.86%

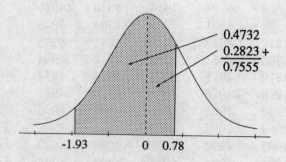

0.4732
$$\frac{0.2823 +}{0.7555}$$

Area between $z=0.78$ and $z=-1.93$ is 0.7555. ie 75.55%

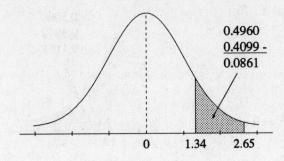

Area between $z=2.65$ and $z=1.34$ is 0.0861. ie 8.61%

0.4960
0.4099 -
0.0861

## Standardisation

Consider the following question:

'What proportion of students are taller than 177 cm ?'

The question corresponds to finding the shaded area in this diagram of the student heights distribution:

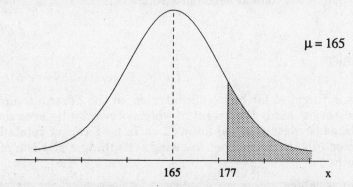

$\mu = 165$

However, the standard normal distribution tables assume that the variable has a mean of 0 and an S.D. of 1. (The heights distribution has a mean of 165 cm and an S.D. of 10 cm).

So, before standard tables can be used, it is necessary to convert the heights distribution into a standard normal distribution. This process is called *standardisation*, and simply measures how many S.D.'s an observation is away from the mean.

To convert a variable $(x)$ into a standardised normal variable $(z)$, use the formula: $z = \dfrac{x - \mu}{\sigma}$

$$\text{i.e. standardised value} = \frac{\text{observation} - \text{mean}}{\text{standard deviation}}$$

In the example: $z = \dfrac{177 - 165}{10} = 1.2$

So, a height of 177 cm is 1.2 standard deviations above the mean height of 165 cm; that is:

$$P(x > 177) \equiv P(z > 1.2)$$

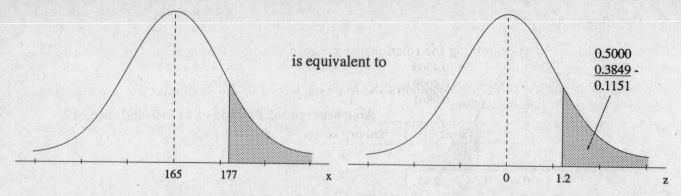

From tables, the area above $z = 1.2$ is 0.1151; this can be interpreted as meaning that approximately 11.5% of students are taller than 177 cm.

So, the steps in using standardisation in the solution of problems can be summarised as:

Step 1: Illustrate the problem with a sketch of the required area.

Step 2: Standardise the variable.

Step 3: Refer to standard normal distribution tables.

Step 4: Interpret the solution in the context of the problem.

## Correlation and regression

All the statistical techniques outlined so far have concentrated on the description of a single variable. However, it is very often necessary to study the extent to which two variables are related to one another e.g. 'Is computing ability related to mathematical ability?' or 'Is lung cancer related to smoking?'. The two variables may be connected in such a way that knowing something about one of them may help to predict the behaviour of the other.

For instance, consider the two variables:

1. the amount that Dale Institute spends on advertising

2. the number of students that enrol on Dale Institute courses

The number of students that enrol may be related to the amount spent on advertising; *correlation* techniques can help to determine (a) whether such a relationship exists and (b) the strength of the relationship.

Once a relationship is shown to exist, *regression* techniques can be used to establish its nature so that predictions can be made. For example, estimating the number of students that can be expected to enrol for a given amount spent on advertising.

### Independent and dependent variables

Since two variables are being considered, it is important to know which is the independent variable and which is the dependent variable. The *independent variable* is the variable that is not affected by changes in the other variable; the *dependent variable* is the variable that is affected by changes in the other variable. In the example, a change in advertising expenditure is likely to bring about a change in the number of students; however, a change in the number of students is not likely to directly affect advertising expenditure.

So, 'advertising expenditure' is the independent variable and 'student enrolments' is the dependent variable. In this case, there is said to be a *causal* (or *direct*) relationship between the two variables; that is, a change in the amount spent on advertising *causes* a change in the number of students enrolling.

## Scatter diagrams

The simplest method of examining the relationship between two variables is to construct a *scatter diagram*.

For instance, consider Table 7 which shows the marks obtained by ten Computer Science students in theory and practical examinations:

| Student | Theory score | Practical score |
|---------|--------------|-----------------|
| A | 68 | 73 |
| B | 58 | 51 |
| C | 71 | 55 |
| D | 44 | 32 |
| E | 61 | 59 |
| F | 80 | 84 |
| G | 47 | 43 |
| H | 52 | 51 |
| I | 75 | 66 |
| J | 64 | 47 |

*Table 7*

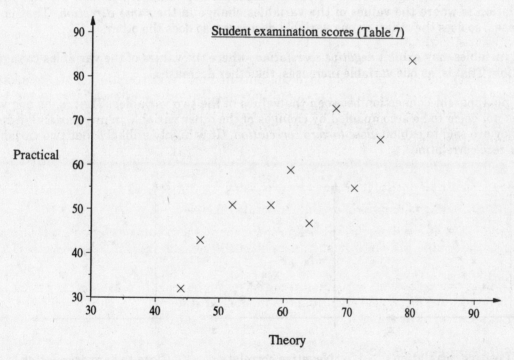

*Figure 20: Scatter diagram*

The basic function of a scatter diagram is to establish visually whether there is a pattern within the data values. The more definite the pattern of points, the more closely the two variables are likely to be related.

In this case, there does appear to be some sort of pattern since the points tend to slope upwards from left to right. This is explained by the fact that students who score low marks in one examination also seem to be those scoring low marks in the other examination; similarly, for high-scoring students. So, there is evidence of correlation between these two variables.

*Note*

i)    Each pair of values is treated as coordinates and plotted as a single point.

ii)   The axes do not need to be scaled from an origin of (0, 0).

iii)  In general, the horizontal axis is used for the independent variable and the vertical axis used for the dependent variable.

iv)   As in this example, it is not always easy to decide which is the independent variable and which is the dependent variable. For example, does a student's score in the practical examination depend on their score in the theory examination, or vice-versa?

v)    Evidence of correlation does not imply that a causal relationship exists. In the example, for instance, a low score in the theory examination is unlikely to be *directly* responsible for a low score in the practical examination. Both scores are linked to other variables such as general intelligence, ability in examinations etc; these factors are likely to influence the students' scores in both of the examinations. Where there appears to be correlation between two variables, but one variable does not *directly* affect the other, there is said to be a *spurious* (or *indirect*) relationship between the variables.

## Types and strength of correlation

In the example, the scatter diagram shows evidence of *positive correlation* between the two variables. Positive correlation is where the values of the variables change in the *same direction*. That is, as one variable increases, so does the other; as one variable decreases, so does the other.

Other pairs of variables may exhibit *negative correlation*, where the values of the variables change in the *opposite direction*. That is, as one variable increases, the other decreases.

There may be no apparent connection between the values of the two variables. That is, as one variable changes it does not seem to be accompanied by changes of the other variable in any particular direction. In this case, they are said to exhibit *close-to-zero correlation*. (It is highly unlikely that two variables will exhibit exactly zero correlation).

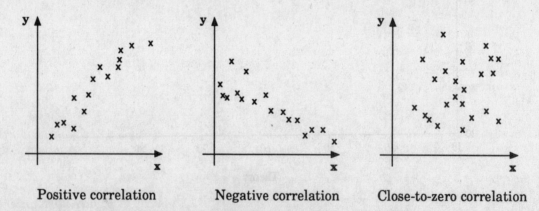

Positive correlation          Negative correlation          Close-to-zero correlation

There is obviously an endless variety of scatter diagrams that can be drawn; some will show stronger relationships than others. The closer the plotted points are to a straight line, the stronger the relationship between the two variables. When the plotted points lie exactly in a straight line, (very unlikely in statistical studies), they are said to exhibit *perfect correlation*.

The following diagrams show some possibilities:

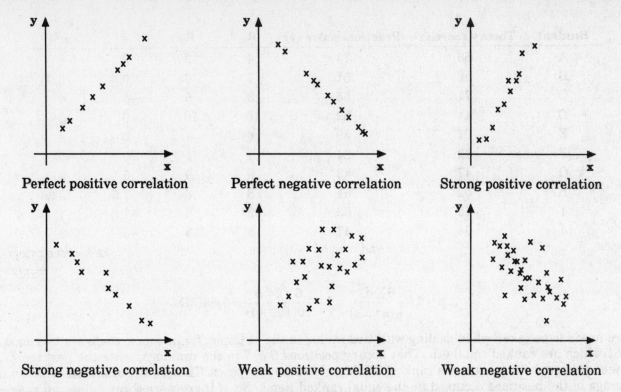

Perfect positive correlation  Perfect negative correlation  Strong positive correlation

Strong negative correlation  Weak positive correlation  Weak negative correlation

It is straightforward to construct a scatter diagram in order to visualise the relationship between two variables. However, there is a need for a precise measure of the strength of the relationship. Such a measure is called a *correlation coefficient*; two of the more common coefficients are described below:

## Measures of correlation (1) – Spearman's coefficient

The full name of this coefficient is *Spearman's rank correlation coefficient* and, as its name implies, involves ranking the values of the variables in order. For instance, using the student examination score data of Table 7, the method can be summarised as follows (data – Table 7a):

Step 1      Write, in columns, the values of the two variables (call these 'x' and 'y')

Step 2      Arrange the x-values in rank order and write them in a column (call these $R_x$) (the highest value has rank 1, the lowest has rank $n$; $n$ is the number of data items)

Step 3      Repeat Step 2 for the y-values (call these $R_y$)

Step 4      Calculate a 'd' column, where $d$ is the difference between the two sets of rankings

$(d = R_x - R_y)$

Step 5      Calculate a $d^2$ column

Step 6      Calculate $\Sigma d^2$, the sum of the $d^2$ column

Step 8      Calculate *Spearman's rank correlation coefficient* ($\rho$) using the formula:

$$\rho = 1 - \frac{6\Sigma d^2}{n(n^2 - 1)}$$

($\rho$ is rho, the Greek letter $r$, and is pronounced 'row')

215

| Student | Theory score (x) | Practical score (y) | $R_x$ | $R_y$ | d | $d^2$ |
|---|---|---|---|---|---|---|
| A | 68 | 73 | 4 | 2 | 2 | 4 |
| B | 58 | 51 | 7 | 6= | 0.5 | 0.25 |
| C | 71 | 55 | 3 | 5 | −2 | 4 |
| D | 44 | 32 | 10 | 10 | 0 | 0 |
| E | 61 | 59 | 6 | 4 | 2 | 4 |
| F | 80 | 84 | 1 | 1 | 0 | 0 |
| G | 47 | 43 | 9 | 9 | 0 | 0 |
| H | 52 | 51 | 8 | 6= | 1.5 | 2.25 |
| I | 75 | 66 | 2 | 3 | −1 | 1 |
| J | 64 | 47 | 5 | 8 | −3 | 9 |

$$\Sigma d^2 = 24.5$$

*Table 7a*

$$\therefore \rho = 1 - \frac{6\Sigma d^2}{n(n^2-1)} = 1 - \frac{6\times 24.5}{10(100-1)} \approx 0.85 (2D)$$

Care needs to be taken when dealing with tied ranks; in the example, for instance, there are two marks of 51 which are ranked equal 6th. They occupy positions 6 & 7 in the rankings, since the next score is ranked 8th; so, both are given a rank of 6.5 for calculation purposes. That is, the allocated rank is the average of the positions occupied by the equal ranked items. So, if there were three values all ranked equal 4th, each would be given a rank of 5 (the average of 4, 5 & 6).

### Interpreting the correlation coefficient

The value of the correlation coefficient is *always* between −1 and +1, inclusive; that is, $-1 \le \rho \le 1$. The interpretation of the value is shown on this number line:

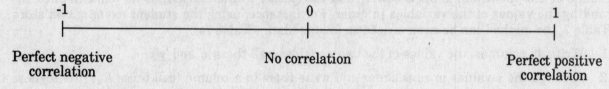

Perfect negative correlation      No correlation      Perfect positive correlation

The closer the value of $\rho$ is to −1 or 1, the stronger the relationship between the variables. For example:

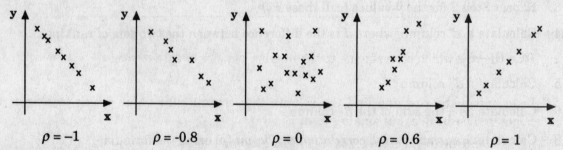

$\rho = -1$      $\rho = -0.8$      $\rho = 0$      $\rho = 0.6$      $\rho = 1$

As a rough guide:

| Value of correlation coefficient | Evidence of relationship (ignoring sign) |
|---|---|
| 0.0 to 0.2 | Very weak |
| 0.2 to 0.4 | Quite weak |
| 0.4 to 0.7 | Reasonable |
| 0.7 to 0.9 | Quite strong |
| 0.9 to 1.0 | Very strong |

So, in the example, a value of $\rho = 0.85$ seems to indicate that there is quite strong evidence that there is a relationship between the students' theory examination scores and the practical examination scores.

Note, however, that a large correlation coefficient on its own does not necessarily imply a strong relationship between the two variables. The correlation coefficient is affected by the number of data items (since it is easier for a small sample size to show evidence of correlation than it is for a large sample; for example, it is easier for five points on a scatter diagram to look correlated than it is for fifty points). Its correct interpretation can therefore be difficult when the number of data items is small. So, tables have been produced which allow a certain amount of confidence to be attached to the interpretation; the tables take account of sample size.

The table below can be used to interpret the significance of the calculated value of Spearman's rank correlation coefficient (ignoring sign) and takes into account the sample size:

### Critical values for Spearman's rank correlation coefficient

(Value of $\rho$ must be > the critical value to be significant)

| n | Level of significance | | |
|---|---|---|---|
| | 10% | 5% | 1% |
| 5 | 0.900 | 1.000 | |
| 6 | 0.829 | 0.886 | 1.000 |
| 7 | 0.714 | 0.786 | 0.929 |
| 8 | 0.643 | 0.738 | 0.881 |
| 9 | 0.600 | 0.683 | 0.833 |
| 10 | 0.564 | 0.648 | 0.746 |
| 12 | 0.506 | 0.591 | 0.777 |
| 14 | 0.456 | 0.544 | 0.715 |
| 16 | 0.425 | 0.506 | 0.665 |
| 18 | 0.399 | 0.475 | 0.625 |
| 20 | 0.377 | 0.450 | 0.591 |
| 22 | 0.359 | 0.428 | 0.562 |
| 24 | 0.343 | 0.409 | 0.537 |
| 26 | 0.329 | 0.392 | 0.515 |
| 28 | 0.317 | 0.377 | 0.496 |
| 30 | 0.306 | 0.364 | 0.478 |

To use the table:

Step 1: Find the row which corresponds to the number of pairs of data items (n)

*e.g. n = 10.*

Step 2: Read across the row and find the column that contains the value which is nearest to the calculated value of $\rho$, but smaller than it.

*e.g. $\rho$ = 0.85: nearest value (0.746) is in last column.*

Step 3: Look at the column heading to find the significance of the result.

*e.g. Level of significance is 1%.*

*Note:*

Suppose that the correlation coefficient is calculated from sample pairs of data items and that the calculated value of $\rho$ suggests that there is a relationship between the two variables. There are four possibilities:

a) there is no relationship between the two variables

b) there is *no* relationship between the two variables but the sample data items just happen, because of the sample size, to produce a value of ρ which suggests that there *is* a relationship

c) there is a relationship between the two variables

d) there *is* a relationship between the two variables but the sample data items just happen, because of the sample size, to produce a value of ρ which suggests that there is *no* relationship

The significance level gives an indication of how likely it is that the value of the correlation coefficient has been affected by the sample size. For instance, in the example, the result is significant at the 1% level. This means that there is only a 1 in 100 chance that the calculated value for the correlation coefficient has been affected by the sample size. In other words, the conclusion:

'There is a relationship between the students' theory exam scores and practical exam scores'

has only a 1% chance of being incorrect (i.e. a 99% chance of being correct).

## Measures of correlation (2) – Pearson's coefficient

The full name of this coefficient is *Pearson's product moment correlation coefficient*. Again, using the student examination score data of Table 7, the method can be summarised as follows (data – Table 7b):

Step 1: Write, in columns, the values of the two variables (call these '$x$' and '$y$')

Step 2: Calculate columns for: (a) $x^2$ (b) $y^2$ (c) $xy$

Step 3: Calculate: (a) $\Sigma x$ (b) $\Sigma y$ (c) $\Sigma x^2$ (d) $\Sigma y^2$ (e) $\Sigma xy$

Step 4: Calculate: (a) $\bar{x}$ (b) $\bar{y}$

Step 8: Calculate Pearson's correlation coefficient ($r$) using the formula:

$$r = \frac{\frac{\sum xy}{n} - \bar{x}.\bar{y}}{\sqrt{\frac{\sum x^2}{n} - \bar{x}^2} \times \sqrt{\frac{\sum y^2}{n} - \bar{y}^2}}$$

| Student | Theory score (x) | Practical score (y) | $x^2$ | $y^2$ | xy |
|---------|------------------|---------------------|-------|-------|------|
| A | 68 | 73 | 4624 | 5329 | 4964 |
| B | 58 | 51 | 3364 | 2601 | 2958 |
| C | 71 | 55 | 5041 | 3025 | 3905 |
| D | 44 | 32 | 1936 | 1024 | 1408 |
| E | 61 | 59 | 3721 | 3481 | 3599 |
| F | 80 | 84 | 6400 | 7056 | 6720 |
| G | 47 | 43 | 2209 | 1849 | 2021 |
| H | 52 | 51 | 2704 | 2601 | 2652 |
| I | 75 | 66 | 5625 | 4356 | 4950 |
| J | 64 | 47 | 4096 | 2209 | 3008 |
| | 620 | 561 | 39720 | 33531 | 36185 |

*Table 7b*

$$\bar{x} = \frac{620}{10} = 62; \quad \bar{y} = \frac{561}{10} = 56.1$$

$$r = \frac{\frac{36185}{10} - 62 \times 56.1}{\sqrt{\frac{39720}{10} - 62^2} \times \sqrt{\frac{33531}{10} - 56.1^2}} = \frac{140.3}{\sqrt{128} \times \sqrt{205.89}} = 0.86 (2D)$$

The possible values of Pearson's coefficient also lie between −1 and +1. The table below can be used to interpret the significance of the result (ignoring sign). Again, sample size is taken into account:

### Critical values for Pearson's product moment correlation coefficient

(Value of $r$ must be > the critical value to be significant)

| n − 2 | Level of significance | | | |
|---|---|---|---|---|
| | 10% | 5% | 1% | 0.1% |
| 2 | 0.900 | 0.950 | 0.990 | 0.999 |
| 3 | 0.805 | 0.878 | 0.959 | 0.991 |
| 4 | 0.729 | 0.811 | 0.917 | 0.974 |
| 5 | 0.669 | 0.754 | 0.875 | 0.951 |
| 6 | 0.621 | 0.707 | 0.834 | 0.924 |
| 7 | 0.582 | 0.666 | 0.798 | 0.898 |
| 8 | 0.549 | 0.632 | 0.765 | 0.872 |
| 9 | 0.521 | 0.602 | 0.735 | 0.847 |
| 10 | 0.497 | 0.576 | 0.708 | 0.823 |
| 11 | 0.476 | 0.553 | 0.684 | 0.801 |
| 12 | 0.457 | 0.532 | 0.661 | 0.780 |
| 13 | 0.441 | 0.514 | 0.641 | 0.760 |
| 14 | 0.426 | 0.497 | 0.623 | 0.742 |
| 15 | 0.412 | 0.482 | 0.606 | 0.725 |
| 16 | 0.400 | 0.468 | 0.590 | 0.708 |
| 17 | 0.389 | 0.456 | 0.575 | 0.693 |
| 18 | 0.378 | 0.444 | 0.561 | 0.679 |
| 19 | 0.369 | 0.433 | 0.549 | 0.665 |
| 20 | 0.360 | 0.423 | 0.537 | 0.652 |
| 25 | 0.323 | 0.381 | 0.487 | 0.597 |
| 30 | 0.296 | 0.349 | 0.449 | 0.554 |
| 35 | 0.275 | 0.325 | 0.418 | 0.519 |
| 40 | 0.257 | 0.304 | 0.393 | 0.490 |
| 45 | 0.243 | 0.288 | 0.372 | 0.465 |
| 50 | 0.231 | 0.273 | 0.354 | 0.443 |
| 60 | 0.211 | 0.250 | 0.325 | 0.408 |
| 70 | 0.195 | 0.232 | 0.302 | 0.380 |
| 80 | 0.183 | 0.217 | 0.283 | 0.357 |
| 90 | 0.173 | 0.205 | 0.267 | 0.338 |
| 100 | 0.164 | 0.195 | 0.254 | 0.321 |

*Note:*

i)  The method of reading and interpreting the table is similar to that described earlier in the case of Spearman's coefficient.

ii) The left-hand column represents values of $n − 2$; so, in the example, since there are 10 students it is necessary to locate row 8.

In the example, the table value which is nearest to, but smaller than, the calculated value (0.86) is 0.765. So, the result is significant at the 1% level. Therefore, as before, the conclusion:

'There is a relationship between the students' theory exam scores and practical exam scores'

has only a 1% chance of being incorrect (i.e. a 99% chance of being correct).

## Which correlation coefficient to use?

There are several points to note:

a)   Pearson's correlation coefficient measures the degree to which two variables are linked by a linear relationship. For instance, consider the two scatter diagrams shown below:

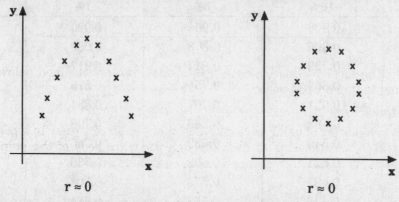

In each case the value of $r$ would be close-to-zero, although there is clearly a relationship between the two variables. So, if the data show any sign of a non-linear relationship then Pearson's correlation coefficient will give misleading values.

b)   Where a linear relationship is indicated, Pearson's $r$ gives a more precise value for the amount of correlation than Spearman's $\rho$. This has to be weighed against the relative complexity of the calculations needed to obtain it.

c)   Spearman's $\rho$ can be used:

i)    where it is difficult or impossible to assign measured values to variables;

ii)   to give a rough idea of the degree of correlation prior to calculating Pearson's $r$.

## The coefficient of determination

This is a helpful means of assessing how much of the change in one variable can be explained by changes in the other variable. It is calculated simply by squaring the correlation coefficient.

For instance, in the case of the students' theory and practical examination scores, $r = 0.86$. So, the coefficient of determination = $0.86^2 = 0.74$. This means that 74% of the variation in the students' practical examination scores can be explained by variations in their theory examination scores. That is, 26% of the variation must be attributed to other factors.

## Linear regression

Scatter diagrams and correlation coefficients show whether there is evidence of a linear relationship between two variables; that is, they establish whether the pairs of values of the variables lie approximately along a straight line.

*Linear regression* is the art of line-fitting and is a collection of techniques that are used to determine precisely which straight line fits the points of the scatter diagram most closely. For this reason, the straight line is called the *line-of-best-fit*. Once the line-of-best-fit is determined, it is then possible to use it for forecasting purposes.

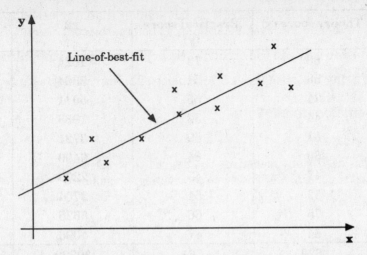

Several methods of fitting straight lines to data points exist; two are outlined below. The degree of accuracy varies according to the method used:

i) *The 'eye-ball' method*

   In this method it is a matter of using personal judgement to place a ruler in a position on the scatter diagram in a position which seems to pass through the main body of the points. Clearly, the accuracy of this method is questionable since it relies on individual skill.

ii) *The method of least-squares*

   This is the method favoured by statisticians. It is based on the idea that, wherever the fitted line is drawn, each point will be a certain distance (called its deviation) from the line. Some points will lie above the line (positive deviation), others will lie below the line (negative deviation). In order to prevent the positive deviations and negative deviations cancelling out, each deviation is squared. Calculating the total of these squared deviations gives a measure of how well the line fits the points. The method of least-squares ensures that the line is chosen such that the total of the squared deviations is as small as possible.

## The method of least-squares

The equation of the line-of-best-fit has the form: $y = mx + c$. This is determined by using the pairs of data values to calculate:

   i)   the gradient ($m$)

   ii)  the intercept on the $y$-axis (c)

The formulas make use of calculations already used in determining Pearson's correlation coefficient; so, not much extra work is involved if this has been previously calculated. Using the student examination score data of Table 7, the least-squares method can be summarised as follows (data – Table 7c):

Step 1:   Write, in columns, the values of the two variables (call these '$x$' and '$y$')

Step 2:   Calculate columns for: (a) $x^2$ (b) $xy$

Step 3:   Calculate: (a) $\Sigma x$ (b) $\Sigma y$ (c) $\Sigma x^2$ (d) $\Sigma xy$

Step 4:   Calculate: (a) $\bar{x}$  (b) $\bar{y}$

Step 8:   Calculate the gradient (m) using the formula:

$$m = \frac{\sum xy - n\bar{x}\,\bar{y}}{\sum x^2 - n\bar{x}^2}$$

Step 9:   Calculate the intercept (c) using the formula:

$$c = \bar{y} - m\bar{x}$$

221

| Student | Theory score (x) | Practical score (y) | x2 | xy |
|---------|------------------|---------------------|------|------|
| A | 68 | 73 | 4624 | 4964 |
| B | 58 | 51 | 3364 | 2958 |
| C | 71 | 55 | 5041 | 3905 |
| D | 44 | 32 | 1936 | 1408 |
| E | 61 | 59 | 3721 | 3599 |
| F | 80 | 84 | 6400 | 6720 |
| G | 47 | 43 | 2209 | 2021 |
| H | 52 | 51 | 2704 | 2652 |
| I | 75 | 66 | 5625 | 4950 |
| J | 64 | 47 | 4096 | 3008 |
|  | 620 | 561 | 39720 | 36185 |

*Table 7c*

$$\bar{x} = \frac{620}{10} = 62; \quad \bar{y} = \frac{561}{10} = 56.1$$

$$m = \frac{36185 - 10 \times 62 \times 56.1}{39720 - 10 \times 62^2} = \frac{1403}{1280} = 1.096 \text{ (3D)}$$

$$c = 56.1 - 1.096 \times 62 = -11.852 \text{ (3D)}$$

So, the equation of the line-of-best-fit is:

$$y = 1.096x - 11.852$$

This is shown on the scatter diagram below:

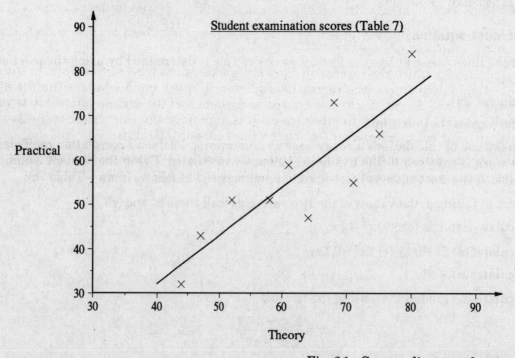

*Fig. 21 - Scatter diagram showing line-of-best-fit*

To draw the line-of-best-fit on the scatter diagram it is a simple matter of plotting two points. In each case:

i)   choose a value of $x$

ii)  use the regression equation to calculate the corresponding value of $y$

iii) plot the point $(x, y)$ on the scatter diagram

Joining the two points gives the position of the line-of-best-fit.

So, in the example:

a)  when $x = 40$, $y = 1.096 \times 40 - 11.852 = 31.99$ (2D)

b)  when $x = 80$, $y = 1.096 \times 80 - 11.852 = 75.83$ (2D)

*Note:*

i)   The line-of-best-fit *always* passes through the point $(\bar{x}, \bar{y})$; this is a useful method of checking its correctness.

ii)  Care should be taken in choosing the number of decimal places to work with when calculating the values of $m$ and $c$. Rounding off too soon may cause error accumulation in later calculations.

iii) The formulas give the regression equation for the value of $y$ in terms of $x$ (' the regression line of y upon $x$'). If the 'regression line of $x$ upon $y$' is required, to give values of $x$ in terms of $y$, then different formulas are needed in the calculation procedure.

iv)  It is pointless fitting a line to the data if the value of the correlation coefficient indicates that there is little evidence of a relationship between the two variables. For this reason, it is useful to calculate the correlation coefficient prior to attempting to fit a line to the data.

Once calculated, the regression line can be used for forecasting purposes. For example, consider the case of a student who obtains a score of 63 in the theory examination but is absent for the practical examination. Using the regression equation, or by reading the graph, a forecast can be obtained for how that student might have performed in the practical examination.

When $x = 63$, $y = 1.096 \times 63 - 11.852 = 57.2$ (1D); so, the best estimate for the student's score is 57.

Caution needs to be taken in using regression for forecasting purposes. There are two main factors that can affect the validity of the value obtained:

1)  the range of values for which the regression equation is likely to be true; for instance, in the case of the student examination scores, the regression equation is based on data values that lie approximately between 40 and 80. So, it may not be wise to assume that the same relationship is valid for values that lie outside this range. In other words, it is appropriate to *interpolate* (estimate values inside the range), but not to *extrapolate* (estimate values outside the range).

2)  the sample size; for instance, the example regression equation is based on only ten pairs of data values. A larger sample size would give a more reliable relationship.

# Unit 7: Inferential statistics 1 – Probability

> This section aims to help you to:
>
> 1. understand the principles of probability
> 2. distinguish between empirical and theoretical approaches to probability
> 3. become familair with the basic laws of probability
> 4. understand what is meant by a 'probability distribution'
> 5. be able to use the Binomial and Poisson probability distributions

## Simple ideas of probability

Many aspects of life are uncertain and it is necessary, in many instances, to be able to predict as accurately as possible the outcomes of such things as general elections, the weather, horse races, experiments involving a new drug, and so on. Probability is a branch of Mathematics that is concerned with analysing such outcomes and the degree of certainty that can be attached to them.

People often express the degree of certainty of outcomes in everyday language such as:

| | |
|---|---|
| Maybe | No chance |
| Perhaps | One in a million |
| Even stevens | Fifty-fifty |
| Probably | Possibly |

So, for example:

'The traffic is likely to be heavy in town on Saturday morning'

'It looks as though it might rain this afternoon'

'Perhaps it will be too expensive to stay in London'

'There's no chance of Switzerland beating England'

'My program will probably work this time'

'You'll be lucky!'

'There's a fifty-fifty chance that a tossed coin will come down heads'

Most of these statements are rather imprecise and are judgements based on past experience. It is necessary, therefore, to try to develop ways of expressing the degree of certainty with more precision.

Consider the case of tossing a coin. Most people, whether they have studied probability or not, would say that the chance of the coin landing 'heads' is fifty-fifty. There are two ways of arriving at this conclusion: the *empirical* approach and the *theoretical* approach.

## The empirical approach to probability

Using this approach, a coin is tossed a certain number of times and the result observed in each case.

The author carried out such an experiment 50 times, the results being as follows:

|   |   |   |   |   |   |   |   |   |   |
|---|---|---|---|---|---|---|---|---|---|
| T | H | T | T | H | H | H | H | T | H |
| H | H | H | T | H | H | T | T | T | T |
| T | T | T | T | H | T | T | T | H | H |
| T | T | T | H | T | T | H | H | H | T |
| H | T | H | H | H | H | T | H | T | T |

In this sample of throws, the coin has shown 'heads' on 24 occasions out of the 50 trials so the chance (or *probability*) that the coin shows heads is $\frac{24}{50} = 0.48$.

The results can be shown another way by calculating the *relative frequency* of heads; this is the proportion of heads obtained at each stage of the experiment. For example, after 5 throws, 2 heads have appeared; so, the relative frequency of heads is $\frac{2}{5} = 0.4$. Tabulating the relative frequencies gives:

| No. of throws | 1 | 2 | 3 | 4 | 5 | 6 | 7 | 8 | 9 | 10 |
|---|---|---|---|---|---|---|---|---|---|---|
| No. of heads | 0 | 1 | 1 | 1 | 2 | 3 | 4 | 5 | 5 | 6 |
| Relative frequency | 0 | 0.5 | 0.33 | 0.25 | 0.4 | 0.5 | 0.57 | 0.63 | 0.55 | 0.6 |

| No. of throws | 11 | 12 | 13 | 14 | 15 | 16 | 17 | 18 | 19 | 20 |
|---|---|---|---|---|---|---|---|---|---|---|
| No. of heads | 7 | 8 | 9 | 9 | 10 | 11 | 11 | 11 | 11 | 11 |
| Relative frequency | 0.63 | 0.67 | 0.69 | 0.64 | 0.67 | 0.69 | 0.65 | 0.61 | 0.58 | 0.55 |

| No. of throws | 41 | 42 | 43 | 44 | 45 | 46 | 47 | 48 | 49 | 50 |
|---|---|---|---|---|---|---|---|---|---|---|
| No. of heads | 19 | 19 | 20 | 21 | 22 | 23 | 23 | 24 | 24 | 24 |
| Relative frequency | 0.46 | 0.45 | 0.47 | 0.48 | 0.49 | 0.5 | 0.49 | 0.5 | 0.49 | 0.48 |

In graphical form:

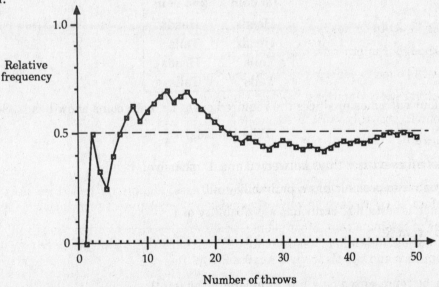

The graph shows that the fluctuations in the relative frequency decrease as the number of throws increases. That is, any runs of heads or tails later in the experiment do not have as much effect as similar runs early in the experiment. For instance, the run of 4 heads in the first 10 throws changes the relative frequency from 0.25 to 0.43 (a change of 0.18); on the other hand, the run of 4 heads in the last 10 throws changes the relative frequency from 0.45 to 0.5 (a change of only 0.05).

So, over a large number of trials the relative frequency begins to settle down; the value that it settles down to is the probability of the coin showing heads (that is, 0.5). In general, the probability of a certain event occurring is given by the long-term relative frequency. The estimate of the probability improves as the number of trials increases.

In the case of tossing a coin, it is not necessary to employ an empirical approach since a theoretical approach can be taken. However, there are plenty of situations where the empirical approach is the only feasible way of obtaining an estimate of the probability. For instance, suppose that a computer user wants to assess the likelihood that a newly-purchased floppy disc is faulty; an empirical estimate can be obtained by calculating the number of faulty discs bought as a proportion of the total number bought. As with coin-tossing, the accuracy of the estimate improves as the number of trials increases. (In this case, a trial is defined as 'buying a disc'):

$$P(\text{faulty disc}) = \frac{\text{No. of faulty discs bought}}{\text{No. of discs bought altogether}}$$

Note that P(faulty disc) is shorthand notation for 'the probability of a disc being faulty'.

## The theoretical approach to probability

There are only two possible outcomes when a coin is tossed (heads or tails), both equally likely.

So, the probability of it showing heads is:    $P(\text{heads}) = \frac{1}{2}$

In general, the probability of an event occurring is given by:

$$P(\text{event}) = \frac{\text{No. of outcomes producing that event}}{\text{Total no. of outcomes}}$$

Now consider the case of tossing a pair of coins.; what is P(both coins showing heads)?

There are four possible outcomes to this experiment:

| 1st coin | 2nd coin |
|----------|----------|
| Heads    | Heads    |
| Heads    | Tails    |
| Tails    | Heads    |
| Tails    | Tails    |

Only one of the four outcomes produces the required event i.e. both coins show heads. So:

$$P(\text{both heads}) = \frac{1}{4}$$

The probability of an event is *always* between 0 and 1, inclusive:

i)    an event which is impossible has a probability of 0

ii)    an event which is certain to occur has a probability of 1

So, for any given event X:

$$0 \leq P(X) \leq 1$$

Probabilities can be represented on a line numbered from 0 to 1:

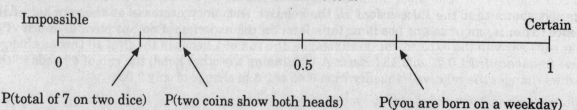

# Some probability terminology

## Possibility spaces

A *possibility space* is the set of all possible outcomes to an experiment. For instance, if two dice are rolled together the possibility space for the experiment is:

|  |  | 2nd die | | | | | |
|---|---|---|---|---|---|---|---|
|  |  | 1 | 2 | 3 | 4 | 5 | 6 |
|  | 1 | (1, 1) | (1, 2) | (1, 3) | (1, 4) | (1, 5) | (1, 6) |
|  | 2 | (2, 1) | (2, 2) | (2, 3) | (2, 4) | (2, 5) | (2, 6) |
| 1st die | 3 | (3, 1) | (3, 2) | (3, 3) | (3, 4) | (3, 5) | (3, 6) |
|  | 4 | (4, 1) | (4, 2) | (4, 3) | (4, 4) | (4, 5) | (4, 6) |
|  | 5 | (5, 1) | (5, 2) | (5, 3) | (5, 4) | (5, 5) | (5, 6) |
|  | 6 | (6, 1) | (6, 2) | (6, 3) | (6, 4) | (6, 5) | (6, 6) |

The first number in each bracket is the outcome of rolling the first die; the second number is the outcome of rolling the second die.

It is then quite straightforward to calculate the probability of any desired event occurring.

For example:

$$P(\text{total of 7 on two dice}) = \frac{6}{36}$$

No. of ways of getting a total of seven

No. of possibilities altogether

$$\approx 0.17$$

So, if two dice are rolled together 100 times, a total of seven could be expected to occur about 17 times.

## Complementary events

Events which, between them, cover the entire set of possibilities are said to be *complementary events*. So, 'heads' and 'tails' are complementary events when a coin is tossed since no other event is possible.

Since either 'head' or 'tail' is certain to occur:

$$P(\text{head}) + P(\text{tail}) = 1$$

and in general:

$$P(\text{event X occurring}) = 1 - P(\text{event X not occurring})$$

For example, if two dice are rolled, $P(\text{not obtaining a total of 7}) = 1 - P(\text{obtaining a total of 7})$
$$= 1 - 0.17$$
$$= 0.83$$

## Independent events

If the outcome of event A does not influence the outcome of event B, they are are said to be *independent events*. For instance, if a coin is tossed and a dice is rolled, the outcome of tossing the coin does not influence the outcome of rolling the dice; these are, therefore, independent events. So, events A and B are:

Event A:   obtaining a head
Event B:   rolling a 6

In this case, A and B are independent events.

## Mutually exclusive events

If two events cannot occur together, they are said to be *mutually exclusive*. For instance, if a single dice is rolled once and the events A and B are:

Event A:   rolling an even number
Event B:   rolling an odd number

In this case, A and B are mutually exclusive events.

# Combining probabilities

## Probability trees

Consider families which have two children; assume that the P(girl) = 0.5 and P(boy) = 0.5.

A *probability tree* is another type of diagram which shows all the possible outcomes, in this case:

It is assumed that the two events are independent; that is, the first child being a boy or a girl does not influence the second child being a boy or a girl.

Each of the four outcomes (B, B), (B, G), (G, B) or (G, G) is equally likely, so:

$$P(B, B) = \frac{1}{4}$$

$$P(B, G) = \frac{1}{4}$$

$$P(G, B) = \frac{1}{4}$$

$$P(G, G) = \frac{1}{4}$$

It can be seen that, for example, P(both children are boys) can be obtained by multiplying the two separate probabilities P(1st child is a boy) and P(2nd child being a boy):

$$P(\text{both boys}) = P(\text{1st is a boy}) \times P(\text{2nd is a boy})$$

$$= 0.5 \times 0.5$$

$$= 0.25$$

This is an example of the basic multiplication law for the probabilities of separate events (see below).

## The basic multiplication law

If A and B are two independent events, the probability of *both* events occurring is given by:

$$P(A \text{ } and \text{ } B) = P(A) \times P(B)$$

For obvious reasons, the multiplication law is sometimes referred to as the '*and*' law.

## The basic addition law

If A and B are two mutually exclusive events, the probability of either one *or* the other of the events occurring is given by:

$$P(A \text{ } or \text{ } B) = P(A) + P(B)$$

For example, if a single die is rolled once and events A and B are:

Event A: rolling a 3

Event B: rolling a 5

Events A and B are mutually exclusive since the dice cannot show a 3 and a 5 simultaneously; so:

$$P(3 \text{ or } 5) \quad = \frac{1}{6} + \frac{1}{6}$$

$$\approx 0.33$$

For obvious reasons, the addition law is sometimes referred to as the '*or*' law.

## The general addition law

If a single dice is rolled once and a coin is tossed once and events A and B are:

Event A: rolling a 6

Event B: obtaining a head

Events A and B are not mutually exclusive since both events can occur simultaneously. The situation can be shown on a possibility space diagram:

|  |  | **Die** | | | | | |
|---|---|---|---|---|---|---|---|
|  |  | 1 | 2 | 3 | 4 | 5 | 6 |
| **Coin** | H | (H, 1) | (H, 2) | (H, 3) | (H, 4) | (H, 5) | (H, 6) |
|  | T | (T, 1) | (T, 2) | (T, 3) | (T, 4) | (T, 5) | (T, 6) |

Since the two events overlap, (circled in the diagram), adding the probabilities together would count the event of (H, 6) twice; so, the probability must be calculated as follows:

$$P(\text{head or 6}) = \frac{6}{12} + \frac{2}{12} - \frac{1}{12} = \frac{7}{12} \approx 0.58$$

P(head)        P(6)        P(head *and* 6)

So, in general, the addition law for two events A and B is:

$$P(A \text{ or } B) = P(A) + P(B) - P(A \text{ and } B)$$

In the example,

$$P(\text{a head or a } 6) = P(\text{head}) + P(6) - P(\text{head and } 6)$$

$$= \frac{6}{12} + \frac{2}{12} - \frac{1}{2} \times \frac{1}{6}$$

$$= \frac{7}{12}$$

$$\approx 0.58$$

## The general multiplication law

The basic multiplication law only applies when the two events are independent. When the events are not independent, a modified version is necessary:

$$P(A \text{ and } B) = P(A) \times P(B \mid A)$$

where $B \mid A$ means 'B given A' and $P(B \mid A)$ is called a *conditional probability*.

For example, consider the case of drawing two cards from a full deck of 52 cards, one after the other, *without replacing* the first card. Suppose that events A and B are:

Event A:    drawing the Queen of Spades

Event B:    drawing the Queen of Hearts

It is required to calculate P(obtaining the Queen of Spades and the Queen of Hearts in that order).

The two events are not independent since the probability of drawing the Queen of Hearts on the second card is dependent on whether the Queen of Spades is drawn on the first card; so:

$$P(\text{QoS and QoH}) = P(\text{QoS}) \times P(\text{QoH} \mid \text{QoS})$$

P(drawing the QoS)

P(drawing the QoH given that the QoS has already been drawn)

$$\backslash \ P(\text{QoS and QoH}) = \frac{1}{52} \yen \frac{1}{51} \approx 0.00038$$

If A and B are independent the conditional probability given by $P(B \mid A)$ is equivalent to $P(B)$ since the probability of event B occurring is the same whether or not event A has occurred. The general multiplication law then takes the same form as the basic multiplication law.

Note also that $P(A \text{ and } B) = P(B) \times P(A \mid B)$

## Expectation

The *expectation*, or *expected value*, of an event is its long-term value.

For example, suppose that a two-person game is based on a standard deck of playing cards; one person is the 'dealer', the other person is the 'gambler'. A card is drawn and if it is a heart then the dealer pays a prize of £5 to the gambler; otherwise, the gambler pays a penalty of £1 to the dealer.

The gambler's expectation is the amount of money that he may expect to win. The probability of winning is given by:

$$P(\text{winning}) = \frac{1}{4}$$

So, on average, he can expect to gain this proportion of £5; that is, $0.25 \times £5 = £1.25$. In other words, winning £5 one-quarter of the time is equivalent to winning £1.25 all of the time. Likewise, he can expect to pay an average penalty of $0.75 \times £1 = 75p$. The gambler's expected net profit is, therefore, £1.25 – 75p = 50p; that is, a profit of 50p. Similarly, the dealer's expected net profit is $0.75 \times £1 - 0.25 \times £5 = -50p$; that is, a loss of 50p. So, in the long-term, this game favours the gambler by 50p per game.

In general, the expectation is:

$$E(x) = \sum x P(x)$$

which is calculated by multiplying each value of $x$ by its probability of occurrence, and summing the results.

## Probability distributions

A probability distribution is an example of a *stochastic* model. Situations that are subject to unpredictable behaviour (for instance: traffic movement, the weather, national economy) need to be represented by models which contain elements of chance. That is, the model is constructed in terms of:

i)    outcomes (what can happen)

ii)   probabilities (how likely the outcomes are)

Different probability distributions are used to model different types of situations.

For example, it is possible to model the behaviour of continuous variables such as students' heights with the Normal Distribution (see Section 2 Unit 6). The model can then be used to make statements such as:

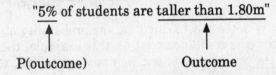

"5% of students are taller than 1.80m"

P(outcome)              Outcome

In other words, there is a 5% chance that a student selected at random is taller than 1.80m.

However, the Normal Distribution is only suitable for continuous variables. Many situations involve discrete variables, for which the Normal Distribution is not appropriate; so, other probability distributions have been developed to model these.

### The Binomial Distribution

As an example of the sort of situation which can be modelled by this distribution, consider a multiple-choice test, consisting of 5 questions, in which each question has 4 possible answers. A student is sitting the test and decides to guess the answer to each question; so:

'How many questions is the student likely to get correct?'

The main features of this situation are:

i)    a fixed number of trials (in this case, 5)

ii)   each trial has only two possible outcomes (correct guess / incorrect guess)

iii)  the trials are independent (the probability of a successful guess is unaffected by previous guesses)

iv)   a discrete variable (the number of correct guesses)

All the possible results are listed below (e.g. CCIIC means that the student correctly guesses the answers to questions1, 2 & 5, and incorrectly guesses the answers to questions 3 & 4):

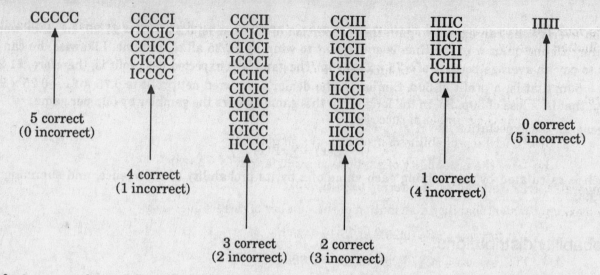

So, for instance, the probability of making exactly 3 correct guesses (and 2 incorrect guesses) is given by:

$$P(3C, 2I) = 10 \times 0.25 \times 0.25 \times 0.25 \times 0.75 \times 0.75$$

$$= 10 \times 0.25^3 \times 0.75^2 = 0.088$$

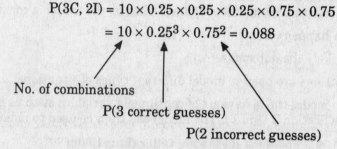

No. of combinations

P(3 correct guesses)

P(2 incorrect guesses)

For each calculation it is not only necessary to calculate the probability of an event but also the number of ways that the event can occur (the *combinations*). In this example, the student can obtain 3 correct answers in 10 different ways; the probability of one way such as CCIIC, therefore, has to be multiplied by 10.

*Note:*

Obviously it would be impractical to list all possible combinations for more complex situations. Fortunately, there is a formula which gives the number of different ways of arranging $r$ items within a group of $n$ items:

$$_nC_r = \frac{n!}{r!(n-r)!}$$

where:

i) $_nC_r$ means 'the number of combinations of $r$ items within $n$ items'

ii) $n!$ (pronounced 'factorial $n$') is equivalent to: $n(n-1)(n-2)(n-3)\ldots\ldots 3 \times 2 \times 1$

So, for example:   $5! = 5 \times 4 \times 3 \times 2 \times 1 = 120$

and:   $_5C_2 = \dfrac{5!}{2!3!} = \dfrac{120}{2 \times 6} = 10$

Note also that, by convention, $0! = 1$

The Binomial Distribution is used, therefore, to model situations where each trial has only two outcomes, often termed *success* and *failure*. In the example, making a correct guess might be considered as a success, so making an incorrect guess is a failure.

232

If the four features mentioned earlier are present then the discrete variable ($r$) has a probability distribution given by:

$$P(r \text{ successes in } n \text{ trials}) = {}_nC_r \, p^r \, q^{n-r}$$

where:
    i)   $n$ is the number of trials

    ii)   $r$ is the number of successes

    iii)  $p$ is the probability of a success in a single trial

    iv)  $q$ is the probability of a failure in a single trial ($q = 1 - p$)

In general, such a distribution is referred to as B($n$, $p$).

In the example, the probability distribution of the number of correct guesses is:

$$P(0 \text{ correct}) = {}_5C_0 \, (0.25)^0 \, (0.75)^5 = 0.237$$

$$P(1 \text{ correct}) = {}_5C_1 \, (0.25)^1 \, (0.75)^4 = 0.396$$

$$P(2 \text{ correct}) = {}_5C_2 \, (0.25)^2 \, (0.75)^3 = 0.263$$

$$P(3 \text{ correct}) = {}_5C_3 \, (0.25)^3 \, (0.75)^2 = 0.088$$

$$P(4 \text{ correct}) = {}_5C_4 \, (0.25)^4 \, (0.75)^1 = 0.015$$

$$P(5 \text{ correct}) = {}_5C_5 \, (0.25)^5 \, (0.75)^0 = 0.001$$

This distribution is B(5, 0.25); that is, a Binomial Distribution with $n = 5$ and $p = 0.25$.

It is important to be able to put the calculations back into context. For instance, if all students were to adopt a guessing tactic in this multiple-choice test, it would be expected that about 8.8% of them would obtain 3 correct answers and only about 0.1% of them would get them all correct.

*Note:*

i)    The total of the calculated probabilities is always 1.

ii)   For a Binomial Distribution $\mu = np; \sigma = \sqrt{npq}$ So, in the example, the mean number of correct guesses is $5 \times 0.25 = 1.25$ and the standard deviation is $\sqrt{5 \times 0.25 \times 0.75} = \sqrt{0.9375} = 0.968$

## The Poisson Distribution

This distribution is used to model the number of successes when the trials happen over a period of time or space. This contrasts with the Binomial Distribution where the number of trials is fixed. For instance, the arrival of customers at a bank automatic cash dispenser is a situation that cannot be modelled with the Binomial Distribution since the number of trials (that is, the occasions when customers could arrive) is infinitely large. So, a Poisson Distribution is appropriate if:

i)    the events happen in a given period of time or space

ii)   the number of events that could occur in that period is theoretically unlimited

The discrete variable ($r$) has a Poisson Distribution given by:

$$P(r) = \frac{e^{-\mu} \mu^r}{r!}$$

where:

i)    m is the mean number of occurrences in a given period

ii)   $e$ is a constant ($\approx 2.71828$)

For example, suppose that during a busy Saturday afternoon an average of 2 customers per minute arrive at a bank cash dispenser:

$$P(0 \text{ customers arrive}) = \frac{e^{-2}2^0}{0!} = 0.135$$

$$P(1 \text{ customer arrives}) = \frac{e^{-2}2^1}{1!} = 0.271$$

$$P(2 \text{ customers arrive}) = \frac{e^{-2}2^2}{2!} = 0.271$$

$$P(3 \text{ customers arrive}) = \frac{e^{-2}2^3}{3!} = 0.180$$

$$P(4 \text{ customers arrive}) = \frac{e^{-2}2^4}{4!} = 0.090$$

$$P(5 \text{ customers arrive}) = \frac{e^{-2}2^5}{5!} = 0.036$$

and so on.

What this means, for instance, is that there is a 9% chance of 4 customers arriving in a one-minute period if there is normally an average of 2 customers per one-minute period. In other words, if 100 one-minute periods were observed then it could be expected to observe 4 customers during about 9 of them (all other factors being equal).

Note that the mean and variance of a Poisson Distribution are equal. So, in the example, the mean number of goals scored is 2 and the variance is 2 (that is, the standard deviation is $\sqrt{2}$)

## The mean and standard deviation of a probability distribution

It can be shown that, for a probability distribution, the mean and standard deviation are given by:

$$\mu = \Sigma x \, P(x)$$

$$\sigma = \sqrt{\Sigma (x - \mu)^2 P(x)}$$

# Unit 8: Inferential statistics 2 – Estimation and hypothesis testing

This section aims to help you to:
1. distinguish between 'estimation' and 'hypothesis testing'
2. understand what is meant by a 'sampling distribution'
3. be able to use 'confidence intervals' in estimation
4. be able to formulate and test hypotheses
5. become familiar with 'goodness-of-fit' tests

## Types of inference

Statistical inference can be divided into two types, *estimation* and *hypothesis* testing.

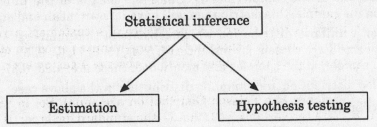

### Estimation

This is concerned with estimating population characteristics (such as the population mean) from sample characteristics (such as the sample mean). For instance, if a sample of 50 students taken from the student population have a mean I.Q. of 115, the main questions that might be asked are:

'Does it follow that the student population also have a mean I.Q. of 115?'

'How confident can I be that the mean I.Q. of the student population is also 115'?

'How accurate an estimate of the population mean is the sample mean'?

The answers to questions like these will depend on factors such as sample size (samples greater than 30 are considered to be large) and sample selection methods.

### Hypothesis testing

This is concerned with formulating ideas about a population and then sampling in order to test the validity of the idea. For instance, a hypothesis might be that:

'Female students spend more time than male students revising for examinations'

In order to test this particular hypothesis it would be necessary to:
i) select a sample of male students and female students to survey their examination revision times
ii) compare the two sets of data to see if there is any difference between them
iii) consider whether the difference between the two sets of data is sufficient to support the hypothesis; this involves the use of a *significance test*, to determine how much importance can be attached to the observed results

In general, the type of significance test that is used depends on the nature of the hypothesis and the sample size. In this section, since the range of different possible tests is vast, only some of the more common ones will be considered as applied to large samples. Once the general principles of hypothesis testing are understood, however, it is then simply a matter of choosing the appropriate test for any given situation.

Again, the sampling techniques that are employed play a critical part in ensuring that the conclusions inferred from the hypothesis test are as accurate and as valid as possible. So, before looking estimation and hypothesis testing in more detail it is necessary to look at some underlying principles of sampling.

## Sampling distributions

The characteristics of a population are referred to as population *parameters*; the characteristics of a sample are referred to as sample *statistics*. Different terminology and notation is employed to distinguish between them:

| Population parameters | Sample statistics | |
|:---:|:---:|---|
| $\mu$ | $\bar{x}$ | (Mean) |
| $\sigma$ | $s$ | (Standard deviation) |
| $N$ | $n$ | (Size) |

If a sample of size $n$ is selected from a population which has a mean $\mu$ and standard deviation $\sigma$, it is a simple matter to calculate the mean, $\bar{x}$, and standard deviation, $s$, for this sample. The process can be repeated for many more samples. The collection of means can then be displayed on a distribution, called the *sampling distribution* of the sample means. Since the means of the different samples may be different depending on the sample, this distribution will have its own mean and standard deviation.

For example, consider a uniform distribution which consists of the numbers: 4, 5, 6, 7, 8. From this population, samples of size 3 are chosen; for instance: (4, 5, 4), (5, 8, 7), (7, 8, 5), (6, 6, 6) etc. A mean can be calculated for each sample; in the samples just mentioned, these are: 4.33, 6.67, 6.67, 6.

Consider the population distribution and sampling distribution in the above case:

a)    Population distribution:

| x | P(x) | xP(x) | $(x - \mu)^2$ | $(x - \mu)^2 P(x)$ |
|:---:|:---:|:---:|:---:|:---:|
| 4 | 0.2 | 0.8 | 4 | 0.8 |
| 5 | 0.2 | 1.0 | 1 | 0.2 |
| 6 | 0.2 | 1.2 | 0 | 0.0 |
| 7 | 0.2 | 1.4 | 1 | 0.2 |
| 8 | 0.2 | 1.6 | 4 | 0.8 |
| | | $\Sigma xP(x) = 6.0$ | | $\Sigma(x - \mu)^2 P(x) = 2.0$ |

So:  Mean, $\mu = \Sigma xP(x) = 6$;  Standard deviation, $\sigma = \sqrt{\Sigma(x-\mu)^2 P(x)} = \sqrt{2} = 1.414 (3D)$

A graph of the population distribution looks like:

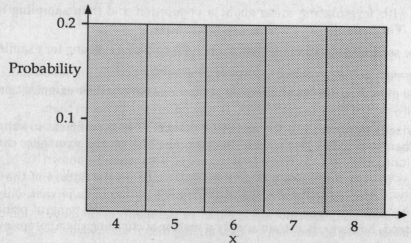

b)   Sampling distribution ($n = 3$)

Note that different samples can have the same mean e.g. (4, 6, 7) and (5, 8, 4). In the table below, therefore, the sample means and the number of different ways of obtaining each mean are shown.

| Sample total | Sample mean (x) | No. of different ways of obtaining mean | P(x) | xP(x) | $(x - m)^2$ | $(x - m)^2 P(x)$ |
|---|---|---|---|---|---|---|
| 12 | 4 | 1 | 0.008 | 0.032 | 4.00 | 0.032 |
| 13 | 4.33 | 3 | 0.024 | 0.104 | 2.78 | 0.066 |
| 14 | 4.67 | 6 | 0.048 | 0.224 | 1.78 | 0.085 |
| 15 | 5 | 10 | 0.080 | 0.400 | 1.00 | 0.080 |
| 16 | 5.33 | 15 | 0.120 | 0.640 | 0.45 | 0.054 |
| 17 | 5.67 | 18 | 0.144 | 0.816 | 0.11 | 0.016 |
| 18 | 6 | 19 | 0.152 | 0.912 | 0.00 | 0.000 |
| 19 | 6.33 | 18 | 0.144 | 0.912 | 0.11 | 0.016 |
| 20 | 6.67 | 15 | 0.120 | 0.800 | 0.45 | 0.054 |
| 21 | 7 | 10 | 0.080 | 0.560 | 1.00 | 0.080 |
| 22 | 7.33 | 6 | 0.048 | 0.352 | 1.78 | 0.085 |
| 23 | 7.67 | 3 | 0.024 | 0.184 | 2.78 | 0.066 |
| 24 | 8 | 1 | 0.008 | 0.064 | 4.00 | 0.032 |
| | | 125 | 1.000 | $\Sigma xP(x) = 6.0$ | | $\Sigma(x - \mu)^2 P(x) = 0.666$ |

So:   Mean $\mu = \sum x P(x) = 6 = 6$

Standard deviation $\sigma = \sqrt{\sum (x - \mu)^2 P(x)} = \sqrt{0.666} = \sqrt{0.816}$ (3D)

A graph of the sampling distribution looks like:

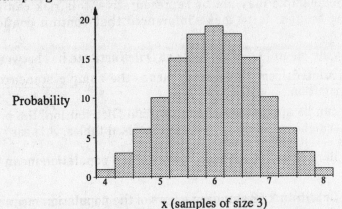

x (samples of size 3)

There are several important points to note about a sampling distribution:

i)   The sample means have a tendency to cluster around the population mean much more so than the original data values. The larger the sample size, the greater the clustering of the sample means around the population mean.

ii)   If the sample size is large ($n > 30$), the sampling distribution approximates a Normal Distribution. Even in the example, which has a small sample size ($n = 3$), the sampling distribution has the characteristic shape of the Normal Distribution. This can be shown to always be the case, irrespective of the shape of the population distribution. In the example, the rectangular population distribution gives rise to a Normal sampling distribution.

iii)   The mean of the sampling distribution is equal to the mean of the population distribution; in the example: population distribution mean = 6; sampling distribution mean = 6.

iv) The standard deviation of the sampling distribution is equal to $\dfrac{\sigma}{\sqrt{n}}$.

So that this does not get confused with the standard deviation of the population distribution, it is called the *standard error*; in the example:

standard deviation = 1.414;

$$\text{standard error} = \frac{1.414}{\sqrt{3}} = 0.816.$$

## Estimating the mean of a population

### Point estimates

If a sample is selected from a population and its mean, $\bar{x}$, is calculated, then $\bar{x}$ is said to be a *point estimate* for m, the population mean. A point estimate is one which does not have reliability factor attached to it. For instance, suppose a group of 50 students are sampled from a population of all the students at Dale Institute and calculations show that their mean I.Q. is 110 with S.D. of 15; that is, $\bar{x} = 110$ and $s = 15$. So, $\bar{x} = 110$ is a point estimate of the population mean, m, which is not known; similarly, $s = 15$ is a point estimate of the population standard deviation, $\sigma$, which is also not known.

What is missing, though, from a statement such as:

'The mean I.Q. of students at Dale Institute is 110'

is any indication of how much reliance can be placed on it. *Confidence intervals* (or *confidence limits*) are used to give just such an indication.

### Confidence intervals

When a sample is selected from a population, some inferences are made about the population based on findings from the sample. If the sample is representative, then the inferences will be valid. However, there is always the risk that a sample may not be representative; this risk can never be completely removed. What can be done, though, is to make inferences that contain confidence intervals; for instance:

'We are 95% certain that the mean I.Q. of students at Dale Institute lies between 106 and 114'

Confidence intervals are calculated from the sample mean, the sample standard deviation and the properties of the Normal Distribution.

Since sampling distributions can be approximated by a Normal Distribution, the proportions under the curve between any two values can be calculated using standardised tables. It is easy to verify that:

i) 95% of all sample means lie within 1.96 standard errors of the population mean $(\mu \pm 1.96\dfrac{\sigma}{\sqrt{n}})$

ii) 99% of all sample means lie within 2.58 standard errors of the population mean $(\mu \pm 2.58\dfrac{\sigma}{\sqrt{n}})$

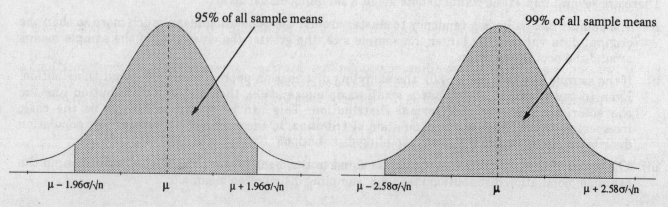

In practice, $\mu$ is estimated by $\bar{x}$ and $\sigma$ is estimated by $s$; so:

i)    a 95% confidence interval for $\mu$ is:   $\bar{x} \pm 1.96 \dfrac{s}{\sqrt{n}}$

ii)   a 99% confidence interval for $\mu$ is:   $\bar{x} \pm 2.58 \dfrac{s}{\sqrt{n}}$

What this means, for example, is:

i)    A 95% confidence interval for the mean I.Q. of students is $110 \pm 1.96 \times \dfrac{15}{\sqrt{50}} = 110 \pm 4$ (1S)

     So, a statement can be made such as:

     'We are 95% certain that the mean I.Q. of students at Dale Institute lies between 106 and 114'

ii)   A 99% confidence interval for the mean I.Q. of students is $110 \pm 2.58 \times \dfrac{15}{\sqrt{50}} = 110 \pm 5$ (1S)

     So, a statement can be made such as:

     'We are 99% certain that the mean I.Q. of students at Dale Institute lies between 105 and 115'

*Note:*

i)    Raising the confidence level from 95% to 99% increases confidence but makes the estimate less precise.

ii)   It is possible to define any level of confidence, but 95% and 99% are the two most widely used levels of confidence.

iii)   The process can be reversed; that is, if a certain level of confidence is required, then an appropriate sample size can be calculated. So, if it is required that the estimate is within $u$ units of the population mean the appropriate sample sizes are given by:

$$n = \left( 1.96 \times \frac{\sigma}{u} \right)^2 \qquad \text{for a 95\% level of confidence}$$

$$n = \left( 2.58 \times \frac{\sigma}{u} \right)^2 \qquad \text{for a 99\% level of confidence}$$

     For example, if it is required to have an estimate for the mean I.Q. that is within 2 I.Q. units of the population mean, a sample size of: $n = \left( 1.96 \times \dfrac{15}{2} \right)^2 = 216$ is required for 95% confidence, and a sample size of: $n = \left( 2.58 \times \dfrac{15}{2} \right)^2 = 374$ is required for 99% confidence

iv)   As the sample size ($n$) increases, the value of $s/\sqrt{n}$ respondingly decreases and gives a narrower confidence interval.

v)    Confidence limits can also be used in estimating other population parameters such as the standard deviation.

vi)   If two samples are taken from different populations it is often necessary to set up confidence limits for the difference between the two means. If two sample sizes of $n_1$ and $n_2$ have means of $\bar{x}_1$ and $\bar{x}_2$, with standard deviations of $s_1$ and $s_2$ respectively, then the 95% confidence interval is given by:

$$\left( \bar{x}_1 - \bar{x}_2 \right) \pm 1.96 \sqrt{\frac{s_1^2}{n_1} + \frac{s_2^2}{n_2}}$$

99% confidence levels can be set up in a similar manner, 1.96 being replaced by 2.58.

# Estimating proportions in a population

The population mean is one of the most important population parameters that needs to be estimated. In many situations, however, it is required to estimate the proportion of the population which have a certain attribute. For instance:

'What proportion of students are aged over 55?'

Suppose a sample of 50 students are chosen and 9 of these students are aged over 55; that is, the proportion of students who are aged over 55 is $\frac{9}{50} = 0.18$

The standard error for the proportion is given by:

$$\text{Standard error} = \sqrt{\frac{pq}{n}}$$

where:

$p$ = the proportion of occurrences of the attribute
$q$ = the proportion of non-occurrences of the attribute $(1 - p)$
$n$ = the sample size

As in the case of estimating the mean, 95% and 99% confidence intervals can be determined for the population proportion (P) which is estimated by the sample proportion, $p$. So:

i)  a 95% confidence interval for P is :

$$p \pm 1.96 \sqrt{\frac{pq}{n}}$$

ii) a 99% confidence interval for P is:

$$p \pm 2.58 \sqrt{\frac{pq}{n}}$$

So, a 95% confidence interval for the proportion of all students at Dale Institute who are aged over 55 is:

$$0.18 \pm 1.96 \times \sqrt{\frac{0.18 \times 0.82}{50}} = 0.18 \pm 0.11 (2D)$$

A statement can now be made such as:

'We are 95% certain that the proportion of students aged over 55 lies between 0.07 and 0.29'

Likewise, a 99% confidence interval for the same proportion is:

$$0.18 \pm 2.58 \times \sqrt{\frac{0.18 \times 0.82}{50}} = 0.18 \pm 0.14 (2D)$$

The corresponding statement is:

'We are 99% certain that the proportion of students aged over 55 lies between 0.04 and 0.32'

# Hypothesis testing

## What is a hypothesis?

A *hypothesis* is an idea or opinion that can be tested statistically; the process of assessing its validity using statistical methods is called *hypothesis testing* (or *significance testing*). There are different types of hypotheses; so, there are different types of test. For example, the hypothesis:

'Male students obtain better marks in Mathematics than female students'

is different to the hypothesis:

'The mean weekly income of a British family is £250'

The first hypothesis is concerned with comparing two populations with one another, whilst the second hypothesis is an opinion about a parameter from a single population. In general, the type of significance test used depends on the nature of the hypothesis; so, it is important to use the appropriate type of significance test in each case.

## Types of hypothesis

Sample data is used to decide whether the stated hypothesis seems reasonable. If it does not seem reasonable then the original hypothesis (the *null hypothesis*) is rejected in favour of another hypothesis (the *alternative hypothesis*). The two types of hypothesis are quite distinct and should not be confused.

i) The null hypothesis is the notion of 'no difference'. In the second example given above, the null hypothesis is the statement that:

'The mean weekly income of a British family is £250'

In other words, there is no difference between the population parameter and the stated value; that is, the mean equals 250. The symbol $H_0$ is used to represent the null hypothesis; so:

$$H_0: \mu = 250$$

This null hypothesis states that the mean equals 250.

ii) The alternative hypothesis, which is represented by the symbol $H_1$, is the notion of 'some difference'. Alternative hypotheses can either be *one-tailed* (one-sided) or *two-tailed* (two-sided). For example:

$H_1: \mu > 250$      (The population mean is greater than 250)

$H_1: \mu < 250$      (The population mean is less than 250)

$H_1: \mu \neq 250$      (The population mean is not equal to 250)

The first two alternative hypotheses are one-sided since values on only one side of 250 are specified. The third alternative hypothesis is two-sided since values on either side of 250 are mentioned.

## Stages of hypothesis testing

There are certain well-defined steps in carrying out a hypothesis test; these are:

Step 1: State a null hypothesis and an alternative hypothesis

Step 2: Decide on a significance level

Step 3: Calculate the appropriate test statistic

Step 4: Use tables to find the critical value of the test statistic

Step 5: Compare calculated value and tabulated critical value to decide whether to reject $H_0$

The underlying principle of a *significance level* is similar to that of a confidence interval. That is:

i) with confidence intervals there is a certain *confidence* (e.g. 95%) attached to stating that a population parameter lies within a given interval

ii) with significance levels there is a certain *risk* (e.g. 5%) attached to rejecting the null hypothesis $H_0$ in favour of the alternative hypothesis $H_1$ when the null hypothesis is actually true

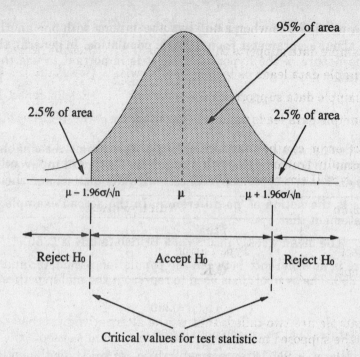

Critical values for test statistic

The *test statistic* is a value which is calculated from (a) the sample data and (b) the value that is used in the null hypothesis; it determines the type of test used. *Critical values* are those values of the test statistic that mark the boundary between acceptance and rejection of the null hypothesis.

For example, consider again the hypothesis:

'The mean weekly income of a British family is £250'

Now, suppose that a selected sample of 50 families living in the Chelford area has a mean weekly income of £253 and a standard deviation of 12. It is required to carry out a significance test on this sample.

Step 1:   $H_0: \mu = 250$           (The population mean is 250)

         $H_1: \mu \neq 250$          (The population mean is not equal to 250)

Step 2:   Significance level: 5%     (This could be any level, but 5% and 1% are common)

Step 3:   Standard error (s.e.) is: $\dfrac{12}{\sqrt{50}} = 1.7$

         The test statistic is:   $z = \dfrac{x - \mu}{\text{s.e.}} = \dfrac{253 - 250}{1.7} = 1.76$

         (Note that, in this case, the test statistic represents the number of standard errors that the observed mean is away from the supposed population mean).

Step 4:   From normal distribution tables, at the 5% significance level, this must be within ± 1.96.

         That is, ± 1.96 is the critical value.

Step 5:   1.76 is within the ± 1.96 range, so the null hypothesis is accepted at the 5% level.

         In other words, even though the sample mean is different from the supposed population mean, it is not *sufficiently* different to make us believe that the original hypothesis is false. In fact, there is only a 5% chance that this inference is wrong, given the available data.

In practice, there are four possibilities when a null hypothesis $H_0$ is tested:

i)   $H_0$ is true and the sample data supports this assertion          (Result: Accept $H_0$; O.K.)

ii)  $H_0$ is true but the sample data leads us to believe otherwise  (Result: Reject $H_0$; Accept $H_1$; Error)

iii) $H_0$ is false and the sample data supports this assertion        (Result: Reject $H_0$; Accept $H_1$; O.K.)

iv)  $H_0$ is false but the sample data leads us to believe otherwise  (Result: Accept $H_0$; Error)

So, two different type of error can be made in testing a hypothesis; that is, *either* rejecting a null hypothesis when it is actually true *or* accepting a null hypothesis when it is actually false. These are called Type I errors and Type II errors respectively. In table form:

| Decision | Null hypothesis | |
|---|---|---|
| | True | False |
| Reject | Type I error | O.K. |
| Accept | O.K. | Type II error |

*Note:*

i)   The tests in the example are two-tailed; that is, the alternative hypothesis is that the population mean is *different* to the supposed mean. A one-tailed test would be used if the alternative hypothesis were, for example, $H_1: \mu < 250$. The critical values for one-tailed tests are different to those associated with two-tailed tests, and for the common 5% and 1% significance levels are:

| Significance level | Number of standard errors | |
|---|---|---|
| | Two-tailed test | One-tailed test |
| 5% | 1.96 | 1.65 |
| 1% | 2.58 | 2.33 |

ii)  The method for carrying out a hypothesis test of a proportion in a population is similar, but makes use of the standard error for the proportion; that is:

$$\text{Standard error} = \sqrt{\frac{pq}{n}}$$

The test statistic is calculated using:   $z = \dfrac{p - P}{\text{s.e.}}$

where:

   $p$ = proportion found in the sample

   $P$ = supposed proportion in the population

iii) The method for carrying out hypothesis testing of the difference between the means ($\bar{x}_1$ and $\bar{x}_2$) of two samples, makes use of the following standard error for the difference:

$$\text{Standard error} = \sqrt{\frac{s_1^2}{n_1} + \frac{s_2^2}{n_2}}$$

where:

   $s_1$ = standard deviation of first sample

   $s_2$ = standard deviation of second sample

   $n_1$ = first sample size

   $n_2$ = second sample size

The test statistic is calculated using: $z = \dfrac{\bar{x}_1 - \bar{x}_2}{\text{s.e.}}$

iv) The method for carrying out significance testing of the difference between the proportions ($p_1$ and $p_2$) of some attribute contained within two samples, makes use of the following standard error for the difference:

$$\text{Standard error} = \sqrt{\frac{n_1 p_1 + n_2 p_2}{n_1 + n_2}\left(\frac{1}{n_1} + \frac{1}{n_2}\right)}$$

where:

$n_1$ = first sample size

$n_2$ = second sample size

The test statistic is calculated using: $z = \dfrac{p_1 - p_2}{\text{s. e.}}$

## The $\chi^2$ (Chi-squared) test

One use of this test is to compare observed and expected frequencies. For this reason, it is often referred to as a 'goodness-of-fit' test. The $\chi^2$ test statistic is calculated using the formula:

$$\chi^2 = \sum \frac{(O - E)^2}{E}$$

where:    $O$ = observed frequencies

$E$ = Expected frequencies

The method can be summarised as follows:

Step 1:   Write, in columns:

a)   the values

b)   the frequencies with which each value is observed to occur (call these $O$)

c)   the frequencies with which each value is expected to occur (call these $E$)

Step 2:   Calculate an ($O - E$) column

Step 3:   Calculate an $\dfrac{(O - E)^2}{E}$ column

Step 4:   Calculate $\sum \dfrac{(O - E)^2}{E}$

Step 5:   Compare the total obtained at step 4 with the critical value of $\chi^2$

For instance, consider an experiment in which a die that is suspected of not being fair is thrown 120 times. The following results are observed:

| Score on die | 1 | 2 | 3 | 4 | 5 | 6 |
|---|---|---|---|---|---|---|
| Frequency | 15 | 19 | 23 | 24 | 13 | 26 |

The null hypothesis is $H_0$: the die is fair

The $\chi^2$ test statistic calculations can be set out as shown in the following table:

| | Expected Frequency | Observed Frequency | (O - E) | (O - E)²/E |
|---|---|---|---|---|
| 1 | 20 | 15 | -5 | 1.25 |
| 2 | 20 | 19 | -1 | 0.05 |
| 3 | 20 | 23 | 3 | 0.15 |
| 4 | 20 | 24 | 4 | 0.80 |
| 5 | 20 | 13 | -7 | 2.45 |
| 6 | 20 | 26 | 6 | 1.80 |
| | | | $\sum \dfrac{(O-E)^2}{E} = 6.50$ | |

The smaller the total of the last column, the closer the die is to its expected behaviour. The larger the total of the last column, the further the die is away from its expected behaviour. The $\chi^2$ table lists the critical values needed to interpret the result. However, caution should be exercised since:

a) the die may be fair but behaved in an unfair manner, producing a large total

b) the die may be unfair but behaved in a fair manner, producing a small total

From tables (see below), the critical value of $\chi^2_5$ at the 5% level is 11.07. The total of 6.50 is smaller, so accept $H_0$; that is, the die is fair. This does not *prove* that the dice is fair, merely that the observed frequencies are not significantly different from the expected frequencies to suspect it of being unfair.

*Note:*

In the chi-squared notation, $\chi^2_\upsilon$ the symbol $\upsilon$ (pronounced 'eta') represents *degrees of freedom*. The number of degrees of freedom for a variable which can take $n$ values is $(n - 1)$. So, in the example, $\upsilon = 5$.

| Critical values of $\chi^2$ (Value of $\chi^2$ must be > the critical value to be significant) | | | |
|---|---|---|---|
| | Level of significance | | |
| u | 10% | 5% | 1% |
| 1 | 2.706 | 3.841 | 6.635 |
| 2 | 4.605 | 5.991 | 9.210 |
| 3 | 6.251 | 7.815 | 11.34 |
| 4 | 7.779 | 9.488 | 13.28 |
| 5 | 9.236 | 11.07 | 15.09 |
| 6 | 10.64 | 12.59 | 16.81 |
| 7 | 12.02 | 14.07 | 18.48 |
| 8 | 13.36 | 15.51 | 20.09 |
| 9 | 14.68 | 16.92 | 21.67 |
| 10 | 15.99 | 18.31 | 23.21 |
| 11 | 17.28 | 19.68 | 24.73 |
| 12 | 18.55 | 21.03 | 26.22 |
| 13 | 19.81 | 22.36 | 27.69 |
| 14 | 21.06 | 23.68 | 29.14 |
| 15 | 22.31 | 25.00 | 30.58 |
| 16 | 23.54 | 26.30 | 32.00 |
| 17 | 24.77 | 27.59 | 33.41 |
| 18 | 25.99 | 28.87 | 34.81 |
| 19 | 27.20 | 30.14 | 36.19 |
| 20 | 28.41 | 31.41 | 37.57 |

## Contingency tables

This is another application of the $\chi^2$ test and is used to test for the independence of two or more category variables. For instance, suppose that students and staff at Dale Institute are given a questionnaire that is designed to analyse attitudes towards certain aspects of student life. One of the questions is concerned with whether students should be allowed to have visitors in their study-bedrooms after midnight. The responses to this question are: Agree, Disagree, Indifferent. The results are collected and tabulated as follows, according to the type of person completing the questionnaire:

| | Observed results | | | |
| | Agree | Disagree | Indifferent | Totals |
|---|---|---|---|---|
| Staff | 50 | 30 | 10 | 90 |
| Students | 190 | 40 | 30 | 260 |
| Totals | 240 | 70 | 40 | 350 |

The question is:

       'Is there any significant difference between the attitudes of staff and students?'

In other words:

       'Is there any relationship between a respondent's status and their response?'

The null hypothesis is $H_0$: There is no difference between the attitudes of staff and students

Calculating the expected frequencies is a little more involved than in previous applications of $\chi^2$. For instance, the proportion of those who 'Agreed' is $\dfrac{240}{350} = 0.686 = 68.6\%$. So, it might be expected that 68.6% of the staff ($0.686 \times 90 = 61.7$) and 68.6% of the students ($0.686 \times 260 = 178.3$) would agree.

The other expected frequencies are calculated similarly; the completed table is shown below right:

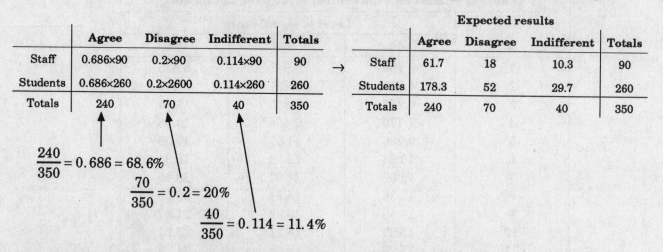

| | Agree | Disagree | Indifferent | Totals | | | Expected results | | | |
| | | | | | | | Agree | Disagree | Indifferent | Totals |
|---|---|---|---|---|---|---|---|---|---|---|
| Staff | 0.686×90 | 0.2×90 | 0.114×90 | 90 | $\rightarrow$ | Staff | 61.7 | 18 | 10.3 | 90 |
| Students | 0.686×260 | 0.2×2600 | 0.114×260 | 260 | | Students | 178.3 | 52 | 29.7 | 260 |
| Totals | 240 | 70 | 40 | 350 | | Totals | 240 | 70 | 40 | 350 |

$$\frac{240}{350} = 0.686 = 68.6\%$$

$$\frac{70}{350} = 0.2 = 20\%$$

$$\frac{40}{350} = 0.114 = 11.4\%$$

An $(O - E)$ table can be constructed by subtracting the corresponding elements in each table:

| | (O - E) | | |
| | Agree | Disagree | Indifferent |
|---|---|---|---|
| Staff | -11.7 | 12 | -0.3 |
| Students | 11.7 | -12 | 0.3 |

So, working element by element from these tables, it is possible to calculate the $\chi^2$ statistic:

$$\sum \frac{(O-E)^2}{E} = \frac{(-11.7)^2}{61.7} + \frac{12^2}{18} + \frac{(-0.3)^2}{10.3} + \frac{11.7^2}{178.3} + \frac{(-12)^2}{52} + \frac{0.3^2}{29.7}$$

$$= 13.77$$

The critical value of $\chi^2{}_2$, at the 5% level is 5.991.

The result is therefore significant and $H_0$ is rejected. In other words, there appears to be a significant difference, at the 5% level, in attitudes between staff and students.

*Note:*

i)  The critical value of $\chi^2{}_2$, at the 1% level is 9.210; so, the result is also significant at the 1% level.

ii) The number of degrees of freedom in a contingency table with $r$ rows and $c$ columns is $(r-1)(c-1)$. The example table has 2 rows and 3 columns; so, degrees of freedom $= (2-1)(3-1) = 1 \times 2 = 2$.

iii) The sum of each row and each column of the $(O-E)$ table is always 0.

# Unit 9: Problem-solving techniques 1 – Simulation

This section aims to help you to:

1. understand the principles of simulation
2. appreciate the value of simulation as a problem-solving technique
3. become familiar with Monte Carlo techniques
4. be able to find solutions to problems using simulation

## What is simulation?

*Simulation* is a common technique for obtaining information about the behaviour of a *system* without actually dealing with the system. The word 'system' is used here to describe any set of connected things; for example: a supermarket's stock levels, a flock of migrating birds, goods in a depot or a queue of people in a Post Office. Simulation involves the construction of a mathematical model with properties that are similar to, but simpler than, those of the real system. This model system is constructed in such a way that the results obtained by using it indicate the results that can be expected from the real system.

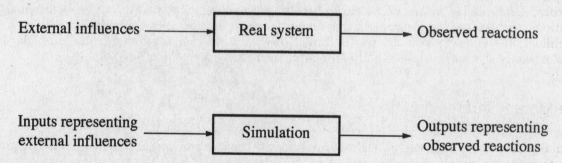

Any system interacts with the outside world in some way; it is subjected to external influences and reacts accordingly. For instance, a supermarket's stock levels are affected by demand for the various items and will cause reordering to take place when stocks run low. A simulation must, therefore, mimic the interactions of the real system:

The complexity of the systems being studied almost always gives rise to mathematical models that need the use of a computer for their manipulation and solution. The computer-based simulation model has inputs that correspond to the external influences on the real system; it then produces outputs which are interpreted as the real system's reactions. So, by varying the model's inputs and observing its corresponding outputs, it is possible to study the real system's likely behaviour. The technique has been used in the study of transport networks, nuclear reactors, ecological systems, fire and ambulance station location, airport layout design etc. whose study by other means would be too complex. Consequently, using such models can save much time, money and risk.

## Simulation models

Any mathematical model that forms the basis of a simulation is not expected to be an exact representation of the system under study; a balance needs to be found between the model's realism and its ease of use. In general, a simulation model should be:

i)   simple enough to be manipulated and understood by those who make use of it

ii)  representative of the real system without being too complex to use

In Section 1 Unit 1– 'Mathematical models' – it was noted that a mathematical model can be classified as being either *deterministic* (that is, the exact outcome of any activity can be predicted exactly) or *stochastic* (in which case activities are included that behave in an unpredictable fashion).

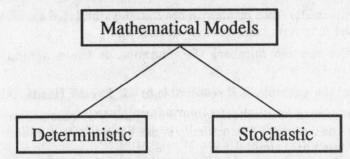

The type of model constructed is governed by the nature of the system to be modelled. Since most real-life systems involve unpredictable features, stochastic models are usually necessary to represent them.

Many deterministic models of real systems have been developed but these have their shortcomings. For instance, it is possible to model the flow of traffic on a roundabout entirely in terms of mathematical equations; the deterministic nature of these equations can then be used to predict, for any given number of vehicles, the behaviour of the traffic flow. However, as in many other situations of this kind, the complexities of the real system (e.g. the human factor) always adds an unpredictable part.

## The Monte Carlo technique

Simulation is particularly useful in those applications that include stochastic elements. The presence of such elements in many systems means that a simulation model is likely to make use of *random* or *pseudo-random* numbers (Appendix A gives a table of such numbers). These sequences of 'unpredictable' numbers are used to represent the unpredictable features of a system.

For instance, suppose that it is required to model the behaviour of a coin when it is tossed. The first four rows of the table of random numbers are:

| 53 | 74 | 23 | 99 | 67 | 98 | 33 | 41 | 19 | 95 | 47 | 53 | 53 | 38 | 09 |
|----|----|----|----|----|----|----|----|----|----|----|----|----|----|----|
| 63 | 38 | 06 | 86 | 54 | 79 | 62 | 67 | 80 | 60 | 75 | 91 | 12 | 81 | 19 |
| 35 | 30 | 58 | 21 | 46 | 49 | 28 | 24 | 00 | 49 | 55 | 65 | 79 | 78 | 07 |
| 63 | 43 | 36 | 82 | 69 | 32 | 92 | 85 | 88 | 65 | 54 | 34 | 81 | 85 | 35 |

The random numbers can be assigned to the possible outcomes of tossing a coin. So, an even number could represent 'Heads' and an odd number could represent 'Tails'. (This is the mathematical model of the situation). The first two rows then represent the following simulated tosses of a coin:

| T | H | T | T | T | H | T | T | T | T | T | T | T | H | T |
|---|---|---|---|---|---|---|---|---|---|---|---|---|---|---|
| T | H | H | H | H | T | H | T | H | H | T | T | H | T | T |
| T | H | H | T | H | T | H | H | H | T | T | T | T | H | T |
| T | T | H | H | T | H | H | T | H | T | H | H | T | T | T |

This 'run' of the model produces 25 Heads and 35 Tails.

This is not the only possible model. For example, numbers in the range 00 – 49 could represent Heads and numbers in the range 50 – 99 could represent Tails. The simulated tosses then become:

| T | T | H | T | T | T | H | H | H | T | H | T | T | H | H |
| T | H | H | T | T | T | T | T | T | T | T | T | H | T | H |
| H | H | T | H | H | H | H | H | H | H | T | T | T | T | H |
| T | H | H | T | T | H | T | T | T | T | T | H | T | T | H |

This run produces 26 Heads and 34 Tails.

The success of the simulation depends on:

i) the number of runs of the model (that is, many more than 60 simulated tosses would be necessary to gain a true picture of the long-term behaviour of the real coin)

ii) the 'randomness' of the random numbers (for instance, is there a hidden bias towards odd numbers?)

iii) the validity of the model (for example, is it reasonable to use Even = Heads; Odd = Tails?)

The technique of assigning ranges of numbers to different possible outcomes and then using random numbers to decide which of the outcomes has occurred is most important. Simulations that make use of this technique are called *Monte Carlo* simulations.

# Random numbers

The widespread use of random numbers in simulation studies means that any computer-based simulation must have some way of producing them.

## True random numbers

These can only be generated by some physical process: throwing a dice, tossing a coin, playing roulette etc. They are not particularly suitable for computer simulation since the sequence of numbers produced cannot be reproduced at a later stage. The ability to reproduce a sequence of random numbers is important in simulation studies since it allows, for instance, the comparison of two different models under exactly the same set of 'random' conditions. The obvious method of storing the true random numbers as look-up tables is too demanding of computer memory. So, mathematical methods of generating sequences of numbers that are sufficiently random in appearance (pseudo-random numbers) have been developed.

## Pseudo-random numbers

These are sequences of numbers that possess the properties of true random numbers but which are deterministic and reproducible. Many different methods of producing them exist, some being more effective than others. (See Section 1: Unit 48 – 'Pseudo-random numbers').

Computer-based pseudo-random number generators are common. Most spreadsheet packages and programming languages have a built-in generator; for instance, the RAND function of Lotus 1-2-3 and the RND function in BASIC. Where no such standard function exists, algorithms have been developed which can form the basis for user-written procedures. Also, once a uniform distribution of pseudo-random numbers has been produced, other distributions (for instance, a Normal Distribution) can easily be obtained.

# Manual simulations

Computer power is obviously necessary to run a model to analyse its long-term behaviour. However, as in computer programming generally, it is always helpful to examine how a person would tackle the computational aspects *before* writing a program to perform the same task. In this respect, *manual simulations*, which are pencil-and-paper runs of a simulation model, are extremely valuable since they can be used to:

i)   validate the model by comparing its behaviour to the real system under existing conditions

ii)  give insights into the construction of an appropriate computer program / spreadsheet model

iii) validate output from computer runs of the model

The table of two-digit random numbers given in Appendix A are uniformly distributed.

That is, any integer in the range 00 – 99 is equally likely to occur in the table.

They can be used to carry out a manual Monte Carlo simulation of events, as follows:

| | |
|---|---|
| Step 1: | Calculate the probability of each event occurring |
| Step 2: | Allocate a range of numbers to each of the different events in proportion to the probability of that event occurring |
| Step 3: | Choose a random number from the uniform distribution |
| Step 4: | Find the event corresponding to the chosen random number |
| Step 5: | Update the state of the simulation |
| Step 6: | Repeat from Step 3 |

## An example of a manual simulation

A small supermarket operates one checkout and is concerned about the build-up of customers at certain times of the day. As a result it is undertaking a simulation study of the congestion at the checkout with a view to providing an extra 'quick checkout' point for customers with a small number of items. The data on which to base the simulation is collected by monitoring customer arrivals and the rate at which they are served during selected 10-minute intervals.

The number of customers arriving at one of the checkouts has been observed for a total of 50 such periods at selected times during a fortnight in March. The probability distribution of arrivals, and assigned random numbers, is as follows:

| Number of arrivals | Frequency(/50) | Probability | Random numbers |
|---|---|---|---|
| 5 | 3 | 0.06 | 00 – 05 |
| 6 | 12 | 0.24 | 06 – 29 |
| 7 | 17 | 0.34 | 30 – 63 |
| 8 | 10 | 0.20 | 64 – 83 |
| 9 | 8 | 0.16 | 84 – 99 |

For instance, in 17 of the 50 observed time periods 7 customers arrive; so, the probability of 7 customers arriving for service is $0.34 \left( \frac{17}{50} \right)$. Therefore, 34 of the available 100 random numbers (30-63) have been assigned to represent that event.

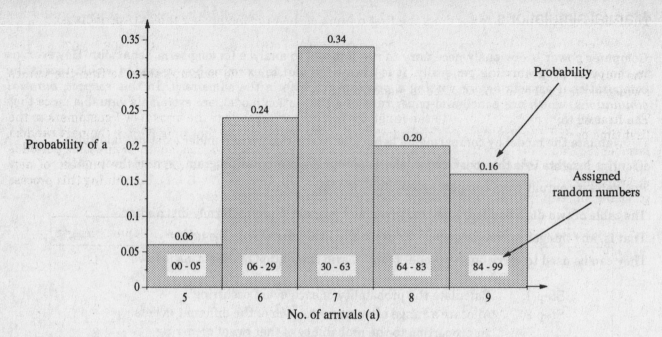

A similar study of the checkout service rate gives the following results:

| Number of services | Frequency(/50) | Probability | Random numbers |
|---|---|---|---|
| 4 | 4 | 0.08 | 00 – 07 |
| 5 | 9 | 0.18 | 08 – 25 |
| 6 | 20 | 0.40 | 26 – 65 |
| 7 | 14 | 0.28 | 66 – 93 |
| 8 | 3 | 0.06 | 94 – 99 |

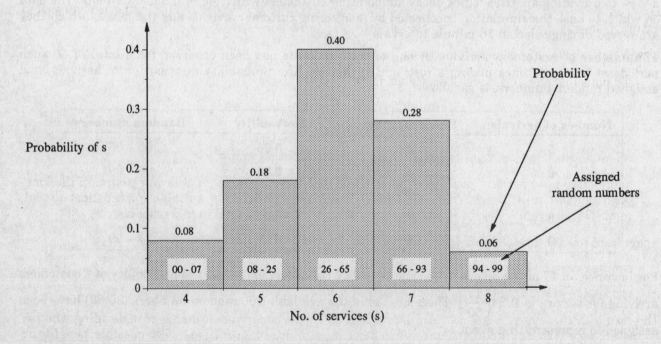

These look-up tables can now be used to simulate the system over many time periods.

The following sequence is taken from the first column of the random number tables (Appendix A):

53    63    35    63    98    02    64    85    58    34    03    62    08    07

The number of arrivals and services are determined by using the look-up tables to find the values corresponding to the numbers in the sequence, one at a time.

The first random number (53) is in the range 30-63; this corresponds to the arrival of 7 customers in the first time period. Similarly, to find the number of customers served in that time period, the next random number (63) is in the range 26-65, and corresponds to 6 services. The queue length in any time period is calculated by considering the queue length in the previous time period, adding the number of new arrivals and subtracting the number of people served (in this case, $0 + 7 - 6 = 1$). Continuing this process gives the following results, which are written in tabulated form for clarity:

| Time period | Random no. | Arrivals | Random no. | Services | Queue length |
|:---:|:---:|:---:|:---:|:---:|:---:|
| 1 | 53 | 7 | 63 | 6 | 1 |
| 2 | 35 | 7 | 63 | 6 | 2 |
| 3 | 98 | 9 | 02 | 4 | 7 |
| 4 | 64 | 8 | 85 | 7 | 8 |
| 5 | 58 | 7 | 34 | 6 | 9 |
| 6 | 03 | 5 | 62 | 6 | 8 |
| 7 | 08 | 6 | 07 | 4 | 10 |
| 8 | .. | .. | .. | .. | .. |
| 9 | .. | .. | .. | .. | .. |

and so on.

Even on this short pencil-and-paper run, it would seem that the model is mimicking the congested nature of the real system; that is, the queue appears to be steadily increasing.

However, it should be borne in mind that:

i)    the model is only as good as the assembled data; for instance:

    a)    is March representative of the supermarket's business pattern?

    b)    at what time of day were the observations made?

    c)    was the same checkout person on duty during the observations?

ii)    many more time periods would need to be simulated in order to get an accurate picture of the long-term behaviour of the system. Obviously, the development of a suitable spreadsheet model, computer program or use of an appropriate software package is vital in this respect.

Apart from the average queue length, other items of interest in this example might be:

i)    average customer waiting time

ii)    proportion of time that the checkout assistant is idle.

The results of these observations / calculations will assist the supermarket manager in deciding whether to install an extra checkout and may lead to a more efficient operation, with possible benefits to employees and customers. Simulation enables possible modifications to be trialled before being put into operation.

*Note:*

When using the random number tables:

i)   The table can be read by starting at any point.

ii)  The numbers can be read in any order – horizontally, vertically, diagonally, backwards.

iii) Although the table is printed in the form of two-digit numbers, this grouping can be ignored if required. For instance, it can be treated as single digits 0 – 9 or, if the probabilities are calculated to 3D, it can be read in groups of three digits, giving a range of 000 – 999; so:

    53   63   35   63   98   02   64   85   58   34   03   62   08   07

can be read as:

    5    3    6    3    3    5    6    3    9    etc

or as:

    536   335   639   802   648   558   340   362   080   etc

# Sampling from distributions

## Empirical distributions

Much of the information used in simulation studies is *empirical*. That is, it has usually been collected as a result of observing the past behaviour of the system under study. This type of data is normally assembled in the form of a probability distribution histogram, which can be thought of as a diagrammatic form of look-up table. As seen earlier in the supermarket checkout simulation, random numbers are used to select values from the histogram (similar to using a look-up table). This process is called *sampling from a distribution*.

For computer purposes, the process is made easier by using instead:

i)   a cumulative probability distribution

ii)  random real numbers in the range 0 -1

For instance, the cumulative probability distribution of customer arrivals at the checkout is:

| Number of arrivals | Frequency(/50) | Probability | Cumulative probability |
|---|---|---|---|
| 5 | 3 | 0.06 | 0.06 |
| 6 | 12 | 0.24 | 0.30 (= 0.06 + 0.24) |
| 7 | 17 | 0.34 | 0.64 (= 0.30 + 0.34) |
| 8 | 10 | 0.20 | 0.84 (= 0.64 + 0.20) |
| 9 | 8 | 0.16 | 1.00 (= 0.84 + 0.16) |

The chart for this data is shown on the following page.

Having chosen a random number between 0 and 1, it is a simple matter to determine the corresponding value. For instance, the random number 0.48 samples the value 7, since it is greater than 0.30 and less than 0.64. (Note that this procedure can also be carried out within a manual simulation, since two-digit random numbers such as 53 can be read as 0.53)

A similar cumulative probability distribution could be constructed for the customer service times.

Within a computer program, sampling a value from a cumulative probability distribution requires the input of the histogram details (number of blocks, associated values, cumulative probabilities).

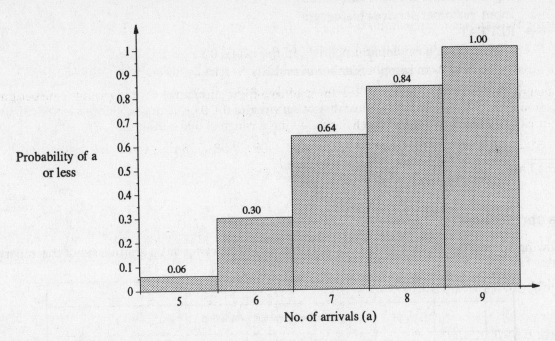

The outline of a program segment / procedure which performs this task is shown below. Its conversion into a suitable programming language is left as an exercise for the reader:

Input the number of histogram blocks, $b$     (e.g. 5)

Input values, $v_b$, one for each histogram block     (e.g. 5, 6, 7, 8, 9)

Input cumulative probabilities, $cp_b$     (e.g. 0.06, 0.30, 0.64, 0.84, 1.00)

Generate a random number, $r$, in the range $0 \leq r < 1$

    IF $r \leq cp_1$ THEN sampled_value = $v_1$

        ELSE IF $r \leq cp_2$ THEN sampled_value = $v_2$

            ELSE IF $r \leq cp_3$ THEN sampled_value = $v_3$

.

.

            ELSE sampled_value = $v_b$

*Note:*

i) Since cumulative *probabilities* are used to define the histogram, random *real numbers* are used in the sampling process.

ii) Only minor adjustments to the outline are needed so that a cumulative *frequencies* histogram can be sampled. This is convenient if it is required to program a simulation to mimic exactly a manual simulation which uses two-digit random *integers*. Most programming languages have facilities for generating random integers in any specified range.

iii) Similarly, it is straightforward to modify the structure to convert input data in the form of a probability distribution into a cumulative probability distribution.

The outline program segment below simulates the supermarket checkout system and incorporates aspects of the sampling process given above. Again, its conversion into a programming language is left as an exercise for the reader. Note that some aspects could be improved; for instance, an output of the system status at the end of each time period would be helpful.

Input customer arrivals histogram
Input customer services histogram
REPEAT
    Generate a random number, $r_1$, in the range $0 \le r_1 < 1$
       Use $r_1$ to sample number of arrivals
    Generate a random number, $r_2$, in the range $0 \le r_2 < 1$
       Use $r_2$ to sample number of services
    Calculate queue length
    Update Time = Time + 1
UNTIL enough time periods simulated
Output summary results

## Using a spreadsheet

The following spreadsheet model shows one possible way of carrying out a simulation of the supermarket checkout:

| | A | B | C | D | E | F |
|---|---|---|---|---|---|---|
| 1 | | | | Supermarket checkout simulation | | |
| 2 | | Arrivals | Cum. Prob. | | Services | Cum. Prob. |
| 3 | | 5 | 0.06 | | 4 | 0.08 |
| 4 | | 6 | 0.30 | | 5 | 0.26 |
| 5 | | 7 | 0.64 | | 6 | 0.66 |
| 6 | | 8 | 0.84 | | 7 | 0.94 |
| 7 | | 9 | 1.00 | | 8 | 1.00 |
| 8 | | | | | | |
| 9 | Time period | Random no | Arrivals | Random no | Services | Queue length |
| 10 | 1 | RND(1) | | RND(1) | | c10-e10 |
| 11 | 2 | RND(1) | ... | RND(1) | ... | f10+c11-e11 |
| 12 | 3 | RND(1) | ... | RND(1) | ... | f11+c12-e12 |
| .. | ... | ... | ... | - | ... | ... |
| | ... | ... | ... | ... | ... | ... |
| 58 | 49 | RND(1) | ... | RND(1) | ... | f57+c58-e58 |
| 59 | 50 | RND(1) | ... | RND(1) | ... | f58+c59-e59 |
| 60 | | | | | Mean queue length = | AV(f10:f59) |

IF(b10≤C3,B3,IF(b10≤C4,B4,IF(b10≤C5,B5,IF(b10≤C6,B6,B7))))

IF(d10≤F3,E3,IF(d10≤F4,E4,IF(d10≤F5,E5,IF(d10≤F6,E6,E7))))

*Notes:*

1. Details of customer arrivals and services are entered into the spreadsheet as cumulative probability distributions (columns B, C, E, F; rows 3 – 7).

2. Formulas are shown in italics. (Lower case letters denote relative cell references; upper case letters denote absolute cell references).

3. a) **AV(XX:YY)** calculates the mean of all cells from XX to YY inclusive.

   b) **RND(1)** generates a random number in the range 0 – 1.

   c) **IF(T, P, Q)** performs P if the statement T is true, otherwise it performs Q.

   For instance, suppose that cell XX contains the function **IF(B10 ≤ C6, B6, B7)** then:

   i)   it is determined whether the contents of cell B10 are ≤ the contents of cell C6

   ii)  if so, then cell XX displays the contents of cell B6

   iii) if not, then cell XX displays the contents of cell B7

   d) Nested **IF** functions are needed to implement the method of selecting values from cumulative probability distributions, as illustrated in the earlier computer program segment.

4. Formulas similar to those shown are replicated into the remaining cells of the columns.

## Standard distributions

Empirical data in histogram form can sometimes be approximated by a standard probability distribution. If this is the case, then there is a definite advantage in using the standard distribution. This is because the standard distribution can be summarised by a small number of parameters. For example, a variable with a Normal Distribution can be expressed solely in terms of the mean and standard deviation. This avoids the need to build up the cumulative probability histograms from which the sampling usually takes place.

Standard distributions are common in simulation studies, particularly those involving queues. For instance, the number of arrivals in a given time period is usually distributed according to a Poisson Distribution and service times distributed according to a Normal Distribution. Also, inter-arrival times (time gaps between arrivals) are usually distributed according to a Negative Exponential Distribution. However, approximating collected data by a standard distribution may not always be appropriate. If the approximation is a poor one, then this will lead to a loss of realism in the simulation model and subsequently in the results. Care must therefore be taken when deciding whether to use an empirical distribution or standard distribution.

As an example, listed below is the outline of a short procedure for sampling from a Normal Distribution.

This can easily be incorporated into a larger simulation program.

```
        Input μ and σ of Normal distribution
        Initialise running_total = 0
      → REPEAT
     |      Generate a random number, r, in the range 0 ≤ r < 1
     |      Calculate running_total = running_total + r
      — UNTIL 12 random numbers generated
        Calculate: μ + σ (running_total – 6)
```

# Simulation studies – the stages

Undertaking a simulation study requires careful planning, organisation and structured record keeping. The various stages are shown diagrammatically below and are explained in more detail with reference to the supermarket checkout example:

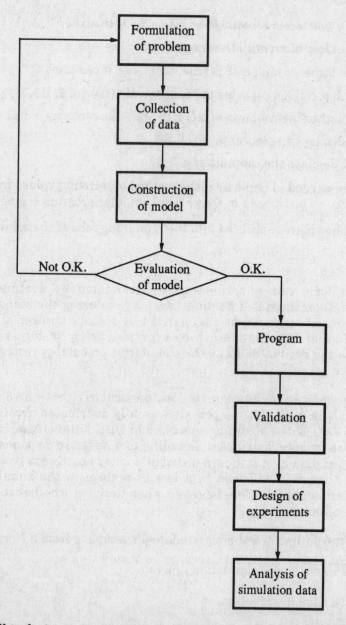

Within this overall technique, certain statistical aspects are extremely important since:

i) the quality of a simulation model depends entirely on the quality of the information on which the model is based

ii) the generation and manipulation of random numbers generation is vital to the successful modelling of stochastic elements within a system

iii) sampling from probability distributions is fundamental to manual / computer simulation.

1. *Formulation of problem*

   Clearly define the purposes of the simulation in terms of:

   a) Questions to be answered

   b) Hypotheses to be tested

   c) Effects to be estimated

   *e.g. Would the provision of a quick checkout at the supermarket increase efficiency?*

   *What efficiency increases would arise if service times on all checkouts were reduced by 10%?*

2. *Collection of data*

   Some knowledge of the available data is required before the problem can be formulated since:

   a) Data may suggest hypotheses to formulate model

   b) Data may be necessary to estimate the system's parameters

   c) Data is necessary to test the validity of the simulation

   d) There may be problems associated with the collection / organisation / storage of data

   *e.g. How much data about customers is necessary?*

   *What data should be collected?*

   *When should the data be collected?*

3. *Construction of model*

   a) Specification of variables / parameters / relationships

   This is dependent on model complexity, program writing time, running time, realism

   b) Estimation of parameters – use of historical data

   *e.g. Customer arrival rates, rate of service.*

4. *Evaluation of model*

   Requires some manual calculation to test model:

   a) Has sufficient data been collected?

   b) Have any non-relevant variables been included?

   c) Have any important variables been omitted?

   d) Have the variables in the form of probability distributions been estimated correctly?

   e) Do the results compare with past experience?

   *e.g. Carry out a manual simulation of checkout queue using random numbers.*

5. *Program*

   a) Should a general or special-purpose programming language be used?

   b) If a general programming language is used, there is a need to consider:

   i) the generation of random numbers

   ii) the generation of variables that fit standard distributions e.g. Normal Distribution

   ii) the collection / display / analysis of statistics e.g. histogram, means, standard deviations

   iii) the readability of the program

   *e.g. Should Pascal or ECSL (Extended Control and Simulation Language) be used?*

6.  *Validation*

    a)  How well do the simulated results compare with historical data?

    b)  How accurate are the predictions of the behaviour of the real system in the future?

    *e.g.* *Do the simulated checkout queue lengths match the actual checkout queue lengths?*

    *Does the predicted customer flow through the simulated system with the extra quick checkout seem reasonable?*

7.  *Design of experiments*

    Now that the model exists, how is it to be used?

    *e.g.* *What if extra checkouts were provided at key times during the day?*

    *What if packers were provided to help with customers' shopping?*

8.  *Analysis of simulation data*

    a)  Presentation of simulated data

    b)  Interpretation of results; there may be problems associated with:

    i)  relative significance of each of a large number of parameters

    ii) the stochastic nature of some of the elements in the model may cause difficulties at the interpretation stage

    *e.g.* *Minute-by-minute status of the checkouts in terms of queue length.*

    *Graphical display of simulation results, including customer queueing times etc.*

## Time-based and event-based simulations

The majority of simulation studies are concerned with systems whose events are time-ordered. Any computer program, therefore, must take account of the time factor in the model. The flow of time in a simulation model can be represented either by the *uniform-increment* method or the *variable-increment* method. Simulations that make use of these methods are often referred to as *time-based* simulations and *event-based* simulations respectively.

With the uniform-increment method, an increment of time is chosen that is suitable in the context of the problem. For instance, considering the state of a supermarket checkout every 10 minutes seems appropriate, whereas considering its state every 2 seconds is not so sensible. So, the simulation begins and, once an increment of time has passed, the system is examined to see what events have occurred. If so, any calculations are made, the computer program's 'clock' is advanced by one increment and the process repeated.

The supermarket checkout simulation, as given earlier, makes use of the uniform-increment method. That is, the model is advanced through fixed 10-minute time periods, observing any changes that take place during each period and then updating the state of the model. So, during each time period the number of arrivals and services is considered and the queue length recalculated. The model is then moved forward in time by 10 minutes and the process repeated.

In the variable-increment method the simulation is proceeded through by incrementing from one event to the next. That is, the model is advanced through time only when an event occurs. For instance, an event in the supermarket checkout example might be a customer arriving. When a particular event has occurred the computer program's clock is advanced to the time when the next event occurs; for instance, the time at which the customer leaves the checkout after being served. Intervening time periods, when no events occur and there are no changes in the system, can be skipped over.

In order to simulate the supermarket checkout by the variable increment method it would be necessary to collect data about the inter-arrival times of customers (that is, the time gaps between the arrival of individual customers) and their individual service times. For instance, suppose that the simulation starts at T=0, the inter-arrival time of the first three customers are 2, 1 and 1 minutes and their service times are 1, 3 and 3 minutes. The state of the model is therefore only examined at T=2 (first customer arrives), T=3 (second customer arrives, first customer leaves), T=4 (third customer arrives), T=6 (second customer leaves), and T=7 (third customer leaves).

## An example of event-based simulation

A small garage serves petrol from a single pump. The forecourt is only big enough to hold 2 other vehicles in the queue apart from the vehicle being served; other vehicles turn away. The distribution of inter-arrival times and service times, in minutes, are as follows:

| Inter-arrival time | Probability | Random numbers | | Service time | Probability | Random numbers |
|---|---|---|---|---|---|---|
| 1 | 0.50 | 00 – 49 | | 3 | 0.10 | 00 – 09 |
| 2 | 0.30 | 50 – 79 | | 4 | 0.20 | 10 – 29 |
| 3 | 0.10 | 80 – 89 | | 5 | 0.30 | 30 – 59 |
| 4 | 0.10 | 90 – 99 | | 6 | 0.40 | 60 – 99 |

Using the first column from the table of random numbers in Appendix A:

| Vehicle | Random number | Inter-arrival time | Clock time of arrival | Random number | Service time | Clock time of departure |
|---|---|---|---|---|---|---|
| A | 53 | 2 | 2 | 63 | 6 | 8 ( 2 + 6) |
| B | 35 | 1 | 3 (2 + 1) | 63 | 6 | 14 ( 8 + 6) |
| C | 98 | 4 | 7 (4 + 3) | 02 | 3 | 17 (14 + 3) |
| D | 64 | 2 | 9 (7 + 2) | 85 | 6 | 23 (17 + 6) |
| E | 58 | 2 | 11 (9 + 2) | (Turns away: 3 departure times > arrival time) | | |
| F | 34 | 1 | 12 (11 + 1) | (Turns away: 3 departure times > arrival time) | | |
| G | 03 | 1 | 13 (12 + 1) | (Turns away: 3 departure times > arrival time) | | |
| H | 62 | 2 | 15 (13 + 2) | 08 | 3 | 26 (23 + 3) |
| I | 07 | 3 | 17 (14 + 3) | 01 | 3 | 29 (26 + 3) |
| J | 72 | 2 | 19 (17 + 2) | (Turns away: 3 departure times > arrival time) | | |
| K | 88 | 3 | 22 (19 + 3) | (Turns away: 3 departure times > arrival time) | | |
| L | 45 | 1 | 23 (22 + 1) | 96 | 6 | 35 (29 + 6) |
| M | 43 | 1 | 24 (23 + 1) | (Turns away: 3 departure times > arrival time) | | |
| N | 50 | 2 | 26 (24 + 2) | 22 | 4 | 39 (35 + 4) |
| O | 96 | 4 | 30 (26 + 4) | 31 | 5 | 44 (39 + 5) |

etc

In some cases, the departure times of 3 vehicles are greater than the arrival time of a new vehicle. This means that there are 3 vehicles still in the system (one at the pump, two in the queue), so the new vehicle has to turn away.

The details of the system's behaviour can also be tabulated as:

| Clock time | Events | System status | |
| --- | --- | --- | --- |
| | | At pump | In queue |
| 1 | | | |
| 2 | A arrives | A | |
| 3 | B arrives | A | B |
| 4 | | A | B |
| 5 | | A | B |
| 6 | | A | B |
| 7 | C arrives | A | B, C |
| 8 | A departs | B | C |
| 9 | D arrives | B | C, D |
| 10 | | B | C, D |
| 11 | E arrives / turns away | B | C, D |
| 12 | F arrives / turns away | B | C, D |
| 13 | G arrives / turns away | B | C, D |
| 14 | B departs | C | D |
| 15 | H arrives | C | D, H |
| 16 | | C | D, H |
| 17 | C departs; I arrives | D | H, I |
| 18 | | D | H, I |
| 19 | J arrives / turns away | D | H, I |
| 20 | | D | H, I |
| 21 | | D | H, I |
| 22 | K arrives / turns away | D | H, I |
| 23 | D departs; L arrives | H | I, L |
| 24 | | H | I, L |
| 25 | | H | I, L |
| 26 | H departs; N arrives | I | L, N |
| 27 | | I | L, N |
| 28 | | I | L, N |
| 29 | I departs | L | N |
| etc | | | |

It is not normally necessary to include times when no events occur. For instance, at clock times 4, 5, 6, 10, 16, 18, 20, 21, 24, 25, 27 and 28 no vehicles arrive, depart or turn away; however. they are included here for clarity. The sort of information that is available from this event chart includes: the proportion of vehicles that turn away; the proportion of time that the pump is busy; the mean queue length; the mean amount of time that each vehicle spends in the system.

# Unit 10: Problem-solving techniques 2 – Linear programming

This section aims to help you to:

1.  understand the principles of linear programming
2.  be able to formulate linear programming problems
3.  be able to solve linear programming problems graphically
4.  be able to apply the simplex method using slack variables
5.  be able to use the duality principle in the solution of problems

## What is linear programming?

Suppose that a local council wishes to build a new housing development consisting of houses and flats. Such a project is likely to be subject to conditions and limiting factors which might include:

☐   a restriction on the amount of land available

☐   a restriction on the amount of time available

☐   a correct balance of houses and flats

☐   a minimum number of people to be housed

Alongside these conditions, the council will probably have an overall goal in mind. This might be, for instance, to provide the accommodation at the least possible cost.

Within a problem like this, it is possible to identify different entities:

i)   variables

    *e.g.*  *the number of houses to be built;*

         *the number of flats to be built*

ii)  parameters

    *e.g.*  *the amount of space required by each type of housing unit;*

         *the number of people that can be accommodated in each type of unit;*

         *the cost of each type of unit*

iii) constraints

    *e.g.*  *the total amount of land available ;*

         *the number of people that need to be housed*

iv)  an objective

    *e.g.*  *to minimise the total cost of the project*

The task of the local council is to build the type and quantity of accommodation that provides sufficient housing without exceeding any of the limits imposed on land, time etc. That is, determine the values of the variables that achieve the objective whilst at the same time satisfying the constraints. There are likely to be several alternative solutions to the problem; of these, some will be better than the others.

*Linear programming* is a systematic method for determining the best solution (*optimum solution*) from a range of possible alternative solutions (*feasible solutions*). It is one of a collection of techniques that has been designed for deciding how to meet some desired *objective* (e.g. minimising costs, maximising profits) subject to the various *constraints* on available resources (e.g. time, equipment, materials).

The term 'linear programming' is applied to any problem where the relationships between the variables can be stated in linear terms. For instance, suppose that a house can accommodate 5 people and a flat can accommodate 2 people; suppose also that at least 100 people need accommodation. The problem is to determine the number of houses and flats to build in order to satisfy this requirement. So, if $x$ houses and $y$ flats are built, the following linear relationship must hold true:

$$5x + 2y \geq 10$$

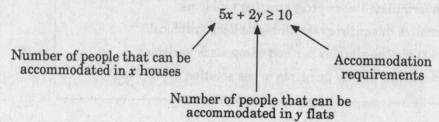

Number of people that can be accommodated in $x$ houses

Accommodation requirements

Number of people that can be accommodated in $y$ flats

It is usually the case in linear programming problems that constraints are specified in terms of *inequalities* (statements involving the use of >, <, ≤ and ≥) rather than *equalities* (statements involving the use of = ). This is because the nature of constraints is to specify relationships in terms of upper limits or lower limits.

*Inequality symbols*

> means 'is greater than'

≥ means 'is greater than or equal to'

< means 'is less than'

≤ means 'is less than or equal to'

So, the statement: $5x + 2y = 100$ is not expressing the same relationship as the statement: $5x + 2y \geq 100$.

The first statement implies that *exactly* 100 people must be accommodated; the second statement implies that *at least* 100 people must be accommodated.

The remaining relationships arising from the context of the problem can be specified in a similar manner. Once it has been formulated as a linear programming problem, the process of solving it can begin.

## Solving linear programming problems

There are two basic approaches that can be used to solve linear programming problems:

1.   The graphical method
2.   The simplex algorithm

The graphical method has limited usefulness since it can only deal with two variables, although it can handle virtually an unlimited number of constraints. Its main advantage is that it is relatively straightforward to understand and apply.

The simplex algorithm, on the other hand, is a method that is appropriate for problems involving any number of variables and constraints. It is a systematic iterative procedure that gradually converges to the optimum solution. Each iteration in the process represents a solution that improves on the previous solution; the process continues until no further improvements are possible. The iterative nature of the process makes it ideally suited to computer implementation; software packages are readily available.

# The graphical method

Step 1   Formulate the linear programming problem

Step 2   Plot each constraint as a region of points on a graph:

    i)  draw a line representing the region boundary

    ii) highlight the region on the appropriate side of the boundary

Step 3   Identify the feasible region (the overlap of all constraints)

Step 4   Plot the objective function

Step 5   Optimise the objective function by drawing a line that is:

    i)  parallel to the objective function

    ii) passing through the vertex of the feasible region that is either:

        a)  as far as possible from the origin if the objective function is to be maximised or

        b)  as near as possible to the origin if the objective function is to be minimised

Step 6   Determine the optimum solution:

    i)  identify the point of intersection of the objective function and the vertex

    ii) the values of $x$ and $y$ at this point represent the optimum solution

## An example of the graphical method

A small firm on an industrial estate need to purchase some new equipment. The machines that they requires are of two types: the Mega and the Hyper. Each Mega costs £6000 and occupies 10m$^2$ of floor space; each Hyper costs £10000 and occupies 5m$^2$ of floor space. The total amount of money available is £60000 and their industrial unit has a floor space of 50m$^2$. The firm have won a substantial contract, the nature of which requires them to buy at least two of each machine. They also want to buy as many machines as possible; how many Megas and Hypers should they purchase?

*Step 1   Formulate the problem*

Define the variables:

i)   $x$: the number of Mega machines purchased

ii)  $y$: the number of Hyper machines purchased

The constraints are:

i)   no more than £60000 is available:                $6000x + 10000y \leq 60000 \rightarrow 3x + 5y \leq 30$

ii)  no more than 50m$^2$ of floor space is available:     $10x + 5y \leq 50 \rightarrow 2x + y \leq 10$

iii) at least two Mega machines must be purchased:    $x \geq 2$

iv) at least two Hyper machines must be purchased:   $y \geq 2$

The objective is to maximise the number of machines purchased ($N$); that is, maximise $N = x + y$.

Note that dividing both sides of i) by 2000 and dividing both sides of ii) by 5 allows these inequalities to be simplified. So, the original problem can now be summarised as the linear programming problem:

$$Maximise: \quad N = x + y$$

Subject to:  i)    $3x + 5y \leq 30$

              ii)   $2x + y \leq 10$

              iii)  $x \geq 2$

              iv)  $y \geq 2$

## Step 2    *Show the constraints on a graph*

The following diagrams show the same pair of axes, each with one of the above constraints:

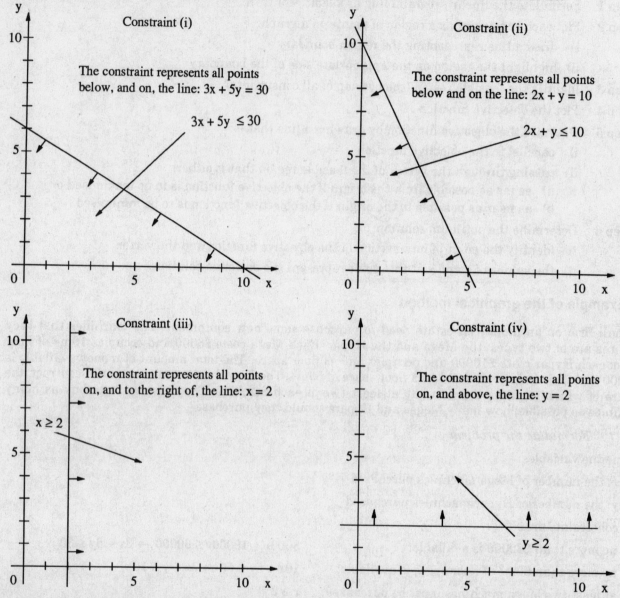

Note that inequalities represent *regions* of points, not just *lines* of points.

Firstly, for each constraint draw a line representing its boundary; for example, for the region:

$3x + 5y \leq 30$, draw the line: $3x + 5y = 30$. To do this, plot and join two suitable points, such as:

   i)   the value of $y$ when $x = 0$ (in this case, $y = 6$); so, the line passes through the point (0, 6)

   ii)  the value of $x$ when $y = 0$ (in this case, $x = 10$); so, the line passes through the point (10, 0)

Secondly, highlight the appropriate side of the boundary line; (shown by small arrows in the diagrams).

## Step 3    *Identify the feasible region*

Showing all the constraints on a single diagram gives:

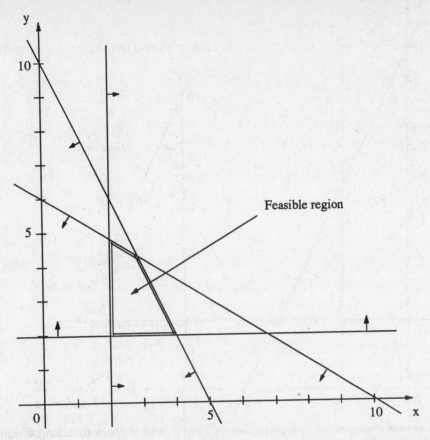

The outlined area represents the region that is common to all constraints; this is called the *feasible region*. Points lying within the feasible region satisfy all the constraints; so, each point $(x, y)$ represents a *feasible solution* to the linear programming problem.

For instance, it can be seen that the point (3, 4) lies within the feasible region. A feasible solution, therefore, is for the manufacturing firm to purchase 3 Mega machines and 4 Hyper machines. This can be confirmed by checking in the original problem:

i)   The cost is: $3 \times £6000 + 4 \times £10000 = £58000$ (less than the available £60000).

ii)  The floor space requirements are: $3 \times 10m^2 + 4 \times 5m^2 = 50m^2$ (does not exceed available $50m^2$).

iii) The machines purchased are 3 Megas, 4 Hypers (at least two of each type have been bought).

*Step 4:*   *Draw the objective function*

The objective is to maximise the number of machines purchased ($N$); that is, maximise:

$$N = x + y$$

To proceed, select an arbitrary value for N. For instance, if 5 machines are purchased, then the objective function becomes: $5 = x + y$ Add this to the diagram (shown by the dotted line, A):

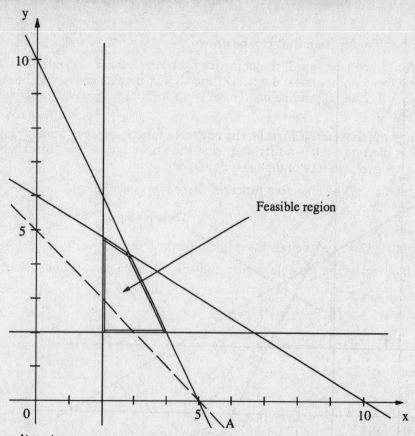

Any point $(x, y)$ on line A represents a combination of Megas and Hypers totalling 5 machines. However, only those points that also lie within the feasible region are feasible solutions to the problem.

*Step 5: Optimise the objective function*

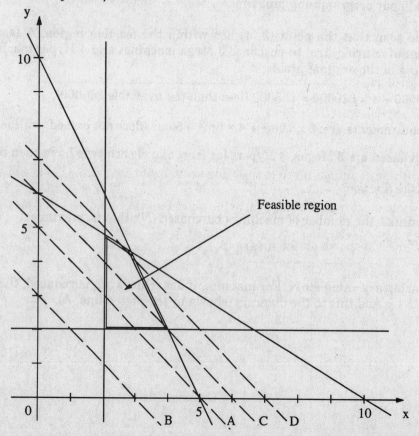

Line A is not the only objective function that can be drawn.

For instance, if 3 machines are purchased, the objective function is: $3 = x + y$ (line B); if 6 machines are purchased, the objective function becomes: $6 = x + y$ (line C); if 7 machines are purchased, the objective function becomes: $7 = x + y$ (line D), and so on. There is an infinite number of possible objective functions, all of which are parallel.

Now, the more machines purchased the further the objective function moves away from the origin. So, the optimum solution is the one that lies furthest from the origin but still within the feasible region. This is usually, but not always, a vertex of the feasible region.

To find the optimum position of the objective function there is no need to draw lines B, C etc. It is only necessary to draw the line that:

i)   is parallel to line A

ii)  passes through the vertex of the feasible region, furthest from the origin

A diagram showing a blow-up of the feasible region and the optimum position for the objective function is shown below.

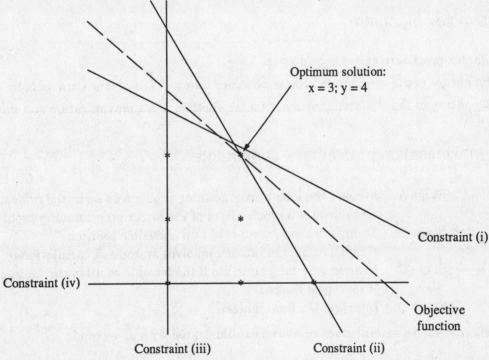

Note that, in this particular example, there is the added constraint that values of $x$ and $y$ are limited to integer values. This constraint is necessary because of the nature of the problem; that is, it is only possible to purchase whole machines. Consequently the objective function does not pass through a vertex of the feasible region.

There are 7 feasible solutions (shown on the diagram):

| x | y |
|---|---|
| 2 | 2 |
| 2 | 3 |
| 2 | 4 |
| 3 | 2 |
| 3 | 3 |
| 3 | 4 | ← Optimum solution |
| 4 | 2 |

When the objective function is optimised according to the procedure it passes through the point (3, 4).

The firm should therefore buy 3 Mega machines and 4 Hyper machines; the total cost is £58000 and the floor space occupied is 50m$^2$.

*Note*

Linear programming techniques normally assume that the variables involved are continuous. However, there are many situations when the variables can only take integer values (as in the example). Where this is the case it can be very tempting to employ normal linear programming techniques and round any fractional quantities that appear in the solution. For instance, in the example, the vertex of the feasible region where constraints i) and ii) intersect is the point (2.86, 4.29); rounding these gives the solution (3, 4) as before. So, in this case, no error has been introduced; however, in general, rounding results is not advisable since serious errors could result.

In these circumstances, *integer programming* (which is a linear programming technique designed for solving problems involving integer variables) is better used.

## The simplex algorithm

The simplex procedure varies according to:

i)   the nature of the constraints; that is, whether they are $\leq$, $\geq$ or a mixture of both

ii)  the nature of the objective function; that is, whether it is a maximisation or a minimisation problem

## 1.   Maximisation problems; $\leq$ constraints

Stage A:   Prepare the linear programming problem as an initial *tableau*
(A tableau is a concise form of the linear programming problem)

Stage B:   *Transform* the tableau to obtain a feasible solution
(Transforming the tableau involves systematic calculations)

Stage C:   Examine the tableau to see if the feasible solution can be improved
If so, repeat Stage B

Stage D:   Interpret the final tableau

Each stage involves several steps that are best illustrated with an example.

### An example of the simplex algorithm applied to a maximisation problem

The small firm in the earlier example manufactures two types of product, the Thingy and the Wotsit. Each product needs processing in three ways in the course of their manufacture. Each Thingy requires 2 hours of process A, 1 hour of process B and 6 hours of process C. Each Wotsit requires 2 hours of process A, 5 hours of process B and 2 hours of process C. Workforce restrictions means that in a given shift there are 24 hours of process A, 44 hours of process B and 60 hours of process C available. The profit on each Thingy is £30 and the profit on each Wotsit is £45. The firm wishes to maximise its profit; how many of each product should it manufacture?

**Stage A:   Prepare initial tableau**

*Step 1   Formulate the problem*

Define the variables:

i)   $x$: the number of Thingys produced

ii)  $y$: the number of Wotsits produced

The constraints are:

i)     no more than 24 hours of process A are available:  $2x + 2y \leq 24$

ii)    no more than 44 hours of process B are available:  $x + 5y \leq 44$

iii)   no more than 60 hours of process C are available:  $6x + 2y \leq 60$

The objective is to maximise the profit (P); that is, maximise $P = 30x + 45y$.

So, the original problem can now be summarised as the linear programming problem:

Maximise:    $P = 30x + 45y$

Subject to:    i)        $2x + 2y \leq 24$

ii)       $x + 5y \leq 44$

iii)      $6x + 2y \leq 60$

**Step 2**    *Rewrite the constraints as equalities*

The constraints i) - iii) and the objective function can be written as:

$$2x + 2y + S_1 = 24$$
$$x + 5y + S_2 = 44$$
$$6x + 2y + S_3 = 60$$
$$(-P) + 30x + 45y = 0$$

$S_1$, $S_2$ and $S_3$ are called *slack variables*; they represent the amount by which the left-hand side of each inequality falls short of the limit specified on the right-hand side.

The simplex algorithm ensures that the value of the variable $P$ is made as large as possible. This corresponds to maximising the profit.

**Step 3**    *Set up an initial tableau*

Write down the equalities in the form of a tableau, similar to:

### Initial tableau

*Coefficients*

| Row no. | Basis | Value | $x$ | $y$ | $S_1$ | $S_2$ | $S_3$ | |
|---------|-------|-------|-----|-----|-------|-------|-------|---|
| 1 | $S_1$ | 24 | 2 | 2 | 1 | 0 | 0 | |
| 2 | $S_2$ | 44 | 1 | 5 | 0 | 1 | 0 | |
| 3 | $S_3$ | 60 | 6 | 2 | 0 | 0 | 1 | |
| 4 | $-P$ | 0 | 30 | 45 | 0 | 0 | 0 | |

The 'Basis' column contains the variables that form the basis of a feasible solution.

The 'Value' column contains the values of each of the basis variables.

The 'Coefficients' columns contain the coefficients of the different variables in the equalities.

Initially, $x$ and $y$ are set equal to 0; so, the basis is: $S_1 = 24$; $S_2 = 44$; $S_3 = 60$ (see tableau). This means that:

i)     0 Thingys and 0 Wotsits are produced (which is a feasible solution, even if it is not profitable!)

ii)    24 hours of process A, 44 hours of process B and 60 hours of process C are unused

iii)   the profit is 0 for this initial feasible solution

## Stage B:     Transform the tableau

Step 4     Identify the pivotal column

Inspect the last row and choose the variable with the largest *positive* coefficient. The column containing this coefficient is the *pivotal column*.

In the last row, the variable with the largest coefficient is $y$ (see Tableau 1).

*Step 5     Identify the pivotal row*

Divide each element in the 'Value' column by the corresponding element in the pivotal column. Write the values so obtained in the spare column on the right-hand side of the tableau. The row with the smallest value is the *pivotal row*.

The values are: $\frac{24}{2} = 12$; $\frac{44}{5} = 8.8$; $\frac{60}{2} = 30$. So, Row 2 is the pivotal row (see Tableau 1).

### Tableau 1
*Coefficients*

| Row no. | Basis | Value | $x$ | $y$ | $S_1$ | $S_2$ | $S_3$ | |
|---------|-------|-------|-----|-----|-------|-------|-------|----|
| 1 | $S_1$ | 24 | 2 | 2 | 1 | 0 | 0 | 12 |
| 2 | $S_2$ | 44 | 1 | (5) | 0 | 1 | 0 | 8.8 ← Pivotal row |
| 3 | $S_3$ | 60 | 6 | 2 | 0 | 0 | 1 | 30 |
| 4 | $-P$ | 0 | 30 | 45 | 0 | 0 | 0 | |

↑
Pivotal column

Step 6:     Identify the pivot

The *pivot* (sometimes called the *pivotal element*) lies at the intersection of the pivotal column and the pivotal row. The pivot is circled in Tableau 1.

Step 7:     Divide each element in the pivotal row by the pivot.

The purpose of this is to change the pivot to 1.

Each element in Row 2 is divided by 5 (see Tableau 2a).

### Tableau 2a
*Coefficients*

| Row no. | Basis | Value | $x$ | $y$ | $S_1$ | $S_2$ | $S_3$ | |
|---------|-------|-------|-----|-----|-------|-------|-------|----|
| 1 | $S_1$ | 24 | 2 | 2 | 1 | 0 | 0 | |
| 2 | $S_2$ | 8.8 | 0.2 | 1 | 0 | 0.2 | 0 | ← Pivotal row |
| 3 | $S_3$ | 60 | 6 | 2 | 0 | 0 | 1 | |
| 4 | $-P$ | 0 | 30 | 45 | 0 | 0 | 0 | |

↑
Pivotal column

Step 8:     Reduce each other element in the pivotal column to 0

This is achieved by performing *row operations*. These are carried out by subtracting multiples of the pivot row from each of the other rows, in turn, so that all other elements in the pivotal column are reduced to zero.

Performing row operations on Tableau 2a:

i) The pivot column element in Row 1 is 2; this needs reducing to 0.

So, subtract: $2 \times$ Row 2 from Row 1; this can be written as: $R_1 - 2R_2$. Repeat this operation for each element in Row 1 (see Tableau 2)

ii) The pivot column element in Row 3 is 2; this need reducing to 0.

So, subtract: $2 \times$ Row 2 from Row 3; this can be written as: $R_3 - 2R_2$. Repeat this operation for each element in Row 3 (see Tableau 2).

ii) The pivot column element in Row 4 is 45; this need reducing to 0.

So, subtract: $45 \times$ Row 2 from Row 4; this can be written as: $R_4 - 2R_2$. Repeat this operation for each element in Row 4 (see Tableau 2).

### Tableau 2

*Coefficients*

| Row no. | Basis | Value | $x$ | $y$ | $S_1$ | $S_2$ | $S_3$ | | Row ops. |
|---------|-------|-------|-----|-----|-------|-------|-------|---|----------|
| 1 | $S_1$ | 6.4 | (1.6) | 0 | 1 | −0.4 | 0 | 4 ← Pivotal row | $R_1 - 2R_2$ |
| 2 | $y$ | 8.8 | 0.2 | 1 | 0 | 0.2 | 0 | 44 | |
| 3 | $S_3$ | 42.4 | 5.6 | 0 | 0 | −0.4 | 1 | 7.57 | $R_3 - 2R_2$ |
| 4 | $-P$ | −396 | 21 | 0 | 0 | −9 | 0 | | $R_4 - 45R_2$ |

↑
Pivotal column

*Step 9*    *Replace 'Basis' variable in pivotal row by variable in pivotal column*

$S_2$ is replaced by $y$ (see Tableau 2).

The calculations in Steps 4 - 8 have produced a solution that is an improvement on the initial feasible solution (see initial tableau). Setting $y = 8.8$ yields a profit of £396 instead of £0. So, $y$ enters the basic feasible solution and $S_2$ leaves it.

## Stage C:    Determine whether the feasible solution can be improved

*Step 10*    *Examine last row of tableau for any positive values*

If all values in the last row are negative or zero, the optimum solution has been reached.

If not, repeat the tableau transformation process from Step 4.

The new pivotal column, pivotal row and pivot are shown in Tableau 2.

The results of carrying out Steps 6 - 9 on Tableau 2 are shown in Tableau 3.

### Tableau 3

*Coefficients*

| Row no. | Basis | Value | $x$ | $y$ | $S_1$ | $S_2$ | $S_3$ | | Row ops. |
|---------|-------|-------|-----|-----|-------|-------|-------|---|----------|
| 1 | $x$ | 4 | 1 | 0 | 0.625 | −0.25 | 0 | | |
| 2 | $y$ | 8 | 0 | 1 | 0.875 | 0.25 | 0 | | $R_2 - 0.2R_1$ |
| 3 | $S_3$ | 20 | 0 | 0 | −3.5 | 1 | 1 | | $R_3 - 5.6R_1$ |
| 4 | $-P$ | −480 | 0 | 0 | −13.125 | −3.75 | 0 | | $R_4 - 21R_1$ |

All values in the last row are either negative or zero; so, this is the final tableau.

## Stage D:    Interpret the final tableau

Step 11   The final tableau represents the optimum solution to the problem.

The important information is contained in the 'Basis' and 'Values' columns.

These columns give:

i)    the variables that appear in the optimum solution and their optimum values;

ii)   slack variables and the amount by which that constraint is under-utilised.

The optimum solution to the problem is: $x = 4$; $y = 8$; $P = 480$.

So, the firm should produce 4 Thingys and 8 Wotsits per shift, yielding a profit of £480.

The slack variable $S_3$ has a value of 20; this means that in a given shift there is 20 hours of unused time on process C.

The absence of the slack variables $S_1$ and $S_2$ in the optimum solution indicates that all of the available time on processes A and B is being utilised.

*Notes:*

i)    The final tableau shows negative coefficients on the last row; each one represents the *shadow cost* of a scarce resource. The shadow cost measures the effect on the objective if an extra available unit of the scarce resource could be used. For instance, for each extra hour of process A that could be obtained, the firm would increase their profit by £13.125; similarly each extra hour of process B would provide a profit increase of £3.75. The shadow cost of any resource not fully utilised is 0 (for example, process C has unused hours). There comes a point, however, beyond which additional units of the scarce resource would not increase profits since other constraints may become binding.

ii)   Since the example involves just two variables, the solution can be verified graphically. The diagram on the following page shows the constraints, feasible region and optimised objective function. The optimum solution is confirmed to be (4, 8) which is also a vertex of the feasible region.

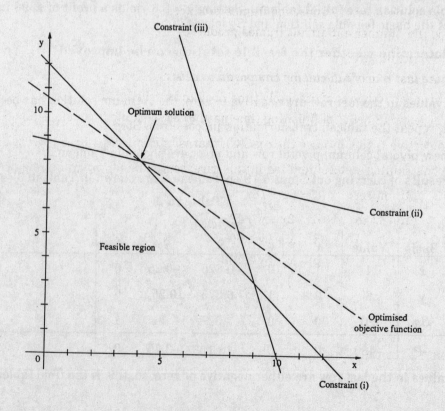

## 2. Minimisation problems; ≥ constraints

For every linear programming problem (called the *primal* problem) there exists an associated problem called the *dual* problem. This duality principle is most important since the two problems are linked in such a way that knowing how to solve one can help in the solution of the other. For instance, if the primal problem is a minimisation problem then its dual is a maximisation problem and vice-versa. So, since it is not as straightforward to solve minimisation problems, one method for their solution is:

Stage A:  Formulate the dual of the linear programming problem

(This reformulates the minimisation problem into a maximisation problem)

Stage B:  Solve this maximisation problem, as described earlier

Stage C:  Interpret the final tableau

The different stages are best illustrated with an example.

### An example of the simplex algorithm applied to a minimisation problem

A manufacturer of picture frames produces two kinds of frame, the Landscape and the Portrait. Each frame has to be cut, assembled and finished. A Landscape frame takes 20 minutes to be cut, 10 minutes to be assembled, 10 minutes to be finished and costs £6 to produce; a Portrait frame takes 10 minutes to cut, 20 minutes to assemble, 60 minutes to finish and costs £18 to produce. On any production run, it is necessary to schedule at least 8 hours of cutting, at least 10 hours of assembling and at least 18 hours of finishing. How many frames of each type should be made during a production run in order to minimise costs ?

**Stage A:    Formulate the dual problem**

Step 1:  Formulate the primal problem

Define the variables:

i)    $x$: the number of Landscape frames produced

ii)   $y$: the number of Portrait frames produced

The constraints are:

i)    at least 8 hours of cutting time need to be scheduled:    $20x + 10y \geq 480$

ii)   at least 10 hours of assembly time need to be scheduled:    $10x + 20y \geq 600$

iii)  at least 18 hours of finishing time need to be scheduled:    $10x + 60y \geq 1080$

The objective is to minimise the cost ($C$); that is, minimise $C = 6x + 18y$.

The constraints can be simplified in this case; so, the linear programming problem is:

Minimise:    $C = 6x + 18y$

Subject to:    i)    $2x + y \geq 48$

ii)   $x + 2y \geq 60$

iii)  $x + 6y \geq 108$

Step 2:  Formulate the dual problem

To formulate the dual problem it is necessary to:

a)  transpose the primal problem coefficients; that is, interchange rows and columns

b)  change all $\geq$ symbols to $\leq$ and vice-versa

So, the primal problem:

$$\text{Minimise:} \quad C = 6x + 18y$$

Subject to:  i)   $2x + y \geq 48$

ii)  $x + 2y \geq 60$

iii) $x + 6y \geq 108$

becomes the dual problem:

$$\text{Maximise:} \quad c = 48X + 60Y + 108Z$$

Subject to:  i)  $2X + Y + Z \leq 6$

ii) $X + 2Y + 6Z \leq 18$

Different variables $(X, Y, Z, c)$ have been used in the dual problem to distinguish them from the primal problem variables $(x, y, C)$.

Note how the rows of coefficients in the primal problem:

| | | |
|---|---|---|
| 2 | 1 | 48 |
| 1 | 2 | 60 |
| 1 | 6 | 108 |
| 6 | 18 | |

have become columns of coefficients in the dual:

| | | | |
|---|---|---|---|
| 2 | 1 | 1 | 6 |
| 1 | 2 | 6 | 18 |
| 48 | 60 | 108 | |

Note also that whereas the primal problem consists of 2 variables and 3 constraints, the dual problem consists of 3 variables and 2 constraints.

**Stage B:   Solve the maximisation problem**

Introducing slack variables, the constraints and objective function can be written as:

$$2X + Y + Z + S_1 = 6$$

$$X + 2Y + 6Z + S_2 = 18$$

$$(-c) + 48X + 60Y + 108Z = 0$$

So, the initial tableau is:

**Initial tableau**

*Coefficients*

| Row no. | Basis | Value | $X$ | $Y$ | $Z$ | $S_1$ | $S_2$ | |
|---|---|---|---|---|---|---|---|---|
| 1 | $S_1$ | 6 | 2 | 1 | 1 | 1 | 0 | 6 |
| 2 | $S_2$ | 18 | 1 | 2 | ⑥ | 0 | 1 | 3 ← Pivotal row |
| 3 | $-c$ | 0 | 48 | 60 | 108 | 0 | 0 | |

↑
Pivotal column

Successive tableaux are:

**Tableau 1**

Coefficients

| Row no. | Basis | Value | X | Y | Z | $S_1$ | $S_2$ | | Row ops. |
|---------|-------|-------|-----|-----|-----|-------|-------|----------------------|----------|
| 1 | $S_1$ | 3 | (11/6) | 2/3 | 0 | 1 | -1/6 | 18/11 ← Pivotal row | $R_1 - R_2$ |
| 2 | Z | 3 | 1/6 | 1/3 | 1 | 0 | 1/6 | 18 | |
| 3 | -c | -324 | 30 | 24 | 0 | 0 | -18 | | $R_3 - 108R_2$ |

↑
Pivotal column

**Tableau 2**

Coefficients

| Row no. | Basis | Value | X | Y | Z | $S_1$ | $S_2$ | | Row ops. |
|---------|-------|----------|---|--------|---|--------|---------|---------------------|----------|
| 1 | X | 18/11 | 1 | (4/11) | 0 | 6/11 | -1/11 | 4.5 ← Pivotal row | |
| 2 | Z | 30/11 | 0 | 3/11 | 1 | -1/11 | 2/11 | 10 | $R_2 - 1/6R_1$ |
| 3 | -c | -4104/11 | 0 | 144/11 | 0 | -180/11 | -168/11 | | $R_3 - 30R_1$ |

↑
Pivotal column

**Tableau 3**

Coefficients

| Row no. | Basis | Value | X | Y | Z | $S_1$ | $S_2$ | | Row ops. |
|---------|-------|-------|-------|---|---|-------|-------|---|----------|
| 1 | Y | 4.5 | 2.75 | 1 | 0 | 1.5 | -0.25 | | |
| 2 | Z | 1.5 | -0.75 | 0 | 1 | -0.5 | 0.25 | | $R_2 - 3/11R_1$ |
| 3 | -c | -432 | -36 | 0 | 0 | -36 | -12 | | $R_3 - 144/11R_1$ |

All values in the last row are either negative or zero; so, this is the final tableau.

(Note that fractions have been used in places since the decimal equivalent may have introduced rounding errors into the calculations).

**Stage C:** **Interpret the final tableau**

The optimum values for the variables in the original primal problem are given by the coefficients of the slack variables on the last row. Note that shadow costs appear under 'Values'.

The optimum solution is: $x = 36$; $y = 12$; $P = 432$.

So, the manufacturer should produce 36 Landscape frames and 12 Portrait frames per production run, with associated costs of £432.

## 3. Problems involving a mixture of ≤ and ≥ constraints

An earlier example, solved graphically, was to solve the linear programming problem:

Maximise:     $N = x + y$

Subject to:   i)   $3x + 5y \leq 30$

ii)   $2x + y \leq 10$

iii)  $x \geq 2$

iv)  $y \geq 2$

Here the constraints contain a mixture of ≤ and ≥ constraints. Forming the dual of this problem would not help since the mixture of constraints would still exist.

However, one possible way of dealing with this is to change any $\geq$ constraints into $\leq$ constraints and then solve the new linear programming problem using normal simplex procedures. So:

i) multiply both sides of each $\geq$ constraint by $-1$

ii) reverse those constraint signs to $\leq$

iii) solve as a normal maximisation problem

The linear programming problem therefore becomes:

Maximise: $N = x + y$

Subject to:  i) $3x + 5y \leq 30$

ii) $2x + y \leq 10$

iii) $-x \leq -2$

iv) $-y \leq -2$

Adding slack variables in the normal way, the initial tableau is:

**Initial tableau**

Coefficients

| Row no. | Basis | Value | x | y | $S_1$ | $S_2$ | $S_3$ | $S_4$ | |
|---------|-------|-------|---|---|-------|-------|-------|-------|---|
| 1 | $S_1$ | 35 | 3 | 5 | 1 | 0 | 0 | 0 | |
| 2 | $S_2$ | 10 | 2 | 1 | 0 | 1 | 0 | 0 | |
| 3 | $S_3$ | $-2$ | $-1$ | 0 | 0 | 0 | 1 | 0 | |
| 4 | $S_4$ | $-2$ | 0 | $-1$ | 0 | 0 | 0 | 1 | |
| 5 | $-N$ | 0 | 1 | 1 | 0 | 0 | 0 | 0 | |

This can be solved using the normal simplex procedure for maximisation problems; it is left as an exercise for the reader.

Another method, which is more mathematically involved, involves the use of *artificial variables*. These are not dealt with here.

# Unit 11: Problem-solving techniques 3 – Transportation and assignment

> This section aims to help you to:
> 1. understand the principles of transportation and assignment problems
> 2. be able to solve problems using the transportation algorithm
> 3. be able to solve problems using the assignment algorithm
> 4. understand a variety of methods of obtaining initial feasible solutions

## What are transportation problems?

Transportation problems are concerned with determining optimum schedules when commodities are transported from one place to another. For instance, when goods are moved from factories to warehouses, there may be limitations on the stocks available at each factory, each warehouse may have its own requirements and there may be several possible routes each incurring different transport costs. The problem is to try and determine which routes should be used to transport the goods, and in what quantities, in order to minimise the total transport costs.

The usual assumptions underlying problems of this nature are that:

i) a commodity originates at sources where fixed amounts are available

ii) the commodity is sent to destinations where fixed amounts are required

iii) the total available quantity of the commodity equals its total requirement

iv) the cost of each shipment is in proportion to the amount shipped

## The transportation algorithm

This is a systematic iterative process that, like the simplex algorithm for solving linear programming problems, starts from a basic feasible solution gradually improving on it until no more improvements are possible and the optimum solution is reached. The algorithm is as follows:

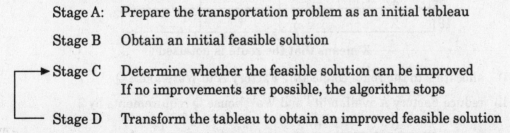

Stage A: Prepare the transportation problem as an initial tableau

Stage B Obtain an initial feasible solution

Stage C Determine whether the feasible solution can be improved
If no improvements are possible, the algorithm stops

Stage D Transform the tableau to obtain an improved feasible solution

Since some of these stages involve several steps, the algorithm is best illustrated with an example.

## An example of the transportation algorithm

Kitchens Inc. manufactures a variety of kitchen items including dishwashers. It has three factories (A, B and C) that manufacture quantities of the dishwasher and these need distributing to its four warehouses (P, Q, R and S). The availability of the dishwashers at each factory, the warehouse requirements and the transport costs per dishwasher are given in the table below:

| Warehouse / Factory | Unit transport cost (£) | | | | Factory availabilities |
|---|---|---|---|---|---|
| | P | Q | R | S | |
| A | 19 | 30 | 50 | 10 | 7 |
| B | 70 | 30 | 40 | 60 | 9 |
| C | 40 | 8 | 70 | 20 | 18 |
| Warehouse requirements | 5 | 8 | 7 | 14 | 34 |

The problem is to determine the number of dishwashers that should be sent from each factory to each warehouse in order to minimise total transport costs.

**Stage A:    Prepare an initial tableau**

Construct a tableau showing availability and requirements, such as:

| | 5 | 8 | 7 | 14 |
|---|---|---|---|---|
| 7 | | | | |
| 9 | | | | |
| 18 | | | | |

**Stage B:    Obtain an initial feasible solution**

One method of obtaining an initial feasible solution is to use the North-West corner rule.

As its name implies, as much as possible is allocated to the North-West corner of the tableau.

So,   i)    allocate 5 to the route connecting Factory A  to Warehouse P

ii)   reduce Factory A availability and Warehouse P requirements by 5

| | 0 | 8 | 7 | 14 |
|---|---|---|---|---|
| 2 | 5 | | | |
| 9 | X | | | |
| 18 | X | | | |

X means that the route is not used

Next,    i)    allocate 2 to the route connecting Factory A to Warehouse Q

ii)   reduce Factory A availability and Warehouse Q requirements by 2

| | 0 | 6 | 7 | 14 |
|---|---|---|---|---|
| 0 | 5 | 2 | X | X |
| 9 | X | | | |
| 18 | X | | | |

The method continues in a 'staircase' fashion, allocating as much as possible to the North-West corner of the remaining rectangular block of routes.

So, i) allocate 6 to the route connecting Factory B to Warehouse Q
ii) reduce Factory B availability and Warehouse Q requirements by 6

| | 0 | 0 | 7 | 14 |
|---|---|---|---|---|
| 0 | 5 | 2 | X | X |
| 3 | X | 6 | | |
| 18 | X | X | | |

Next, i) allocate 3 to the route connecting Factory B to Warehouse R
ii) reduce Factory B availability and Warehouse R requirements by 3

| | 0 | 0 | 4 | 14 |
|---|---|---|---|---|
| 0 | 5 | 2 | X | X |
| 0 | X | 6 | 3 | X |
| 18 | X | X | | |

Next, i) allocate 4 to the route connecting Factory C to Warehouse R
ii) reduce Factory C availability and Warehouse R requirements by 4

| | 0 | 0 | 0 | 14 |
|---|---|---|---|---|
| 0 | 5 | 2 | X | X |
| 0 | X | 6 | 3 | X |
| 14 | X | X | 4 | |

Next, i) allocate 14 to the route connecting Factory C to Warehouse R
ii) reduce Factory C availability and Warehouse R requirements by 14

| | 0 | 0 | 0 | 0 |
|---|---|---|---|---|
| 0 | 5 | 2 | X | X |
| 0 | X | 6 | 3 | X |
| 0 | X | X | 4 | 14 |

This represents an initial feasible solution, shown in more detail (Tableau 0) with route costs in the top left-hand corner of each cell and allocations in the bottom right-hand corner of each cell (boxed numbers):

| Tableau 0 | Warehouse | | | | Factory availabilities |
|---|---|---|---|---|---|
| Factory | P | Q | R | S | |
| A | 19 | 30 | 50 | 10 | 7 |
| | | [5] | [2] | | |
| B | 70 | 30 | 40 | 60 | 9 |
| | | | [6] | [3] | |
| C | 40 | 8 | 70 | 20 | 18 |
| | | | | [4] | [14] |
| *Warehouse requirements* | 5 | 8 | 7 | 14 | 34 |

The total transport cost of this allocation is:

$$5 \times 19 + 2 \times 30 + 6 \times 30 + 3 \times 40 + 4 \times 70 + 14 \times 20 = \text{\pounds}1015$$

**Stage C:    Determine whether an improved feasible solution is possible**

Each unused route is examined in turn to see whether the cost can be reduced by using it.

The procedure for doing this depends on considering the cost for each route as consisting of two components, called its *shadow costs:*

i)    the cost of despatch from a supply point

ii)   the cost of reception at a destination point

The cost of each route is, therefore, the sum of its 'despatch' cost and its 'reception' cost. (These costs can be referred to as a route's *d* value and *r* value).

For instance, the cost of transporting each dishwasher along route (B, R), that is, from Factory B to Warehouse R, is £40. This might consist of a £25 despatch cost from Factory B and a £15 reception cost at Warehouse R. So, the shadow costs for route (B, R) are given by: $d=25$; $r=15$.

*Step 1:    Determine the shadow costs for those routes that are currently being used*

Initially, arbitrarily set one of the supply points despatch cost to 0.

In the feasible solution tableau below (Tableau 1), the d value for Factory A is set to 0. This is written in the right-hand column opposite Factory A.

| Tableau 1 Factory | Warehouse | | | | Factory availabilities |
|---|---|---|---|---|---|
| | P | Q | R | S | |
| A | 19 | 30 | 50 | 10 | 7 |
| | | 5 | 2 | | $d = 0$ |
| B | 70 | 30 | 40 | 60 | 9 |
| | | | 6 | 3 | $d = 0$ |
| C | 40 | 8 | 70 | 20 | 18 |
| | | | | 4    14 | $d = 30$ |
| Warehouse requirements | 5 $r = 19$ | 8 $r = 30$ | 7 $r = 40$ | 14 $r = -10$ | 34 |

Now, route (A, P) has a route cost of 19; since the *d* value for Factory A is 0, this means that the *r* value for Warehouse P is 19. This is written in the bottom row, opposite Warehouse P.

The remainder of the shadow costs can now be deduced and entered into the tableau.

For instance, examining the cost for route (A, Q) implies that the *r* value for Warehouse Q is 30 since the *d* value for Factory A is 0.

By examining the remaining used routes, it can be determined that:

i)    the *d* value for Factory B is 0

ii)   the *r* value for Warehouse R is 40

iii)  the *d* value for Factory C is 30

iv)   the *r* value for Warehouse R is -10

(See Tableau 1).

**Step 2:** *Determine the potential benefits of using those routes that are currently not in use*

The potential benefit of each unused route is the amount that could be saved by using it.

This amount is called the *relative cost factor* and is calculated by subtracting the sum of its $d$ value and its $r$ value from its transport cost.

For instance, for route (C, P), the sum of its $d$ value and its $r$ value is: $30 + 19 = 49$.

Subtracting this from its transport cost gives: $40 - 49 = -9$. This relative cost factor is written as a signed number in the bottom left-hand corner of the corresponding cell (see Tableau 2).

| **Tableau 2** | Warehouse | | | | *Factory availabilities* |
|---|---|---|---|---|---|
| Factory | P | Q | R | S | |
| **A** | 19 | 30 | 50 | 10 | 7 |
| | 5 | 2 | +10 | +20 | $d = 0$ |
| **B** | 70 | 30 | 40 | 60 | 9 |
| | +51 | 6 | 3 | +70 | $d = 0$ |
| **C** | 40 | 8 | 70 | 20 | 18 |
| | −9 | −52 | 4 | 14 | $d = 30$ |
| *Warehouse requirements* | 5 | 8 | 7 | 14 | 34 |
| | $r = 19$ | $r = 30$ | $r = 40$ | $r = -10$ | |

The remainder of the unused routes can be dealt with in a similar way (see Tableau 2):

i)   route (A, R):  $50 - (0 + 40) = 50 - 40 = +10$

ii)   route (A, S):  $10 - (0 + -10) = 10 + 10 = +20$

iii)   route (B, P):  $70 - (0 + 19) = 70 - 19 = +51$

iv)   route (B, S):  $60 - (0 + -10) = 60 + 10 = +70$

v)   route (C, Q):  $8 - (30 + 30) = 8 - 60 = -52$

Note that:

a)   a negative relative cost factor means that a saving on the total cost can be made by using that route; so, for instance, the total cost would decrease by £9 for each dishwasher sent by route (C, P).

b)   a positive relative cost factor means that the total cost increases if that route is used; so, for instance, the total cost would increase by £20 for each dishwasher sent by route (A, S).

c)   if none of the relative cost factors are negative then the tableau represents the optimum allocation and the algorithm stops.

**Stage D:    Transform the tableau to obtain improved feasible solution**

**Step 3:** *Determine the most beneficial unused route to bring into use*

Choose the unused route with the largest negative relative cost factor arising from Step 2.

In Tableau 2, it can be seen that route (C, Q) has the largest negative relative cost factor. That is, this route is the most beneficial for reducing the total transport cost (£52 for each dishwasher); so, as many dishwashers as possible should be sent by this route.

**Step 4:** *Allocate units to the most beneficial route, maintaining totals*

Allocating units to the most beneficial route will upset the row totals and the column totals. So, other routes must be adjusted to counterbalance this allocation.

i) Write an '$x$' in the bottom right-hand corner of the most beneficial unused route; this represents the number of units to be allocated to this route

ii) Find a group of used routes that can be modified by the amount $x$, in order to keep the row totals and the column totals the same.

Tableau 3 shows the result of this procedure.

| **Tableau 3** | Warehouse | | | | *Factory availabilities* |
|---|---|---|---|---|---|
| Factory | P | Q | R | S | |
| **A** | 19 | 30 | 50 | 10 | 7 |
| | 5 | 2 | +10 | +20 | $d = 0$ |
| **B** | 70 | 30 | 40 | 60 | 9 |
| | +51 | 6-$x$ | 3+$x$ | +70 | $d = 0$ |
| **C** | 40 | 8 | 70 | 20 | 18 |
| | −9 | −52 | $x$ | 4-$x$ | 14 | $d = 30$ |
| *Warehouse requirements* | 5 | 8 | 7 | 14 | 34 |
| | $r = 19$ | $r = 30$ | $r = 40$ | $r = -10$ | |

Allocating an extra $x$ units to route (C, Q) can be balanced by subtracting $x$ units from those already allocated to route (B, Q); so, this becomes 6-$x$. However, this upsets the row total for Factory B; so, this needs balancing by increasing the allocation to route (B, R) by $x$ units. In turn, this upsets the column total for Warehouse R; so, this needs balancing by decreasing the allocation to route (C, R) by $x$ units.

The modified routes are, therefore, (B, Q), (B, R) and (C, R); these form a 'closed path' that leave the row totals and the column totals unchanged, as follows:

i) for Warehouse Q, total requirements = $2 + (6 - x) + x = 8$

ii) for Factory B, total availability = $(6 - x) + (3 + x) = 9$

iii) for Warehouse R, total requirements = $(3 + x) + (4 - x) = 7$

iv) for Factory C, total availability = $x + (4 - x) + 14 = 18$

The closed path is shown below:

Note that no other closed path is possible.

There are some general points to consider when trying to find a closed path through the tableau:

i)     the path starts and finishes at the cell with the largest negative relative cost factor

ii)    alternately add and subtract $x$ units in the cells on the closed paths

iii)   moves can only be made horizontally and vertically

iv)    only 90° turns can be made at each intersection

v)     any number of cells with units already allocated can be skipped over; that is, it is not a requirement that the path changes direction every time such a cell is encountered

vi)    there is only one possible closed path through the tableau

vii)   closed paths need not be rectangular (as is the case in the example)

*Step 5:*     *Determine the maximum number of units that can be sent by the most beneficial route*

Allocate as many units as possible to the most beneficial route; that is, determine the maximum value of $x$ that results in non-negative allocations. The allocations to the remaining routes on the closed path are then revised accordingly.

In Tableau 3, the routes on the closed path are allocated $x$, $6 - x$, $3 + x$ and $4 - x$ units; so, the maximum possible value of $x$ is 4. (If, for instance, $x$ is set to 6, then the allocation to route (C, R) is -2 units; that is, a negative number of dishwashers !).

The new tableau showing revised route allocations is:

| **Tableau 4** | Warehouse | | | | *Factory availabilities* |
|---|---|---|---|---|---|
| Factory | P | Q | R | S | |
| A | 19 | 30 | 50 | 10 | 7 |
| | | 5 | 2 | | | |
| B | 70 | 30 | 40 | 60 | 9 |
| | | | 2 | 7 | |
| C | 40 | 8 | 70 | 20 | 18 |
| | | | 4 | | 14 |
| *Warehouse requirements* | 5 | 8 | 7 | 14 | 34 |

The total transport cost of this allocation is:

$$5 \times 19 + 2 \times 30 + 2 \times 30 + 7 \times 40 + 4 \times 8 + 14 \times 20 = £807$$

This represents a saving of £208 on the initial feasible solution (Tableau 0).

The process is now repeated from Step 1 to determine whether any further improvements can be made. Successive tableaux are shown below; the reader should confirm the results.

## Step 1

| Tableau 5 Factory | Warehouse | | | | Factory availabilities |
|---|---|---|---|---|---|
| | P | Q | R | S | |
| A | 19 | 30 | 50 | 10 | 7 |
| | 5 | 2 | | | d = 0 |
| B | 70 | 30 | 40 | 60 | 9 |
| | | 2 | 7 | | d = 0 |
| C | 40 | 8 | 70 | 20 | 18 |
| | | 4 | | 14 | d = -22 |
| Warehouse requirements | 5 r = 19 | 8 r = 30 | 7 r = 40 | 14 r = 42 | 34 |

## Step 2

| Tableau 6 Factory | Warehouse | | | | Factory availabilities |
|---|---|---|---|---|---|
| | P | Q | R | S | |
| A | 19 | 30 | 50 | 10 | 7 |
| | 5 | 2 | +10 | −32 | d = 0 |
| B | 70 | 30 | 40 | 60 | 9 |
| | +51 | 2 | 7 | +18 | d = 0 |
| C | 40 | 8 | 70 | 20 | 18 |
| | +43 | 4 | +52 | 14 | d = −22 |
| Warehouse requirements | 5 r = 19 | 8 r = 30 | 7 r = 40 | 14 r = 42 | 34 |

## Steps 3 & 4

| Tableau 7 Factory | Warehouse | | | | Factory availabilities |
|---|---|---|---|---|---|
| | P | Q | R | S | |
| A | 19 | 30 | 50 | 10 | 7 |
| | 5 | 2-x | +10 | −32   x | d = 0 |
| B | 70 | 30 | 40 | 60 | 9 |
| | +51 | 2 | 7 | +18 | d = 0 |
| C | 40 | 8 | 70 | 20 | 18 |
| | +43 | 4+x | +52 | 14-x | d = −22 |
| Warehouse requirements | 5 r = 19 | 8 r = 30 | 7 r = 40 | 14 r = 42 | 34 |

**Step 5**

| Tableau 8 | Warehouse | | | | Factory availabilities |
|---|---|---|---|---|---|
| Factory | P | Q | R | S | |
| A | 19 | 30 | 50 | 10 | 7 |
| | 5 | | | 2 | |
| B | 70 | 30 | 40 | 60 | 9 |
| | | 2 | 7 | | |
| C | 40 | 8 | 70 | 20 | 18 |
| | | 6 | | 12 | |
| Warehouse requirements | 5 | 8 | 7 | 14 | 34 |

The total transport cost of this allocation is:

$$5 \times 19 + 2 \times 10 + 2 \times 30 + 7 \times 40 + 6 \times 8 + 12 \times 20 = £743$$

**Step 1**

| Tableau 9 | Warehouse | | | | Factory availabilities |
|---|---|---|---|---|---|
| Factory | P | Q | R | S | |
| A | 19 | 30 | 50 | 10 | 7 |
| | 5 | | | 2 | $d = 0$ |
| B | 70 | 30 | 40 | 60 | 9 |
| | | 2 | 7 | | $d = 32$ |
| C | 40 | 8 | 70 | 20 | 18 |
| | | 6 | | 12 | $d = 10$ |
| Warehouse requirements | 5 | 8 | 7 | 14 | 34 |
| | $r = 19$ | $r = -2$ | $r = 8$ | $r = 10$ | |

**Step 2**

| Tableau 10 | Warehouse | | | | Factory availabilities |
|---|---|---|---|---|---|
| Factory | P | Q | R | S | |
| A | 19 | 30 | 50 | 10 | 7 |
| | 5 | +32 | +42 | 2 | $d = 0$ |
| B | 70 | 30 | 40 | 60 | 9 |
| | +19 | 2 | 7 | +18 | $d = 32$ |
| C | 40 | 8 | 70 | 20 | 18 |
| | +11 | 6 | +52 | 12 | $d = 10$ |
| Warehouse requirements | 5 | 8 | 7 | 14 | 34 |
| | $r = 19$ | $r = -2$ | $r = 8$ | $r = 10$ | |

Since none of the relative cost factors are negative, Tableau 8 cannot be improved upon. This therefore represents the optimum route allocation, the minimum transport cost being £743.

287

# Alternative methods for obtaining an initial feasible solution

The amount of effort required to solve transportation problems is substantially reduced if the initial feasible solution is close to the optimum solution. This reduces the number of further tableau transformations that are needed before the optimum solution is reached, so saving time. Although the North-West corner rule is an adequate method for obtaining an initial feasible solution, more efficient methods are available.

## The least cost rule

This method uses the principle of allocating, in turn, as many units as possible to the routes of least cost. The method is illustrated below using the data of the previous example in a modified tableau form:

|    | 5 | 8 | 7 | 14 |
|----|----|----|----|----|
| 7  | 19 | 30 | 50 | 10 |
| 9  | 70 | 30 | 40 | 60 |
| 18 | 40 | 8   **8** | 70 | 20 |

|    | 5 | 0 | 7 | 14 |
|----|----|----|----|----|
| 7  | 19 | 30   X | 50 | 10   **7** |
| 9  | 70 | 30   X | 40 | 60 |
| 10 | 40 | 8   **8** | 70 | 20 |

|    | 5 | 0 | 7 | 7 |
|----|----|----|----|----|
| 0  | 19   X | 30   X | 50   X | 10   **7** |
| 9  | 70 | 30   X | 40 | 60 |
| 10 | 40 | 8   **8** | 70 | 20   **7** |

| | 5 | 0 | 7 | 0 |
|---|---|---|---|---|
| **0** | 19  X | 30  X | 50  X | 10  [7] |
| **9** | 70 | 30  X | 40  [7] | 60  X |
| **3** | 40 | 8  [8] | 70 | 20  [7] |

| | 5 | 0 | 0 | 0 |
|---|---|---|---|---|
| **0** | 19  X | 30  X | 50  X | 10  [7] |
| **2** | 70  [2] | 30  X | 40  [7] | 60  X |
| **3** | 40  [3] | 8  [8] | 70  X | 20  [7] |

In turn:

i)   the least route cost is chosen and as many units as possible allocated to it, the corresponding row totals  and column totals being reduced by that amount

ii)  if a row total or a column total becomes equal to 0, (that is, all available units at a supply point have been despatched or all requirements at a destination point have been met), the remaining routes in that row or column are marked with an X to show that they cannot now be used for transporting units

The total transport cost of this allocation is:

$$7 \times 10 + 2 \times 70 + 7 \times 40 + 3 \times 40 + 8 \times 8 + 7 \times 20 = £814$$

Note that this initial feasible solution is closer to the optimum solution (£743) than the corresponding initial feasible solution obtained by the North-West corner rule (£1015).

## Vogel's rule

This method is even more efficient than either of the previous rules for obtaining an initial feasible solution.

It is so effective that the initial feasible solution is also, frequently, the optimum solution.

When using the method, consideration is given not only to the least cost route but also the difference between  the least cost route and the next least cost route, in any row or column. The principle is that, if the least cost route in any row or column cannot be used then the second least cost route is the next best to use. The cost difference indicates the minimum penalty incurred for not using that route.

The algorithm is:

Step 1    Considering available routes, determine the cost difference between the least cost route and the second least cost route

Step 2    Choose the row or column with the mimum cost difference and allocate as much as possible to the least cost route

Step 3    Reduce the availabilities and requirements by the amount allocated and delete any routes that are no longer available

Step 4    Repeat from step 1, continuing until all availabilities have been allocated

So, for the previous example:

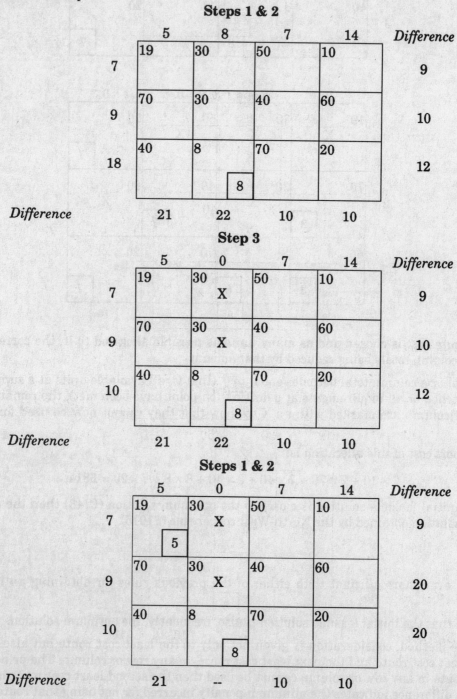

**Steps 1 & 2**

**Step 3**

**Steps 1 & 2**

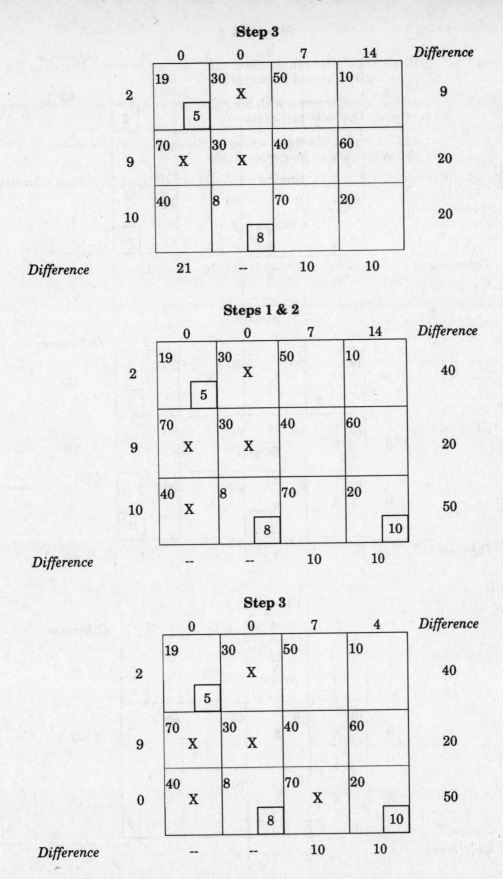

### Step 3

| | 0 | 0 | 7 | 14 | *Difference* |
|---|---|---|---|---|---|
| 2 | 19 | 30 **X** | 50 | 10 | 9 |
| | 5 | | | | |
| 9 | 70 **X** | 30 **X** | 40 | 60 | 20 |
| 10 | 40 | 8 | 70 | 20 | 20 |
| | | 8 | | | |

*Difference*  21  --  10  10

### Steps 1 & 2

| | 0 | 0 | 7 | 14 | *Difference* |
|---|---|---|---|---|---|
| 2 | 19 | 30 **X** | 50 | 10 | 40 |
| | 5 | | | | |
| 9 | 70 **X** | 30 **X** | 40 | 60 | 20 |
| 10 | 40 **X** | 8 | 70 | 20 | 50 |
| | | 8 | | 10 | |

*Difference*  --  --  10  10

### Step 3

| | 0 | 0 | 7 | 4 | *Difference* |
|---|---|---|---|---|---|
| 2 | 19 | 30 **X** | 50 | 10 | 40 |
| | 5 | | | | |
| 9 | 70 **X** | 30 **X** | 40 | 60 | 20 |
| 0 | 40 **X** | 8 | 70 **X** | 20 | 50 |
| | | 8 | | 10 | |

*Difference*  --  --  10  10

291

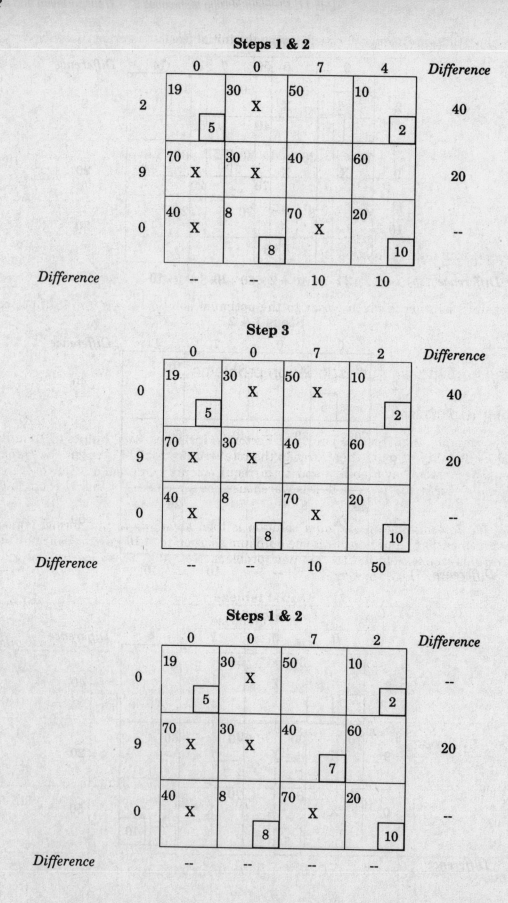

## Steps 1 & 2

|        | 0 | 0 | 7 | 4 | Difference |
|--------|---|---|---|---|------------|
| 2 | 19 | 30 X | 50 | 10 | 40 |
|        | 5 |   |   | 2 |            |
| 9 | 70 X | 30 X | 40 | 60 | 20 |
| 0 | 40 X | 8 | 70 X | 20 | -- |
|        |   | 8 |   | 10 |            |
| Difference | -- | -- | 10 | 10 | |

## Step 3

|        | 0 | 0 | 7 | 2 | Difference |
|--------|---|---|---|---|------------|
| 0 | 19 | 30 X | 50 X | 10 | 40 |
|        | 5 |   |   | 2 |            |
| 9 | 70 X | 30 X | 40 | 60 | 20 |
| 0 | 40 X | 8 | 70 X | 20 | -- |
|        |   | 8 |   | 10 |            |
| Difference | -- | -- | 10 | 50 | |

## Steps 1 & 2

|        | 0 | 0 | 7 | 2 | Difference |
|--------|---|---|---|---|------------|
| 0 | 19 | 30 X | 50 | 10 | -- |
|        | 5 |   |   | 2 |            |
| 9 | 70 X | 30 X | 40 | 60 7 | 20 |
| 0 | 40 X | 8 | 70 X | 20 | -- |
|        |   | 8 |   | 10 |            |
| Difference | -- | -- | -- | -- | |

The remaining allocations are straightforward, giving the initial feasible solution:

| 19 | 30 | 50 | 10 |
|---|---|---|---|
| 5 | | | 2 |
| 70 | 30 | 40 | 60 |
| | | 7 | 2 |
| 40 | 8 | 70 | 20 |
| | 8 | | 10 |

The total transport cost of this allocation is:

$$5 \times 19 + 2 \times 10 + 7 \times 40 + 2 \times 60 + 8 \times 8 + 10 \times 20 = £779$$

This initial feasible solution is much closer to the optimum solution of £743 than those calculated earlier.

## Complications arising with transportation problems

### Unequal supply and demand

Suppose, in the example, that the availability at Factory A increases from 7 units to 10 units. In this case, the total availability of units then exceeds the total requirements. However, the transportation algorithm depends on total availability and total requirements being equal. So, to overcome this problem, a 'dummy' warehouse is created; this warehouse has a requirement that is equal to the excess availability.

The procedure for determining an optimum solution is then according to the normal transportation algorithm described earlier. Shown below is the optimum solution to the original problem, which can be used as an initial feasible solution to this new problem. Note that the 3 excess units have been arbitrarily allocated to route (A, Dummy).

**Initial tableau**

| Factory | Warehouse | | | | | *Factory availabilities* |
|---|---|---|---|---|---|---|
| | P | Q | R | S | Dummy | |
| A | 19 | 30 | 50 | 10 | 0 | 10 |
| | 5 | | | 2 | 3 | |
| B | 70 | 30 | 40 | 60 | 0 | 9 |
| | | 2 | 7 | | | |
| C | 40 | 8 | 70 | 20 | 0 | 18 |
| | | 6 | | 12 | | |
| *Warehouse requirements* | 5 | 8 | 7 | 14 | 3 | 37 |

Allocation to the dummy warehouse indicates, in practice, those units that are available at the factories but not allocated. (The dummy allocations are equivalent to the use of slack variables in linear programming techniques). For calculation purposes, the cost of the dummy routes is set equal to 0.

The final tableau, representing the optimum solution is shown below; it is left as an exercise for the reader to confirm the intermediate calculations.

**Final tableau**

| Factory | Warehouse | | | | | Factory availabilities |
|---|---|---|---|---|---|---|
| | P | Q | R | S | Dummy | |
| A | 19 | 30 [5] | 50 | 10 [5] | 0 | 10 |
| B | 70 | 30 | 40 [7] | 60 | 0 [2] | 9 |
| C | 40 | 8 [8] | 70 | 20 [9] | 0 [1] | 18 |
| Warehouse requirements | 5 | 8 | 7 | 14 | 3 | 37 |

The total transport cost of this allocation is:

$$5 \times 19 + 5 \times 10 + 7 \times 40 + 2 \times 0 + 8 \times 8 + 9 \times 20 + 1 \times 0 = £669$$

Note that this amount is less than the cost of the optimum allocation with no excess availability.

A similar procedure can be adopted for problems in which requirements are in excess of availability; in that case, a dummy factory is created.

## Degeneracy

Suppose that the number of rows in a tableau is $r$ and the number of columns is $c$; then, at any stage of the transportation algorithm the number of routes in use should not be less than $r + c - 1$. So, in the original example, which has 3 rows and 4 columns, there should not be less than 6 routes in use.

However, at some stages in certain problems it may occur that there are less than $r + c - 1$ routes in use. this situation is called *degeneracy*. When this happens, it is found to be impossible to calculate all the shadow costs and the algorithm cannot be continued.

The complication is overcome by:

i)  increasing one or more warehouse's requirements by a small amount, $\varepsilon$

(the number of warehouses whose requirements are increased is as many as necessary in order that the number of routes in use becomes $r + c - 1$).

ii)  increasing the availability at one factory by $n\varepsilon$, where $n$ is the number of warehouses whose requirements are increased

iii)  continuing with the transportation algorithm as normal

iv)  when the tableau ceases to be degenerate, or the optimum solution is reached, setting the value of $\varepsilon$ equal to 0

For example, consider this tableau which shows a transportation problem and an initial feasible solution:

**Initial tableau**

| Factory | Warehouse | | | Factory availabilities |
|---|---|---|---|---|
| | X | Y | Z | |
| J | 5 | 2 | 1 | 10<br>d = 0 |
| | | 10 | | |
| K | 3 | 3 | 4 | 15<br>d = ? |
| | 8 | | 7 | |
| Warehouse requirements | 8<br>r = ? | 10<br>r = 2 | 7<br>r = ? | 25 |

Notice, however, that the solution is degenerate since there are less than 4 routes in use, making it impossible to calculate all of the shadow costs. So, the requirement of Warehouse Y is increased by ε and the availability of Factory K is increased by ε. The new tableau is as follows:

| Factory | Warehouse | | | Factory availabilities |
|---|---|---|---|---|
| | X | Y | Z | |
| J | 5 | 2 | 1 | 10<br>d = 0 |
| | | 10 | | |
| K | 3 | 3 | 4 | 15 + ε<br>d = 1 |
| | 8 | ε | 7 | |
| Warehouse requirements | 8<br>r = 2 | 10 + e<br>r = 2 | 7<br>r = 3 | 25 |

Notice that it is now also possible to calculate all of the shadow costs. The remainder of Stages C & D in the normal transportation algorithm can then be followed:

**Steps 2,3 & 4**

| Factory | Warehouse | | | Factory availabilities |
|---|---|---|---|---|
| | X | Y | Z | |
| J | 5 | 2 | 1 | 10<br>d = 0 |
| | +3 | 10-x | -2 | x |
| K | 3 | 3 | 4 | 15 + ε<br>d = 1 |
| | 8 | ε+x | 7-x | |
| Warehouse requirements | 8<br>r = 2 | 10 + ε<br>r = 2 | 7<br>r = 3 | 25 |

**Steps 5, 1 & 2**

| Factory | Warehouse | | | Factory availabilities |
|---|---|---|---|---|
| | X | Y | Z | |
| J | 5 | 2 | 1 | 10 $d = 0$ |
| | +3 | 3 | 7 | |
| K | 3 | 3 | 4 | 15 + ε $d = 1$ |
| | 8 | ε+7 | +2 | |
| Warehouse requirements | 8 $r = 2$ | 10 + ε $r = 2$ | 7 $r = 1$ | 25 |

$x$ is set equal to 7

Note that now there are 4 routes in use, the solution is no longer degenerate and:

i)    the value of ε can be set to 0

ii)   all shadow costs can be determined

Also, since none of the relative cost factors are negative, this tableau represents the optimum route allocation; so, the final tableau is:

**Final tableau**

| Factory | Warehouse | | | Factory availabilities |
|---|---|---|---|---|
| | X | Y | Z | |
| J | 5 | 2 | 1 | 10 |
| | | 3 | 7 | |
| K | 3 | 3 | 4 | 15 |
| | 8 | 7 | | |
| Warehouse requirements | 8 | 10 | 7 | 25 |

## Maximisation problems

The transportation algorithm is a minimisation procedure. However, it is quite easily adaptable to problems where the objective is maximisation. For instance, suppose that the dishwashers produced at the three factories A, B and C can be sold to four distributors P, Q, R and S at the rates of profit given in the following tableau; the objective is to maximise the total profit:

*Unit profit (£)*

| | P | Q | R | S |
|---|---|---|---|---|
| A | 19 | 28 | 30 | 20 |
| B | 40 | 35 | 38 | 29 |
| C | 17 | 18 | 23 | 24 |

This problem can be transformed into a minimisation problem by selecting the largest unit profit (in this case, 40) and subtracting each of the other profits from it. The new tableau, shown below, can then be solved using the normal transportation algorithm.

*Unit profit (£)*

|   | P | Q | R | S |
|---|---|---|---|---|
| A | 21 | 12 | 10 | 20 |
| B | 0 | 5 | 2 | 11 |
| C | 23 | 22 | 17 | 16 |

This approach is the equivalent of the primal/dual technique in linear programming.

### Inadmissible routes

There may be occasions when certain routes must not, or cannot, be used; so, no units must be allocated to them. This may be because there is some geographical or political reason why they are not to be used. Such a complication can easily be overcome by assigning any inadmissible routes a very high route cost. This then makes it virtually impossible for the transportation algorithm to allocate any units to the route, since the algorithm is designed to keep costs to a minimum.

For instance, in the original dishwasher problem, if route (A, P) becomes inadmissible its route cost could be changed from 19 to 500. With such a high transport cost, it is extremely unlikely to be allocated any units.

## What are assignment problems ?

Assignment problems are concerned with situations where there are a number of resources and a variety of uses to which each of the resources can be put; the objective is to assign the resources to the given uses to maximise the effectiveness of the total assignment. For example, suppose four teachers are to be assigned to teach an assortment of topics to four different classes. Every teacher is capable of teaching every topic but, because each teacher cannot be an expert in everything, their effectiveness varies from topic to topic. The problem is to assign teachers to classes so that the students receive the best teaching possible.

The usual assumptions in problems of this nature are:

i)   there are $n$ resources

ii)  there are $n$ uses to which the resources can be put

iii) there is a measure of effectiveness attached to each resource and its corresponding uses

## The assignment algorithm

The following algorithm is the most well known of those that have been designed to solve assignment problems. It is referred to as the *Hungarian method* and proceeds as follows:

Step 1    For each row in the tableau:

     i)    find the smallest element

     ii)    subtract this value from all of the other elements in the same row

Step 2    Repeat step 1 similarly for each column

Step 3    Draw the least number of vertical/horizontal lines needed to cover all zeros
If the number of lines is equal to the tableau's dimensions, then:

     i)    it is possible to inspect the tableau and make the optimum assignment

     ii)    the algorithm stops

(The *dimension* of an assignment tableau is the number of rows/columns)

Step 4    Find the smallest uncovered element and:

     i)    subtract it from all uncovered elements

     ii)    add it to any element at the intersection of two lines

     iii)    do not change elements covered by one line

Step 5    Repeat from step 3

## An example of the assignment algorithm

A hire company has to arrange for five clients (a, b, c, d, e) to be collected by chauffeur driven limousine. The company has a limousine available at each of five depots (A, B, C, D, E); the mileages from the depots to the clients are given in the following tableau:

|   | a | b | c | d | e |
|---|-----|-----|-----|-----|-----|
| A | 160 | 130 | 175 | 190 | 175 |
| B | 135 | 120 | 130 | 160 | 175 |
| C | 140 | 110 | 155 | 170 | 185 |
| D | 50  | 50  | 80  | 80  | 110 |
| E | 55  | 35  | 70  | 80  | 105 |

The problem is to assign the limousines to the clients so that the total mileage is a minimum.

### Step 1

| | | | | |
|----|---|----|----|----|
| 30 | 0 | 45 | 60 | 70 |
| 15 | 0 | 10 | 40 | 55 |
| 30 | 0 | 45 | 60 | 75 |
| 0  | 0 | 30 | 30 | 60 |
| 20 | 0 | 35 | 45 | 70 |

**Step 2**

| | | | | |
|---|---|---|---|---|
| 30 | 0 | 35 | 30 | 15 |
| 15 | 0 | 0 | 10 | 0 |
| 30 | 0 | 35 | 30 | 20 |
| 0 | 0 | 20 | 0 | 5 |
| 20 | 0 | 25 | 15 | 15 |

**Step 3**

| | | | | |
|---|---|---|---|---|
| 30 | 0 | 35 | 30 | 15 |
| ~~15~~ | ~~0~~ | ~~0~~ | ~~10~~ | ~~0~~ |
| 30 | 0 | 35 | 30 | 20 |
| ~~0~~ | ~~0~~ | ~~20~~ | ~~0~~ | ~~5~~ |
| 20 | 0 | 25 | 15 | 15 |

The number of lines is less than 5 (the dimension of the tableau), so proceed to Step 4.

**Step 4**

| | | | | |
|---|---|---|---|---|
| 15 | 0 | 20 | 15 | 0 |
| 15 | 15 | 0 | 10 | 0 |
| 15 | 0 | 20 | 15 | 5 |
| 0 | 15 | 20 | 0 | 5 |
| 5 | 0 | 10 | 0 | 0 |

**Step 3**

| | | | | |
|---|---|---|---|---|
| 15 | 0 | 20 | 15 | 0 |
| ~~15~~ | ~~15~~ | ~~0~~ | ~~10~~ | ~~0~~ |
| 15 | 0 | 20 | 15 | 5 |
| ~~0~~ | ~~15~~ | ~~20~~ | ~~0~~ | ~~5~~ |
| ~~5~~ | ~~0~~ | ~~10~~ | ~~0~~ | ~~0~~ |

The number of lines is equal to 5, so it is possible to use this tableau to find the optimum solution. The tableau below shows the optimum assignment:

|   | a | b | c | d | e |
|---|---|---|---|---|---|
| A | 15 | 0 | 20 | 15 | [0] |
| B | 15 | 15 | [0] | 10 | 0 |
| C | 15 | [0] | 20 | 15 | 5 |
| D | [0] | 15 | 20 | 0 | 5 |
| E | 5 | 0 | 10 | [0] | 0 |

| Limousine | Client |
|-----------|--------|
| A | e |
| B | c |
| C | b |
| D | a |
| E | d |

The minimum mileage with this assignment is:

$$200 + 130 + 110 + 50 + 80 = 570 \text{ miles}$$

## Mismatched rows and columns

In order to make use of the assignment algorithm, the number of rows and columns in a tableau need to be the same. If they are not, then dummy rows (or columns) must be added. After giving each dummy cell a value of 0, it is possible to apply the algorithm.

## Assignment maximisation problems

Like the transportation algorithm, the assignment algorithm is a minimisation procedure. If the objective is to maximise the total assignment effectiveness, the problem must firstly be converted into a minimisation problem. This can be achieved by subtracting each element in the initial tableau from the largest element (as described earlier in the treatment of transportation maximisation problems). The normal assignment algorithm can then be applied.

# Unit 12: Problem-solving techniques 4 – Routing

This section aims to help you to:

1. understand what is meant by a 'network'

2. understand what is meant by a 'routing' problem

3. distinguish between the various classes of routing problems

4. be able to use appropriate algorithms to solve routing problems

## What is a network ?

The transportation algorithm is used to solve problems where it is required to minimise transport costs. When the algorithm is used, no account needs to taken of the physical layout of the different locations involved. However, it is possible to construct a diagrammatic representation of the locations (a *network*) that shows relative positions and distances. It is usual to think of distances as being measurements of length (for instance, in miles); however, it perfectly reasonable in problems of this type for the measurement to be in terms of time, cost or quantity.

This is an example of a network:

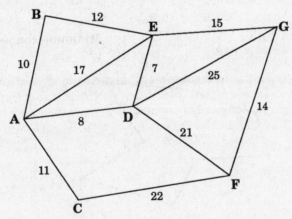

The network is a collection of interconnected lines and can be described by using the following terms:

i) Node – this is a point on the network where two or more lines meet; for instance, in the example network, the nodes are A, B, C, D, E, F and G

ii) Arc – this is a line joining the nodes and usually referred to by the nodes at the start and finish of the arc; for instance, in the example network, arcs include AB, AC, DF and FG

*Note*

i) It is not necessary for there to be arcs connecting every pair of nodes; for instance, there is no arc between nodes B and D or between nodes C and E.

ii) The distances on the arcs need not be to scale.

301

# What are routing problems?

*Routing* problems are concerned with minimising network distances. They can be classified according to the nature of the problem and are usually of 4 types:

    i)    shortest path

    ii)   minimum connector

    iii)  travelling salesman

Shortest path:            Concerned with finding the shortest continuous route between two specified nodes in a network.

Minimum connector:       Also referred to as the *minimal spanning tree*; concerned with connecting all nodes in a network so that the total distance is a minimum.

Travelling salesman:      Concerned with determining a circular tour of all nodes (that is, starting and finishing at the same node) so that the total distance covered is a minimum

These are illustrated in the following diagrams, for a simple network of 8 nodes:

Shortest path                          Minimum connector

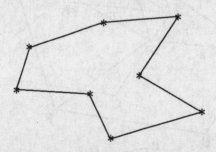

Travelling salesman

For problems concerned with small networks, (that is, for those networks with few nodes and arcs) it is possible to find solutions simply by evaluating every conceivable route. However, for serious applications this approach is impractical. For instance, to solve the travelling salesman problem for this simple network (which has only 8 nodes) would mean evaluating 5040 possible routes; for 10 nodes this number rises to 362880! So, a variety of algorithms have been developed to reduce the work involved; these can be used on either simple or complex networks and are, by definition, ideally suited to computer implementation.

## Shortest path algorithm

Step 1    Form two lists, List 1 and List 2;
List 1 initially contains only the start node;
List 2 initially contains all the other nodes.

Step 2    Label the start node with a 0.

Step 3    Consider all the arcs joining a node in List 1 to a node in List 2; in each case, calculate the sum of its length and the label on its List 1 node.

Step 4    Choose the arc with the smallest total; if there are equal totals, choose any one of them.

Step 5    Label the List 2 node on that arc with the total;
transfer that node from List 2 to List 1.
Repeat from Step 3 until the final node has been transferred to List 1.

Step 6    Determine the shortest path by working backwards from the finish node; choose only those arcs whose length is equal to the difference in its node labels.

The algorithm is best demonstrated using the earlier example, by finding the shortest path from A to G:

*Steps 1 & 2*

| List 1 | List 2 |
|--------|--------|
| A | B, C, D, E, F, G |

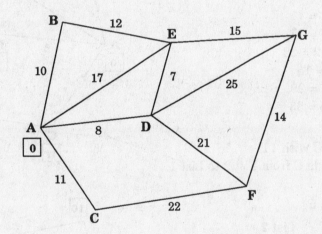

*Steps 3, 4 & 5*

Arc lengths:
AB = 0 + 10 = 10
AC = 0 + 11 = 11
AD = 0 + 8 = 8
AE = 0 + 17 = 17

Choose AD.
Label node D with 8.
Transfer node D from List 2 to List 1.

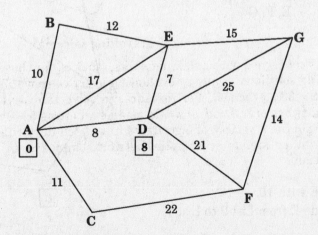

*Steps 3, 4 & 5*

| List 1 | List 2 |
|--------|--------|
| A, D | B, C, E, F, G |

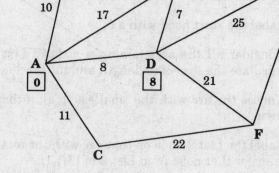

Arc lengths:
AB = 0 + 10 = 10
AC = 0 + 11 = 11
AE = 0 + 17 = 17
DE = 8 + 7 = 15
DF = 8 + 21 = 29
DG = 8 + 25 = 33

Choose AB.
Label node B with 10.
Transfer node B from List 2 to List 1.

*Steps 3, 4 & 5*

| List 1 | List 2 |
|--------|--------|
| A, B, D | C, E, F, G |

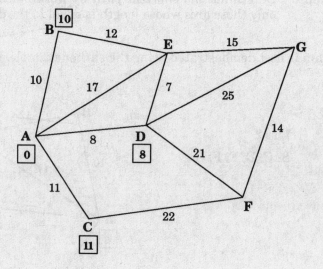

Arc lengths:
AC = 0 + 11 = 11
AE = 0 + 17 = 17
BE = 10 + 12 = 22
DE = 8 + 7 = 15
DF = 8 + 21 = 29
DG = 8 + 25 = 33

Choose AC.
Label node C with 11.
Transfer node C from List 2 to List 1.

*Steps 3, 4 & 5*

| List 1 | List 2 |
|--------|--------|
| A, B, C, D | E, F, G |

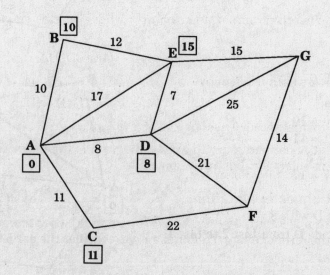

Arc lengths:
AE = 0 + 17 = 17
BE = 10 + 12 = 22
CF = 11 + 22 = 33
DE = 8 + 7 = 15
DF = 8 + 21 = 29
DG = 8 + 25 = 33

Choose DE.
Label node E with 15.
Transfer node E from List 2 to List 1.

*Steps 3, 4 & 5*

| List 1 | List 2 |
|---|---|
| A, B, C, D, E | F, G |

Arc lengths:
CF = 11 + 22 = 33
DF = 8 + 21 = 29
DG = 8 + 25 = 33
EG = 15 + 15 = 30

Choose DF.
Label node F with 29.
Transfer node F from List 2 to List 1.

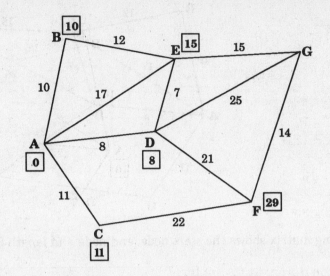

*Steps 3, 4 & 5*

| List 1 | List 2 |
|---|---|
| A, B, C, D, E, F | G |

Arc lengths:
DG = 8 + 25 = 33
EG = 15 + 15 = 30
FG = 29 + 14 = 43

Choose EG.
Label node G with 30.
Transfer node G from List 2 to List 1.

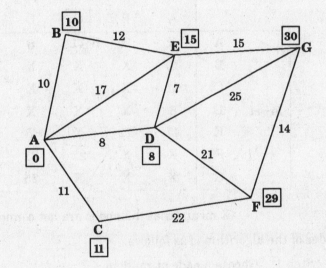

*Step 6*

Working backwards from node G, the arcs whose lengths equal the difference between their two node labels are:

GE, ED, DA.

So, the shortest path is given by:

A – D – E – G

The minimum distance between A and G is 30.

In practice, it is not necessary to draw a diagram of the network for each step of the algorithm; they are included here solely for illustrative purposes.

## Minimum connector algorithm

This algorithm is known as *Prim's algorithm* and is easier to work with when the network information is written in the form of a matrix. For example, consider the earlier network:

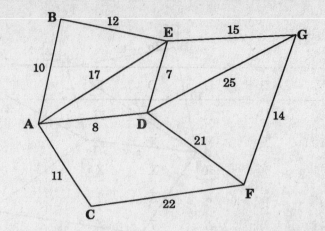

The following matrix shows the start node, end node and length for each route on the network:

|  |  | To | | | | | | |
|---|---|---|---|---|---|---|---|---|
|  |  | A | B | C | D | E | F | G |
| **From** | A | X | 10 | 11 | 8 | 17 | X | X |
|  | B | 10 | X | X | X | 12 | X | X |
|  | C | 11 | X | X | X | X | 22 | X |
|  | D | 8 | X | X | X | 7 | 21 | 25 |
|  | E | 17 | 12 | X | 7 | X | X | 15 |
|  | F | X | X | 22 | 21 | X | X | 14 |
|  | G | X | X | X | 25 | 15 | 14 | X |

(X means that the nodes are not connected directly)

The remainder of the algorithm is as follows:

Step 1: Choose a node at random.
Mark its row as 'connected' and cross out its column.

Step 2: Look at the 'connected' rows (ignore any numbers already crossed out).
Circle the minimum value.

Step 3: Cross out the column containing this minimum value.

Step 4: Find the row corresponding to the column that you have just removed and mark it as 'connected'.

Step 5: Repeat from Step 2 until all rows are marked as 'connected'.

Step 6: Calculate the total of all the circled numbers.

The rows and columns that intersect at the circled numbers represent the minimum connector.

So, in the example, choosing node F as the starting point:

Step 1

To

|  | A | B | C | D | E | F | G |  |
|---|---|---|---|---|---|---|---|---|
| A | X | 10 | 11 | 8 | 17 | X | X |  |
| B | 10 | X | X | X | 12 | X | X |  |
| C | 11 | X | X | X | X | 22 | X |  |
| D | 8 | X | X | X | 7 | 21 | 25 |  |
| E | 17 | 12 | X | 7 | X | X | 15 |  |
| F | X | X | 22 | 21 | X | X | 14 | Connected |
| G | X | X | X | 25 | 15 | 14 | X |  |

From

Steps 2, 3 & 4

To

|  | A | B | C | D | E | F | G |  |
|---|---|---|---|---|---|---|---|---|
| A | X | 10 | 11 | 8 | 17 | X | X |  |
| B | 10 | X | X | X | 12 | X | X |  |
| C | 11 | X | X | X | X | 22 | X |  |
| D | 8 | X | X | X | 7 | 21 | 25 |  |
| E | 17 | 12 | X | 7 | X | X | 15 |  |
| F | X | X | 22 | 21 | X | X | (14) | Connected |
| G | X | X | X | 25 | 15 | 14 | X | Connected |

From

Steps 2, 3 & 4

To

|  | A | B | C | D | E | F | G |  |
|---|---|---|---|---|---|---|---|---|
| A | X | 10 | 11 | 8 | 17 | X | X |  |
| B | 10 | X | X | X | 12 | X | X |  |
| C | 11 | X | X | X | X | 22 | X |  |
| D | 8 | X | X | X | 7 | 21 | 25 |  |
| E | 17 | 12 | X | 7 | X | X | 15 | Connected |
| F | X | X | 22 | 21 | X | X | (14) | Connected |
| G | X | X | X | 25 | (15) | 14 | X | Connected |

From

*Steps 2, 3 & 4*

**To**

| From | A | B | C | D | E | F | G | |
|---|---|---|---|---|---|---|---|---|
| A | X | 10 | 11 | 8 | 17 | X | X | |
| B | 10 | X | X | X | X | 12 | X | |
| C | 11 | X | X | X | X | 22 | X | |
| D | 8 | X | X | X | 7 | 21 | 25 | Connected |
| E | 17 | 12 | X | (7) | X | X | 15 | Connected |
| F | X | X | 22 | 21 | X | X | (14) | Connected |
| G | X | X | X | 25 | (15) | 14 | X | Connected |

*Steps 2, 3 & 4*

**To**

| From | A | B | C | D | E | F | G | |
|---|---|---|---|---|---|---|---|---|
| A | X | 10 | 11 | 8 | 17 | X | X | Connected |
| B | 10 | X | X | X | 12 | X | X | |
| C | 11 | X | X | X | X | 22 | X | |
| D | (8) | X | X | X | 7 | 21 | 25 | Connected |
| E | 17 | 12 | X | (7) | X | X | 15 | Connected |
| F | X | X | 22 | 21 | X | X | (14) | Connected |
| G | X | X | X | 25 | (15) | 14 | X | Connected |

*Steps 2, 3 & 4*

**To**

| From | A | B | C | D | E | F | G | |
|---|---|---|---|---|---|---|---|---|
| A | X | (10) | 11 | 8 | 17 | X | X | Connected |
| B | 10 | X | X | X | 12 | X | X | Connected |
| C | 11 | X | X | X | X | 22 | X | |
| D | (8) | X | X | X | 7 | 21 | 25 | Connected |
| E | 17 | 12 | X | (7) | X | X | 15 | Connected |
| F | X | X | 22 | 21 | X | X | (14) | Connected |
| G | X | X | X | 25 | (15) | 14 | X | Connected |

*Steps 2, 3 & 4*

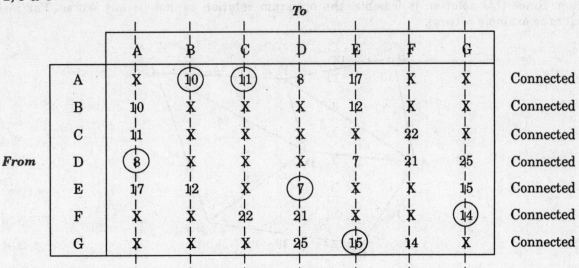

| | To | | | | | | |
|---|---|---|---|---|---|---|---|
| | A | B | C | D | E | F | G |
| A | X | ⑩ | ⑪ | 8 | 17 | X | X | Connected |
| B | 10 | X | X | X | 12 | X | X | Connected |
| C | 11 | X | X | X | X | 22 | X | Connected |
| D | ⑧ | X | X | X | 7 | 21 | 25 | Connected |
| E | 17 | 12 | X | ⑦ | X | X | 15 | Connected |
| F | X | X | 22 | 21 | X | X | ⑭ | Connected |
| G | X | X | X | 25 | ⑮ | 14 | X | Connected |

So, the minimum connector has a length of: 14 + 15 + 7 + 8 + 10 + 11 = 65.

The minimum connector is made up of the arcs FG, GE, ED, DA, AB and AC; its diagram looks like:

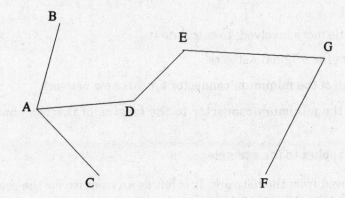

*Note:*

i) The word 'connected' means that the node has been added to the minimum connector.

ii) Crossing out a column signifies that the node need not be considered for adding to the minimum connector.

## The travelling salesman problem

There is no known algorithm that provides an efficient method for finding the solution to the travelling salesman problem. A feasible way of providing a solution is to consider every possible route in turn and choose the shortest. This method of approach is fine for networks that consist of a small number of nodes and arcs but for larger networks this becomes impractical even with the aid of a computer. For instance, the number of possible routes on a network with 20 nodes is about $1.2 \times 10^{17}$; so, even a computer capable of evaluating 1 million routes a second would be kept busy for approximately 4000 years!

In this situation, the best that can be achieved is an approximate idea of the size of the minimum travelling distance. This is usually specified in terms of a *lower bound* and an *upper bound*; that is, a pair of values between which it is known that the minimum travelling distance lies.

Calculating an upper bound is straightforward and consists of using common sense to arrive at any solution. Since this solution is feasible, the optimum solution cannot be any worse. For instance, consider the example network:

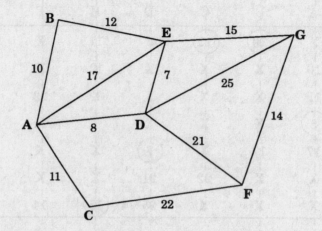

It is relatively easy to see that, if the travelling salesman starts at A, then ABEGDFCA is a feasible route. The length of this route is: $10 + 12 + 15 + 25 + 21 + 22 + 11 = 116$; so, 116 is an upper bound for the optimum route. In other words, there may be many routes shorter than 116, but the best solution cannot be longer than 116. (Note that it may be possible to find an even better upper bound simply by trial and error).

Finding a lower bound is a little more involved; to calculate it:

    i)   Remove a node from the original network

    ii)  Calculate the length of the minimum connector for this new network

    iii) Add the length of the minimum connector to the lengths of the two shortest arcs from the removed node

Consider this procedure as it applies to the example:

a)   Suppose vertex G is removed from the network. It is left as an exercise for the reader to confirm that the minimum connector for the remaining nodes is:

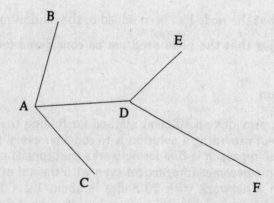

b)    The minimum connector has a length of: 7 + 8 + 10 + 11 + 21 = 57.

c)    The two shortest arcs from node G are: GE = 15 and GF = 14; so, a lower bound for the travelling salesman problem is: 57 + 15 + 14 = 86. This means that the optimum solution must be at least 86.

The optimum solution to this travelling salesman problem, therefore, lies between 86 and 116.

*Note:*

i)    The optimum solution may, in fact, be longer than the value obtained as a lower bound; the lower bound is not a guarantee that a route as short as it actually exists.

ii)   If, by trial-and-error or good luck, a solution is found that is equal to the lower bound, then that solution must be an optimum solution.

# Unit 13: Problem-solving techniques 5 – Critical path analysis

This section aims to help you to:

1. understand what is meant by an 'activity network'
2. be able to construct activity networks
3. be able to determine the critical path through an activity network
4. be able to apply critical path analysis to activity-based problems

## What is Critical Path Analysis?

*Critical Path Analysis* (CPA) is a technique for solving problems concerned with the organisation and scheduling of several *activities*. In CPA terminology, a task consisting of a number of separate activities is called a *project*. For instance, the 'project' of making a cup of tea includes these activities:

> Fill kettle with water
> Boil water
> Find teapot and cups
> Put tea in teapot
> Pour water into teapot
> Allow tea to brew
> Put milk in cups
> Pour tea into cups

Some of these activities can be carried out simultaneously (this is the principle of *concurrence*); examples of concurrent activities are 'boil water' and 'find teapot and cups'. Certain activities cannot be started until others have been completed (this is the principle of *precedence*); for example, the activity 'find teapot and cups' must precede the activity 'put tea in teapot'. The start / finish of an activity is called an *event*. So, for example, one event indicates the start of 'fill kettle'; another event marks the completion of 'fill kettle' and the start of 'boil water'. The relationship between activities and events can be shown as follows:

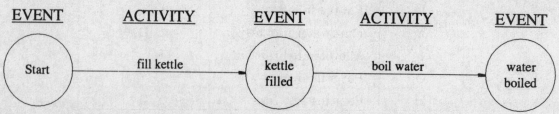

The important distinction between activities and events is that an activity takes time but an event merely indicates a moment in time when something has been completed.

Note also that some items on the above list are not usually thought of as being 'activities' in the normal sense of the word of using energy or money; for instance, the activity 'allow tea to brew'. However, 'allow tea to brew' has an associated time factor which in turn contributes to the total time needed to complete the overall task and affects the minimum possible completion time. So, any activities that take time to complete must be included.

The timings for the activities might be:

| Activity | Activity description | Duration (secs) |
|----------|----------------------|-----------------|
| A | Fill kettle with water | 8 |
| B | Boil water | 60 |
| C | Find teapot and cups | 25 |
| D | Put tea in teapot | 6 |
| E | Pour water into teapot | 10 |
| F | Allow tea to brew | 45 |
| G | Put milk in cups | 10 |
| H | Pour tea into cups | 20 |

The total of the separate activity times is 194s. This means that if each activity on the list is not started before the previous activity is completed then the tea-making takes 194s; (so, 194s is an upper bound on the completion time). It is obviously possible to reduce this time since some activities can take place concurrently. However, even in this simple example, it is not immediately apparent what the minimum project completion time might be.

## Precedence tables

To help with the task of determining the minimum completion time, it is normal to construct an *activity network*. This is a diagrammatic form of the information showing the relationships between the different activities. Once it has been produced, CPA techniques can be applied to analyse the network and determine the minimum completion time.

However, before producing the activity network it is sensible to construct a *precedence table* that gives a list showing each activity and its immediately preceding activities. This makes the job of network construction far easier; for instance, the precedence table for the tea-making activities looks like:

| Activity | Activity description | Preceding activity |
|----------|----------------------|--------------------|
| A | Fill kettle with water | — |
| B | Boil water | A |
| C | Find teapot and cups | — |
| D | Put tea in teapot | C |
| E | Pour water into teapot | B, D |
| F | Allow tea to brew | E |
| G | Put milk in cups | C |
| H | Pour tea into cups | F, G |

Note that activities A and C are not dependent on any preceding activities.

# Activity networks

This is a completed activity network for the tea-making example:

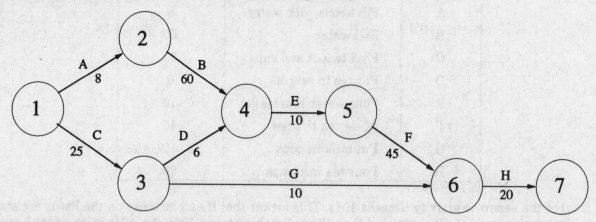

The network consists of two basic components:

i) Arcs (Arrows)

ii) Nodes (Circles)

*Arcs*: These represent the activities.

The activity letter is shown above the arc; its duration is shown below the arc.

The length of an arc is not in proportion to the activity duration.

The arcs are arrowed to give the feeling of flow of time from left to right.

The orientation of an arc is not significant; some need to be angled for drawing purposes.

*Nodes*: These represent the start and finish of the activities; that is, the events.

The node at the beginning of an activity is called the 'tail' node; the node at the end of the activity is called the 'head' node.

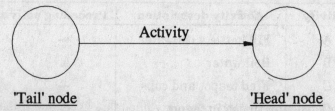

'Tail' node            'Head' node

Network nodes are numbered so that the head node number is greater than the tail node number. (This provides a useful way of describing an activity; for example, the activity 'boil water' can be described as activity 2-4).

There must be only one start node and one finish node in the network.

Note that, where more than one arc enters a node, this represents the completion of all activities leading to that node (this is referred to as a *merge* node). For instance, since activity B and activity D enter node 4, *both* activities must be completed before activity E can begin; so, node 4 is a merge node. Similarly, some nodes generate a number of emerging arcs (this is referred to as a *burst* node). For instance, neither activity D nor activity G can begin until activity C has been completed; so, node 3 is a burst node.

Constructing a network from a precedence table is not always straightforward and it may be helpful to draw 'subnetworks', each of which represents a line of the precedence table. So, in the example:

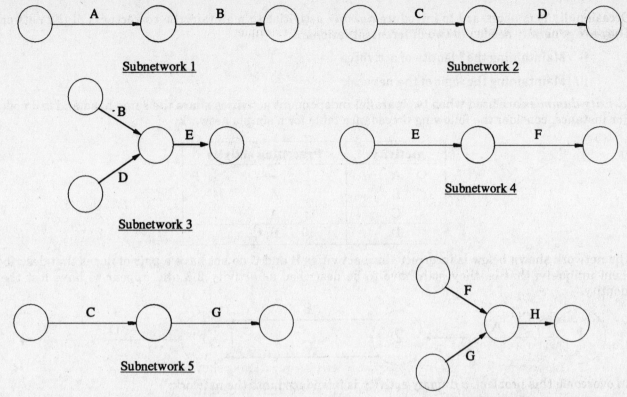

The subnetworks can then be linked together so that any duplicate arcs appearing in different subnetworks are combined into a single arc. For instance, subnetwork 3 and subnetwork 4 can be combined to give:

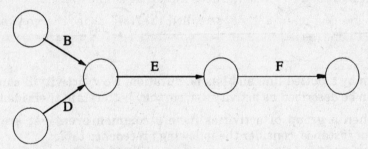

Continuing in this fashion, ensuring that there is only one start node, one finish node and angling arcs where necessary, the complete network looks like:

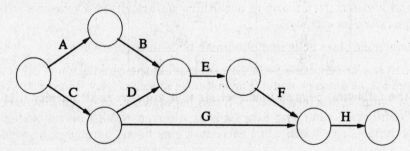

## Dummy activities

Occasionally it is necessary to introduce *dummy* activities to maintain the correctness of the network. They are generally needed in two different situations:

i)   Maintaining the identity of activities

ii)  Maintaining the logic of the network

*Identity dummies* are used when two parallel independent activities share the same head and tail nodes. For instance, consider the following precedence table for a simple network:

| Activity | Preceding activity |
|----------|--------------------|
| A | — |
| B | A |
| C | A |
| D | B, C |

The network shown below is incorrect since activities B and C do not have a pair of nodes that describes them uniquely; that is, they both have to be described as activity 2-3 and appear to have lost their identity.

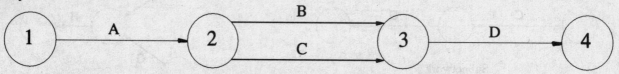

To overcome this problem, a dummy activity is introduced into the network:

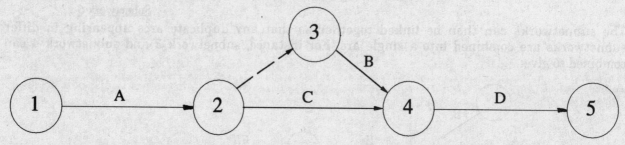

The dummy activity is shown by a dotted line and has no duration. Now, activity B can be described as activity 3-4 and activity C can be described as activity 2-4; so, they both retain their identities.

*Logic dummies* are used when a group of activities have a common event yet are at least partly independent of each other. For instance, consider the following precedence table:

| Activity | Preceding activity |
|----------|--------------------|
| P | — |
| Q | — |
| R | P, Q |
| S | Q |

The network shown on the following page is incorrect since it appears that activity S is dependent on both activity P and activity Q:

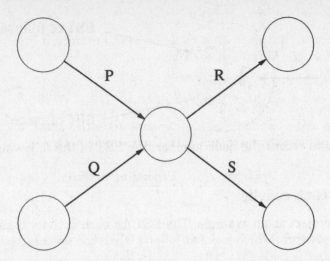

The correct representation is shown here with a dummy activity introduced into the network:

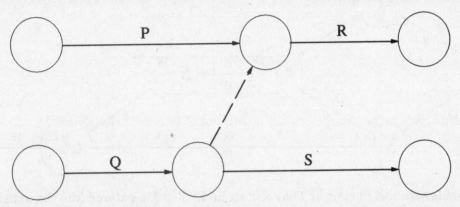

Again, the dummy does not have a duration; it has been introduced into the network only to maintain the logical dependencies between the different activities.

## Critical path analysis

There are two stages of calculation necessary to determine the critical path through an activity network. These are the calculation of:

   i)   the earliest start time (EST) for each activity

   ii)  the latest finish time (LFT) for each activity

The EST for each activity is calculated by performing a *forward pass* through the network. The LFT for each activity is calculated by performing a *backward pass* through the network.

The critical path is then determined by locating those activities which have an identical EST and LFT.

The results of calculating the EST and LFT for each activity are written on the network; this requires a slight modification to the nodes so that they can accommodate all the information.

Each node on the network is drawn as shown below:

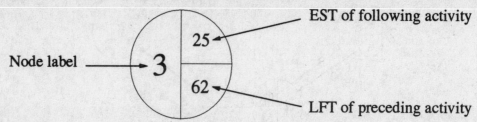

The node can now be used to record the node number, the EST of the following activity and the LFT of the preceding activity.

## Calculating the EST for each activity

Consider the tea-making project as an example. The EST for each activity is calculated by performing a forward pass through the network, which looks as follows when the process is completed:

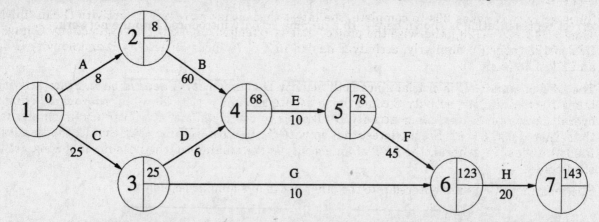

i) The project is assumed to start at Time = 0; so, an EST of 0 is entered into the upper half of node 1.

This simply means that the earliest time that activity A and activity C can start is 0.

ii) Since activity A has to be completed before activity B can start, this means that activity B cannot start until Time = 0 + 8 = 8. Activity B, therefore, has an EST of 8 (node 2).

Similarly, both activity D and activity G have an EST of 25 (node 3).

iii) Activity E cannot start until both activity B and activity D are complete. Now, activity B is not completed until Time = 8 + 60 = 68; activity D is not completed until Time = 25 + 6 = 31. So, the earliest that activity E can start is Time = 68; that is, the largest of the two activity completion times. In general, the EST of an activity is the largest of the completion times of its preceding activities.

iv) The remaining ESTs are entered into the other nodes in a similar fashion.

Note that the minimum time for making the tea is 143s; this is considerably less than the 194s upper bound obtained earlier and is due to performing parallel activities where possible.

## Calculating the LFT for each activity

The LFT for each activity is calculated by performing a backward pass through the network, which looks as follows when the process is completed:

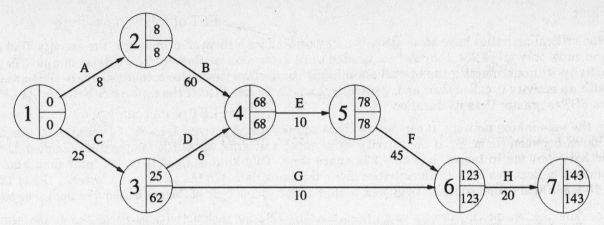

i) The project finishes at Time = 143; so, a value of 143 is entered into the lower half of node 7.

ii) Since activity H takes 20s to complete, the latest that either activity F or activity G can finish is Time = 143 - 20 = 123, otherwise the project time is extended. So, activity F and activity G have an LFT of 123 (node 6). Similarly, activity E has an LFT of 78 (node 5); activity B and activity D have an LFT of 68 (node 4).

iii) The LFT of activity C is crucial since both activity D and activity G depend on it. Since activity G takes 10s to complete, activity C could finish as late as Time = 123 - 10 = 113, without delaying the overall project; however, since activity D takes 6s to complete, activity C cannot finish any later than Time = 68 - 6 = 62. So, the latest that activity C can finish is Time = 62; that is, the smallest of the two times. In general, the LFT of an activity is the smallest of the possible following activity start times.

iv) The remaining LFTs are entered into the other nodes in a similar fashion.

## The critical path

*Critical* activities are those activities that must begin on time and finish on time if the project completion time is not to be delayed. For instance, it is clear that 'boil water' is a critical activity; that is, any delay in completing this activity will have a knock-on effect and delay the end of the tea-making. Together, critical activities such as 'find kettle', 'boil water', 'pour water into teapot' etc. make up the critical path. Generally, the critical path can be determined by noting those activities that have an identical EST and LFT. In the example, therefore, the critical path is: A - B - E - F - H and is highlighted in the diagram below. Delaying any activity on the critical path will increase the overall project time.

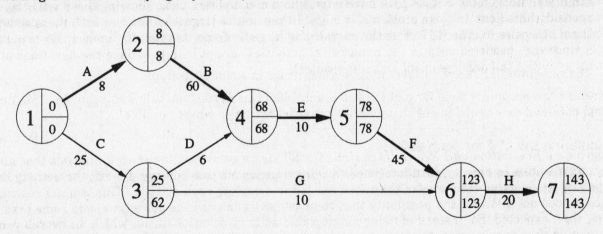

## Float

Non-critical activities have some spare time associated with them. For instance, the activity 'find teapot and cups' only takes 25s; they are not needed until Time = 62, so there can be a delay of upto 37s in this activity without affecting the overall tea-making completion time. The amount of spare time associated with an activity is called *float* and, generally, an activity has float if the difference between its LFT and its EST is greater than its duration.

In the tea-making network, it can be seen that activity C and activity D have 37s spare time; this time is shared between them. So, if the activity 'find teapot and cups' takes 10s longer than planned, then the activity 'put tea in teapot' has only 27s spare time. This kind of float is called *total* float and is the amount of float available to all activities along the same path. On the other hand, activity G has 123 - 25 - 10 = 88s spare time which belongs just to that activity; this type of float is called *free* float. For each activity:

i)   Total float = Head LFT - Tail EST - duration

   e.g. for activity C, total float = 62 - 0 - 25 = 37

ii)  Free float = Head EST - Tail EST - duration

   e.g. for activity G, free float = 123 - 25 - 10 = 88

The total float for an activity is always larger than, or equal to, its free float.

An analysis of the activity floats for the tea-making project is shown below:

| Activity | Nodes | Head node | | Tail node | | Duration | Total float | Free float |
|----------|-------|-----|-----|-----|-----|----------|-------------|------------|
|          |       | EST | LFT | EST | LFT |          |             |            |
| A | 1 - 2 | 8   | 8   | 0   | 0   | 8  | 0  | 0  |
| B | 2 - 4 | 68  | 68  | 8   | 8   | 60 | 0  | 0  |
| C | 1 - 3 | 25  | 62  | 0   | 0   | 25 | 37 | 0  |
| D | 3 - 4 | 68  | 68  | 25  | 62  | 6  | 37 | 37 |
| E | 4 - 5 | 78  | 78  | 68  | 68  | 10 | 0  | 0  |
| F | 5 - 6 | 123 | 123 | 78  | 78  | 45 | 0  | 0  |
| G | 3 - 6 | 123 | 123 | 25  | 62  | 10 | 88 | 88 |
| H | 6 - 7 | 143 | 143 | 123 | 123 | 20 | 0  | 0  |

Note that activities on the critical path have a total float of 0, the table also showing those activities that have considerable float. In some problems, it might be possible to transfer resources from these activities to critical activities in order to reduce the overall project time. In the tea-making project this is not possible, since the resources used in the non-critical activities cannot help to reduce the durations of the critical activities (all are dependent on boiling water).

# PERT

*Programme Evaluation and Review Technique* (PERT) is an extension to network analysis that allows for uncertainties in activity duration times. For instance, in the tea-making project, the activity durations are single-value estimates of the times needed to complete each activity. This is quite restrictive since it does not allow for the possibility that some activities might take more time, and some take less time, than expected. So, instead of using single-value activity durations from which an overall project completion time is calculated, it is more sensible to have an indication of the likely range of durations for each activity; from these it is then possible to gain an idea of the range of project completion times.

In the long run, there are likely to be more activities that overrun their expected duration than there are activities that are completed quicker than expected. In fact, the distribution of times can be shown to follow a probability distribution called a *beta* distribution.

Knowing this makes it possible to:

i)    approximate the mean and standard deviation for the duration of each activity

ii)   combine the results of i) to determine the mean and standard deviation for the overall project time

For each activity, suppose that:

$a =$    the most optimistic time for completion of an activity;
that is, the shortest possible time

$b =$    the most likely time for completion of an activity;
that is, the time used in the network analysis

$c =$    the most pessimistic time for completion of an activity;
that is, the worst conceivable time

Estimates for the mean and standard deviation of each activity duration can then be calculated, as follows:

$$\text{Mean duration} = \frac{a+4b+c}{6}$$

$$\text{Standard deviation} = \frac{(c-a)}{6}$$

Once these have been calculated for each activity along the critical path, estimates for the mean and standard deviation of the overall project can be calculated by combining the results, as follows:

$$\text{Project mean } = \sum(\text{Individual activity means})$$

$$\text{Project standard deviation } = \sqrt{\sum(\text{Individual activity standard deviations})^2}$$

For instance, consider the following table which gives the optimistic time, expected time and pessimistic time for each activity along the critical path of the tea-making project:

| Activity | Optimistic duration | Most likely duration | Pessimistic duration | Mean | Standard deviation |
|---|---|---|---|---|---|
| A | 7 | 8 | 12 | $\frac{(7+32+12)}{6} = 8.5$ | $\frac{(12\text{-}7)}{6} = 0.83$ |
| B | 50 | 60 | 75 | $\frac{(50+240+75)}{6} = 60.83$ | $\frac{(75\text{-}50)}{6} = 4.17$ |
| E | 8 | 10 | 13 | $\frac{(8+40+13)}{6} = 10.17$ | $\frac{(13\text{-}8)}{6} = 0.83$ |
| F | 40 | 45 | 55 | $\frac{(40+180+55)}{6} = 45.83$ | $\frac{(55\text{-}40)}{6} = 2.5$ |
| H | 16 | 20 | 26 | $\frac{(16+80+26)}{6} = 20.33$ | $\frac{(26\text{-}16)}{6} = 1.67$ |

So, for the overall project:

$$\text{Project mean } = 8.5 + 60.83 + 10.17 + 45.83 + 20.33 = 145.66$$

$$\text{Project standard deviation } = \sqrt{\left(0.83^2 + 4.17^2 + 0.83^2 + 2.5^2 + 1.67^2\right)} = 5.27$$

From these results, it can be concluded that the average tea-making time is 145.66s with a standard deviation of 5.27s. Assuming that the final distribution is normal, what this means is that there is a 95% chance that the tea-making will take between 145.66 + 1.96 × 5.27s and 145.66 − 1.96 × 5.27s. That is, rounding the results, there is a 95% chance that the tea-making will take between 135s and 156s.

Note that, when there are uncertainties about activity durations, it cannot always be assumed that the critical path found by using the most likely durations will always be the critical path. It is wise, therefore, to treat the results of PERT analysis with some caution.

# Section 3

---

**Further tasks and investigations**

The sequence of topics in this section is the same as that in Section 2 and contains the following:

(i)  Further tasks based on the material in Sections 1 and 2. These are designed to help you consolidate the  skills and techniques developed in those sections.

(ii) Extended investigations which provide the stimulus for you to research information, undertake further reading and answer additional questions. The extended work is related to topics developed in Section  2 but not necessarily dealt with explicitly within that section.

This section is intended for students studying on a taught course. The lecturer may wish you to do further investigations, either on your own or as part of a team, in order to assess your progress. For this reason, no answers are provided to tasks in this section.

If you are studying independently, you can check that you have understood the concepts in Section 2 by checking your answers to all the Section 1 tasks in Appendix B.

# Unit 1: Modelling, graphs and functions

1. *Day nursery*

   The Institute has decided to establish a day nursery at the Brooklands campus, for children of staff and students. A large room (18m long, 12m wide, 3.5m high) has been earmarked for the nursery and a sum of money allocated to buy toys, play equipment, furnishings etc. It is decided to decorate the walls with brightly coloured patterned wallpaper. The room has two doors (each 2m by 80cm) and two windows (each 3m by 1.5m).

   a) Estimate the number of rolls of wallpaper needed for the room. You should:

      i) Make a list of the relevant variables

      ii) Write down any simplifying assumptions you make

      iii) Make a note of the sort of calculations you need to perform

      iv) Obtain any other necessary information and solve the problem

   b) Construct a mathematical model which can be used to estimate the number of rolls of wallpaper required for any given room.

   c) i) Implement your model on a spreadsheet

      ii) Validate it using the data in (a)

      iii) Use it to calculate the number of rolls of wallpaper required for a room measuring 6m by 4m by 2.5m with one door (2m by 80cm) and two windows (each 1.5m by 1.2m).

2. *Library book fines*

   a) Make a list of the variables which are involved in deciding how much fine has to be paid if library books are returned after the due date.

   b) Formulate a model which gives the amount of fine to be paid as a function of these variables.

3. *'Student Saver'*

   A special 'Student Saver' account is available at the Chelford Building Society. It has been designed to appeal to students by offering: a £1 minimum account opener, instant access to funds, cashcard and attractive rates, arranged in bands according to the amount invested. The current rates of interest are:

   | Amount invested (£) | Net rate of interest (% p.a.) |
   |---|---|
   | 1 – 499 | 4.5 |
   | 500 – 2499 | 6.73 |
   | 2500 – 4999 | 6.85 |
   | 5000 – 9999 | 7.16 |
   | 10000 – 24999 | 7.64 |
   | > 25000 | 7.85 |

   Draw a graph which shows the interest received (*i*) as a function of the amount invested (*a*).

**Information Bank:** *Mathematical models, pages 95 – 104*
*Functions and graphs, pages 105 – 107; 112 – 117*

4. *Relationships*

Produce a graph for these situations, showing the relationship between the variables in brackets. (The independent variable is given first). State any assumptions that you are making in each case.

a) Riding in a lift (time, height)

b) Driving over 'sleeping policeman' speed restriction humps (time, speed)

c) Raising the flag on a flagpole (time, height)

d) Winning a raffle with your solitary ticket (no. of tickets sold, chance of winning)

e) Lighting-up times (month, lighting-up time)

f) Life expectancy (no. of years alive, % of people still alive)

g) Car insurance premiums (age, premium)

5. *Theme park*

Each year a group of Mechanical Engineering students are taken on a visit to a theme park to observe the mechanics of some of the rides. Part of their task is to sketch motion graphs which represent the movement of each ride. Shown below are some of their incorrect attempts. In each case:

a) say why the graph is incorrect

b) produce a better graph

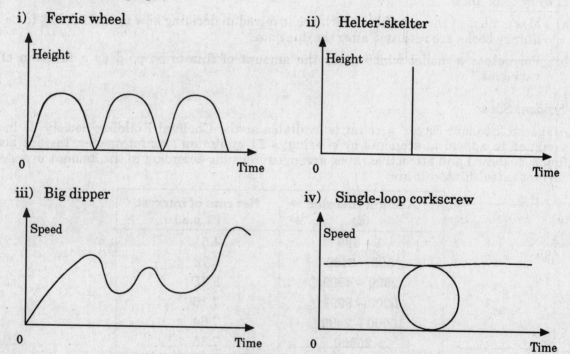

i) Ferris wheel

ii) Helter-skelter

iii) Big dipper

iv) Single-loop corkscrew

**Information Bank:** *Functions and graphs, pages 108 – 111*

6. *Playground*

The Brooklands campus day nursery, run for the children of students and staff, provides a very useful service, especially for mature students with young children who might otherwise have difficulties attending the Institute. One of the other benefits is that students on the Primary B.Ed. course can observe the social behaviour of children in a pre-school setting. With this in mind, students operate a rota system to take some of the children to a nearby adventure playground once each week. There is the usual variety of play apparatus available. One of the more mathematically inclined students sketched graphs to show the behaviour of each piece of apparatus. She took several attempts to get them right, and they are shown below. In each case, say which of the graphs A, B, C or D is the most accurate representation:

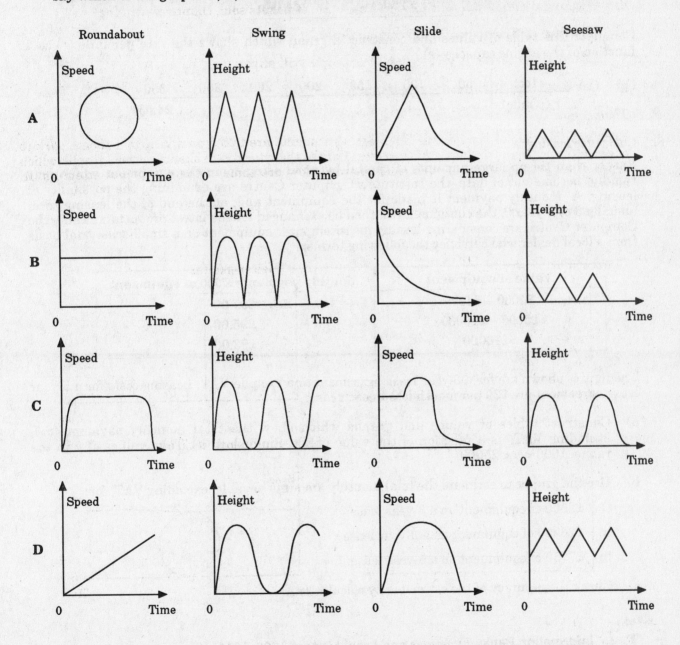

7. *Motor cycle allowances*

The Institute operates a scheme for reimbursing travel expenses to staff, if they are incurred as part of their normal daily work (see Section 1 Unit 5 – 'Car Allowances'). The current rates for motor cycle users are given in the table below. The rate varies according to the engine capacity, as follows:

| Engine size | Rate / mile |
|---|---|
| Up to 150cc | 14.00p |
| 151 – 250cc | 18.03p |
| > 250cc | 24.03p |

Complete this table of values and construct a graph which shows the rate per mile ($r$) as a function of the engine capacity ($e$):

| $e$ (cc) | 50 | 100 | 150 | 200 | 250 | 300 | 350 |
|---|---|---|---|---|---|---|---|
| $r$ (p/mile) | | 14 | | | | | 24.03 |

8. *Computer leasing*

Rather than tie up large amounts of capital by purchasing computer equipment which may rapidly become out of date, the Institute's Computer Centre are examining the possibility of leasing. A monthly payment is made for the equipment and, at the end of the leasing term (usually 3 or 5 years), the equipment can then be exchanged for the latest products. Initially the Computer Centre are considering leasing microcomputer equipment on a small-scale trial basis from a local dealer who can offer the following terms:

| Value of equipment | Monthly payment / £'000 of equipment |
|---|---|
| £1000 – £4999 | £97.00 |
| £5000 – £10000 | £95.00 |
| >£10000 | £93.00 |

The figures shown are for a 3-year lease agreement and exclude VAT. Leasing costs for a 5-year lease agreement are £20 per month less in each case.

a) Construct tables of values and graphs which show the total monthly payment ($m$), excluding VAT, as a function of the value of the equipment ($v$). Take values of $v$ in the range: $1000 < v < 25000$.

b) Use the graphs to estimate the total monthly amounts payable, excluding VAT, for:

i) £3500 of equipment on a 3-year lease

ii) £23250 of equipment on a 3-year lease

iii) £7750 of equipment on a 5-year lease

c) Check the accuracy of the estimates by calculation.

**Information Bank:** *Functions and graphs, pages 105 – 107; 113*

## 9. Linear functions (1)

This is the graph of $y = x$:

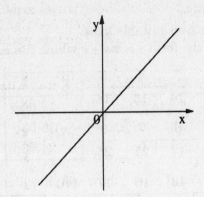

Write down possible equations for each of the graphs A – I:

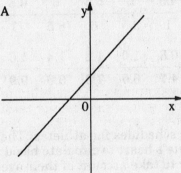

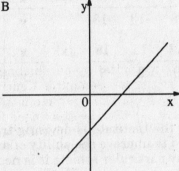

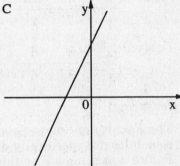

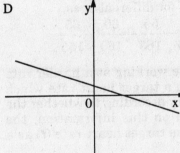

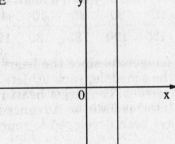

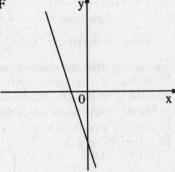

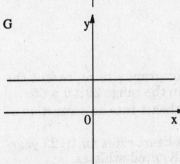

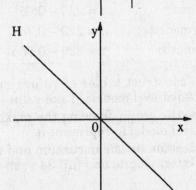

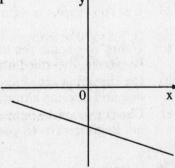

**Information Bank:** *Functions and graphs, pages 112 – 117*

## 10. Linear functions (2)

For each of these tables of values:

a) Plot them as a set of points on suitable axes

b) Find a linear function in the form $y = mx + c$ which fits each set of points

(i)

| x | 0 | 1 | 2 | 3 | 4 | 5 |
|---|---|---|---|---|---|---|
| y | 8 | 10 | 12 | 14 | 16 | 18 |

(ii)

| x | 0 | 1 | 2 | 3 | 4 | 5 |
|---|---|---|---|---|---|---|
| y | 12 | 9 | 6 | 3 | 0 | -3 |

(iii)

| x | 3 | 4 | 5 | 6 | 7 | 8 |
|---|---|---|---|---|---|---|
| y | 5 | 9 | 13 | 17 | 21 | 25 |

(iv)

| x | 3 | 4 | 5 | 6 | 7 | 8 |
|---|---|---|---|---|---|---|
| y | 14 | 15 | 16 | 17 | 18 | 19 |

(v)

| x | 7 | 9 | 11 | 13 | 15 | 17 |
|---|---|---|---|---|---|---|
| y | 6 | 10 | 14 | 18 | 22 | 26 |

(vi)

| x | -2 | -1 | 0 | 1 | 2 | 3 |
|---|---|---|---|---|---|---|
| y | 5 | 6 | 7 | 8 | 9 | 10 |

(vii)

| x | -14 | -12 | -10 | -8 | -6 | -4 |
|---|---|---|---|---|---|---|
| y | 7 | 2 | -3 | -8 | -13 | -18 |

(viii)

| x | 4 | 4.5 | 5 | 5.5 | 6 | 6.5 |
|---|---|---|---|---|---|---|
| y | -1.5 | 1 | 3.5 | 6 | 8.5 | 11 |

(ix)

| x | 3 | 6 | 9 | 12 | 15 | 18 |
|---|---|---|---|---|---|---|
| y | 3 | 3 | 3 | 3 | 3 | 3 |

(x)

| x | 0.6 | 0.8 | 1.0 | 1.2 | 1.4 | 1.6 |
|---|---|---|---|---|---|---|
| y | 3.4 | 4.7 | 6.0 | 7.3 | 8.6 | 9.9 |

## 11. Heart rates

The Faculty of Sports Science at the Institute is devising training schedules for athletes. The schedules are specifically designed to improve the ability of an athlete's heart to circulate blood. Before allocating a schedule to any particular athlete it is necessary to take account of their age in order that it is safe to undertake the training. The faculty draw up the following table, which gives estimates of the fastest possible rate at which a heart can beat, for different ages:

| Age (years) | 20 | 25 | 30 | 35 | 40 | 45 | 50 | 55 | 60 | 65 |
|---|---|---|---|---|---|---|---|---|---|---|
| Max. rate (beats / min.) | 200 | 195 | 190 | 185 | 180 | 175 | 170 | 165 | 160 | 155 |

Reaching the maximum could be dangerous since the heart could be working at a harder rate than the it can cope with. So, in the schedule, each athlete is given a target heart rate which should provide the required improvement. The target heart rates vary according to whether the athlete is classed as Beginner, Intermediate or Advanced. Based on this information, the following mathematical models have been developed to represent the target heart rate ($t$) as a function of age ($a$):

| Beginner: | $t = 220 - 0.6a$ |
|---|---|
| Intermediate: | $t = 220 - 0.7a$ |
| Advanced: | $t = 220 - 0.85a$ |

a) Using the same set of axes, construct tables of values and plot graphs to represent the Beginner, Intermediate and Advanced models. Take values of a in the range $20 \leq a \leq 65$.

b) On the same set of axes draw the graph showing the maximum heart rate as a function of age and develop a mathematical model to represent it.

c) Use the graphs and models to estimate the maximum and target heart rates for (i) 23 year-old Beginner (ii) 46 year-old Intermediate and (iii) 34 year-old Advanced athletes.

**Information Bank:** *Functions and graphs, pages 112 – 117*

## 12. *Quadratic functions (1)*

This is the graph of $y = x^2$:

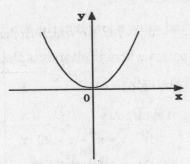

Write down possible equations for each of the graphs A – I:

A
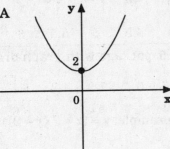

B
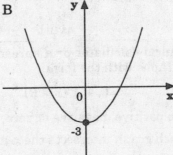

C
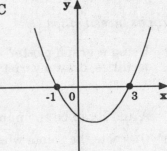

D
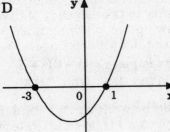

E
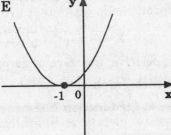

F
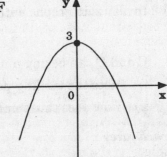

G
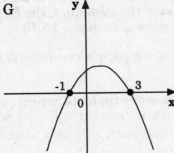

H
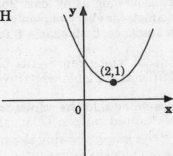

I
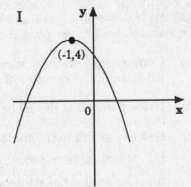

**Information Bank:** *Functions and graphs, pages 117 – 122*

## 13. Quadratic functions (2)

For each of the following quadratic functions:

a) Construct a table of values and draw a graph of the function

b) Find the coordinates of the points where it intersects the $x$-axis

c) Find the coordinates of the turning-point

d) Find the equation of the line of symmetry

| | | |
|---|---|---|
| i) $\quad y = x^2 - 7x + 10$ | ii) $\quad y = x^2 - x + 20$ | iii) $\quad y = x^2 - 25$ |
| iv) $\quad y = x^2 + 3x + 4$ | v) $\quad y = 16 - 6x - x^2$ | vi) $\quad y = -1 - 5x - 2x^2$ |
| vii) $\quad y = 24 - 7x - 6x^2$ | viii) $\quad y = 2x^2 - 11x + 12$ | ix) $\quad y = -7 + 3x - x^2$ |

## 14. Graphs investigation (1)

a) Using a graph-plotter, graphical calculator or a spreadsheet package with graph-drawing facilities, draw a variety of graphs with the form:

$$y = (x + A)(x + B)$$

A and B can be any numbers; positive, negative or zero; for example: $y = (x + 7)(x - 2)$

i) note the points where each graph intersects the $x$-axis

ii) how do these points relate to the function ?

b) Investigate graphs with the form:

$$y = (x + C)^2 + D$$

C and D can be any numbers; positive, negative or zero; for example: $y = (x - 3)^2 + 5$

i) note the turning-point of each graph

ii) how does this point relate to the function ?

## 15. Coach fares

The student's union is organising an outing to an open-air concert. A local bus company will hire out one of its 60-seater coaches as long as at least 25 people travel. The fare is £6.10 per person if this minimum number is met; for every person in excess of the minimum, the fare will be reduced by 10p per person. For instance, if 32 people travel, each will each pay £5.40.

a) Construct a mathematical model which represents the bus company's revenue (£$r$) as a function of the number of *additional* students who travel ($s$).

b) Draw a graph of the model, assuming that the minimum number of students travel.

c) Use the graph to calculate:

i) the maximum amount of revenue that the bus company can expect

ii) the number of students needed for this amount of revenue

iii) the cost to each student, in this case

**Information Bank:** *Functions and graphs, pages 117 – 122*

16. *Leisure development*

It is proposed to develop an area of ground, on the embankment of the River Dale, as a leisure complex. The complex would include a swimming pool, cinema, fast-food takeaways, nightclub and bowling alley. The radical architectural design of the complex makes it a point of controversy; a group consisting of local residents argues that the development will detract from the quiet beauty of the river surrounds; the developers stress the benefits to the local economy.

The residents say that the more money is spent on developing the site, the more it loses its appeal. After analysing the results of a survey carried out among people living in the vicinity of the development, the attractiveness of the site is shown to behave according to the mathematical model:

$$a = 50 - 6x$$

where *a* is a measure of the site's attractiveness if £*x* million is spent on development.

The developers say that the more money is spent on developing the site, the more it gains in value. A similar survey carried out in the local business community suggest that a more appropriate model is:

$$a = 50 + 8x$$

a)   Using the same set of axes, draw a graph for each model; take values of *x* in the range $0 \leq x \leq 10$.

b)   Use the graphs to find out:

   i)    what would be the value of *a*, according to the developers, if £6 million were to be invested ?

   ii)   what would be the residents' value of *a*, for the same amount ?

   iii)  what is the site's measure of attractiveness without the development ?

   iv)   what amount of investment would destroy the site's attractiveness ?

c)   To take account of the different viewpoints both models are combined to make the following:

$$a = (50 - 6x)(50 + 8x)$$

Construct a table of values, draw a graph and use it find out what level of investment will maximise the site's attractiveness in this situation.

**Information Bank:** *Functions and graphs, pages 112 – 122*

17. **Which graph?**

Match each of the graphs A – I with a function from this list:

1. $y = -2x^2$

2. $y = -x^3$

3. $y = (x - 2)(x + 3)(x - 4)$

4. $y = \dfrac{1}{x}$

5. $y = x + \dfrac{1}{x}$

6. $y = \sqrt{x}$

7. $y = x(x - 3)^2$

8. $y = \dfrac{(2x - 5)}{x}$

9. $y = \dfrac{1}{(x + 2)}$

A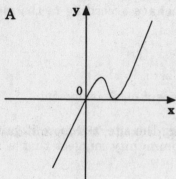

B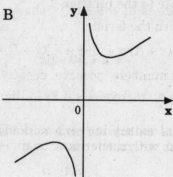

C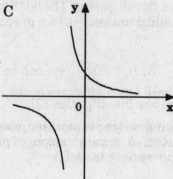

D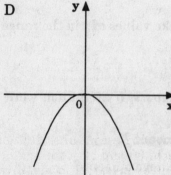

E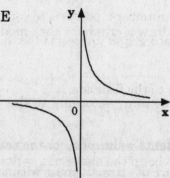

F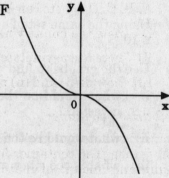

G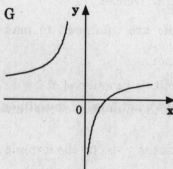

H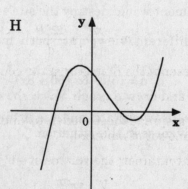

I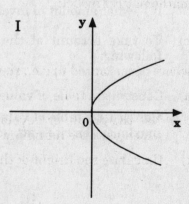

**Information Bank:** *Functions and graphs, pages 112 – 129*

18. *Graphs investigation (2)*

    a)  Using a graph-plotter, graphical calculator or a spreadsheet package with graph-drawing facilities, draw a variety of graphs with the form:

    $$y = (x + A)(x + B)(x + C)$$

    A, B and C can be any numbers: positive, negative or zero; for example:

    $$y = (x + 7)(x - 2)(x + 3)$$

    i)   note the points where each graph intersects the *x*-axis

    ii)  how do these points relate to the function ?

    b)  Repeat part (a) for graphs with the form:

    $$y = (x + A)(x + B)(x + C)(x + D) \ldots \ldots$$

    A, B, C, D . . . etc can be any numbers: positive, negative or zero.

19. *Graphs investigation (3)*

    Using a graph-plotter, graphical calculator or a spreadsheet package with graph-drawing facilities, draw a variety of graphs with the form:

    $$y = \frac{Ax + B}{Cx + D}$$

    A, B, C, D . . . etc can be any numbers: positive, negative or zero.

    i)   note the points where each graph intersects the axes

    ii)  note the asymptotes

    iii) how do (i) and (ii) relate to the function ?

20. *Soft drinks container*

    As part of a design project, students were given the task of designing a container suitable for soft drinks. The container had to be in the shape of a cylinder, hold 300 ml of drink and use the minimum amount of material in its construction. The amount of material is given by the mathematical model:

    $$m = \frac{\pi d^2}{2} + \frac{1200}{d}$$

    where *d*, measured in cm., represents the diameter of the container.

    a)  Construct a table of values and draw a graph which shows *m* as a function of *d*; $0 \leq d \leq 10$.

    b)  Use the graph, or develop a spreadsheet model, to find out the diameter of the container which uses the minimum amount of material.

    c)  Calculate the height of this container; the volume of a cylinder is given by the formula:

    $$V = \pi r^2 h$$

    where *h* is the height and *r* is the radius.

**Information Bank:** *Functions and graphs, pages 122 – 133*

21. *Bit patterns*

Four distinct bit patterns can be formed when two binary digits are used: 00, 01, 10 and 11. Using three binary digits gives eight possible patterns: 000, 001, 010, 011, 100, 101, 110 and 111.

a) Complete this table which gives the number of possible bit patterns when various numbers of binary digits are used:

| No. of binary digits (n) | 0 | 1 | 2 | 3 | 4 | 5 | 6 | 7 | 8 |
|---|---|---|---|---|---|---|---|---|---|
| No. of bit patterns (p) | | | 4 | 8 | | | | | |

b) Construct a graph showing the relationship between $n$ and $p$.

c) Formulate a mathematical model which represents this relationship.

d) Use your model to predict the number of possible bit patterns when 32 binary digits are used.

22. *Population growth*

The population of Chelford, which was approximately 75000 in 1985 has grown at the rate of about 5% per year since.

a) Formulate a mathematical model which represents the population ($p$) as a function of the number of years elapsed since 1985 ($t$).

b) Draw a graph which shows the population growth since 1985.

c) Use the model to estimate:

   i) the population this year

   ii) the population in the year 2000

d) How reliable are the answers to part c)?

23. *Maze running*

As part of their studies into the way that learning takes place, students of Psychology investigate mazes. Each person is timed according to how long they take to trace through a maze without making an error. They are then timed again over several 'runs', using the same maze, and their successive timings noted. As a result of the experiments, the time taken can be represented by the mathematical model:

$$T = \frac{t}{\sqrt[3]{n}}$$

where: $t$ represents the amount of time (in minutes) taken on the first run

$n$ is the number of the run

a) One student takes 8 minutes for his first run of a particular maze. Construct a graph which shows $T$ as a function of $n$, for this student.

b) Use your graph to estimate:

   i) the number of runs required for this student to reduce his time to 5 minutes

   ii) whether the running time is halved when the number of runs is doubled

   iii) the number of runs likely to be needed before the student runs the maze in 1 minute

c) How reliable are the answers to part (b)?

**Information Bank:** *Functions and graphs, pages 122 – 133*

# Unit 2: Numerical methods

1. *Rounding*

   a) Complete this table, which shows numbers rounded off to different levels of accuracy:

   | Number | 2D | 1D | 2S | 1S |
   |---|---|---|---|---|
   | 32.168 | 32.17 | 32.2 | 32 | 30 |
   | 16.483 | | | | |
   | 8.456 | | | | |
   | 26.093 | | | | |
   | 145.635 | | | | |
   | 3672.165 | | | | |
   | 0.6176 | | | | |
   | 0.07542 | | | | |

   b) Change these rational numbers to decimals and write down the answer correct to 3D:

   i) $\dfrac{7}{9}$   ii) $\dfrac{5}{7}$   iii) $\dfrac{3}{11}$   iv) $\dfrac{9}{13}$   v) $\dfrac{23}{17}$

   c) Write down the value of these irrational numbers as decimals correct to 4D:

   i) $\sqrt{2}$   ii) $\sqrt{5}$   iii) $\sqrt{23}$   iv) $\sqrt[3]{9}$   v) $\pi$

2. *Errors*

   a) Complete this table:

   | Measurement | Measurement is to the nearest: | Absolute error | Relative error |
   |---|---|---|---|
   | 25 cm | 1 cm | 0.5 cm | 0.02 |
   | 10.9 secs | 0.1 sec | | |
   | 126.5 m | 0.1 m | | |
   | 1850 cc | 10 cc | | |
   | 93000000 miles | 1000000 miles | | |
   | 57.6 kg | 10 g | | |
   | 0.006 m | 1 mm | | |

   b) Calculate the answers to the following and give an error bound in each case; every number has been rounded:

   i) $46.48 + 95.61$   ii) $57.92 - 12.48$   iii) $916.4 + 0.642 - 52.67$

   iv) $32.1 - 8.56 - 0.26$   v) $48.32 \times 3.76$   vi) $27.98 \times 7.51 \times 92.74$

   vii) $\dfrac{72.13 \times 7.5}{13.2}$   viii) $(16.2 + 6.7) \times (28.9 - 7.8)$

   c) The dimensions of some shapes are measured to the nearest cm. Calculate the perimeter and area of each shape and give error bounds for the answers:

   i) a square, 14 cm × 14 cm   ii) a rectangle, 13 cm × 8 cm   iii) a circle, radius 9 cm

**Information Bank:** *Numerical methods, pages 134 – 137*

3. *Laboratory measurements*

   In each of the following scenarios, which relate to small-scale experiments undertaken by students on an introductory Science course, assume that all measurements are correct to the number of significant figures given. Give an error bound for the answer in each case:

   a) The gross weight of a bag of crisps is measured as 29.7 g, and the weight of the bag alone as 0.6 g. Estimate the net weight of the crisps.

   b) A model parachute is dropped to the ground from a height of 3.2 m; it is timed as taking 2.92 secs. Estimate its speed in m/s.

   c) A box containing 50 similar steel ball-bearings weighs 825 g. Estimate the weight of a ball-bearing.

   d) A bottle, initially containing 675 cc of acid, is used by 15 students each of whom required 25 cc for an experiment. Estimate the amount of acid remaining in the bottle.

   e) Measurements from a rainfall gauge, taken over a period of 30 days, produce an average daily rainfall figure of 2 mm. Estimate the total amount of rain falling over that time.

4. *Floating-point*

   a) Convert each of the following numbers to floating-point decimal form:

   | | | | |
   |---|---|---|---|
   | i) 62.45 | ii) 5328 | iii) 673000000 | iv) -731.52 |
   | v) 0.08 | vi) 0.00000046 | vii) -0.00059 | viii) -193000000 |
   | ix) $10^6$ | x) $-10^{-3}$ | | |

   b) Represent each of the following decimal numbers in floating-point binary form, using 10 bits for the mantissa and 6 bits for the exponent:

   | | | | |
   |---|---|---|---|
   | i) 37.25 | ii) -4.5 | iii) 0.375 | iv) 27.625 |
   | v) -0.0625 | vi) 154.03125 | vii) 934 | viii) 0.8125 |
   | ix) -276.609375 | x) $10^4$ | | |

5. *Repeating patterns (1)*

   Determine which of the following decimal numbers are represented in binary notation

   i) exactly

   ii) as a repeating sequence of digits or

   iii) as a non-repeating sequence of digits

   | | | | | |
   |---|---|---|---|---|
   | a) $\frac{15}{16}$ | b) 0.1 | c) $\frac{3}{8}$ | d) $\frac{1}{3}$ | e) $\frac{17}{128}$ |
   | f) $\frac{5}{7}$ | g) 0.6125 | h) $\frac{1}{9}$ | i) $\sqrt{11}$ | |

6. *Repeating patterns (2)*

   Consider the numbers in Q.5 and calculate the relative error when they are represented as floating-point binary numbers if 8 bits are used for each of the mantissa and exponent.

**Information Bank:** *Numerical methods, pages 134 – 141*

7. *Consider these program segments, which are supposed to give an exact total of 10, and determine:*

   a) the total that each program actually produces   b) the relative error, where appropriate

   i)   FOR loop = 1 TO 10 DO
        total = total + 1

   ii)  FOR loop = 1 TO 40 DO
        total = total + 0.25

   iii) FOR loop = 1 TO 50 DO
        total = total + 0.2

   iv)  FOR loop = 1 TO 80 DO
        total = total + 0.125

   v)   FOR loop = 1 TO 30 DO
        total = total + $\frac{1}{3}$

   vi)  FOR loop = 1 TO 7.75 STEP 0.75 DO
        total = total + 1

   Assume that the variable 'total' is initialised to zero prior to each program run and that the mantissa and exponent of floating-point binary numbers are each allocated 8 bits.

8. *Flower-beds*

   a) As part of a programme to improve the Brooklands campus environment, several areas within the grounds are to be redesigned. The diagram below shows a rectangular piece of of ground (measuring 8m by 8m) which is to be mostly laid with turf; it will have two corner sections for a selection of plants. In order to calculate the area of turf required, one side is taken as a base-line and the distance from the base-line to the edge of the border is measured. Measurements are taken every 1m:

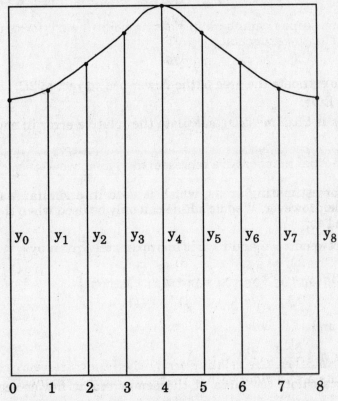

| Horizontal distance ($x$) | Vertical distance ($y$) |
|---|---|
| 0 | 6.00 |
| 1 | 6.20 |
| 2 | 6.75 |
| 3 | 7.40 |
| 4 | 8.00 |
| 5 | 7.40 |
| 6 | 6.75 |
| 7 | 6.20 |
| 8 | 6.00 |

   Use the Trapezium Rule and Simpson's Rule to calculate the area of turf, correct to 2D.

**Information Bank:** *Numerical methods, pages 139 – 148*

b) A flower-bed is to be in the shape of a semi-circle with a diameter of 6m, as shown below. The precise mathematical shape means that the base-line measurement method need not be used. Instead, the area can be represented more precisely by:

$$\text{Area of semi-circle} = \int_{-3}^{3} \sqrt{9-x^2}\,dx$$

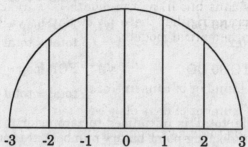

i) Complete this table of values for $y = \sqrt{9-x^2}$ :

| $x$ | $y$ | |
|-----|-----|-----|
| -3 | 0 | $(y_0)$ |
| -2 | | $(y_1)$ |
| -1 | 2.828 | $(y_2)$ |
| 0 | | $(y_3)$ |
| 1 | | $(y_4)$ |
| 2 | | $(y_5)$ |
| 3 | | $(y_6)$ |

ii) Use the Trapezium Rule to estimate the area of the flower-bed correct to 2D.

iii) Repeat ii)using Simpson's Rule.

iv) The true value of the area is $28.27\text{m}^2$ (2D); calculate the relative error in each of the solutions.

9. *Weddle's Rule*

This is a little known rule, also for estimating areas, which is used in a similar way to the Trapezium Rule and Simpson's Rule. However, Weddle's Rule can only be used when the area is divided into 6 strips; it can be stated as:

The area under the curve $y = f(x)$ between $x = a$ and $x = b$ is approximately given by:

$$\int_{-3}^{3} f(x)dx \approx 0.3h\{y_0 + y_2 + y_3 + y_4 + y_6 + 5(y_1 + y_3 + y_5)\}$$

where

i) $y_0, y_1, \ldots . y_6$ are the ordinates and

ii) h is the width of a strip; that is, $h = \dfrac{b-a}{6}$

a) Use Weddle's Rule to recalculate the area of the semi-circular flower-bed in the previous question.

b) Find the relative error in the answer and state whether it is more accurate in this case.

**Information Bank:** *Numerical methods, pages 144 – 148*

10. *Canned vegetables*

The cafeteria on the Harper campus takes delivery of 90 cans of processed vegetables at the beginning of each month to supplement a single purchase of fresh vegetables. The number of cans which are in stock at any given time tends to follow the same monthly pattern. That is: i) in the early part of the month, when there are plenty of fresh vegetables available, it is not necessary to open many cans but ii) as the month goes by and the fresh vegetables dwindle more cans are opened. Assuming that there are 30 days in each month, this stock situation can be represented by the mathematical model:

$$n = 90 - 0.1d^2$$

where:  $n$ represents the number of cans in stock

$d$ represents the number of days elapsed

a) Complete the following table for the model and draw a graph of the situation:

| d | 0 | 5 | 10 | 15 | 20 | 25 | 30 |
|---|---|---|----|----|----|----|----|
| n | 90 |  |  |  |  |  | 0 |

b) Storage costs are 0.5p per can, per day. Estimate the area under the curve and find the total storage costs for the month.

11. *Accounting package*

The Institute decides to invest in a financial accounting software package which is expected to save money. It is estimated that the annual amount of money likely to be saved by using the package can be represented by the mathematical model:

$$s = 10t - t^2$$

where:  $s$ represents the savings, in £'000s

$t$ represents the time, in years

A certain amount of expenditure is involved not only in the initial purchase of the package but also in a continual programme of staff training and development, monitoring the package's effectiveness and so on. It is estimated that the annual expenditure can be represented by the mathematical model:

$$e = 0.5t^2 + 4$$

where:  $e$ represents the expenditure, in £'000s

$t$ represents the time, in years

a) Using the same pair of axes, construct graphs which show the two models ($0 \le t \le 10$).

b) Estimate the area under the appropriate curve to find:

i) the total savings after 5 years

ii) the total expenditure after 5 years

**Information Bank:** *Numerical methods, pages 144 – 148*

12. *Decimal search*

    For each of the following equations:

    a)  Draw a suitable graph for values of $x$ in the range $-6 \leq x \leq 6$

    b)  Use the decimal search method to calculate the roots correct to 2D

        i)   $x^2 - 6x + 3 = 0$

        ii)  $x^2 - 4x - 7 = 0$

        iii) $x^2 + 4x + 1 = 0$

        iv)  $2x^2 + 12x + 9 = 0$

        v)   $5x^2 + 12x - 5 = 0$

        vi)  $x^3 - 3x^2 - 9x - 3 = 0$

13. *Interval bisection*

    Use the interval bisection method to calculate the specified roots (correct to 2D) of these equations:

    i)   $x^3 + 2x^2 - 5 = 0$ has a root which lies between $x = 1$ and $x = 2$

    ii)  $x^3 - 3x^2 - 6 = 0$ has a root which lies between $x = 3$ and $x = 4$

    iii) $x^3 - 2x - 5 = 0$ has a root which lies between $x = 2$ and $x = 3$

    iv)  $x^3 - x^2 - 2x + 1 = 0$ has a root which lies between $x = 1$ and $x = 2$

14. *Iteration investigation*

    The quadratic equation: $x^2 + x - 2 = 0$ can be solved by using the iterative process:

    $$x_{n+1} = \frac{2}{x_n + 1}$$

    a)  Use a variety of initial values and investigate what happens in each case.

        A spreadsheet layout similar to the one below may be helpful.

| Initial $x_0$ = | -4 | -3 | -2 | -1 | 0 | 1 | 2 | 3 | 4 |
|---|---|---|---|---|---|---|---|---|---|
| $x_1$ | -0.7 | -1 | -2 | ? | 2 | 1 | 0.7 | 0.5 | 0.4 |
| $x_2$ | .. | .. | .. | .. | .. | .. | .. | .. | .. |
| $x_3$ | .. | .. | .. | .. | .. | .. | .. | .. | .. |
| $x_4$ | .. | .. | .. | .. | .. | .. | .. | .. | .. |
| $x_5$ | .. | .. | .. | .. | .. | .. | .. | .. | .. |
| $x_6$ | .. | .. | .. | .. | .. | .. | .. | .. | .. |
| etc. | .. | .. | .. | .. | .. | .. | .. | .. | .. |

    b)  Try to summarise the results of the investigation.

**Information Bank:** *Numerical methods, pages 148 – 154*

15. *Simple Iterative Processes (1)*

Three possible iterative processes for solving the equation $x^2 - 5x - 8 = 0$ are:

    i)   $x_{n+1} = \dfrac{(x_n{}^2 - 8)}{5}$
                                ii)   $x_{n+1} = \dfrac{8}{(x_n - 5)}$

    iii)  $x_{n+1} = \sqrt{(5x_n + 8)}$
                              iv)   $x_{n+1} = 5 + \dfrac{8}{x_n}$

In each case, use the process and comment on the results.

16. *Simple Iterative Processes (2)*

Devise simple iteration processes for each of these quadratic equations, and use them to calculate the roots, correct to 2D:

    i)   $x^2 - 4x - 1 = 0$
                 ii)   $x^2 + 10x + 8 = 0$
              iii)   $4x^2 + 5x - 3 = 0$

    iv)  $3x^2 - 3x - 1 = 0$
               v)   $11x^2 + 7x - 9 = 0$

17. *Simple Iterative Processes (3)*

    a)   Use the following simple iterative processes to obtain the solution (correct to 1D) of the cubic equation: $x^3 + x - 1 = 0$; the equation only has one root, lying between 0 and 1.

          Draw a graph to show each process.

          i)   $x_{n+1} = 1 - x_n{}^3$
                                ii)   $x_{n+1} = \sqrt[3]{1 - x_n}$

          iii)  $x_{n+1} = \dfrac{1}{(1 + x_n{}^2)}$
                        iv)   $x_{n+1} = \dfrac{1}{x_n{}^2} - \dfrac{1}{x_n}$

          Which is the best process?

    b)   Devise your own simple iterative process to solve the cubic equation: $x^3 - 3x + 3 = 0$.

18. *Newton-Raphson Processes*

    a)   i)   Devise a Newton-Raphson process for each of the equations in Question 16.

          ii)   Compare the results with those already obtained.

    b)   Devise a Newton-Raphson process to solve the equation in Question 17.

    c)   Devise a Newton-Raphson process to solve the equation:

          $x^4 - 4x^3 + x + 12 = 0$.

19. *Chaos*

Some functions behave in strange ways under iteration. For instance, in Section 1 Unit 16 – The Fish Pond, the population function displays so-called chaotic behaviour under certain conditions.

    a)   In the same way, investigate the iterative process: $x_{n+1} = 2x_n{}^2 - 1$ for different initial values.

    b)   Try to find other examples of functions which exhibit chaotic behaviour.

**Information Bank:** *Numerical methods, pages 150 – 158*

20. *Strange Attractors*

It has already been seen (Section 1 Unit 16 and Section 3 Q.19) that some iterative processes, under certain conditions, refuse to settle down. That is, while most initial values produce sequences that eventually either converge or diverge, others produce sequences that behave in an unpredictable fashion i.e. chaos.

Similar behaviour can also be generated by using *pairs* of iterative processes and initial values. Again, the sequence of numbers which is produced appears to dart about in a random manner. However, plotting the values on a graphics screen reveals an odd phenomenon called a 'strange attractor'. The one outlined in this activity is called the 'Henon attractor', after the mathematician who studied it.

Start with *two* initial values e.g. $x_0 = 0.1$, $y_0 = 0.2$

Use the following pair of iterative processes to generate two new values:

$$x_{n+1} = 1 + y_n - 1.4x_n^2; \qquad y_{n+1} = 0.3x_n$$

So, for example:

$x_0 = 0.1$ $\qquad\qquad\qquad\qquad\qquad$ $y_0 = 0.2$

$x_1 = 1 + 0.2 - 1.4 \times 0.1^2 = 1.186$ $\qquad\qquad$ $y_1 = 0.3 \times 0.1 = 0.03$

$x_2 = 1 + 0.03 - 1.4 \times 1.186^2 = -0.939$ $\qquad\quad$ $y_2 = 0.3 \times 1.186 = 0.356$

$x_3 = 1 + 0.356 - 1.4 \times (-0.939)^2 = 0.122$ $\qquad$ $y_3 = 0.3 \times (-0.939) = -0.282$

etc. $\qquad\qquad\qquad\qquad\qquad\qquad\qquad\qquad$ etc.

a)  Develop a spreadsheet model, or write a computer program, to help with the calculations.

For instance, a spreadsheet might have the following general structure:

|   | A | B | C | D | E |
|---|---|---|---|---|---|
| 1 |   |   | Henon Attractor Spreadsheet |   |   |
| 2 |   |   |   |   |   |
| 3 |   | n | $x_n$ | $y_n$ |   |
| 4 |   | 0 | 0.1 | 0.2 |   |
| 5 |   | 1 | *1+d4–1.4\*c4\*c4* | *0.3\*c4* |   |
| 6 |   | 2 | *1+d5–1.4\*c5\*c5* | *0.3\*c5* |   |
| .. |   | ... | ... | ... |   |
| .. |   | ... | ... | ... |   |

Formulas are shown in italics; lower case letters denote relative cell references.

**Information Bank:** *Numerical methods, pages 150 – 158*

Alternatively, a typical program structure is:

Initialise $x_0 = 0.1$, $y_0 = 0.2$
Initialise $n = 0$
REPEAT
    Calculate $x_{n+1}$
    Calculate $y_{n+1}$
    Increment $n$
UNTIL enough values calculated

b) Treat the values of $x$ and $y$ obtained at each stage of the iteration (for example, columns C and D on the sample spreadsheet above) as a pair of coordinates and plot the $(x, y)$ point. This can be done by using the graph-drawing facilities of the spreadsheet package, *if the spreadsheet automatically scales the coordinates to fill the whole screen display*. If the spreadsheet does not possess automatic scaling, then since the values of $x$ and $y$ obtained at each iteration are relatively small, it will be necessary to adjust the values before they can be plotted as screen coordinates; for example, multiply both the $x$- and $y$-coordinates by 1000. (Two extra columns on the spreadsheet could be used for this purpose). The scaling factors will vary from computer to computer but will depend on the range of numbers used as screen coordinates for the graphics display. So, for instance:

| *Iteration values* | *Screen coordinates* |
| --- | --- |
| $x_0 = 0.1$, $y_0 = 0.2$ | (100, 200) |
| $x_1 = 1.186$, $y_1 = 0.03$ | (1186, 30) |
| $x_2 = -0.939$, $y_2 = 0.356$ | (−939, 356) |
| $x_3 = 0.122$, $y_3 = -0.282$ | (122, -282) |
| etc | etc |

Likewise, modifying the program structure:

Initialise $x_0 = 0.1$, $y_0 = 0.2$
Initialise $n = 0$
REPEAT
    Calculate $x_{n+1}$
    Calculate $y_{n+1}$
    Plot the point $(1000{*}x_{n+1}, 1000{*}y_{n+1})$
    Increment $n$
UNTIL enough values calculated

At first, the points appear to scatter around the screen in a fairly haphazard way. However, as more points are plotted, notice the way that they seem to be 'attracted' to a strange underlying shape.

c) Investigate what happens for:

i) different initial values of $x_0$ and $y_0$

ii) different parameters i.e. try other values instead of the '1.4' and '0.3' in the iterative processes

**Information Bank:** *Numerical methods, pages 150 – 158*

## 21. *The Mandelbrot Set*

This mathematical phenomenon involves iterative processes (similar to those of Q.20) and the plotting of coloured points on a graphics screen. The colours are related to the number of iterations carried out at each stage. The pictures which result from this type of process are both beautiful and intricate.

This activity is designed to introduce the reader to some features of the Mandelbrot set. However, since many books and computer programs have been produced on this fascinating subject, further research is strongly recommended and will be well rewarded.

Imagine that the computer screen represents a piece of graph-paper where:

$$-2 \leq x \leq 2$$

and

$$-2 \leq y \leq 2$$

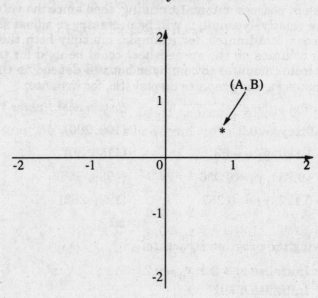

The underlying iterative process is:

Step 1: Choose a point (A, B); for example: (0.9, 0.4)

Step 2: Set initial values $x_0 = 0$, $y_0 = 0$

Step 3: Calculate: $x_{n+1} = x_n{}^2 - y_n{}^2 + A$
$$y_{n+1} = 2x_ny_n + B$$

Step 4: Repeat: Step 3 until $x_{n+1}{}^2 + y_{n+1}{}^2 > 4$

Step 5: Colour the point (A,B) on the graph. The colour will depend on how many times Step 3 has been performed; that is, the value of $n$. A different colour is needed for each value of $n$. eg if 10 iterations are required, plot the point in colour 10; etc ...

Step 6: Choose a new point (A, B)

**Information Bank:** *Numerical methods, pages 150– 158*

So, for example:

Step 1    A = 0.9, B = 0.4

Step 2    $x_0 = 0$;  $y_0 = 0$

Step 3    $x_1 = 0^2 - 0^2 + 0.9 = 0.9$;  $y_1 = 2 \times 0 \times 0 + 0.4 = 0.4$

   Step 4:  $x_1{}^2 + y_1{}^2 = 0.9^2 + 0.4^2 = 0.97$ (this is < 4, so repeat Step 3)

Step 3    $x_2 = 0.9^2 - 0.4^2 + 0.9 = 1.55$;  $y_2 = 2 \times 0.9 \times 0.4 + 0.4 = 1.12$

   Step 4:  $x_2{}^2 + y_2{}^2 = 1.55^2 + 1.12^2 = 3.6569$ (this is < 4, so repeat Step 3)

Step 3    $x_3 = 1.55^2 - 1.12^2 + 0.9 = 2.0481$;  $y_3 = 2 \times 1.55 \times 1.12 + 0.4 = 3.872$

   Step 4:  $x_3{}^2 + y_3{}^2 = 2.0481^2 + 3.872^2 \approx 19.19$ (this is > 4, so process stops)

Step 5    $n = 3$ (i.e. the process has been repeated 3 times). So, (0.9, 0.4) would be plotted in colour 3.

Step 6    Choose another point (A, B); for example: (0.9, 0.5)

   Repeat from Step 2

This whole procedure is repeated for each point (A, B) within the graph area. Obviously, the number of points to be processed is very large and a computer program is essential e.g.:

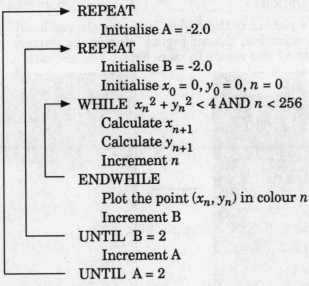

```
REPEAT
    Initialise A = -2.0
    REPEAT
        Initialise B = -2.0
        Initialise x₀ = 0, y₀ = 0, n = 0
        WHILE  xₙ² + yₙ² < 4 AND n < 256
            Calculate xₙ₊₁
            Calculate yₙ₊₁
            Increment n
        ENDWHILE
        Plot the point (xₙ, yₙ) in colour n
        Increment B
    UNTIL  B = 2
    Increment A
UNTIL A = 2
```

a)  Develop this outline program so that it will draw the Mandelbrot Set. Note that:

i)   The maximum value of $n$ is dependent on the number of colours available; in this program it is taken as 256. Any point requiring more than 255 iterations is normally plotted in black.

ii)  Scaling will need to be incorporated (see Q.20).

iii) The amounts by which A and B are incremented will depend on the computer's resolution.

**Information Bank:** *Numerical methods, pages 150 – 158*

So, in the finished drawing, all points which take the same number of iterations have the same colour:

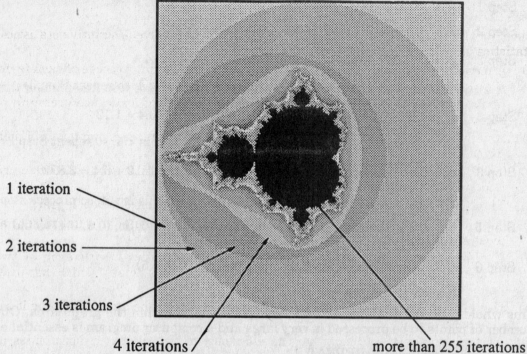

1 iteration

2 iterations

3 iterations

4 iterations

more than 255 iterations

b) The interesting bit of the picture is the region immediately surrounding the central black portion. This is the unpredictable, chaotic region. Modify the original program slightly to 'zoom in' and examine part of this region in more detail. For instance:

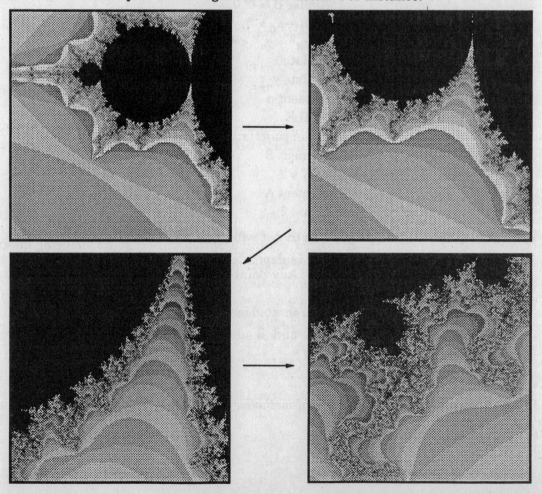

# Unit 3: Statistics – 1

1. *Descriptive or inferential ?*

   Identify which of the following situations are likely to involve descriptive statistics, inferential statistics or both:

   a) A member of the 1st XI cricket team calculates the batting average of each team member.

   b) A 20 year old student, who has just passed her driving test, telephones three different insurance brokers to gain an impression of the sort of insurance premium payable on a second-hand car.

   c) An environmental pressure group analyses the effect of increasing levels of pollution in the River Dale on fish stocks.

   d) The Institute's Educational Research Unit studies the relationship between private tuition and grades obtained in examinations.

   e) The Institute's registry records the number of students enrolled each year.

   f) A group of students, new to the Chelford area, are looking for a flat to rent and examine local newspaper advertisements as a guide to the likely cost.

   g) A Mathematics lecturer uses different teaching methods with each of two groups of students. He then compares the examination scores to see which has been the most successful.

   h) Out of interest, a lecturer asks his students to record the amount of time it takes them to do a piece of coursework.

   i) Agricultural students compare the efficiency of two different insecticides on vegetable crops.

   j) A nutritional analysis is carried out on a meal served at the Brooklands campus cafeteria.

2. *Populations*

   Identify a population from which each of the following samples might be selected:

   a) Computer Science students at Dale Institute

   b) Mount Everest

   c) IBM

   d) The Prime Minister

   e) Positive integers

   f) People leaving King's Cross station between 6 p.m. and 7 p.m. on Friday evening

   g) People arriving at King's Cross station between 6 p.m. and 7 p.m. on Friday evening

   h) BBC2

   i) Garden gnomes

   j) Yorkshire terriers

3. *Samples (1)*

   Which sampling method would be the most appropriate to obtain the following information:

   a) Parents' views about the value of computer games

   b) The state of health of the British people

   c) Student alcohol consumption

   d) Ages of American-born people living in the British Isles

   e) Soap powder sales in London

**Information Bank:** *Statistics, pages 159 – 165*

4. *Samples (2)*

Comment on the appropriateness of obtaining the views of the following groups of people:

| Subject of study | Sample |
|---|---|
| Television advertising | Supermarket customers |
| Soccer hooliganism | Spectators at a cricket match |
| Unemployment | People leaving a travel agency |
| School dinners | Headteachers |
| Police brutality | Teachers at a primary school |
| Abortion | A church congregation |
| Petrol prices | People leaving a railway station |
| Inner city riots | Social workers |
| Drink-driving | Publicans |
| Public transport | People at a bus-stop |
| Football transfer fees | Football team managers |
| The health of elderly people | Residents of an old people's home |

5. *Questionnaire questions*

Comment on the suitability of each of the following, for inclusion on questionnaires:
   a) How fit are you?
   b) What is your socio-economic status?
   c) How much television do you watch?
   d) Are you illegitimate?
   e) When did you last see a doctor?
   f) Would you prefer even more vouchers with petrol?
   g) How often do you have a bath?
   h) When you shop at our store do you find that the checkout assistants are generally friendly and willing to help or do you find them curt and unhelpful?
   i) How much petrol did you use last year?

6. *Computing course questionnaire*

A study is being undertaken about the contribution that computing courses have made to the careers of people who were students at Dale Institute about 5 years ago. Records of their names and addresses are still available, so it is proposed to send a questionnaire to the 200 who were enrolled on computing courses during that year. Devise the questionnaire to obtain the following information:
   a) present employment
   b) any previous employment
   c) current pay
   d) subjects studied as part of their course
   e) grade of certificate awarded, exam results etc
   f) the value of the following areas of study to their present employment: programming / computer architecture / systems analysis and design / quantitative techniques
   g) their opinions about the benefits of the course

**Information Bank:** *Statistics, pages 162 – 167*

7. *Computer Services*

The main function of the Computer Services Unit at Dale Institute is to ensure that staff and students have access to a suitable range of hardware, software and technical support services. A review of these facilities takes place annually and involves consultation between teaching staff, the Head of the Computer Services Unit and student representatives. The purpose of the review is to monitor the quality of computing provision and to maintain a high level of service; suggestions are made for new or replacement items of equipment, software packages and additional support personnel e.g. operators, programmers and technicians. Prior to the latest review, the student representatives decide to obtain the views of a cross-section of students about ways that the current facilities might be improved. Several suggestions are put forward as to how this might be achieved:

- ☐ Individual interviews of students by members of the Computer Services Unit
- ☐ Group interviews of students by members of the Computer Services Unit
- ☐ A questionnaire circulated to all students
- ☐ A suggestion box with a cash prize for the best suggestion
- ☐ A sample survey of students leaving the Brooklands campus computer centre
- ☐ Observation of the computing activities undertaken by students in the computer centres

a) List the advantages and disadvantages of each of the above schemes.

b) After some discussion, it is decided to obtain the information by means of a questionnaire. Devise a set of about ten questions which could form the basis of such a questionnaire.

c) It is also decided that circulating all students with the questionnaire would be impractical and costly. So, it is proposed to send a copy to a sample of five hundred students.

   i) Describe three possible ways of selecting the sample. (Dale Institute caters for approximately 10000 students on a variety of courses, full-time and part-time).

   ii) List the likely practical difficulties of implementing the survey and make suggestions as to how they might be overcome.

8. *People data*

a) Classify each of the following 'people' characteristics as either category variables, discrete variables or continuous variables

b) In each case, give some example categories or a range of possible values

| | | |
|---|---|---|
| Hair colour | Height | Size of family |
| Blood group | Marital status | Shoe size |
| Foot size | Occupation | Sex |
| Nationality | Pulse rate | Religion |
| I.Q. | Age | Inside leg measurement |
| Income | Weight | National Insurance number |

**Information Bank:** *Statistics, pages 162 – 167*
*Descriptive statistics, pages 168 – 169*

9. *Computing data*

   a) Classify each of the following 'computing' characteristics as either category variables, discrete variables or continuous variables

   b) In each case, give some example categories or a range of possible values

   | | |
   |---|---|
   | Microcomputer word length | Pins on dot-matrix printer mechanism |
   | Disc read / write access time | Processor clock speed |
   | Prices of software packages | Hard disc capacity |
   | Microcomputer RAM size | Printer paper width |
   | Monitor resolution | Microcomputer manufacturers |
   | Modem baud rate | Amount of printer paper used |
   | Types of software | Inkjet printer resolution |

10. *Bar chart*

    As it stands, the bar chart shown below is unhelpful, inaccurate and misleading.

    Identify at least *six* features that need modification:

    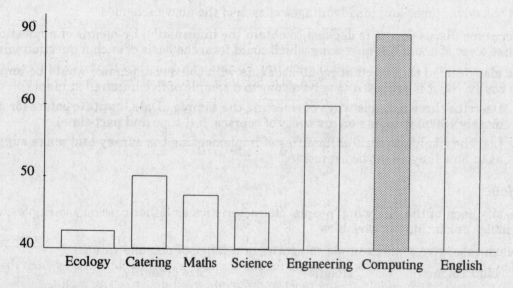

11. *Newspaper graphs*

    a) Observe the different types and styles of graphical representations used in newspapers, magazines, journals etc.

    b) Collect examples of 'good' graphical representations; that is, those that are clear, accurate, do not mislead in any way and present the information in an appropriate, attractive manner.

    c) Collect examples of 'poor' graphical representations; identify why they are poor.

    d) Note the differences, if any, between statistical graphs used in advertising and those used purely for illustrative purposes.

**Information Bank:** *Descriptive statistics, pages 168 – 169; 173 – 182*

12. *The school day*

Use a suitable graph to display the following data, obtained in a study of a Secondary school teacher's annual activities. The daily amount of each activity is approximately as follows:

| Activity | Time (mins) |
|---|---|
| Teaching | 203 |
| Department / school / exam administration | 63 |
| Pastoral work, discipline | 13 |
| Parental consultation | 10 |
| Supervision | 7 |
| Breaks | 46 |
| Assembly, registration | 15 |
| Preparation, marking, recording | 114 |
| Organising displays | 13 |
| Weekend preparation, marking etc | 106 |
| Other activities (clubs, sports etc) | 35 |
| Courses, conferences , travel | 16 |
| Meetings, liaison | 28 |
| Reading | 8 |
| Total = | 677 |

13. *Motor racing*

This table shows the performance of the leading Formula One drivers in the first 10 races in the 1992 World Championship. (1st, 2nd, 3rd, 4th, 5th, 6th place earns 10, 6, 4, 3, 2, 1 points:

| Driver | Race no. | | | | | | | | | |
|---|---|---|---|---|---|---|---|---|---|---|
| | 1 | 2 | 3 | 4 | 5 | 6 | 7 | 8 | 9 | 10 |
| Nigel Mansell | 10 | 10 | 10 | 10 | 10 | 6 | 0 | 10 | 10 | 10 |
| Ricardo Patrese | 6 | 6 | 6 | 0 | 6 | 4 | 0 | 6 | 6 | 0 |
| Ayrton Senna | 4 | 0 | 0 | 0 | 4 | 10 | 0 | 0 | 0 | 6 |
| Michael Schumacher | 3 | 4 | 4 | 6 | 0 | 3 | 6 | 0 | 3 | 4 |
| Gerhard Berger | 2 | 3 | 0 | 3 | 0 | 0 | 10 | 0 | 2 | 0 |
| Martin Brundle | 0 | 0 | 0 | 0 | 3 | 2 | 0 | 4 | 4 | 3 |

a) Calculate the mean, median and mode for the number of points obtained by each driver.

b) State which average would be the most appropriate to summarise the results.

14. *Routes*

A lecturer has a choice of two alternative routes in travelling from home to Dale Institute, both of which involve queueing at traffic lights. Over a series of 10 journeys by each route the lecturer records the time spent in queues. The times in minutes are as follows:

| Route A | 12 | 12 | 13 | 10 | 18 | 11 | 12 | 14 | 15 | 15 |
|---|---|---|---|---|---|---|---|---|---|---|
| Route B | 13 | 12 | 13 | 14 | 13 | 14 | 13 | 14 | 14 | 12 |

a) Calculate the mean and standard deviation of the times for each route.

b) Which is your preferred route ? Why ?

**Information Bank:** *Descriptive statistics, pages 173 – 182; 184 – 185; 193 – 199*

15. *Checkouts*

The following data were collected by observing the customer service rate at two checkouts in a supermarket. The service time, in minutes, was noted for each of 30 customers at checkout A and 30 customers at checkout B:

| No. of minutes to be served | 1 | 2 | 3 | 4 | 5 | 6 | 7 | 8 | 9 | 10 |
|---|---|---|---|---|---|---|---|---|---|---|
| Checkout A customers | 0 | 1 | 1 | 1 | 6 | 8 | 6 | 1 | 1 | 1 |
| Checkout B customers | 2 | 2 | 1 | 3 | 3 | 3 | 3 | 3 | 3 | 3 |

a) Display the information using a suitable graph.
b) Complete the partially finished table below, for checkout A.
c) Construct a similar table for checkout B.
d) Calculate the mean and standard deviation of the service times for each checkout.
e) Comment on the results.

| | Checkout A | | |
|---|---|---|---|
| Time (mins) | Customers | | |
| $x$ | $f$ | $fx$ | $fx^2$ |
| 1 | 0 | 0 | |
| 2 | 1 | 2 | |
| 3 | 1 | 3 | |
| 4 | 2 | 8 | |
| 5 | 7 | | 175 |
| 6 | 8 | | 288 |
| 7 | 7 | | |
| 8 | 2 | | |
| 9 | 1 | | |
| 10 | 1 | | |
| | $\Sigma f = 30$ | $\Sigma fx = 180$ | $\Sigma fx^2 =$ |

16. *Examination marks*

The marks obtained by 100 students in an examination have the following distribution:

| Mark | Frequency | Mark | Frequency |
|---|---|---|---|
| 0 - 9 | 2 | 50 - 59 | 16 |
| 10 - 19 | 5 | 60 - 69 | 13 |
| 20 - 29 | 12 | 70 - 79 | 10 |
| 30 - 39 | 15 | 80 - 89 | 6 |
| 40 - 49 | 19 | 90 - 99 | 2 |

a) Construct a cumulative frequency diagram of the data and use it to estimate the median, quartiles and interquartile range.
b) Students are assigned one of five grades in such a way that the top 15% of the students receive grade A, the next 25%: grade B, the next 25%: grade C, the next 25%: grade D and the remainder receive grade E. Use the cumulative frequency diagram to estimate the lowest mark in each of the grades A, B, C and D.

**Information Bank:** *Descriptive statistics, pages 184 – 190; 193 – 202*

17. *Switchboard*

a)  The number of incoming telephone calls to the Brooklands switchboard in each of 50 one-minute intervals were:

|   |   |   |   |   |   |   |   |   |   |
|---|---|---|---|---|---|---|---|---|---|
| 1 | 0 | 2 | 4 | 0 | 1 | 2 | 4 | 3 | 1 |
| 1 | 0 | 1 | 0 | 0 | 1 | 0 | 1 | 0 | 2 |
| 0 | 0 | 1 | 1 | 1 | 1 | 1 | 2 | 3 | 0 |
| 0 | 0 | 0 | 1 | 0 | 0 | 0 | 4 | 0 | 2 |
| 2 | 5 | 4 | 0 | 2 | 0 | 0 | 3 | 2 | 1 |

   i)   Summarise the data in a suitable table.
   ii)  Use an appropriate graph to display the information.
   iii) Calculate the mean and standard deviation of the number of calls.

b)  At the Wentworth campus, a sample of 50 one-minute intervals showed that the mean number of calls was 2.1 with a standard deviation of 0.5. What conclusions might be drawn about the relative switchboard usage on the two campuses?

18. *Task times*

The times taken by a group of 50 students to complete a task were as follows:

| Time in minutes | 2-4 | 5-7 | 8-10 | 11-13 | 14-19 | 20-23 |
|---|---|---|---|---|---|---|
| No. of students | 2 | 5 | 13 | 17 | 8 | 5 |

a)  Construct a histogram which shows this data.
b)  Use the histogram to estimate the mode of the times.
c)  Calculate the mode using the method described in Q.25 of this section.
d)  Construct a cumulative frequency curve and use it to estimate the median time, quartiles and interquartile range.
e)  Calculate the median time from the frequency distribution.
f)  Calculate the mean and standard deviation of the times.
g)  Another group of 50 students who were given the same task to perform had a mean time of 12 minutes and a standard deviation of 3.2 minutes. What can be said about the comparative performances of the two classes ?

19. *Ages*

The ages of a particular intake of 80 students are distributed as follows:

| Age in years | 17.25- | 17.5- | 17.75- | 18- | 18.25- | 18.5- | 19- | 20- | 20.75- |
|---|---|---|---|---|---|---|---|---|---|
| No. of students | 0 | 10 | 28 | 17 | 9 | 3 | 4 | 2 | 0 |

(Note that 17.25- means: 'ages between 17.25 and 17.5, including 17.25 and excluding 17.5')

a)  Use a cumulative frequency curve to estimate the median age.
b)  Calculate the median age from the frequency distribution.
c)  Calculate the skewness coefficient, using the method described in Q.26 of this section.

**Information Bank:** *Descriptive statistics, pages 169 – 202*

## 20. Distributions

Match each of the frequency distributions with a general distribution curve shape as shown:

| x | 1 | 2 | 3 | 4 | 5 | 6 | 7 | 8 | 9 | 10 | 11 | 12 | 13 |
|---|---|---|---|---|---|---|---|---|---|----|----|----|----|
| a) $f$ | 72 | 59 | 48 | 32 | 23 | 15 | 8 | 17 | 24 | 36 | 45 | 56 | 69 |
| b) $f$ | 1 | 2 | 5 | 11 | 16 | 23 | 34 | 45 | 50 | 32 | 18 | 7 | 3 |
| c) $f$ | 10 | 10 | 10 | 10 | 10 | 10 | 10 | 10 | 10 | 10 | 10 | 10 | 10 |
| d) $f$ | 1 | 2 | 3 | 7 | 11 | 17 | 23 | 16 | 9 | 6 | 4 | 3 | 2 |
| e) $f$ | 80 | 67 | 45 | 31 | 22 | 15 | 12 | 9 | 7 | 6 | 5 | 3 | 1 |
| f) $f$ | 1 | 3 | 6 | 11 | 20 | 17 | 13 | 16 | 19 | 10 | 8 | 2 | 1 |
| g) $f$ | 2 | 10 | 26 | 27 | 22 | 18 | 15 | 11 | 9 | 6 | 4 | 2 | 1 |
| h) $f$ | 1 | 4 | 7 | 10 | 13 | 16 | 19 | 16 | 13 | 10 | 7 | 4 | 1 |
| i) $f$ | 1 | 2 | 3 | 5 | 8 | 12 | 18 | 27 | 39 | 50 | 62 | 75 | 90 |
| j) $f$ | 2 | 4 | 7 | 10 | 18 | 28 | 42 | 60 | 70 | 75 | 78 | 80 | 81 |

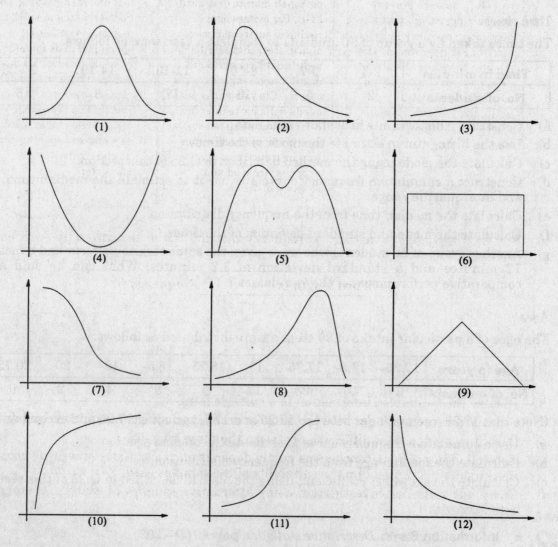

**Information Bank:** *Descriptive statistics, pages 182 – 184*

21. *Distributions (2)*

    a)   Calculate a suitable average and measure of dispersion for each of the distributions in Q.20.

    b)   Investigate the effect on the average of adding (or subtracting) a constant number, such as 5, to each data item.

    c)   Investigate the effect on the average of multiplying (or dividing) each data item by a constant number, such as 5.

22. *Languages*

The extracts below are taken from an instruction leaflet enclosed with a computer monitor. The leaflet is written in many languages; the ones given are the English, Italian and Dutch versions:

| | | |
|---|---|---|
| This colour monitor is suitable for use with home and personal computers equipped with an RGB socket. In order to prevent overheating, ensure that the ventilation openings in the monitor are not covered. The monitor should not be placed near a source of heat nor on a soft surface since this would block the ventilation slots on the bottom. | Questo e un monitor a colori ultramoderno, adatto per l'uso con la maggiore parte dei computer domestici e personali munito di in'uscita RGB. Per evitare ogni rischio di surriscaldamento assicuratevi che le feritoie di ventilazione praticate nel monitor non vengano coperte. Cio vale anche per quelle dalla parte inferiore del monitor: no sistematel o percio su un fondo soffice. Non mettete il monitor neppure vicino ad una sorgente di calore. | Dit is een zeer moderne kleurenmonitor, specifiek voor gebruik met de meeste huis en personal computers met een RGB uitgang. Om oververhitting to voorkomen mogen de ventilatie-openingen in de monitor niet afgedekt worden. De monitor mag niet bij een warmtebron geplaatst worden en evenmin op een zachte ondergrond omdat hierdoor de ventilatie-openingen aan de onderkant worden afgesloten. |

    a)   For each language, construct a frequency distribution of the different word lengths; for example:

*English*

| Word length (x) | Frequency (f) |
|---|---|
| 1 | 2 |
| 2 | 8 |
| 3 | 13 |
| etc | etc |

    b)   Display the assembled information in a suitable form.

    c)   Calculate figures that describe the data for each language e.g. mean, standard deviation.

    d)   Describe any apparent differences between the three languages.

    e)   The reliability of your conclusions partly depends on the samples of writing chosen for the investigation. Comment on the suitability of the samples used.

    f)   Carry out a similar investigation using alternative samples of writing; compare the two sets of results.

**Information Bank:** *Descriptive statistics, pages 173 – 182; 184 – 202*

## 23. *Telephone calls*

As a result of a major modernisation programme, the outdated telephone switchboard on the Harper campus has recently been replaced with a modern system; this links and monitors a large network of extensions. As outgoing calls are made, a logging system monitors their duration and produces a print-out giving details of extension number, telephone number dialled, time of day, duration of call and number of metered units used. After the first month of operation, the Finance Officer requests a summary of the print-out information to ensure that costs are being kept within reasonable limits. So many calls have been made that a member of the administrative staff decides to choose a sample of the print-out on which to base the summary. The table below shows the printout for a Friday between 2 p.m. and 3 p.m.:

| Duration (mins : secs) | Units | Duration (mins : secs) | Units | Duration (mins : secs) | Units |
|---|---|---|---|---|---|
| 0:28 | 0 | 0:41 | 1 | 0:12 | 0 |
| 3:13 | 2 | 0:34 | 0 | 0:46 | 0 |
| 5:00 | 4 | 0:37 | 1 | 7:58 | 6 |
| 0:21 | 0 | 1:39 | 3 | 1:11 | 7 |
| 4:53 | 9 | 1:22 | 2 | 0:24 | 0 |
| 1:10 | 2 | 0:33 | 0 | 3:43 | 3 |
| 1:12 | 1 | 0:42 | 0 | 3:07 | 5 |
| 4:20 | 30 | 6:26 | 5 | 12:20 | 9 |
| 0:48 | 0 | 4:47 | 4 | 2:23 | 2 |
| 1:41 | 1 | 6:06 | 9 | 3:02 | 2 |
| 3:12 | 5 | 7:57 | 6 | 0:48 | 0 |
| 10:42 | 25 | 5:51 | 11 | 6:13 | 5 |
| 0:14 | 0 | 0:42 | 0 | 7:00 | 4 |
| 2:38 | 5 | 2:16 | 4 | 1:41 | 1 |
| 9:32 | 17 | 1:02 | 1 | 5:07 | 4 |

a) Comment on the suitability of the sample chosen.

b) Describe a better method of obtaining the sample.

c) For the 'Units' data:

   i) construct a frequency distribution

   ii) display it in an appropriate form

   iii) find the mean, median and mode

   iv) state which of the averages in iii) is the most representative

   v) calculate the standard deviation

d) Repeat part c) for the 'Duration' data.

e) i) Compare the graphs and calculated figures for the two distributions

   ii) Explain any similarities or differences

**Information Bank:** *Statistics, pages 162 – 167*
*Descriptive statistics, pages 169 – 202*

24. *Statistical investigations*

Use suitable statistical methods to investigate a simple situation and write a report on your activities.

The report should include:

    i)    a description of the data collection procedures

    ii)   tables of results, calculations and graphs where appropriate

    iii)  an analysis of the results

    iv)  any conclusions

Some suggestions for sources of data are:

a)   Student data:
              Age
              Height
              Weight
              Pulse rate
              I.Q.
              Religion
              Opinions

b)   Computing data:
              Number of lines of code in a collection of programs
              Program compilation / execution times
              Number of runs required by different students to get a program working
              Terminal response times
              Number of pages of printout for different programs
              Ages / types of hardware at your educational institution

c)   Other data:
              Goals in football matches (e.g. compare leagues)
              Words in sentences (e.g. compare authors)
               Letters in words (e.g. compare newspapers)
               Ages of cars
              Different digits in telephone numbers
              Postal delivery times (e.g. compare 1st & 2nd class mail)
              Playing times of compact discs / cassettes
              Nutritional analysis of different brands of:
                    Crisps
                    Breakfast cereals
                    Chocolate bars
                    Ice creams
                    etc.
              Queue length / queueing times at:
                    Cafeteria
                    Supermarket checkout
                    Traffic lights
                    Automatic cash dispenser
                    Post Office counter
                    Bus stop
                    etc.

**Information Bank:** *Statistics, pages 162 – 167*
*Descriptive statistics, pages 168 – 202*

25. *Calculating the mode of a grouped frequency distribution*

In Section 2 Unit 6 – 'Descriptive Statistics', various methods were outlined for calculating the mean and median of a grouped frequency distribution. The easiest way to estimate the mode is to use the graphical method described in that section; obtaining its value by calculation is relatively difficult. An approximate value can be found by using the following method:

Step 1:   Locate the modal class (call this class $M$)

Step 2:   Calculate the mode using the formula:

$$\text{Mode} = L + \frac{(N_m - N_b)W}{(N_m - N_b) + (N_m - N_a)}$$

where:   i)   $L$ is the lower limit of class $M$

ii)   $N_m$ is the number of data items in class $M$

iii)   $N_b$ is the number of data items in the class below class $M$

iv)   $N_a$ is the number of data items in the class above class $M$

v)   $W$ is the width of class $M$

a)   Calculate values for the modes of each of the sets of data given in Tables 1 & 2.

b)   Compare the values you obtain with the values obtained by other methods.

26. *Skewness coefficient*

In Section 2 Unit 6 – 'Descriptive Statistics' a skewed distribution was defined as a frequency distribution that is not symmetrical. The amount of skewness can be measured with a coefficient of skewness and the most common measure is *Pearson's No. 2 coefficient of skewness*. This is calculated by using the formula:

$$\text{Skewness} = \frac{3(\text{Mean - Median})}{\text{Standard deviation}}$$

Note also that:

i)   the possible range of values for the coefficient is -3 to 3

ii)   the greater the result, the greater the skewness

iii)   a positive coefficient means positive skewness; a negative coefficient means negative skewness

iv)   for a symmetrical distribution, the coefficient of skewness is zero

a)   Calculate the coefficient of skewness for each of the distributions given in Q.20.

b)   Comment on the results.

**Information Bank:** *Descriptive statistics, pages 182 – 184; 186 – 190*

## 27. *Kurtosis coefficient*

The degree of kurtosis of a distribution can be measured by using the formula:

$$\text{Kurtosis} = \frac{\sum(x - \bar{x})^4}{ns^4} - 3$$

Note that:
  i)   $x - \bar{x}$ is the deviation of each data item from the mean
  ii)  $n$ is the number of data items
  iii) $s$ is the standard deviation
  iv)  a normal distribution has a kurtosis of 0; a platykurtic distribution has a negative kurtosis coefficient, a leptokurtic distribution has a positive kurtosis coefficient.

a) Calculate the coefficient of kurtosis for each of the distributions given in Q.20.

b) Comment on the results.

## 28. *Normal variables ?*

Which of the following variables are likely to be approximately normally distributed?

a) Execution times of a selection of computer programs written by students at Dale Institute.

b) Weights of bottles of washing-up liquid on a supermarket shelf.

c) Shelf-life of cartons of milk on display in a supermarket.

d) Weights of all new-born babies on any given day.

e) I.Q.s of children in a primary school.

f) Estimates obtained from builders' firms for the cost of converting a loft.

g) Number of minutes that pupils are late arriving for school.

h) Number of minutes that staff are late arriving at school.

h) Weights of people attending a keep-fit class.

i) The amount of petrol purchased by people at a garage during a day's trading.

## 29. *Normal distribution tables*

Use tables to find the proportion of area under the standard Normal distribution curve for each of the following; express your answer as a percentage:

a) between the mean and:
  i)   $z = 0.7$
  ii)  $z = 1.53$
  iii) $z = -1.86$

b) between:
  i)   $z = 1.6$ and $z = 1.3$
  ii)  $z = 2.16$ and $z = -0.62$
  iii) $z = -1.59$ and $z = -1.4$

c) i)   above $z = 1.26$
   ii)  above $z = -0.09$
   iii) below $z = -1.48$

**Information Bank:** *Descriptive statistics, pages 186 – 190; 202 – 209*

30. *Normal distribution tables (2)*

 a) Use tables to find the $z$-values which enclose the following areas under the standard Normal distribution curve, above the mean:

   i) 0.4554

   ii) 0.1915

   iii) 0.4115

   iv) 0.4573

   v) 0.2790

 b) Use tables to find the $z$-values which enclose the following areas under the standard Normal distribution curve:

   i) the middle 50%

   ii) the middle 75%

31. *Normal distributions (1)*

Students marks in an examination are approximately normally distributed with a mean of 60 and a standard deviation of 20. Calculate the proportion of students who have marks which are:

 a) between 60 and 90

 b) between 50 and 60

 c) between 35 and 55

 d) between 40 and 110

 e) over 80

 f) less than 50

 g) over 30

 h) less than 75

32. *Normal distributions (2)*

The marks obtained by a student for four different assignments are given below, along with the mean and S.D. of the assignment marks for the 250 students in his year group:

| Assignment | $\mu$ | $\sigma$ | Student's mark |
|---|---|---|---|
| Software Engineering | 74 | 10 | 82 |
| Quantitative Techniques | 56 | 14 | 60 |
| Programming Methodology | 63 | 12 | 70 |
| Computer Architecture | 97 | 25 | 106 |

 a) Standardise each of the students scores and determine his best and worst assignments.

 b) How many students obtained a higher mark than him in each of the assignments ?

**Information Bank:** *Descriptive statistics, pages 206 – 212*

33. *Health and diet*

Use the data in Section 1 Unit 17 - 'Health and diet questionnaire' Page 26 for this question:

a) Assuming that the students' weights are approximately normally distributed, calculate the number of students who, in theory, should weigh:

    i)   more than 70 kg        ii)  less than 50 kg        iii)  between 50 kg and 60 kg

b) How well do the expected results of part a) compare to the actual observations ?

c) Calculate the mean and standard deviation of the 60 students' heights

d) Assuming that the heights are approximately normally distributed, compare the theoretical and observed number of students who have a height:

    i)   over 170 cm        ii)  below 150 cm        iii)  between 140 cm and 160 cm

e) Can you draw any conclusions from your results ?

34. *Positive, negative or close-to-zero ?*

For each of the following pairs of variables, say whether you would expect the correlation between them to be positive, negative or close-to-zero:

a) Age of person; life insurance premium

b) Ability in football; ability in computing

c) Number of vehicles on British roads; number of accidents on British roads

d) Age of a person; height of a person

e) Length of computer program; compilation time

f) Length of computer program; execution time

g) Length of computer program; amount of memory space used

h) Number of runs of computer program; number of bugs detected

h) Absence from lectures; performance in examinations

i) Camcorder sales; camera sales

j) Level of pollution in the River Dale; quantity of fish caught from it

k) Car mileage; depth of tyre tread

l) Daily hours of sunshine; daily maximum temperature

m) Size of feet; quality of handwriting

n) Prison population; number of reported crimes

o) Video-recorder sales; cinema attendances

p) Number of policeman on the beat; number of domestic burglaries

q) Quantity of carrots eaten; quality of eyesight

r) Length of time spent talking to a plant; amount of plant growth

s) Candy-floss sales; number of deaths by drowning in the sea

t) Ability in Mathematics; ability in computing

u) Age of a coin; weight of coin

v) Size of a coin; value of coin

w) Car speed; petrol consumption

x) Age of car; second-hand value

y) Size of skull; general intelligence

z) Foot size; shoe size

 **Information Bank:** *Descriptive statistics, pages 206 – 212*

**35.** *Causal or spurious ?*

For those pairs of variables in Q.1 which are expected to show some correlation, say whether the relationship is likely to be causal or spurious.

**36.** *Cartoons*

As part of an experiment to compare male and female humour, a male student and a female student are shown a selection of cartoons by the same cartoonist. They each rank the cartoons in order of preference. The results of the experiment are as follows:

| Cartoon | A | B | C | D | E | F | G | H | I | J |
|---------|---|---|---|---|---|---|---|---|---|---|
| Male ranking | 8 | 2 | 6 | 3= | 3= | 1 | 7 | 9 | 5 | 10 |
| Female ranking | 6 | 2 | 5 | 4 | 3 | 1 | 7= | 7= | 10 | 9 |

a) Calculate Spearman's correlation coefficient for the data.

b) Interpret the result and comment on its reliability.

**37.** *Marking experiment*

In a marking experiment, two lecturers marked the same pieces of work from a sample of ten students. The first lecturer read through each piece of work and placed them in what she considered to be their order of merit. The pieces of work were then given grades ranging from A for the best through to D for the poorest. The second lecturer adopted a different approach; he identified a number of criteria which he thought should be used for judging that type of work and graded them according to those criteria. The grades awarded by both lecturers are given in this table:

| First lecturer | A | A- | B+ | B | B- | C+ | C | C- | D+ | D |
|----------------|---|----|----|---|----|----|---|----|----|---|
| Second lecturer | B | A- | A | B+ | B- | C- | C+ | C | D+ | D |

a) Calculate Spearman's correlation coefficient for the two sets of grades.

b) Interpret the result and comment on its reliability.

**38.** *Noise levels*

The Engineering section at Dale Institute has been asked to carry out some tests about the noise ratings of several industrial machines. The testers realise that the level of noise is closely related to engine speed and set up an experiment to measure the strength of the relationship. The data collected from the experiments is shown in this table:

| Engine speed (revs / min) | 600 | 800 | 1000 | 1200 | 1400 | 1600 |
|---------------------------|-----|-----|------|------|------|------|
| Noise level (decibels) | 64 | 69 | 73 | 77 | 82 | 84 |

a) Construct a scatter diagram for the data.

b) Calculate Pearson's correlation coefficient and interpret the result.

c) Use the method of least-squares to calculate the line-of-best-fit and draw it on the scatter diagram.

d) Use the regression equation to predict the likely noise level for the following engine speeds:
   i)  1300 revs / min
   ii) 2000 revs / min

e) Comment on the reliability of the results in (d).

 **Information Bank:** *Descriptive statistics, pages 212 – 223*

39. *Heating system*

In a study of the operating efficiency of the heating system on the Brooklands campus, Engineering students collected the following data relating to the units of heat output to units of fuel input:

| Units of fuel input (x) | Units of heat output (y) |
|:---:|:---:|
| 17 | 56 |
| 12 | 41 |
| 8 | 30 |
| 13 | 44 |
| 5 | 17 |
| 7 | 26 |
| 9 | 32 |
| 14 | 43 |
| 10 | 36 |
| 6 | 20 |

a) Construct a scatter diagram which shows the collected data.

b) Use the least-squares method to calculate the equation of the line-of-best-fit relating 'Output' to 'Input' and draw it on the scatter diagram.

c) Use the regression equation to estimate output when input is 20.

d) What input would be required for an output of 28?

e) Explain why it is unreasonable to use the regression equation to estimate output when input is 55.

 **Information Bank:** *Descriptive statistics, pages 220 – 223*

## 40. *League tables*

The final positions in the football league in the 1991-92 season were:

| Team | P | W | D | L | F | A | Pts |
|------|---|---|---|---|---|---|-----|
| Leeds Utd | 42 | 22 | 16 | 4 | 74 | 37 | 82 |
| Manchester Utd | 42 | 21 | 15 | 6 | 63 | 33 | 78 |
| Sheffield Wednesday | 42 | 21 | 12 | 9 | 62 | 49 | 75 |
| Arsenal | 42 | 19 | 15 | 8 | 81 | 46 | 72 |
| Manchester City | 42 | 20 | 10 | 12 | 61 | 48 | 70 |
| Liverpool | 42 | 16 | 16 | 10 | 47 | 40 | 64 |
| Aston Villa | 42 | 17 | 9 | 16 | 48 | 44 | 60 |
| Nottingham Forest | 42 | 16 | 11 | 15 | 60 | 58 | 59 |
| Sheffield Utd | 42 | 16 | 9 | 17 | 65 | 63 | 57 |
| Crystal Palace | 42 | 14 | 15 | 13 | 53 | 61 | 57 |
| Queen's Park Rangers | 42 | 12 | 18 | 12 | 48 | 47 | 54 |
| Everton | 42 | 13 | 14 | 15 | 52 | 51 | 53 |
| Wimbledon | 42 | 13 | 14 | 15 | 53 | 53 | 53 |
| Chelsea | 42 | 13 | 14 | 15 | 50 | 60 | 53 |
| Tottenham Hotspur | 42 | 15 | 7 | 20 | 58 | 63 | 52 |
| Southampton | 42 | 14 | 10 | 18 | 39 | 55 | 52 |
| Oldham Athletic | 42 | 14 | 9 | 19 | 63 | 67 | 51 |
| Norwich City | 42 | 11 | 12 | 19 | 47 | 63 | 45 |
| Coventry City | 42 | 11 | 11 | 20 | 35 | 44 | 44 |
| Luton Town | 42 | 10 | 12 | 20 | 38 | 71 | 42 |
| Notts County | 42 | 10 | 10 | 22 | 40 | 62 | 40 |
| West Ham Utd | 42 | 9 | 11 | 22 | 37 | 59 | 38 |

Each game won earns 3 pts; each game drawn earns 1 pt; games lost earn 0 pts.

| | | | |
|---|---|---|---|
| P | = No. of games played | W | = No. of games won |
| D | = No. of games drawn | L | = No. of games lost |
| F | = No. of goals scored for that team | A | = No. of goals scored against that team |
| Pts | = Total no. of points obtained | | |

a) Construct a scatter diagram showing the relationship between 'Goals for' and 'Points obtained'

b) Calculate Pearson's coefficient for the pair of variables in a) and interpret the result

c) Calculate the coefficient of determination and explain what it means in this case

d) Select other pairs of variables, construct scatter diagrams, measure the strength of the relationship between them and interpret the result in each case; for instance:

i) 'Goals against' and 'Points obtained'

ii) 'Goals for' and 'Goals against'

iii) 'Number of letters in team name' and 'Points obtained'

**Information Bank:** *Descriptive statistics, pages 218 – 220*

# Unit 4: Statistics – 2

1. *Tetrahedral dice*

    A dice is shaped in the form of a tetrahedron (a solid shape with four equal faces) and has its faces numbered 1, 2, 3, 4; another similar dice has its faces numbered 1, 3, 5, 7. Both dice are thrown together.

    a)  Complete this possibility space diagram of the situation:

    |        |        | 1st die |        |        |        |
    |--------|--------|---------|--------|--------|--------|
    |        |        | 1       | 2      | 3      | 4      |
    | 2nd die | 1     | (1, 1)  |        |        |        |
    |        | 3      |         |        |        |        |
    |        | 5      |         |        | (3, 5) |        |
    |        | 7      |         | (2, 7) |        |        |

    b)  If the two dice are thrown together, calculate the probability that the total is:

    i)   9

    ii)  11

    iii) even

    iv)  greater than 4

    v)   not 5

    c)  Draw a probability tree of the situation and use it to calculate the probability that:

    i)   both numbers are different

    ii)  the number on the first dice is greater than the number on the second dice

2. *Cards (1)*

    If a normal pack of fifty-two playing cards is cut once, calculate the probability that the card is:

    i)   red

    ii)  an Ace

    iii) less than eight (Ace counts 1)

    iv)  a red eight

    v)   the Ace of hearts

    vi)  black and even

    vii) black or even

**Information Bank:** *Inferential statistics pages 224 – 228*

3. *Cards (2)*

A selection of three playing cards is drawn at random from a normal pack of fifty-two cards. Each card is drawn, its suit noted, then replaced before the next is drawn.

a) Calculate the probability that:
   i) all three cards are spades
   ii) none of the three cards are hearts
   iii) the cards all have a value greater than 10 (Ace counts as 1)

b) What is the effect on the solutions to a) of not replacing the cards after being drawn ?

4. *Tennis*

Of 60 previous sets that two students have played against one another at tennis, student A has won 45 sets. They are due to play a game of three sets.

a) Draw a probability tree diagram of the situation.

b) Use the diagram to calculate:
   i) P(student A will win all three sets)
   ii) P(student B will lose only one set)
   iii) the number of sets that student A is most likely to win

5. *Strange dice*

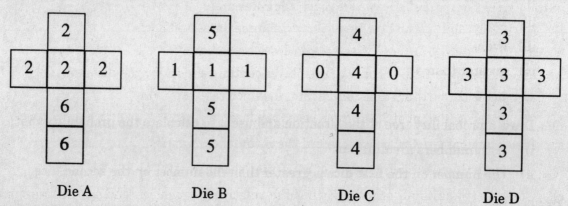

Die A          Die B          Die C          Die D

In a game for two players there are four dice available, the faces being marked as shown on the nets ('flattened' versions) above. The first player chooses one of the dice; the second player chooses one of the remaining dice. The two dice are rolled at the same time and the highest score wins.

a) Draw a tree diagram for each of the following pair of dice in a game:
   i) Die A v. Die B
   ii) Die B v. Die C
   iii) Die C v. Die D
   iv) Die D v. Die A

b) Which die would you choose ?

**Information Bank:** *Inferential statistics pages 228 – 230*

6. *Spinners*

   In a game, you are given the following choices:

   Choice A: One 9-sided spinner with sections numbered 0, 1, 2, 3, 4, 5, 6, 7, 8

   Choice B: Two 5-sided spinners with sections numbered 0, 1, 2, 3, 4

   Choice C: Four 3-sided spinners with sections numbered 0, 1, 2

   If the object of the game is to avoid scoring 7 or 8, which choice gives the best chance of winning ?

7. *The game of '21'*

   In the game of '21' two players take turns to throw a die, keeping a running total of their scores. The first player to reach, or pass, a total of 21 is the winner.

   A standard die is in the shape of a cube and has 1, 2, 3, 4, 5, 6 spots on its faces. This makes a total of 21 spots on all the faces. By redistributing the 21 spots differently on a blank cube, try to design a die which stands a good chance of beating a standard die when a game of '21' is played.

8. *Craps*

   In the game of craps, two dice are thrown; the rules are:
   i)   if the total is 7 or 11, the player wins immediately
   ii)  if the total is 2, 3 or 12, the player loses immediately
   iii) if any other total is thrown, the player continues to throw the dice until they:

   *either* throw that same total again, in which case they win

   *or* throw a total of 7, in which case they lose

   a) Play some games of craps and record the result of each game

   b) Calculate the relative frequency of wins after each game

   c) Construct a suitable graph showing the relative frequencies and use it to estimate the probability of winning.

9. *Dominoes*

   Two dominoes are drawn from a standard set of 28. Calculate the probability that they 'fit'.

10. *Beads*

   A box contains 8 beads - 7 black and 1 white; in a second box are 6 black beads. Five beads are taken out of the first box and put in the second; then five beads are taken from the second box and put in the first. What is the probability that the white bead is in the first box ?

 **Information Bank:** *Inferential statistics pages 224 – 230*

11. *Binomial Distribution*

   a)  Find the probabilities of:
     i)   rolling exactly two 3's in five rolls of a fair die
     ii)  rolling no more than two 3's in five rolls of a fair die
     iii) obtaining exactly four heads in seven tosses of a fair coin
     iv) obtaining at least four heads in seven tosses of a fair coin

   b)  Only 75% of student drivers use seat belts when travelling between campuses. If a sample of five cars are selected at random, what is the probability that all of the drivers are wearing seat belts ?

   c)  The probability that a student entering Dale Institute will survive the first year is 0.65. What is the probability that fewer than three of five new students who are selected at random will survive the first year ?

   d)  The probability that a server at tennis wins a particular point is 0.8. Find the chance that, in four consecutive points, the server:
     i)   wins all four points
     ii)  wins exactly three points
     iii) loses at least three points

   e)  90% of the students on a particular course pass the end-of-year examination. If ten marked examination scripts are selected at random, what is the probability of finding amongst them:
     i)   only five passes
     ii)  at least eight passes

   f)  6% of all biros delivered to the student shop prove to be faulty. What is:
     i)   the probability of opening a packet of 20 biros and finding no faulty ones
     ii)  the mean number of faulty biros

12. *Poisson Distribution*

   a)  Cars arrive at a small local garage at a rate of 1 per five-minute period; there are only two petrol pumps. What is the probability of more than 2 cars arriving in any given five-minute period ?

   b)  Telephone calls come into a switchboard on average at a rate of 3 per minute. What is the probability of receiving more than 5 calls in any given one-minute period.

   c)  Customers enter a store at an average rate of 110 per hour. What is the probability that, during a two-minute period, no customers enter the store ?

   d)  A car insurance firm finds that, on average, it receives claims on 10 student policies each year. What is the probability that the company will have to deal with 14 claims next year ?

   e)  Road accidents in the vicinity of the Brooklands campus occur at the rate of about one every two days. What is the probability of there being more than 5 accidents in a week ?

   f)  In 10 games recently played by a football team, there have been 32 goals. What is the probability that the next game will produce:
     i)   no goals
     ii)  more than 5 goals

**Information Bank:** *Inferential statistics pages 231 – 234*

13. *Left-handedness*

It is estimated that 1 student in 5 at Dale Institute is left-handed.

a) Calculate the probability that, of a random sample of 8 students, more than half are left-handed.

b) Calculate the probability that, of a random sample of 20 students, more than two are left-handed.

c) Calculate the size of sample needed in order that there is a probability of greater than 0.90 that it contains at least one left-handed student.

d) Calculate the size of sample needed in order that there is a probability of greater than 0.95 that it contains at least one left-handed student.

14. *Crosswords*

A newspaper is delivered to the students' common room each day of the week except Saturday and Sunday. A group of students try to complete the crossword and on past performances stand a 75% chance of successfully completing it.

a) Explain why a Binomial Distribution is a suitable model for the distribution of the number of crosswords completed in a week.

b) Calculate the mean and standard deviation for this distribution.

c) Calculate the probability that they complete all the crosswords in any given week.

d) Calculate the probability that they do not complete any crosswords during a given week.

15. *Biassed dice ?*

A die is thrown 3 times and the number of sixes noted. This experiment is performed 180 times, the results shown below:

| Number of 6's | 0 | 1 | 2 | 3 |
|---|---|---|---|---|
| Frequency | 98 | 65 | 14 | 3 |

a) Use the binomial distribution to calculate the probabilities of obtaining 0, 1, 2, 3 sixes for an unbiased die.

b) Use the answers to a) to calculate the expected frequencies for 0, 1, 2, 3 sixes.

c) Use a $\chi^2$ test to compare the expected and observed frequencies and interpret the result.

16. *Forecourt*

Cars arrive at a garage forecourt at a rate of 1 every 2 minutes.

a) Explain why a Poisson Distribution is a suitable model for the distribution of the number of cars arriving at the garage.

b) Calculate the probability that:

i) no cars arrive during a 10-minute period

ii) more than 2 cars arrive during a 1-minute period

iii) 20 cars arrive in a half-hour period

**Information Bank:** *Inferential statistics pages 231 – 234; 244 – 245*

## 17. *Injuries*

The number of injuries to rugby team members during matches played each week at Dale Institute has a Poisson Distribution with a mean of 2.2.

a) Explain why a Poisson Distribution is a suitable model for the distribution of the number of injuries each week.

b) Calculate the probability that there are:
   i)   no injuries in a given week
   ii)  more than 5 injuries in a given week
   iii) more than 5 injuries in a fortnight

## 18. *Guest house*

A guest house on a main road in Chelford has 5 rooms. All of its trade is from business people who require overnight accommodation. The number of people seeking accommodation each day has a Poisson Distribution with a mean of 5.

a) Explain why a Poisson Distribution is a suitable model for the distribution of the number of accommodation requests each day.

b) Calculate the probabilities of 0, 1, 2, 3, 4 . . . . . . .10, >10 accommodation requests each day.

c) Calculate the expected frequencies for accommodation requests over a 300-day period.

d) Calculate the number of people who are refused accommodation in this period.

e) The owner is thinking of providing 2 extra rooms. What effect will this have on the answer to (d)?

## 19. *Photocopiers*

Two photocopiers are provided, in the library, for student use; both photocopiers are rather unreliable. In the case of photocopier A, the number of breakdowns per week has a Poisson Distribution with a mean of 0.5. Similarly, for photocopier B, the number of breakdowns per week has a Poisson Distribution with a mean of 0.2. Assume that A and B break down independently of one another. Calculate the probability that, in the next fortnight:
   i)   Neither A nor B breaks down
   ii)  There are exactly two breakdowns

## 20. *Student shop*

The number of students entering the student shop per minute is observed over 100 one-minute periods, the results being as follows:

| No. of students / min. | 0 | 1 | 2 | 3 | 4 | 5 | 6 | 7 |
|---|---|---|---|---|---|---|---|---|
| Frequency | 5 | 15 | 24 | 25 | 17 | 8 | 4 | 2 |

a) Calculate the mean number of students entering the shop per minute.

b) Use the Poisson Distribution to calculate the probabilities that 0, 1, 2, 3, 4, 5, 6 and 7 students enter the shop during any given one-minute period.

c) Calculate the expected frequencies for the number of students during 100 one-minute periods.

d) Use a $\chi^2$ test to compare the expected and observed frequencies and interpret the result.

**Information Bank:** *Inferential statistics pages 233 – 234; 244 – 245*

21. *Estimation of population mean*

    Determine a) 95% and b) 99% confidence intervals for the mean of the population for each of the following samples:

    i)   $n = 100$; $\bar{x} = 72$; $s = 10$

    ii)  $n = 150$; $\bar{x} = 645$; $s = 4.2$

    iii) $n = 60$; $\bar{x} = 82$; $s = 12$

    iv)  $n = 80$; $\bar{x} = 68$; $s = 3.5$

    v)   $n = 60$; $\bar{x} = 52.3$; $s = 4.8$

22. *Estimation of population proportion*

    Determine a) 95% and b) 99% confidence intervals for the population proportion for each of the following samples:

    i)   $n = 100$; $p = 0.75$

    ii)  $n = 30$; $p = 0.1$

    iii) $n = 60$; $p = 0.02$

    iv)  $n = 75$; $p = 0.92$

    v)   $n = 42$; $p = 0.23$

23. *Printer ribbons*

    The lifetimes of a sample of printer ribbons were noted as follows:

    | Lifetime (hours) | 1 – 20 | 21 – 40 | 41 – 60 | 61 – 80 | 81 – 100 |
    |---|---|---|---|---|---|
    | Frequency | 10 | 16 | 25 | 11 | 8 |

    a) Calculate the mean and standard deviation for this sample.

    b) Determine 95% and 99% confidence intervals for the mean of the population of printer ribbons from which this sample is taken.

24. *Drinks machine*

    A record kept of the number of soft drinks sold from a machine on the Wentworth campus over a period of 60 consecutive days gave the following results:

    | Number of drinks sold | Frequency |
    |---|---|
    | 0 – 9 | 3 |
    | 10 – 19 | 9 |
    | 20 – 29 | 16 |
    | 30 – 39 | 20 |
    | 40 – 49 | 7 |
    | 50 – 59 | 4 |
    | 60 – 69 | 1 |

    Calculate 95% confidence intervals for the mean number of drinks sold daily in the long-term.

**Information Bank:** *Inferential statistics, pages 235 – 240*

25. *Student loans*

A sample of 100 students showed that the mean amount of money arranged through the student loan facility to be £200 with a standard deviation of £25.

a) Determine 95% and 99% confidence intervals for the mean amount loaned to all students.

b) The administrative officer who deals with student loans wishes the estimate of the mean amount loaned to be accurate to within £2 of the true mean. How many students would need to be sampled in order to get this level of accuracy ?

26. *Cigarettes*

A random sample of 50 students showed that 17 regularly smoked 'Hackingcoff' cigarettes.

a) Determine 95% and 99% confidence intervals for the true proportion of all students at Dale Institute who smoke that brand.

b) Given that there are approximately 10000 students at Dale Institute, determine 95 % and 99% confidence intervals for the number who smoke 'Hackingcoff'.

27. *Sweets*

A tube of Smartoes, randomly selected from the shelves of the student shop, contains 60 variously coloured sweets, including 5 blue ones. Determine 95% and 99% confidence intervals for the true proportion of Smartoes that are blue.

28. *Invoices*

A random sample of invoices is taken in order that the mean value for all invoices at Dale Institute can be estimated. 100 invoices are sampled and grouped according to their value as follows:

| Invoice value (£) | Frequency |
|---|---|
| 0 – 49 | 8 |
| 50 – 99 | 11 |
| 100 – 149 | 14 |
| 150 – 199 | 25 |
| 200 – 249 | 12 |
| 250 – 299 | 7 |
| 300 – 349 | 7 |
| 350 – 399 | 6 |
| 400 – 449 | 6 |
| 450 – 500 | 4 |

a) Determine 95% and 99% confidence intervals for the mean amount for all invoices.

b) Determine 95% and 99% confidence intervals for the proportion of invoices that are for amounts of £250 or more.

**Information Bank:** *Inferential Statistics, pages 235 – 240*

29. *Weather*

As part of a project connected with wind speed and direction in East Anglia, students of Environmental Science release a number of balloons on randomly selected days and observe the distance travelled from the Institute. Each balloon has a label attached on which the finder can note the landing-place, returning it to the Institute for processing. The data shown below gives the distances travelled from the Institute of a sample of retrieved balloons:

| Distance (miles) | 0-49 | 50-99 | 100-149 | 150-199 | 200-249 | 250-299 | 300-349 |
|---|---|---|---|---|---|---|---|
| Frequency | 34 | 12 | 25 | 15 | 9 | 5 | 5 |

a) Determine 95% and 99% confidence limits for the mean distance travelled.

b) Determine 95% and 99% confidence intervals for the proportion of balloons that travel a distance of 150 miles or more.

30. *Market research*

In a survey of shoppers at a shopping precinct close to Dale Institute, a market research company found that 27 people out of a random sample of 100 people used 'Whitewash' soap powder.

a) Determine 95% and 99% confidence limits for the proportion of local people who use Whitewash.

b) If there are 1500 residents on a housing estate close to Dale Institute, determine 95% and 99% confidence intervals for the number of these who use Whitewash.

c) Explain why these results should be treated with caution.

31. *Hypotheses*

Decide whether the following are examples of null, one-tailed or two-tailed hypotheses:

a) The Mathematics test scores obtained by children in two different classes are the same

b) Vandalism rises with unemployment

c) Age affects reaction time

d) Vegetarians have a higher incidence of tooth decay

e) Quality of bar staff influences drinks sales

f) Eating carrots improves eye-sight

g) Diet influences intelligence

h) Advertising policy affects sales

i) CFCs have increased the size of the hole in the ozone layer

j) The Guardian is more difficult to read than The Sun

k) Weather affects mood

l) Anxiety influences performance in examinations

m) Talking to plants makes them grow faster

n) The mean I.Q. of students at Dale Institute is 110

o) Recursion is a more efficient programming technique than looping

p) Programming style affects program execution time

q) VDU screen-glare affects concentration span

r) Changing hands has no effect on tiddlywinks skill

s) Drinking blood makes teeth grow longer

t) Exercise slows down the ageing process

**Information Bank:** *Inferential statistics, pages 235 – 241*

32. *Hypothesis tests (1) – Single mean*
    Test the following hypotheses   i) at the 5% level   ii) at the 1% level:
    a)   $H_0$: m = 98
         $H_1$: m ≠ 98
         $\bar{x}$ = 100; s = 5; n = 40

    b)   $H_0$: m = 32
         $H_1$: m ≠ 32
         $\bar{x}$ = 31.4; s = 1.6; n = 64

    c)   $H_0$: $m$ = 1.9
         $H_1$: m ≠ 1.9
         $\bar{x}$ = 1.87; s = 0.08; n = 33

    d)   $H_0$: $m$ = 16.7
         $H_1$: $m$ > 16.7
         $\bar{x}$ = 17.1; s = 1.7; n = 30

33. *Hypothesis tests (2) – Proportion*
    Test the following hypotheses   i)  at the 5% level   ii) at the 1% level:
    a)   $H_0$: P = 0.8
         $H_1$: P ≠ 0.8
         p = 0.9; n = 50

    b)   $H_0$: P = 0.6
         $H_1$: P ≠ 0.6
         p = 0.7; n = 60

    c)   $H_0$: P = 0.25
         $H_1$: P ≠ 0.25
         p = 0.17; n = 125

    d)   $H_0$: P = 0.55
         $H_1$: P > 0.55
         p = 0.65; n = 280

34. *Hypothesis tests (3) – Difference between two means*
    Test the following hypotheses   i) at the 5% level   ii) at the 1% level:
    a)   $H_0$: $\bar{x}_1 - \bar{x}_2$ = 0
         $H_1$: $\bar{x}_1 - \bar{x}_2$ ≠ 0
         $\bar{x}_1$ = 44; $\bar{x}_2$ = 42
         $n_1$ = 80; $n_2$ = 100
         $s_1$ = 8.8; $s_2$ = 5.5

    b)   $H_0$: $\bar{x}_1 - \bar{x}_2$ = 0
         $H_1$: $\bar{x}_1 - \bar{x}_2$ ≠ 0
         $\bar{x}_1$ = 29.7; $\bar{x}_2$ = 31
         $n_1$ = 50; $n_2$ = 50
         $s_1$ = 2.7; $s_2$ = 2.5

    c)   $H_0$: $\bar{x}_1 - \bar{x}_2$ = 0
         $H_1$: $\bar{x}_1 - \bar{x}_2$ ≠ 0
         $\bar{x}_1$ = 49.7; $\bar{x}_2$ = 47.8
         $n_1$ = 50; $n_2$ = 40
         $s1_1$ = 2.1; $s_2$ = 2.2

    d)   $H_0$: $\bar{x}_1 - \bar{x}_2$ = 0
         $H_1$: $\bar{x}_1 - \bar{x}_2$ ≠ 0
         $\bar{x}_1$ = 128; $\bar{x}_2$ = 124
         $n_1$ = 80; $n_2$ = 80
         $s_1$ = 10.7; $s_2$ = 10.7

35. *Hypothesis tests (4) – Difference between two proportions*
    Test the following hypotheses   i) at the 5% level   ii) at the 1% level:
    a)   $H_0$: $p_1 - p_2$ = 0
         $H_1$: $p_1 - p_2$ ≠ 0
         $p_1$ = 0.8; $p_2$ = 0.86
         $n_1$ = 150; $n_2$ = 200

    b)   $H_0$: $p_1 - p_2$ = 0
         $H_1$: $p_1 - p_2$ ≠ 0
         $p_1$ = 0.5; $p_2$ = 0.48
         $n_1$ = 100; $n_2$ = 90

    c)   $H_0$: $p_1 - p_2$ = 0
         $H_1$: $p_1 - p_2$ ≠ 0
         $p_1$ = 0.64; $p_2$ = 0.67
         $n_1$ = 100; $n_2$ = 120

    d)   $H_0$: $p_1 - p_2$ = 0
         $H_1$: $p_1 - p_2$ > 0
         $p_1$ = 0.5; $p_2$ = 0.4
         $n_1$ = 80; $n_2$ = 60

**Information Bank:** *Inferential statistics, pages 241 – 244*

36. *Student shop*

a) Blank music cassettes are advertised as having a playing time of 90 minutes. A sample of 40 tapes are selected and found to have a mean playing time of 89.1 minutes with a standard deviation of 1.3 minutes. Is this sufficient evidence that the mean playing time is not 90 minutes ?

b) Chocolate bars on sale have a mean stated weight of 25 grams. A sample of 100 bars had a mean weight of 23.6 grams with a standard deviation of 0.8 grams. Does this support the idea that the mean weight is not 25 grams ?

c) Two types of blank video tapes are sold in the shop, both with a playing time of 3 hours. A sample of 50 type A tapes are found to have a mean playing time of 185 minutes with a standard deviation of 2.5 minutes. A sample of 40 type B tapes were found to have a mean of 182 minutes with a standard deviation of 2 minutes. Is there a significant difference between the playing times of the two types ?

d) 100 packets of coloured sweets, each of which contains 25 sweets, contain the following number of those that are coloured orange:

| No. of orange sweets | 0 | 1 | 2 | 3 | 4 | 5 |
|---|---|---|---|---|---|---|
| No. of packets | 12 | 32 | 25 | 20 | 8 | 3 |

i) Calculate the proportion of sweets that are coloured orange

ii) Test the null hypothesis $H_0: p = 0.1$ with the alternative hypothesis $H_1: p \neq 0.1$.

iii) A further sample of 50 packets of the same type of sweets have 115 that are coloured orange. Are the proportions of orange coloured sweets in the two samples significantly different ?

37. *Examinations*

a) Two different lecturers mark 100 scripts each in an examination. The first lecturer awards a mean mark of 53 with a standard deviation of 18; the second lecturer awards a mean mark of 57 with a standard deviation of 21. Does this suggest a significant difference in their markings ?

b) In another examination, 60 candidates who have been taught by a certain lecturer have a mean mark of 55 with a standard deviation of 14. The 80 candidates who have been taught by another lecturer obtain a mean mark of 52 with a standard deviation of 16.

Does this suggest that the first lecturer is a significantly better teacher than the second lecturer?

38. *Teaching methods*

A lecturer in the Computing section of Dale Institute believes that his method of teaching structured programming methodology is so good that it brings about an absolute improvement in the level of programming efficiency in his students. He tests a new intake of 70 students on entry to his course and retests them a year later. In each case, he sets a test which is appropriate to their level of programming experience. The test on entry gives a mean score of 85.7 with a standard deviation of 10.8; the retest gives a mean score of 89.5 with a standard deviation of 11.2.

Do these results support his belief ?

**Information Bank:** *Inferential statistics, pages 241 – 244*

## 39. Teaching methods (2)

A lecturer in Mathematics is about to introduce a topic in geometry to two of her classes. In class A there are 36 students and in class B there are 38 students. She has just seen a computer package that is designed to introduce students to this particular topic. She has not previously had the opportunity to use computers within her teaching; so, she decides to use it only with the students in class A so that she can compare their progress with those from class B who she decides to teach in her usual way.

At the end of the topic she gives the same assessment test, maximum score 50, to both classes. Class A have a mean score of 41.6 with a standard deviation of 2.2; class B have a mean score of 39.7 with a standard deviation of 2.8. She also enquired of the students whether they had enjoyed the topic. 27 of the students in class A replied that they had, compared with 21 from class B.

Use appropriate tests to determine whether:

i) there is a significant difference in performance between the two classes

ii) there is a significant difference in attitudes between the two classes

## 40. ESP

A simple experiment is designed by a lecturer to test whether individual students possess powers of ESP (Extra-sensory perception). For the purposes of the experiment she makes a pack of ninety cards each of which contains either a triangle, square or circle. There are an equal number of cards containing each shape. She draws a card from the pack, which the student cannot see, and asks what shape is shown on the card. At the end of one particular experiment, a student has scored forty-five correct answers.

a) How many correct answers should the student obtain by sheer guesswork ?

b) Use a $\chi^2$ test to determine whether this student's results are significantly different.

## 41. Marking

Over a period of time, the grades awarded for the assessment on a particular course by a group of lecturers has been:

A: 10%    B: 20%    C: 40%    D: 20%    E: 10%

A new lecturer gives 21 A's, 35 B's, 67 C's, 15 D's and 12 F's in teaching the same course.

Use a $\chi^2$ test to determine whether the new lecturer seems to be following the same pattern of grades set by the others.

 **Information Bank:** *Inferential statistics, pages 241 – 245*

42. *Car bumpers*

Examination of the cars in the Wentworth campus car parks show that the dents in 400 car bumpers are as follows:

Right front     95

Right rear      80

Left front      115

Left rear       110

Use a $\chi^2$ test to determine whether these results are significantly different to what might be expected.

43. *Karting*

Dale Institute hosts a go-kart competition involving local schools who race against one another over a pre-determined course. Among the top fifty finishers the makes of karts are distributed as follows:

Brand A: 14     Brand B: 12     Brand C: 6     Brand D: 5     Brand E: 13

Each brand represents 20% of all karts entered in the race. Brands C and D are the only ones made in Britain. Those riders using British karts claim that they had an off-day; the others claim that their karts are superior.

a) Use a $\chi^2$ test to determine whether the other riders are justified in their claim.

b) What assumptions have you made ?

44. *Seeds*

A germination experiment undertaken by a group of Science students consists of placing 500 seeds, in rows of 5, on damp filter paper. The number of seeds that germinate in each row is counted and give the following results:

| No. of seeds germinating per row | No. of rows |
|:---:|:---:|
| 0 | 0 |
| 1 | 2 |
| 2 | 12 |
| 3 | 33 |
| 4 | 41 |
| 5 | 12 |

a) Assuming that a Binomial Distribution is appropriate for this situation, calculate the probabilities of obtaining 0, 1, 2, 3, 4, 5 seeds germinating in each row.

b) Use the answers to a) to calculate the number of rows that are expected to contain 0, 1, 2, 3, 4, 5 germinated seeds.

c) Use a $\chi^2$ test to compare the expected frequencies with the observed frequencies.

**Information Bank:** *Inferential statistics, pages 244 – 247*

## 45. *Drinking*

A small-scale survey which asked students to state whether they considered current licensing laws to be satisfactory gave the following information:

|  |  | \multicolumn{3}{c}{Age group} |  |  |
|---|---|---|---|---|
|  |  | 18 – 25 | 26 – 40 | 40+ |
| **Opinion** | Satisfactory | 35 | 50 | 30 |
|  | Not satisfactory | 45 | 20 | 25 |

Carry out a $\chi^2$ test to determine whether opinion is independent of age.

## 46. *Partners*

Use a $\chi^2$ test to determine whether the following set of data obtained about students and their partners supports the hypothesis that stature affects choice of partner:

|  |  | \multicolumn{3}{c}{Partner A} |  |  |
|---|---|---|---|---|
|  |  | Short | Medium | Tall |
|  | Short | 5 | 30 | 9 |
| **Partner B** | Medium | 26 | 49 | 29 |
|  | Tall | 12 | 21 | 22 |

## 47. *Smoking and drinking*

A survey of a large number of students gave the following information regarding their smoking and drinking habits:

|  |  | \multicolumn{4}{c}{Type of drinking} |  |  |  |
|---|---|---|---|---|---|
|  |  | None | Occasional | Moderate | Heavy |
| **Type of smoking** | None | 78 | 147 | 126 | 25 |
|  | Occasional | 22 | 45 | 27 | 7 |
|  | Moderate | 55 | 133 | 102 | 17 |
|  | Heavy | 35 | 75 | 45 | 46 |

Do drinking and smoking seem to be related ?

 **Information Bank:** *Inferential statistics, pages 244 – 247*

48. *Hair and eyes*

Does the following data suggest a connection between hair colour and eye colour ?

|  |  | Eye colour | | |
|---|---|---|---|---|
|  |  | Blue | Brown | Grey |
| **Hair colour** | Black | 6 | 46 | 3 |
|  | Brown | 40 | 40 | 20 |
|  | Blonde | 28 | 7 | 5 |

49. *Interviews*

As part of their course, some students have to be interviewed by examiners and are given either a Merit, Pass or Fail on the basis of the interview. The large number of students means that three examiners are involved. The number of grades awarded by the different examiners are as follows:

|  |  | Examiner | | |
|---|---|---|---|---|
|  |  | A | B | C |
| **Grade awarded** | Merit | 12 | 4 | 12 |
|  | Pass | 28 | 39 | 28 |
|  | Fail | 30 | 22 | 25 |

a) Does there appear to be any significant difference in the standard of grade awarded by the examiners ?

b) What assumptions have been made ?

**Information Bank:** *Inferential statistics, pages 244 – 247*

# Unit 5: Problem-solving techniques

1. *Cash dispenser*

A bank cash dispenser in Chelford is observed over several weeks and is found to have the following distribution of customers in any given 1-minute time period:

| Number of customers | Probability |
|:---:|:---:|
| 0 | 0.65 |
| 1 | 0.20 |
| 2 | 0.10 |
| 3 | 0.03 |
| 4 | 0.02 |
| 5+ | 0.00 |

Also, associated with each customer is the amount of time taken for a transaction. These times are distributed according to the following pattern:

| Transaction time (mins) | Probability |
|:---:|:---:|
| 1 | 0.20 |
| 2 | 0.40 |
| 3 | 0.30 |
| 4 | 0.10 |

a) i) Carry out a manual simulation of the queueing situation at the cash dispenser over a period of 1 hour. Tabulate the results in an appropriate manner.

   ii) Calculate the mean queue length during this time.

   iii) What is the mean queueing time per customer?

b) Write a computer program or develop a spreadsheet model to carry out the simulation and modify it to answer the following questions:

   i) It is reasonable to suppose that if there is a lengthy queue (for instance, 5 customers) then no new customers will join the queue, but will go elsewhere. How many 'lost' customers in a 12-hour day?

   ii) As in i), but customers go away after they have queued for 10 minutes.

   iii) Investigate how sensitive queue length is to any variation in transaction time.

   iv) As in iii), but consider customer arrival rate instead.

   v) Throughout a normal working day, the arrival probabilities are likely to vary – incorporate this factor.

   vi) The bank are considering providing an extra cash-point. Modify your simulation model to incorporate this new feature and investigate its likely effects.

**Information Bank:** *Problem-solving techniques, pages 248 – 257*

2. *Van hire*

A van hire firm has 5 light vans that it rents to customers. The demand for vans has been recorded over a period of time and is found to be distributed as follows:

| Number of vans demanded | Probability |
|---|---|
| 0 | 0.05 |
| 1 | 0.10 |
| 2 | 0.20 |
| 3 | 0.25 |
| 4 | 0.20 |
| 5 | 0.10 |
| 6 | 0.10 |

The amount of time for which each van is hired is distributed as follows:

| Number of days required | Probability |
|---|---|
| 1 | 0.10 |
| 2 | 0.25 |
| 3 | 0.30 |
| 4 | 0.15 |
| 5 | 0.10 |
| 6 | 0.05 |
| 7 | 0.05 |

a) Carry out a manual simulation of the situation over a period of 30 days, tabulating the results in a suitable form.

b) As a result of the simulation, what advice can you offer the firm?

3. *Stock*

Each week the Students' Union order cartons of crisps for the Brooklands campus shop from a local wholesale supplier. At the moment, 15 cartons of crisps are ordered every week. Sales of crisps have been observed over a period of time and are distributed as follows:

| Cartons sold | Probability |
|---|---|
| 13 | 0.04 |
| 14 | 0.13 |
| 15 | 0.31 |
| 16 | 0.35 |
| 17 | 0.12 |
| 18 | 0.05 |

a) Carry out a manual simulation of the crisp stock situation over a period of 20 weeks, tabulating the results in an appropriate form.

b) As a result of the simulation, what advice can you offer the Student Union?

**Information Bank:** *Problem-solving techniques, pages 248 – 257*

4.  *Doctor (1)*

A doctor notes that the lengths of time spent in consultation with patients is distributed as follows:

| Consultation (mins) | Frequency |
|---|---|
| 14 | 25% |
| 15 | 41% |
| 16 | 19% |
| 17 | 11% |
| 18 | 4% |

The doctor's receptionist issues appointments at intervals of 15-minutes, starting at 8.30 a.m. and finishing at 11.00 a.m. It can be assumed that:

1.  Patients arrive on time for appointments
2.  If the doctor is free, the patient is seen immediately on arrival
3.  Any patients who have not been seen by the doctor by 11.00 a.m. are not seen that day and have to make another appointment

The doctor is concerned to improve the situation for patients and so wants to find out how the system operates at the moment.

Carry out a manual simulation of the situation over the period of a 8.30 a.m. – 11.00 a.m. surgery. Tabulate the results in order to obtain:

i)   the mean waiting time for each patient
ii)  the mean number of patients in the waiting room
iii) the amount of time that the doctor is not seeing patients
iv)  the number of patients who do not get seen

5.  *Doctor (2)*

The doctor in Q.4 realises that the assumption that patients arrive on time for their appointments is unrealistic. So, he gathers further data which shows that arrival times are distributed as follows:

| Lateness (mins) | Frequency |
|---|---|
| -3 | 7% |
| -2 | 16% |
| -1 | 28% |
| 0 | 24% |
| 1 | 10% |
| 2 | 8% |
| 3 | 5% |
| 4 | 2% |

(Note that a lateness of -3 minutes means that the patient arrives 3 minutes early).

Assuming that the consultation times are distributed as before, carry out a manual simulation of the situation over the surgery period. Tabulate it in order to obtain the same measures of waiting times, doctor idle time etc. as before.

**Information Bank:** *Problem-solving techniques, pages 248 – 257*

6. *Drinks dispenser*

A dispenser in the student common room on the Harper campus provides a selection of three different brands of canned soft drinks. The dispenser is filled by a member of the catering staff who takes delivery of cartons of drinks from a local wholesale supplier early on Monday morning. Orders for the following week are telephoned to the supplier late on Friday afternoon. The member of staff has kept a record of daily sales for each drink and these are shown to be distributed as follows:

| Drink A | | | | | | |
|---|---|---|---|---|---|---|
| Cans sold: | 10 | 11 | 12 | 13 | 14 | 15 | 16 |
| Probability: | 0.35 | 0.23 | 0.12 | 0.10 | 0.08 | 0.07 | 0.05 |

| Drink B | | | | | | |
|---|---|---|---|---|---|---|
| Cans sold: | 13 | 14 | 15 | 16 | 17 | 18 | 19 |
| Probability: | 0.04 | 0.10 | 0.17 | 0.34 | 0.19 | 0.11 | 0.05 |

| Drink C | | | | | | |
|---|---|---|---|---|---|---|
| Cans sold: | 14 | 15 | 16 | 17 | 18 | 19 | 20 |
| Probability: | 0.05 | 0.10 | 0.10 | 0.15 | 0.20 | 0.25 | 0.15 |

Other relevant facts and assumptions are:
    i)    only a whole number of cartons can be ordered
    ii)   each carton contains 10 cans
    iii)  the dispenser is filled daily; capacity 20 cans of each drink
    iv)  each can has an unlimited shelf life
    v)   all drinks cost the same

a) For each drink, use random numbers to simulate sales over a period of 10 weeks.

b) From the results of a) suggest a sensible ordering policy; that is, determine the number of cartons of each drink that should be ordered each week so that there are sufficient quantities to meet demand while avoiding an excessive build-up of unsold drinks.

c) Either develop a spreadsheet model or write a computer program to simulate the situation.

d) Use the spreadsheet / program to investigate how variations in a drink's sales distribution might affect the ordering policy.

7. *Picture cards*

In an attempt to persuade children to buy 'Choc-o-bloc' chocolate bars, the manufacturer includes a picture card of a pop star with every bar. There are 10 different picture cards to collect and it can be assumed that equal numbers of each picture card are produced.

a) Carry out a simulation of the situation and determine how many bars of Choc-o-bloc, on average, a child needs to buy before s/he has the complete set.

b) Investigate the number of bars of Choc-o-bloc that would need to be purchased if there were a different number of cards in the set; for instance, what about 5 cards, 15 cards, 20 cards etc?

c) Two friends decide to start collecting the cards and agree to swop duplicates with each other when possible. Simulate this situation and determine:
    i)    how many bars of Choc-o-bloc they need to buy between them, on average, before each has a complete set of cards
    ii)   as a result of i), whether it is more expensive to be a single collector

**Information Bank:** *Problem-solving techniques, pages 248 – 257*

8. *Football*

The performance of Dale Institute's 'A' team is the subject of Section 1 Unit 35 – 'Goals'. A student is keen to predict the likely outcome of a forthcoming game and so decides to simulate some games between them and the opposition. The distribution of goals scored by Dale is:

| Goals scored | Frequency |
| --- | --- |
| 0 | 20% |
| 1 | 20% |
| 2 | 35% |
| 3 | 20% |
| 4 | 5% |

Similarly, the distribution of goals scored by the opposition is:

| Goals scored | Frequency |
| --- | --- |
| 0 | 25% |
| 1 | 30% |
| 2 | 30% |
| 3 | 15% |
| 4 | 5% |

a) Simulate 20 games between the two teams and use the results to predict whether the outcome of the game is most likely to be a win for Dale, a win for the opposition or a draw.

b) Extend the model to take account of goals scored against the teams.

9. *Half-life*

In a certain unit of time, some radioactive atoms in a substance become non-radioactive. These atoms are said to have decayed; the remaining atoms stay radioactive. This means that there are now less atoms left to decay, so the rate of decay reduces as more units of time pass. The time taken for half of the initial number of atoms to decay is called the substance's *half-life*.

Suppose the probability of an atom decaying is 10% and initially there are 250 radioactive.

a) Assign a range of random digits to the events 'Decayed' and 'Not decayed' as follows:

| Atom state | Random digits |
| --- | --- |
| Decayed | 0 |
| Not decayed | 1 - 9 |

i) Use the table of random numbers in Appendix A to simulate the decay of the substance, tabulating the results in an appropriate manner. Continue until all atoms have decayed.

ii) How many units of time pass before all of the atoms decay?

iii) Determine the half-life of the substance.

iv) Construct a graph of the results with 'Units of time' on the horizontal axis and 'Atoms of substance remaining' on the vertical axis.

b) Investigate the effect of altering:

i) the initial number of radioactive atoms: 1000, 100000, 1000000 etc.

ii) the decay probability: 20%, 30%, 40% etc.

**Information Bank:** *Problem-solving techniques, pages 248 – 257*

10. *Random walks*

a) A drunk staggers along a line which runs West-East; he takes one step every minute and is equally likely to move W or E. Each step moves him a distance of 1 unit.

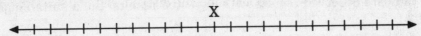

i) Assuming that he starts at point X, allocate ranges of random numbers to 'West' and 'East', simulate the drunk's walk over a series of 50 steps and calculate his final distance from X.

ii) Repeat the simulation for different numbers of steps and determine how far from X he is likely to finish after *n* steps.

b) The drunk now moves onto a square grid, as shown below, with lines that run North-South as well as West-East. When he is at an intersection he is equally likely to move N, S, E, or W. As before, he takes one step every minute and each step moves him a distance of 1 unit.

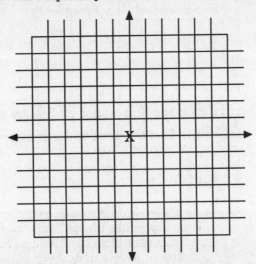

i) Assuming that he starts at point X, allocate appropriate ranges of random numbers and simulate the drunk's walk over a series of 50 steps and calculate his final distance from X (as the crow flies).

ii) Repeat the simulation for different numbers of steps and determine how far from X he is likely to finish after *n* steps.

c) Try the simulation on other grid types; for instance, isometric. Again, determine how far the drunk is from his starting-point after *n* steps,

d) In reality, the drunk would be able to stagger in any direction (not just along grid line); incorporate this feature into the simulation.

e) Also in reality, the drunk's distance would not always be 1 unit. Modify the simulation to allow for random distances moved at each step.

f) Random walks can be used to study the way that diseases spread, molecules move etc. In practice, therefore, random walks are not restricted to movement in 2-D. So, construct a simulation that allows for completely free movement in 3-D; that is, in random directions and for random distances.

**Information Bank:** *Problem-solving techniques, pages 248 – 257*

11. *Tests for randomness*

Various tests have been devised to ascertain the 'randomness' of pseudo-random numbers. Below is a short description of one such test. When carrying out any test for randomness, it is necessary to compare observed results with expected results. So, a suitable goodness-of-fit test should be used.

*Frequency Test*: Each digit should appear approximately one-tenth of the time; for instance, in a group of 100 digits there should be ten 0's, ten 1's, ten 2's etc.

a)  Carry out the frequency test on:

   i)   the random numbers given in the table in Appendix A

   ii)  a sequence of pseudo-random numbers produced by a spreadsheet or computer program

b)  Find out what you can about:

   i)   the poker test

   ii)  the run test

   iii) the gap test

12. *Area under a curve*

It is possible to obtain an estimate for the area under a curve by simulation.

For instance, suppose it is required to find the area under the curve: $y = 2x - x^2$ for $1 < x < 2$.

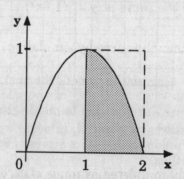

Step 1:    Complete a rectangle surrounding the required area (dotted line)
Step 2:    Generate a random x-coordinate in the range $1 < x < 2$
Step 3:    Calculate the value of $2x - x^2$
Step 4:    Generate a random y-coordinate in the range $0 < y < 1$
Step 5:    If $y$ is less than the calculated value of step 3, accept the point $(x, y)$; otherwise reject it
Step 6:    Repeat steps 2 to 5, 100 times
Step 7:    Area under the curve = $\dfrac{\text{No. of points accepted}}{100} \times \text{Area of rectangle}$

**Information Bank:** *Problem-solving techniques, pages 248 – 251*

a) Study the algorithm and find out how and why the method works.

b) Either develop a spreadsheet or write a computer program to perform this task.

> *Note*: Most computer-based generators produce random numbers, $r$, in the range $0 < r < 1$.
> If random numbers, $R$, in the range $a < R < b$ are required, then calculate:
> $$R = a + r(b - a)$$

c) The more points selected, the closer the simulated value gets to the actual area. Note that the exact value for the area under the curve in the example is $\frac{2}{3}$. Determine how many points need to be used in order to get the area correct to 1D, 2D, 3D etc.

d) Obtain an estimate for $\pi$ from this quadrant of a circle which has a radius of 1 unit:

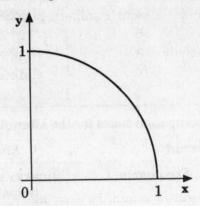

Note that the equation of the curve is: $y = \sqrt{(1 - x^2)}$

To estimate $\pi$:
i) estimate the area under the curve by simulation (100 points)

ii) multiply the area by $4 \left( \text{since the area of the quadrant is } \dfrac{\pi}{4} \right)$

e) Investigate how many points are needed to obtain the value of $\pi$ correct to 1D, 2D, 3D, etc. ($\pi = 3.1415926535897932384 \ldots\ldots\ldots\ldots$)

13. *Garage forecourt*

On pages 261 – 262, a partially completed example of an event-based simulation is given:

a) Complete the simulation for vehicles A – Z.

b) Determine:
   i) the time taken before all vehicles have cleared the system
   ii) the proportion of vehicles that turn away
   iii) the proportion of time that the pump is busy
   iv) the mean length of the queue
   v) the mean time that each vehicle spends in the system

c) The garage owner is looking into the feasibility of the following options:
   i) extending the forecourt to cater for an extra vehicle
   ii) adding an extra pump

   Carry out simulations and make a recommendation as to which is the better option.

d) Construct a spreadsheet model or write a computer program to perform this simulation.

**Information Bank:** *Problem-solving techniques, pages 260 – 262*

14. *Runways*

A commercial airport has two runways which deal with both large and small aircraft. At present one runway only deals with large aircraft and the other runway only deals with small aircraft. The time that an aircraft occupies a runway varies but is generally longer for the large aircraft. The airport deals with roughly equal numbers of large and small aircraft.

The distribution of inter-arrival times is:

| Inter-arrival time (mins) | Frequency |
|:---:|:---:|
| 2 | 8% |
| 4 | 22% |
| 6 | 27% |
| 8 | 18% |
| 10 | 14% |
| 12 | 11% |

The distribution of runway occupation times for the aircraft is:

*Large aircraft*

| Runway time (mins) | Frequency |
|:---:|:---:|
| 10 | 25% |
| 12 | 39% |
| 14 | 26% |
| 16 | 10% |

*Small aircraft*

| Runway time (mins) | Frequency |
|:---:|:---:|
| 6 | 15% |
| 8 | 30% |
| 10 | 36% |
| 12 | 19% |

a) Perform a simulation of the runway congestion if aircraft arrive in the following order:

L, S, L, L, S, S, S, L, S, S, S, S, L, L, L, S, L, L, S, L, L, S, S, L, S, L, L, S, L, S

b) Use the results to determine, for each runway:

i) the time taken before all aircraft have cleared the runway

ii) the proportion of time that the runway is busy

iii) the mean number of aircraft on the runway

iv) the mean time that each aircraft spends on the runway

c) The airport management are looking into the possibility of using each runway for both types of aircraft. With this facility, aircraft would be directed to land at the most appropriate runway. Perform a simulation and determine whether this idea is likely to bring about any improvements in the situation. You will need to decide what is meant by 'the most appropriate runway' and how to measure 'improvements'.

**Information Bank:** *Problem-solving techniques, pages 260 – 262*

15. *Outing*

A group of students at Dale Institute decides to organise an outing for 240 under-privileged children. There are upto 24 adults who are willing to go if required. The group arranges to hire a mixture of coaches and minibuses from a local firm. Each coach can carry 50 passengers, each minibus can carry 16 passengers.

It is decided that there should be 3 adults on each coach and 2 adults on each minibus. Further, since some of the children have special needs, there must be at least 1 minibus.

The cost of hiring a coach is £72 and the cost of hiring a minibus is £30; the organisers wish to keep costs to a minimum.

a) Assuming that the organisers hire $x$ coaches and $y$ minibuses:

   i) Explain why the number of adults to be carried means that:

$$3x + 2y \leq 24$$

   ii) Formulate two more constraints.

   iii) Write down the objective function.

b) Show the constraints on a graph.

c) Highlight the feasible region.

d) Use the graph to determine the number of coaches and minibuses that should be hired.

e) Calculate the total cost of hiring the transport.

16. *Repairs*

A small company specialising in computer repairs employs two part-time service engineers, Paul and Ann. The majority of their work is concerned with repairing monitors, keyboards and disc drives. Their work schedule is allocated at the beginning of each week by the service manager; he decides how many days each engineer should work that week. Paul's rate of pay is £35 per day; Ann's rate of pay is £42 per day. Neither Paul nor Ann can work for more than 6 days each week.

Each day, Paul is capable of repairing 3 monitors, 3 keyboards and 1 disc drive; Ann is capable of repairing 2 monitors, 6 keyboards and 1 disc drive each day.

At the beginning of one particular week there are 12 monitors, 18 keyboards and 5 disc drives awaiting repair. The service manager obviously wishes to keep repair costs to a minimum. How many days should he ask Paul and Ann to work in that week ?

a) Assuming Paul works $x$ days and Ann works $y$ days:

   i) Formulate five constraints.

   ii) Write down the objective function.

b) Show the constraints on a graph.

c) Highlight the feasible region.

d) Use the graph to determine the number of days that Paul and Ann should each work that week.

e) Calculate the total cost of hiring their services.

**Information Bank:** *Problem-solving techniques, pages 263 – 270*

17. *Slimmers foods*

Food Science students have been investigating slimmers' foods and decide to set up an experiment to try to produce their own. From their research they know that each serving of slimming food should contain at least 360 units of Vitamin A, 126 units of Vitamin B and 168 units of Vitamin C.

They have available two ingredients, X and Y, from which to produce their own food; both ingredients contain Vitamins A, B and C. The amount of each vitamin in one millilitre of ingredient is given in the following table:

| Ingredient | Vitamin A (units) | Vitamin B (units) | Vitamin C (units) |
|------------|-------------------|-------------------|-------------------|
| X | 5 | 1 | 1 |
| Y | 4 | 2 | 3 |

Each ingredient costs 1p per millilitre and the students wish to keep the cost to a minimum.

a) Assuming that $x$ millilitres of ingredient X and $y$ millilitres of ingredient Y are used:

   i) Explain why the amount of Vitamin A required means that:

$$5x + 4y \geq 360$$

   ii) Formulate two more constraints.

   iii) Write down the objective function.

b) Show the constraints on a graph.

c) Highlight the feasible region.

d) Use the graph to determine the amount of each ingredient that should be used.

e) Calculate the cost of 1 litre of the mixture.

f) The cost of ingredient X doubles. What effect does this have on the solutions to (d) and (e)?

18. *Cakes*

A cake stall is being organised at a Summer Fair; two types of cake will be sold. 'Butterfly' cakes need 50g of fat and 150g of flour; 'Beeswing' cakes need 75g fat and 75g flour. Altogether, there are 3kg of fat and 4.5kg of flour available. The stallholders wish to bake as many cakes as possible.

a) Assuming that the stallholders bake $x$ Butterfly cakes and $y$ Beeswing cakes:

   i) Formulate (and simplify, where possible) two constraints.

   ii) Write down the objective function.

b) Show the constraints on a graph.

c) Highlight the feasible region.

d) Use the graph to determine the number of each cake that should be baked.

e) Use the simplex algorithm to confirm your solution to (d).

f) i) Use the graphical method to determine how many of each type of cake should be baked if only half the quantities of fat and flour are available.

   ii) Use the simplex algorithm to solve the new problem. Comment on your solution.

**Information Bank:** *Problem-solving techniques, pages 263 – 274*

19. *Pillows*

The Little Wooden Hills Co. of Bedfordshire manufactures two type of pillow: the Sleeptite and the Sweetdream. The production costs for each Sleeptite is £8; for each Sweetdream the figure is £4. Each Sleeptite takes 12 minutes to make; the corresponding time for each Sweetdream is 36 minutes. The amount of packaging time needed for either product is 4 minutes.

There is a production budget of £4000; there are also 240 hours available for manufacture and 40 hours available for packaging.

The profit on each Sleeptite is £5 and for each Sweetdream is £10.

a) Assuming $x$ Sleeptite and $y$ Sweetdream pillows are made:

    i)   Formulate three constraints.

    ii)  Write down the objective function.

b) Show the constraints on a graph.

c) Highlight the feasible region.

d) Use the graph to determine the number of each type of pillow that should be made in order to maximise profit.

e) If the company were forced to reduce the profit on each Sweetdream to £4, what would be the effect ?

f) Use the simplex algorithm to confirm your solutions to (d) and (e).

20. *Graphical calculators*

An electronics company has decided to produce three new models of graphical calculator (called the GT100, GT350 and GT500) specifically for the education market. Each calculator requires time for manufacture, assembly, finishing and testing. The amount of time needed for each process, in minutes, are given below:

|  | GT100 | GT350 | GT500 |
|---|---|---|---|
| Manufacture | 3 | 2.5 | 3 |
| Assembly | 2 | 3 | 1.5 |
| Finishing | 1 | 0.5 | 2 |
| Testing | 1 | 1.5 | 2.5 |

In any given day, the amount of time available (in minutes) for each process are:

        Manufacture: 1200   Assembly: 900   Finishing: 750   Testing: 600

The profit on each type of calculator is:

        GT100: £10     GT350: £12     GT500: £16

The company wishes to know how many of each type of calculator to produce each day in order to maximise profits. It is assumed that all calculators manufactured are sold.

a) Assuming $x$, $y$ and $z$ of the GT100, GT350 and GT500 respectively are made:

    i) Formulate four constraints.      ii) Write down the objective function.

b) Use the simplex algorithm to determine:

    i) the optimum daily production of each calculator   ii) the maximum possible daily profit

**Information Bank:** *Problem-solving techniques, pages 263 – 274*

21. *Simplex algorithm (1)*

Solve the following linear programming problems by using the simplex algorithm, (confirming solutions by the graphical method, if possible) assuming in each case that $x \geq 0$, $y \geq 0$:

a)   Maximise:     $P = x + 2y$

    Subject to:   i)   $4x + 5y \leq 140$

              ii)   $x + 3y \leq 63$

              iii)   $3x + 2y \leq 84$

b)   Maximise:     $P = 2x + 3y$

    Subject to:   i)   $5x + 2y \leq 20$

              ii)   $3x + 10y \leq 30$

              iii)   $4x + 5y \leq 20$

c)   Maximise:     $P = 2x + 3y$

    Subject to:   i)   $3x + y \leq 90$

              ii)   $x + 2y \leq 70$

              iii)   $x + y \geq 40$

d)   Maximise:     $P = 5x + y$

    Subject to:   i)   $5x + 2y \leq 180$

              ii)   $x + y \leq 45$

              iii)   $x \geq 10$

e)   Maximise:     $P = x + 2y$

    Subject to:   i)   $12x + 5y \geq 30$

              ii)   $x + y \leq 10$

              iii)   $x \leq 7$

              iv)   $y \leq 4$

f)   Maximise:     $P = 4x + 3y$

    Subject to:   i)   $2x + y \leq 16$

              ii)   $x + 2y \leq 20$

              iii)   $3x + 4y \leq 30$

              iv)   $x \geq 4$

g)   Maximise:     $P = 3x + 4y$

    Subject to:   i)   $2x + y \leq 50$

              ii)   $2x + 3y \leq 90$

              iii)   $x + y \leq 40$

              iv)   $x \leq 20$

              v)   $y \geq 10$

h)   Maximise:     $P = 4x + 5y + 6z$

    Subject to:   i)   $3x + y + 2z \leq 218$

              ii)   $x + 2y + 2z \leq 134$

              iii)   $2x + 3y + z \leq 150$

**Information Bank:** *Problem-solving techniques, pages 270 – 274*

## 22. *Simplex algorithm (2)*

Solve the following linear programming problems by forming the dual problems and solving using the simplex algorithm (confirm your solutions using the graphical method, if possible):

a)  Minimise:      $C = x + y$

    Subject to:  i)   $x + 2y \geq 14$

                ii)  $x + 3y \geq 18$

                iii) $5x + 4y \geq 40$

b)  Minimise:      $C = x + y$

    Subject to:  i)   $3x + 11y \geq 11$

                ii)  $x + 4y \geq 10$

                iii) $4x + y \geq 14$

c)  Minimise:      $C = x + y$

    Subject to:  i)   $x + 3y \geq 12$

                ii)  $3x + y \geq 6$

                iii) $5x + 4y \geq 20$

d)  Minimise:      $C = 5x + 6y + 8z$

    Subject to:  i)   $2x + 3y + 3z \geq 270$

                ii)  $2x + y + 6z \geq 190$

                iii) $2x + y + z \geq 100$

e)  Minimise:      $C = 6x + 18y + 16z + 9v + 5w$

    Subject to:  i)   $x + y + 2z + 3v + w \geq 20$

                ii)  $12x + 4v + 3w \geq 30$

                iii) $x + 8y + 3z + 4w \geq 10$

                iv)  $2x + 12y + 10z + v + 2w \geq 20$

 **Information Bank:** *Problem-solving techniques, pages 274 – 278*

23. *Satellite dishes*

The Skywards Satellite Dish Company has factories in Leeds, Manchester and Birmingham; daily outputs at the factories are: 75, 50 and 100 respectively. The outputs are sent to wholesale depots in Oxford, Cheltenham and Lincoln which have daily requirements of: 70, 90 and 65 respectively. Transportation costs, in £ per satellite dish, are as follows:

|  | Leeds | Manchester | Birmingham |
|---|---|---|---|
| Oxford | 28 | 23 | 17 |
| Cheltenham | 18 | 14 | 16 |
| Lincoln | 20 | 13 | 15 |

Skywards wishes to minimise its total transport costs.

a)   Formulate an initial tableau suitable for solution by the transportation algorithm.

b)   Obtain an initial feasible solution using the North-West corner rule.

c)   Use the transportation algorithm to determine:

   i)   the optimum allocation of satellite dishes to routes

   ii)   the minimum total transportation costs

d)   The requirements of the depot in Manchester fall to 60 satellite dishes per day. Determine the new optimum allocation and total transport costs.

24. *Solar-powered car*

The Fjord Motor Company of Norway have U.K. factories at Wolverhampton, Slough and Winchester. These factories manufacture the revolutionary new solar-powered car, the Fiasco. Each week the factories produce 200, 260 and 340 Fiascos respectively. Fjord's main distributors are based in Norwich, Swindon, Bristol and Exeter; the distributors have placed orders for 300, 240, 160 and 100 Fiascos respectively.

The costs for transporting each Fiasco between the various factories and dealers are as follows:

|  | Norwich | Swindon | Bristol | Exeter |
|---|---|---|---|---|
| Wolverhampton | 22 | 36 | 50 | 78 |
| Slough | 20 | 29 | 43 | 22 |
| Winchester | 36 | 57 | 85 | 50 |

The company wish to minimise their total transport costs.

a)   Formulate an initial tableau suitable for solution by the transportation algorithm.

b)   Obtain an initial feasible solution using the least cost rule

c)   Use the transportation algorithm to determine:

   i)   the optimum allocation of Fiascos to routes

   ii)   the minimum total transportation costs

d)   Determine the optimum allocation if it becomes impossible to use the Slough / Norwich route.

**Information Bank:** *Problem-solving techniques, pages 279 – 298*

25. *Ships*

Ships containing 15, 12 and 18 loads respectively are in ports A, B and C. They are to proceed to ports P, Q, R and S where they are required to deliver 7, 12, 12 and 14 loads respectively. The profits to be made (in £'00s) by selling the loads in the destination ports vary according to the route as follows:

|   | P | Q | R | S |
|---|---|---|---|---|
| A | 2 | 3 | 4 | 8 |
| B | 2 | 6 | 7 | 4 |
| C | 5 | 3 | 5 | 3 |

The shipping company wish to maximise their total profit

a) Formulate an initial tableau suitable for solution by the transportation algorithm.

b) Obtain an initial feasible solution using Vogel's rule

c) Use the transportation algorithm to determine:

 i) the optimum allocation of loads to routes

 ii) the maximum possible total profit

d) The ship in port A, in fact, has only 10 loads. Determine the new optimum allocation and the maximum possible total profit.

26. *Paper*

A publishing company has paper mills at A, B and C; it also has printing houses at P, Q and R. Paper needs to transported by road from the paper mills to the printing houses. Transport costs are £15 per mile. The distances between the paper mills and printing houses are as follows:

|   | P | Q | R |
|---|---|---|---|
| A | 140 | 220 | 180 |
| B | 60 | 100 | 140 |
| C | 200 | 100 | 60 |

A, B and C have 70, 60 and 30 units of paper available respectively; P, Q and R require 50, 30 and 70 units of paper respectively.

a) Formulate an initial tableau suitable for solution by the transportation algorithm.

b) Obtain an initial feasible solution

c) Use the transportation algorithm to determine:

 i) the optimum allocation pattern

 ii) the minimum total transportation costs

d) The amount of paper at mill A falls to 40 units; at the same time the requirements of printing house Q rises to 60. Determine the new optimum allocation pattern and the total transport costs.

**Information Bank:** *Problem-solving techniques, pages 279 – 298*

27. *Cleaners*

Four cleaners at Dale Institute are to be assigned to clean four different areas A, B, C and D. From experience, the times (in minutes) that the cleaners take to clean these areas are as follows:

|  | A | B | C | D |
|---|---|---|---|---|
| **Cleaner 1** | 24 | 24 | 21 | 23 |
| **Cleaner 2** | 21 | 27 | 22 | 22 |
| **Cleaner 3** | 20 | 23 | 24 | 26 |
| **Cleaner 4** | 26 | 24 | 25 | 23 |

Use the Hungarian method to determine the allocation of cleaners to jobs so that they are completed in the least possible total time.

28. *Teaching practice*

Five mature student teachers are to be assigned to five schools for teaching experience. A shortage of schools means that the students will have to travel daily from their homes to the schools. The distances, in miles, from homes to schools are as follows:

|  | School | | | | |
|---|---|---|---|---|---|
|  | A | B | C | D | E |
| **Student 1** | 7 | 14 | 12 | 15 | 15 |
| **Student 2** | 8 | 11 | 11 | 12 | 10 |
| **Student 3** | 9 | 8 | 7 | 8 | 13 |
| **Student 4** | 10 | 9 | 8 | 12 | 9 |
| **Student 5** | 7 | 10 | 14 | 13 | 14 |

The institute has to pay the students' travelling expenses; they obviously wish this to be a minimum.

Use the Hungarian method to determine the optimum allocation of students to schools.

29. *Quiz*

A group of five students are to take part in an inter-institute trivia quiz. The quiz is in five categories: Sport, Television, Food, Travel and Music; each student can only enter one category. The team manager has kept a record of their best scores (out of 150) in previous competitions:

|  | Sport | Television | Food | Travel | Music |
|---|---|---|---|---|---|
| **Student A** | 113 | 82 | 122 | 77 | 99 |
| **Student B** | 107 | 82 | 118 | 85 | 120 |
| **Student C** | 97 | 71 | 95 | 109 | 123 |
| **Student D** | 80 | 50 | 87 | 65 | 82 |
| **Student E** | 117 | 97 | 132 | 124 | 147 |

a) Determine the assignment of students that maximises the team's overall score.

b) The Music category is dropped from the quiz. What is the new optimum assignment?

**Information Bank:** *Problem-solving techniques, pages 298 – 300*

30. *Happiness*

Three lecturers at Dale Institute are to teach on a modular computing course. The six modules last for 1 hour each week and each lecturer has to teach two of the modules. The lecturers are asked to choose the times of day that they would prefer to teach the modules. They give a preference score out of 10 for each of the 1-hour sessions during a teaching day. (A score of 10 means that they are very happy to teach at that time; a score of 0 means that would be very unhappy about teaching then).

The 'happiness' information for the lecturers is as follows:

|  | 9 a.m. | 10 a.m. | 11 a.m. | 1 p.m. | 2 p.m. | 3 p.m. |
|---|---|---|---|---|---|---|
| **Lecturer A** | 8 | 8 | 5 | 8 | 5 | 6 |
| **Lecturer B** | 5 | 6 | 6 | 5 | 6 | 7 |
| **Lecturer C** | 3 | 3 | 7 | 7 | 8 | 8 |

a)      Formulate an initial tableau suitable for solution by the assignment algorithm.

b)      Use the Hungarian method to determine the allocation of lecturers to classes that maximises their total happiness.

c)      Lecturer B later becomes extremely unhappy about teaching before 11 a.m.; determine the new optimum assignment pattern.

**Information Bank:** *Problem-solving techniques, pages 298 – 300*

## 31. *Networks*

Use Prim's algorithm to determine the minimum connector for each of these networks:

(a)

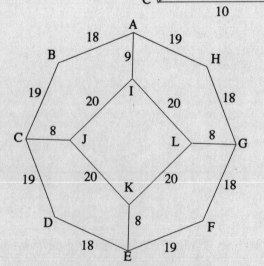

(b)

(c)

(d)

(e)

## 32. *Printed circuit boards*

The diagrams below show printed circuit boards, each with several points that need linking together. In each case, calculate the minimum amount of conductor needed to connect the points.

a)

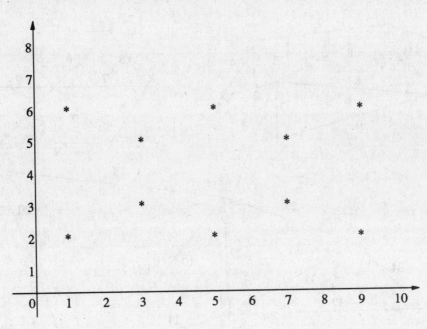

b)

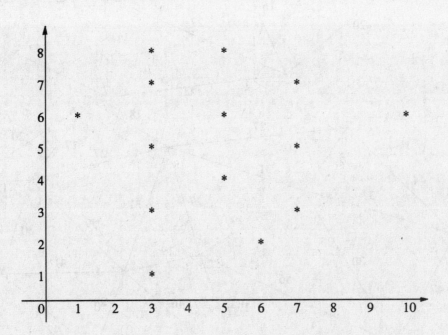

**Information Bank:** *Problem-solving techniques, pages 305 – 309*

33. *Shortest paths*

In each of the networks shown below, use a suitable algorithm to determine the shortest route between the points X and Y.

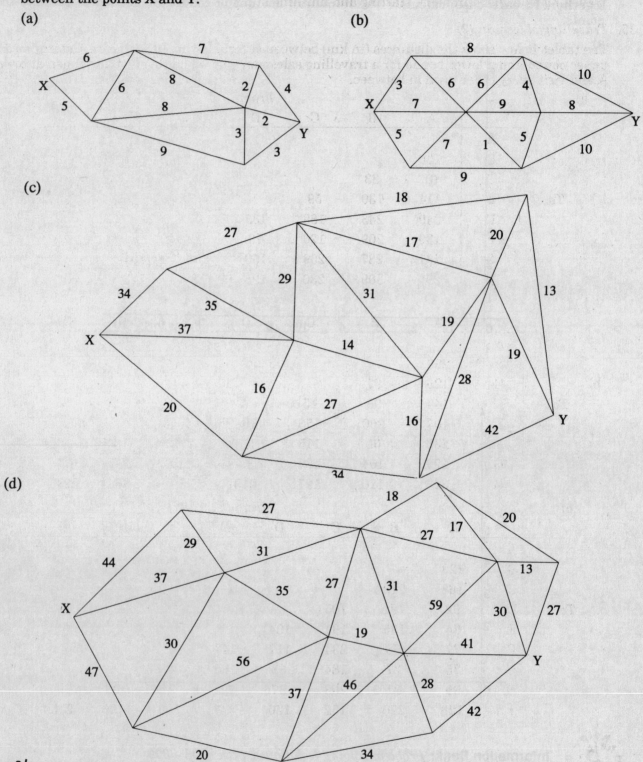

(a)

(b)

(c)

(d)

**34.** *Travelling salesman (1)*

For each of the networks given in Q. 33, determine an upper bound and a lower bound for the 'travelling salesman' problem, starting and finishing at point X.

**35.** *Travelling salesman (2)*

The tables below show the distances (in km) between several towns. In each case, determine an upper bound and a lower bound for a travelling salesman who wishes to start and finish at town A and visit every other town in between.

a)

|  |  | From | | | | | | |
|---|---|---|---|---|---|---|---|---|
|  |  | A | B | C | D | E | F | G |
|  | A |  |  |  |  |  |  |  |
|  | B | 106 |  |  |  |  |  |  |
|  | C | 61 | 83 |  |  |  |  |  |
| To | D | 114 | 130 | 59 |  |  |  |  |
|  | E | 249 | 243 | 188 | 135 |  |  |  |
|  | F | 130 | 209 | 120 | 79 | 187 |  |  |
|  | G | 231 | 287 | 209 | 150 | 156 | 101 |  |
|  | H | 296 | 309 | 230 | 198 | 89 | 179 | 90 |

b)

|  |  | From | | | | | | |
|---|---|---|---|---|---|---|---|---|
|  |  | A | B | C | D | E | F | G |
|  | A |  |  |  |  |  |  |  |
|  | B | 223 |  |  |  |  |  |  |
|  | C | 126 | 97 |  |  |  |  |  |
| To | D | 144 | 98 | 45 |  |  |  |  |
|  | E | 107 | 260 | 156 | 168 |  |  |  |
|  | F | 238 | 61 | 115 | 153 | 270 |  |  |
|  | G | 229 | 104 | 122 | 87 | 255 | 160 |  |
|  | H | 323 | 120 | 197 | 218 | 254 | 86 | 224 |

c)

|  |  | From | | | | | | | |
|---|---|---|---|---|---|---|---|---|---|
|  |  | A | B | C | D | E | F | G | H |
|  | A |  |  |  |  |  |  |  |  |
|  | B | 123 |  |  |  |  |  |  |  |
|  | C | 168 | 212 |  |  |  |  |  |  |
| To | D | 62 | 191 | 105 |  |  |  |  |  |
|  | E | 84 | 195 | 191 | 104 |  |  |  |  |
|  | F | 77 | 68 | 234 | 117 | 147 |  |  |  |
|  | G | 75 | 37 | 184 | 88 | 155 | 47 |  |  |
|  | H | 99 | 31 | 203 | 97 | 195 | 74 | 36 |  |
|  | I | 128 | 220 | 152 | 120 | 62 | 198 | 196 | 215 |

**Information Bank:** *Problem-solving techniques, pages 309 – 311*

## 36. *Network analysis (1)*

Construct networks from the following precedence tables:

a)

| Activity | Preceding activities |
|----------|----------------------|
| A | — |
| B | A |
| C | A |
| D | B |
| E | B, C |
| F | D, E |

b)

| Activity | Preceding activities |
|----------|----------------------|
| A | — |
| B | A |
| C | A |
| D | A |
| E | B |
| F | C |
| G | E |
| H | F |
| I | G, H |
| J | C |
| K | D |
| L | I, J, K |

c)

| Activity | Preceding activities |
|----------|----------------------|
| A | — |
| B | — |
| C | A |
| D | A |
| E | A |
| F | C |
| G | C |
| H | C |
| I | B, D |
| J | F, I |
| K | E, G, H, J |
| L | E, H |
| M | K, L |

**Information Bank:** *Problem-solving techniques, pages 312 – 317*

d)

| Activity | Preceding activities |
|----------|----------------------|
| A | — |
| B | A |
| C | A |
| D | A |
| E | C |
| F | C, D |
| G | E |
| H | B, G |
| I | C, F, G |
| J | F, I |
| K | G, I, J |
| L | H |
| M | G, L |
| N | K, M |

37. *Network analysis (2)*

For each of the following projects:

   i)   construct a network of activities

   ii)  identify the critical path

   iii) calculate the total project time

   iv)  calculate the total float and free float for each activity

a)

| Activity | Preceding activities | Estimated time for completion (hours) |
|----------|----------------------|---------------------------------------|
| A | — | 4 |
| B | — | 16 |
| C | A, B | 2 |
| D | A, B | 4 |
| E | A, B | 8 |
| F | D | 2 |
| G | C, D | 7 |
| H | F | 3 |
| I | F | 4 |
| J | E, I | 2 |
| K | G, H | 5 |
| L | J, K | 4 |

b)

| Activity | Preceding activities | Estimated time for completion (hours) |
|---|---|---|
| A | — | 3 |
| B | A | 3 |
| C | A | 5 |
| D | A | 7 |
| E | B | 2 |
| F | B | 3 |
| G | E | 7 |
| H | F | 4 |
| I | G, H | 4 |
| J | C, D, G, H | 5 |
| K | D | 6 |
| L | I, J, K | 3 |

c)

| Activity | Preceding activities | Estimated time for completion (hours) |
|---|---|---|
| A | — | 28 |
| B | — | 12 |
| C | — | 34 |
| D | A | 43 |
| E | B | 26 |
| F | A, B | 17 |
| G | D | 42 |
| H | E | 19 |
| I | C, D, E, F | 26 |
| J | G, H, I | 13 |

## 38. PERT

The precedence table for a project consisting of 11 activities is as follows:

| Activity | Preceding activities |
|---|---|
| A | — |
| B | — |
| C | A |
| D | B |
| E | B |
| F | F |
| G | C, D |
| H | E |
| I | F |
| J | G, H |
| K | I |

Each activity has been given an optimistic, most likely and pessimistic completion time, in days:

| Activity | Optimistic duration | Most likely duration | Pessimistic duration |
|----------|---------------------|----------------------|----------------------|
| A | 4 | 6 | 8 |
| B | 2 | 4 | 7 |
| C | 1 | 3 | 6 |
| D | 6 | 9 | 12 |
| E | 5 | 10 | 14 |
| F | 7 | 12 | 19 |
| G | 5 | 9 | 14 |
| H | 1 | 2 | 4 |
| I | 2 | 3 | 6 |
| J | 10 | 15 | 22 |
| K | 6 | 9 | 12 |

a) Construct a network diagram for the project.

b) Use the diagram and the most likely durations to determine:

   i) the EST for each activity

   ii) the LFT for each activity

   iii) the minimum possible completion time for the project

   iv) the critical path

   v) the total float and free float for each activity

c) Use PERT principles to calculate, for each activity' duration:

   i) the mean

   ii) the standard deviation

d) Determine:

   i) the mean time and standard deviation for completion of the overall project

   ii) 95% and 99% confidence intervals for completion of the overall project

e) What is the probability that the project is completed within 40 days ?

**Information Bank:** *Problem-solving techniques, pages 317 – 322*

### 39. *Product launch*

A toy manufacturing company have identified certain activities that must be completed before their new toy can be launched; these are:

| Activity | Description |
|----------|-------------|
| A | Product design |
| B | Market research |
| C | Order raw materials |
| D | Receive raw materials |
| E | Construct prototype product |
| F | Develop advertising campaign |
| G | Organise mass production facilities |
| H | Product distribution to outlets |

The company have also determined an optimistic, most likely and pessimistic duration (in weeks) associated with each activity, as follows:

| Activity | Optimistic duration | Most likely duration | Pessimistic duration |
|----------|---------------------|----------------------|----------------------|
| A | 2 | 6 | 11 |
| B | 4 | 5 | 8 |
| C | 2 | 3 | 4 |
| D | 1 | 2 | 4 |
| E | 2 | 4 | 6 |
| F | 3 | 4 | 6 |
| G | 2 | 3 | 6 |
| H | 1 | 2 | 4 |

a) Construct a possible precedence table for the activities.

b) Construct a network diagram for the project.

c) Use the diagram and the most likely durations to determine:
   i) the EST for each activity
   ii) the LFT for each activity
   iii) the minimum possible completion time for the project
   iv) the critical path
   v) the total float and free float for each activity

d) Use PERT principles to calculate, for each activity' duration:
   i) the mean
   ii) the standard deviation

e) Determine:
   i) the mean time and standard deviation for completion of the overall project
   ii) 95% and 99% confidence intervals for completion of the overall project

f) It is now October 1st. What is the probability that the toy will be in shops before Christmas ?

**Information Bank:** *Problem-solving techniques, pages 317 – 322*

# Appendix A

*Random numbers*

| | | | | | | | | | | | | | | |
|---|---|---|---|---|---|---|---|---|---|---|---|---|---|---|
| 53 | 74 | 23 | 99 | 67 | 98 | 33 | 41 | 19 | 95 | 47 | 53 | 53 | 38 | 09 |
| 63 | 38 | 06 | 86 | 54 | 79 | 62 | 67 | 80 | 60 | 75 | 91 | 12 | 81 | 19 |
| 35 | 30 | 58 | 21 | 46 | 49 | 28 | 24 | 00 | 49 | 55 | 65 | 79 | 78 | 07 |
| 63 | 43 | 36 | 82 | 69 | 32 | 92 | 85 | 88 | 65 | 54 | 34 | 81 | 85 | 35 |
| 98 | 25 | 37 | 55 | 26 | 24 | 02 | 71 | 37 | 07 | 03 | 92 | 16 | 66 | 75 |
| 02 | 13 | 22 | 80 | 30 | 74 | 97 | 58 | 70 | 21 | 21 | 22 | 09 | 10 | 05 |
| 64 | 62 | 49 | 52 | 60 | 83 | 34 | 83 | 38 | 30 | 72 | 61 | 38 | 11 | 18 |
| 85 | 28 | 74 | 63 | 81 | 25 | 85 | 33 | 14 | 20 | 68 | 47 | 74 | 55 | 44 |
| 58 | 32 | 01 | 41 | 78 | 42 | 00 | 04 | 17 | 65 | 56 | 79 | 49 | 61 | 71 |
| 34 | 73 | 42 | 90 | 74 | 18 | 32 | 27 | 23 | 23 | 71 | 32 | 65 | 18 | 05 |
| 03 | 59 | 35 | 58 | 46 | 83 | 94 | 89 | 57 | 20 | 40 | 07 | 33 | 23 | 13 |
| 62 | 80 | 10 | 59 | 89 | 68 | 69 | 93 | 52 | 68 | 87 | 06 | 64 | 09 | 49 |
| 08 | 12 | 56 | 74 | 45 | 94 | 23 | 58 | 90 | 92 | 29 | 41 | 28 | 75 | 76 |
| 07 | 88 | 88 | 48 | 06 | 62 | 97 | 96 | 41 | 26 | 11 | 06 | 20 | 58 | 81 |
| 01 | 79 | 68 | 94 | 32 | 88 | 85 | 44 | 36 | 05 | 88 | 64 | 42 | 07 | 52 |
| 72 | 91 | 46 | 37 | 58 | 34 | 95 | 40 | 08 | 79 | 30 | 99 | 91 | 01 | 74 |
| 88 | 64 | 42 | 88 | 78 | 02 | 12 | 18 | 01 | 80 | 80 | 79 | 82 | 41 | 63 |
| 45 | 05 | 78 | 62 | 58 | 50 | 33 | 85 | 04 | 45 | 62 | 93 | 47 | 22 | 78 |
| 96 | 50 | 20 | 14 | 84 | 83 | 02 | 39 | 17 | 33 | 57 | 61 | 47 | 84 | 77 |
| 43 | 72 | 32 | 13 | 06 | 59 | 77 | 29 | 67 | 70 | 33 | 50 | 85 | 43 | 37 |
| 50 | 78 | 38 | 89 | 25 | 06 | 27 | 54 | 46 | 95 | 77 | 61 | 63 | 38 | 97 |
| 22 | 12 | 78 | 96 | 01 | 65 | 89 | 60 | 25 | 95 | 84 | 83 | 04 | 14 | 76 |
| 96 | 63 | 26 | 27 | 39 | 84 | 65 | 01 | 84 | 37 | 76 | 88 | 29 | 16 | 08 |
| 31 | 46 | 00 | 71 | 32 | 93 | 65 | 27 | 01 | 33 | 54 | 70 | 27 | 71 | 91 |
| 78 | 14 | 69 | 55 | 58 | 80 | 48 | 78 | 26 | 86 | 54 | 27 | 64 | 61 | 39 |
| 56 | 41 | 99 | 42 | 63 | 61 | 14 | 03 | 86 | 47 | 41 | 22 | 80 | 06 | 33 |
| 24 | 01 | 07 | 46 | 26 | 13 | 90 | 40 | 63 | 86 | 33 | 37 | 82 | 34 | 24 |
| 80 | 64 | 66 | 50 | 24 | 75 | 43 | 69 | 91 | 40 | 15 | 22 | 06 | 79 | 90 |
| 59 | 44 | 50 | 40 | 24 | 86 | 82 | 90 | 63 | 84 | 66 | 80 | 43 | 74 | 02 |
| 49 | 01 | 07 | 84 | 56 | 85 | 31 | 39 | 00 | 61 | 01 | 51 | 53 | 45 | 55 |

# Appendix B: **Answers to Section 1 Tasks**

## Unit 1: **Paper models**

1. (a) Variables: $l, t, w, e, d$      Parameters: $n, f, s, p$

   (b) e.g. relatively unimportant: size of plates      (c)   Stated relationships are reasonable

   (d) e.g. if $n$ increases, $l$ and $w$ increase

---

**Problem statement**

'How long will it take me to travel between the Wentworth and Brooklands campuses?'

| *Variables / Parameters* | *Relationships* |
|---|---|
| Distance between campuses (d) | |
| Speed (s) | s depends on m, v, t and w |
| Traffic density (v) | if v increases, s decreases |
| Mode of transport (m) | |
| Time of day (t) | t affects v |
| Weekday (w) | w affects v |

---

2. (a) Several possible solutions to each problem; for example:

   In this example, parameters are: $d, m, t, w$; variables are: $s, v$

   (b) In most cases, the model will be a combination of deterministic and stochastic factors. Whether one type of factor predominates is governed by the relative presence of unpredictable elements within the situation. For instance, the arrival of a lift is likely to be subject to more stochastic factors than the siting of a coin-operated telephone.

## Unit 2: **Paint-pots**

1. Length / width / height of room

   Length / height of window

   Width / height of door

   Depth of window sill and surround / area covered by 1 litre of paint

2. Door / depth of window can be ignored minimal amount of paint compared to total required

3. Possible steps   (i)     Calculate areas of: two end walls, two side walls, ceiling, window

                   (ii)    Calculate total area of walls & ceiling; subtract area of window

                   (iii)   Divide area in (ii) by area covered by 1 litre of paint

4. From Task 3:   (i)     $42 \text{ m}^2$ (end walls); $63 \text{ m}^2$ (side walls); $54 \text{ m}^2$ (ceiling); $14 \text{ m}^2$ (window)

                   (ii)     $145 \text{ m}^2$

                   (iii)   14.5 litres

5. (a) Similar to:    Multiply length by width; multiply length by height, double it; multiply width by height, double it; calculate total area; subtract area of window; divide by amount of area covered by 1 litre of paint.

   (b) $P = \dfrac{l \times w + l \times h \times 2 + w \times h \times 2 - (l-2) \times (h-1.5)}{10}$

   i.e.     $P = \dfrac{lw + 2lh + 2wh - (l-2)(h-1.5)}{10}$

   (c) (ii)   19.5 litres

## Unit 3: **Travel expenses**

1. $W = 5(m-d)(r + 0.5n)$

2. e.g. Number of passengers and daily mileage remain the same from day to day

3. (a) £30.48            (b) £33.35

## Unit 4: Sporting graphs

1. (a) Pole vault  (b) 4 × 100m sprint relay
   (c) Swimming  (d) Springboard diving
   (e) Freefall parachuting  (f) Drag racing

2. 

110 m hurdles

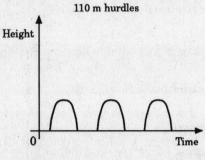

Hammer throwing

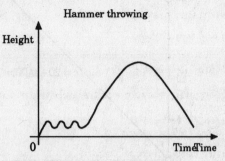

Fishing

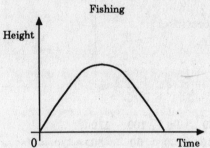

Clay pigeon shooting

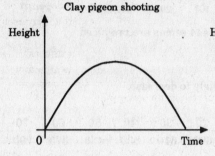

Trampolining

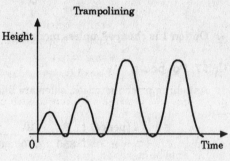

## Unit 5: Car allowances

1.

| m ('000 miles) | 0 | 2 | 4 | 6 | 8 |
|---|---|---|---|---|---|
| t (£) | 0 | 1040 | 1816 | 2543.50 | 3125.50 |
| m ('000 miles) | 10 | 12 | 14 | 16 | |
| t (£) | 3707.50 | 4119.50 | 4361.50 | 4603.50 | |

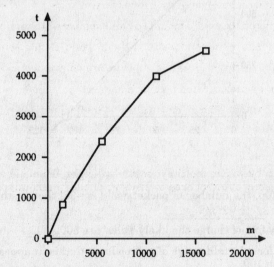

2. (b) Calculated values:

   (i) £45.12  (ii) £1509.48  (iii) £3024.81  (iv) £4174.19

## Unit 6: Leaflets

1. $c = 0.05n$

2. $c = 20 + 0.005n$

3.

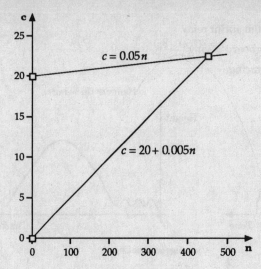

4.  Option 1 is cheaper, unless more than 444 copies are produced.

## Unit 7: Pot-pourri

1.  As selling price increases, sales are likely to decrease.

2.

| s (pence) | 0 | 10 | 20 | 30 | 40 | 50 | 60 | 70 | 80 | 90 | 100 | 110 |
|---|---|---|---|---|---|---|---|---|---|---|---|---|
| n | 850 | 770 | 690 | 610 | 530 | 450 | 370 | 290 | 210 | 130 | 50 | −30 |

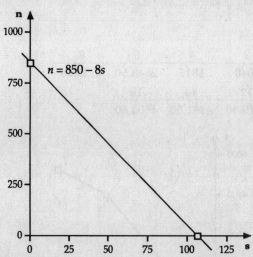

3.  (a) 322

    (b) 75p

    (c) When the selling price is 110p, the number of packets sold is −30; that is, the sellers *increase* their stock by 30 packets !

    (d) If the packets are given away free of charge the likely 'sales' are 800.

    (e) A linear model is valid only for a certain range of values for $s$; that is, it appears not to be valid when $s$ is close to zero or when s is greater than 100.

4.  (a) $r = s(850 - 8s) = 850s - 8s^2$

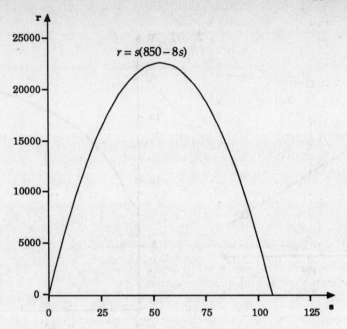

r = s(850 − 8s)

(b) s ≈ 53

## Unit 8: Pot-pourri (2)

1.  (a)  V = s(30 − 2s)(20 − 2s)

    (b)  No overlap for gluing; no card lost in cutting/folding.

    (c)

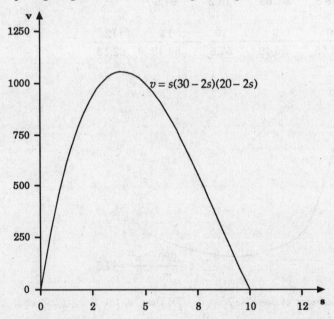

v = s(30 − 2s)(20 − 2s)

    (d)  Maximum volume ≈ 1056 cm$^3$

    (e)  s ≈ 3.9 (1D)

2.  (a)  A = (30−2s)(20−2s) + 2s(30− 2s) + 2s(20 − 2s) = 600− 4s$^2$

    (b)  A ≈ 540 (2S)

## Unit 9: Reading difficulty

1. (d)

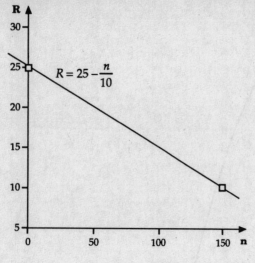

$$R = 25 - \frac{n}{10}$$

2. (c)

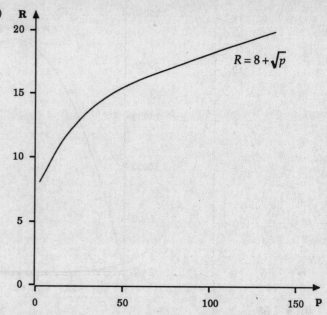

$$R = 8 + \sqrt{p}$$

## Unit 10: Minibus

1.

| m ('000 miles) | 0 | 1 | 2 | 3 | 4 | 5 |
|---|---|---|---|---|---|---|
| c (pence / mile) | 0 | 262.7 | 138.3 | 97.63 | 78.2 | 67.5 |

| m ('000 miles) | 6 | 7 | 8 | 9 | 10 | 11 | 12 |
|---|---|---|---|---|---|---|---|
| c (pence / mile) | 61.37 | 58.01 | 56.55 | 56.48 | 57.5 | 59.43 | 62.13 |

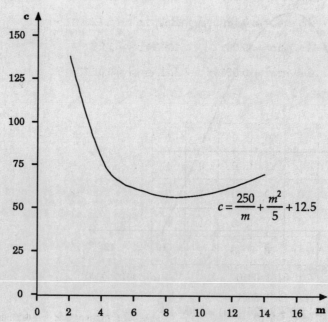

$$c = \frac{250}{m} + \frac{m^2}{5} + 12.5$$

2.  $m \approx 8550$ (3S)

## Unit 11: Bounciness

1. (a)

| Bounce number (n) | 0 | 1 | 2 | 3 | 4 | 5 | 6 | 7 | 8 |
|---|---|---|---|---|---|---|---|---|---|
| Height of bounce in metres (h) | 10 | 5.6 | 3.14 | 1.76 | 0.98 | 0.55 | 0.31 | 0.17 | 0.10 |

(b)

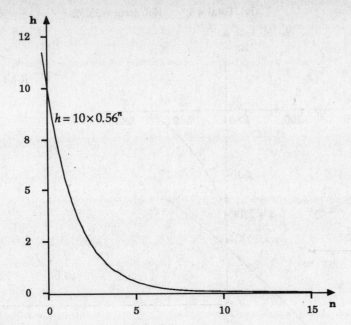

$h = 10 \times 0.56^n$

(c) $h \approx 0.03$ m

(d) (i) $h = 10 \times 0.56^n$  (ii) $h \approx 0.03$ m   (iii) $n = 12$

2. (a) $h = 10 \times b^n$  (b) $b = 0.8, n = 31; b = 0.4, n = 8$   (c) $n$ varies from 11 to 13

## Unit 12: Calculating $\pi$

1. (a) $\pi \approx 3.41(2D)$     Abs. error $= 0.27$;     Rel. error $\approx 8.6\%$

   (b) $\pi \approx 2.83(2D)$     Abs. error $= 0.31$;     Rel. error $\approx 9.9\%$

   (c) $\pi \approx 2.96(2D)$     Abs. error $= 0.18$;     Rel. error $\approx 5.7\%$

   (d) $\pi \approx 3.08(2D)$     Abs. error $= 0.06$;     Rel. error $\approx 1.9\%$

   (e) $\pi \approx 3.1397(4D)$     Abs. error $= 0.0019$;     Rel. error $\approx 0.06\%$

## Unit 13: Calculating device

1. (a)

| 0 | 1 | 1 | 1 | 0 | 0 | 0 | 1 |
|---|---|---|---|---|---|---|---|

(b)

| 0 | 1 | 0 | 1 | 1 | 0 | 0 | 1 |
|---|---|---|---|---|---|---|---|

(c)

| 0 | 1 | 1 | 0 | 0 | 0 | 1 | 0 |
|---|---|---|---|---|---|---|---|

(d)

| 0 | 1 | 1 | 0 | 1 | 0 | 1 | 0 |
|---|---|---|---|---|---|---|---|

(e)

| 1 | 1 | 0 | 1 | 0 | 0 | 1 | 1 |
|---|---|---|---|---|---|---|---|

2. (a) 0100 1001     (b) 0111 0010     (c) 1101 0000

   (d) 0100 0011     (e) 1101 0001

3. (a) Abs. error $= 0.5$;   Rel. error $\approx 9.1\%$     (b) Abs. error $= 0.5$;   Rel. error $\approx 5.9\%$

   (c) Abs. error $= 0.25$;   Rel. error $\approx 7.7\%$     (d) Abs. error $= 1.125$;   Rel. error $\approx 12.3\%$

   (e) Abs. error $= 1.25$;   Rel. error $\approx 9.4\%$

4. (a) Rel. error $\approx 6.7\%$     (b) Rel. error $\approx 5.9\%$     (c) Rel. error $\approx 9.7\%$

   (d) Rel. error $\approx 9.4\%$     (e) Rel. error $\approx 11.1\%$

5. (a) (i) 3   (ii) 3.5     (b) Addition is performed in order of magnitude.

6. (i) Total $= 6$;   Rel. error $= 0$     (ii) Total $= 5$;   Rel. error $\approx 16.7\%$

(iii) Total = 4;     Rel. error ≈ 33.3%         (iv) Total = 4;     Rel. error ≈ 33.3%

(v) Total = 1;     Rel. error ≈ 83.3%

## Unit 14: Computacare

1. (a)

| t | 0 | 1 | 2 | 3 | 4 |
|---|---|---|---|---|---|
| C | 0 | 200 | 380 | 540 | 680 |

See graph below.

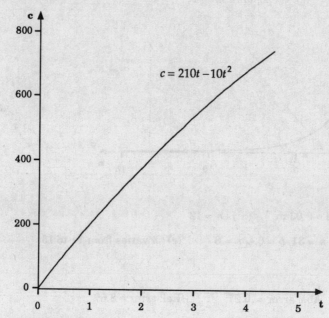

$$c = 210t - 10t^2$$

(b) (i) £1460 (4 strips)     (ii) £1466.67

(c) Abs. error = £6.67;     Rel. error ≈ 0.45%

2.

| t | 0 | 1 | 2 | 3 | 4 |
|---|---|---|---|---|---|
| C | 20 | 191 | 364 | 539 | 716 |

Trapezium Rule: £1462   (4 strips)

Simpson's Rule: £1461.33

Abs. error = £0.67; Rel. error ≈ 0.05%

MaintEase is the slightly cheaper option.

## Unit 15: The Golden Ratio

1. (a)

| x | 0 | 1 | 2 | 3 | 4 |
|---|---|---|---|---|---|
| y | -1 | -1 | 1 | 5 | 11 |

2. $\phi \approx 1.618$ (3D)

3. (a) $x_{n+1} = 1 + \dfrac{1}{x^n}$          Converges to $\phi \approx 1.618$ (3D)

(b) $x_{n+1} = x_n{}^2 - 1$          Divergent process

(c) $x_{n+1} = \sqrt{(1 + x_n)}$          Converges to $\phi \approx 1.618$ (3D)

(d) $x_{n+1} = \dfrac{1}{(x_n - 1)}$          Converges to -0.618 (3D)

## Unit 16: The Fish Pond

1. (a)   (i)   Population → 0        (ii)   Population → 0

       (iii)  Population → 0        (iv)  Population → 0.333 (3D)

       (v)   Population → 0.5       (vi)  Population → 0.615 (3D)

       (vii)  Population → 0.643

2. Initial population has no effect.

3. Population → $1 - \dfrac{1}{r}$ if $1 < r < 3$; if $r < 1$ population → 0.

4. (i)  $r = 0.5$                     (ii)  $r = 1.5$

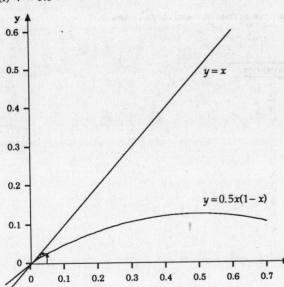 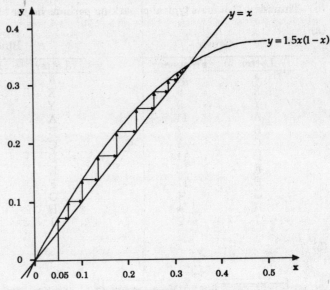

(iii)   $r = 2.5$

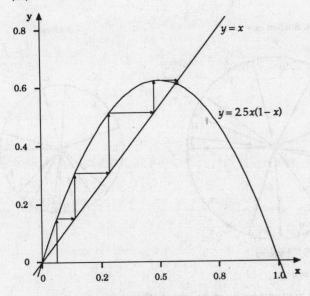

## Unit 17: Health and diet questionnaire

1. (a) Possible criticisms include:

    Confidential, so 'Name' question is unnecessary.

    'Are you male or female' should be answered 'Yes' in its present form.

    Units need to specified for height / weight etc.

    Smoking quantity question is too open; responses could include 'lots', '10 a day' etc.

(Possible improvement: limit range of responses e.g. less than 10 per day, between 10 and 20 per day, etc).

    (b) Stratified sample-proportions to reflect male/female; full-time/part-time; age groupings.

    (c) Include: determining proportions; distributing questionnaires to part-time students.

2. (c) (i)    Actual mean weight = 63.05 kg.

    (ii)    Stratified 'Sex' sample likely to give most accurate result.

## Unit 18: Cars

1. Stratified sample generally satisfactory providing:

    (i)    Harper campus is representative of whole Institute

    (ii)    Thursday 11 a.m. is typical of parking perhaps better to sample across several days/times.

2. (a)

| Green | | | Blue | |
|---|---|---|---|---|
| Letter | Frequency | | Letter | Frequency |
| # | 20 | | # | 6 |
| X | 6 | | X | 2 |
| Y | 9 | | Y | 3 |
| A | 11 | | A | 1 |
| B | 2 | | B | 2 |
| C | 8 | | C | 3 |
| D | 11 | | D | 2 |
| E | 12 | | E | 8 |
| F | 11 | | F | 9 |
| G | 4 | | G | 3 |
| H | 4 | | H | 8 |
| J | 2 | | J | 3 |

(b)

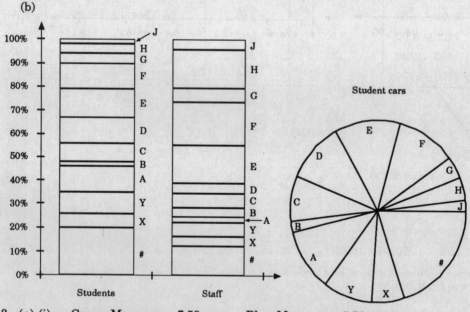

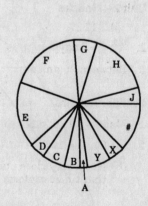

3. (a) (i)    Green: Mean age = 7.59 years    Blue: Mean age = 5.72 years

    (ii)    Green: S.D. ≈ 3.3 years    Blue: S.D. ≈ 3.5 years

    (b) Staff cars appear to be newer than students cars (by comparing average ages); there appears to be similar variation within both groups (by comparing standard deviations)

## Unit 19: Salary negotiations

1. (i)    Mean salary increases by £1100    (ii)    Median salary increases by £1100

    (iii) Quartiles increase by £1100    (iv)    Standard deviation is unchanged

2. (i)    Mean salary increases by 6%    (ii)    Median salary increases by 6%

    (iii) Quartiles increase by 6%    (iv)    Standard deviation increases by 6%

3. (a) (i)    £1100 increase    (ii)    £1100 increase    (iii)    6% increase

   (b) £1100 flat increase probably the cheapest option but will depend on proportion of staff at the extremes of the pay scale.

## Unit 20: Crossing

1. (a) Comprehensive in range of times but may not be typical since only Monday surveyed.

   (c) Means: P ≈ 250, V ≈ 704

   Standard deviations: P ≈ 125,  V ≈ 246

   (d)

| Time period | Time of day | Pedestrians (P) | Vehicles (V) | Conflict (PV2) |
|---|---|---|---|---|
| 1 | 0600 – 0700 | 130 | 380 | $0.19 \times 10^8$ |
| 2 | 0700 – 0800 | 252 | 504 | $0.64 \times 10^8$ |
| 3 | 0800 – 0900 | 495 | 980 | $4.75 \times 10^8$ |
| 4 | 0900 – 1000 | 281 | 962 | $2.60 \times 10^8$ |
| 5 | 1000 – 1100 | 167 | 850 | $1.21 \times 10^8$ |
| 6 | 1100 – 1200 | 183 | 712 | $0.93 \times 10^8$ |
| 7 | 1200 – 1300 | 391 | 820 | $2.63 \times 10^8$ |
| 8 | 1300 – 1400 | 328 | 806 | $2.13 \times 10^8$ |
| 9 | 1400 – 1500 | 185 | 813 | $1.22 \times 10^8$ |
| 10 | 1500 – 1600 | 290 | 809 | $1.90 \times 10^8$ |
| 11 | 1600 – 1700 | 493 | 823 | $3.34 \times 10^8$ |
| 12 | 1700 – 1800 | 297 | 961 | $2.74 \times 10^8$ |
| 13 | 1800 – 1900 | 181 | 843 | $1.29 \times 10^8$ |
| 14 | 1900 – 2000 | 150 | 562 | $0.47 \times 10^8$ |
| 15 | 2000 – 2100 | 124 | 320 | $0.13 \times 10^8$ |
| 16 | 2100 – 2200 | 50 | 116 | $0.01 \times 10^8$ |

## Unit 24: Snacks

1. (i)  12.2%          (ii)  9.2%          (iii) 34.8%

2. (i)  ≈ 7 days       (ii)  ≈1 day

3. Between 20 and 44.

## Unit 25: Repairs

1. Mean ≈ 10.26; S.D. ≈ 3.71

2. (a) (i)   ≈ 10%      (ii)   ≈ 12.5%      (iii)   ≈ 28.3%

   (b) Not a very close match between calculated proportions and observed proportions, so may be not sensible to assume that times conform to a Normal Distribution.

## Unit 26: Printer test

1. (b) ρ ≈ -0.62 (2D) (assumes most expensive printer is ranked 1; highest quality is ranked 1).

   Significant at 10% level.

2. ρ ≈ -0.78 (2D) (assumes highest quality is ranked 1; greatest speed is ranked 1).

   Significant at 1% level.

3. Quality is inversely related to both price and speed; that is, print quality tends to improve as price and speed become lower.

   Reliability likely to be affected by small sample size.

### Unit 27: Wheat

1. Variables exhibit positive correlation.

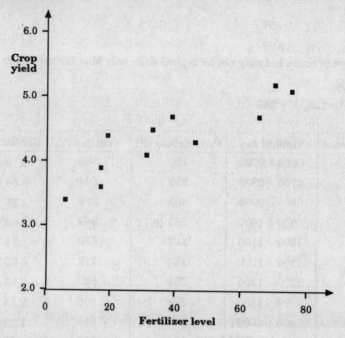

2. (a) $r \approx 0.89$ (2D)

   (b) Very strong evidence of positive correlation (significant at the 0.1% level).

3. (a) $y = 0.022x + 3.53$

   (c) (i) 3.79$t$      (ii) 4.74$t$      (iii) 5.44$t$      (iv) 6.28t

   (d) (i) & (ii) are within range of available data, so are likely to be reliable.

   (iii) & (iv) are outside range, so are less reliable.

### Unit 28: Jumpers

1. (b) e.g. Height v. Jump time: $r \approx -0.078$ i.e. two variables very unlikely to be related.

   Most of the variables exhibit very little evidence of correlation with jump times.

2. There is no real evidence to support the idea that males and females are significantly different in their experimental performances.

3. Possible errors in measurements.

   Consistency in the way that the measurements are made (e.g. definition of 'arm length').

### Unit 30 – Computer delivery

1. (i) 0.96      (ii) 0.90      (iii) 0.0024

   (iv) 0.0192      (v) 0.0000048

2. (a) (i) 0.815      (ii) 0.904      (iii) 0.590

   (b) Faults between systems are independent.

3. 0.0099

### Unit 31 – One-armed bandit

1. (i) 0.2      (ii) 0.04      (iii) 0.2304

2. (i) 0.0016      (ii) 0.0032      (iii) 0.0064

   (iv) 0.0128      (v) 0.0001638      (vi) 0.000087

3. Expected loss of £25.75

4. (i) 0.0000128      (ii) 0.0000512

5.  (i)  0.000064          (ii)  0.000256          (iii)  0.005888

## Unit 32: Hardware components

1.  (i)  0.81          (ii)  0.8655          (iii)  0.99
    (iv)  0.919          (v)  0.9898

## Unit 33: Games

1.  (a) 0.40
    (b)  (i)  0.06          (ii)  0.04          (iii)  0.21
    (c)  Expected loss of approximately 20p

2.  Expected profit of approximately £1.67

3.  (a) Expected loss of 11p per game.
    (b) No effect.

4.  (a)  (i)  0.2          (ii)  0.2          (iii)  0.3          (iv)   0.5
    (b)  9p profit

5.  0.16

## Unit 34: Passengers

1.  Success or failure situation; that is, a passenger seat is either filled or not filled.
    Fixed number of trials; that is, 8 seats on the bus.

2.  (a)

|  |  |  | *Probability* |
|---|---|---|---|
| P(0 passengers) | = | $_8C_0 (0.7)^0 (0.3)^8$ | = | 0.00006561 |
| P(1 passenger) | = | $_8C_1 (0.7)^1 (0.3)^7$ | = | 0.00122472 |
| P(2 passengers) | = | $_8C_2 (0.7)^2 (0.3)^6$ | = | 0.01000188 |
| P(3 passengers) | = | $_8C_3 (0.7)^3 (0.3)^5$ | = | 0.04667544 |
| P(4 passengers) | = | $_8C_4 (0.7)^4 (0.3)^4$ | = | 0.13613670 |
| P(5 passengers) | = | $_8C_5 (0.7)^5 (0.3)^3$ | = | 0.25412184 |
| P(6 passengers) | = | $_8C_6 (0.7)^6 (0.3)^2$ | = | 0.29647548 |
| P(7 passengers) | = | $_8C_7 (0.7)^7 (0.3)^1$ | = | 0.19765032 |
| P(8 passengers) | = | $_8C_8 (0.7)^8 (0.3)^0$ | = | 0.05764801 |

    (b)  (i)  0.0113          (ii)  0.0576          (iii)  0.8059

3.  (b)  (i)  5.6          (ii)  1.296

## Unit 35: Goals

1.  (a) 1.7
    (b)  (i)  0.18268          (ii)  0.31056          (iii)  0.26398          (iv)  0.14959
         (v)  0.06357          (vi)  0.02162          (vii)  0.008

2.  (i)  0.14957          (ii)  0.28418          (iii)  0.26997
    (iv)  0.17098          (v)  0.08122          (vi)  0.03086          (vii)  0.01322

3.  (a) (i)    0.04
        (ii)    0.3027
        (iii)    0.218
    (b)  1 – 1 draw
    (c)  Dale and the opposition score goals independently.

## Unit 36: Administration

1. (a) (i) 0.224      (ii) 0.084      (iii) 0.043

    (b) 0.00248

    (c) 0.132

2. 0.00004096      3. 0.135      4. 0.0000454

5. (i) 0.0062 (ii) 0.3085      6. 0.1681      7. 0.2212

8. £47      9. 21.4%      10. 0.043

## Unit 38: The Fish Pond (2)

1. (a) $0.422 < p < 0.728$      (b) 95% confidence interval: 68 to 119

2. 99% confidence interval: 64 to 134

3. 95% confidence interval: 47 to 65

    99% confidence interval: 45 to 69

## Unit 39: Crisps

1. Mean weight $\approx$ 29.29g; S.D. $\approx$ 0.919g

2. $z \approx -4.23$; Reject $H_0$ at 1% level

3. Reject $H_0$

## Unit 40: Chinese proverb

1. (a) 'Hear' mean score $= 10.2$; S.D. $\approx 3.18$    'See' mean score $\approx 12.67$; S.D. $\approx 3.71$

    (b) s.e. $\approx 0.959$; $z \approx 2.57$

2. (i) Reject $H_0$ at 5% level      (ii) Accept $H_0$ at 1% level

3. Some evidence, since significant at 5% level. However, result should be treated with caution since it is based on the assumption that the two student samples are equivalent in all other respects.

## Unit 42: Pitches

1. $H_0$: Team performance is not affected by the quality of pitch

    Result (5.03) not significant; accept $H_0$

2. (a) $H_0$: There is no difference between the smoking habits of males and females

       Result (3.86) not significant; accept $H_0$

    (b) $H_0$: Temperament is not related to hair colour

       Result (2.31) not significant; accept $H_0$

## Unit 43: Students

1. $H_0$:     There is no difference between 1983 and 1988 mean points scores

    $H_1$:     The 1988 mean points score is less than 1983 mean points score

    $z \approx 1.116$

    One-tailed test; result not significant – accept $H_0$

2. $H_0$:     There is no difference between the proportions of the 1983 and 1988 intakes that enter teaching

    $H_1$:     The proportion of the 1988 intake entering teaching is less than that of the 1983 intake

    $z \approx 6.37$

    One-tailed test; result highly significant – reject $H_0$ at 1% level

3. (a) (i) $H_0$: There is no difference between the mean number of 'A'-level passes gained by male students and female students

        $H_1$: There is a difference between the mean number of 'A'-level passes gained by male students and female students

        $z \approx 0.72$

Two-tailed test; result not significant – accept $H_0$

(ii)   Result (1.117) is not significant at 10% level.

(b) (ii)  Table B:     Mean ≈ 8.36 hours; S.D. ≈ 4.45 hours

Table C:     Mean ≈ 6.33 hours; S.D. ≈ 4.23 hours

(iii)  $z ≈ 0.267$; not significant

## Unit 44: Cafeteria

1. (a) Time; difficulty of mathematical analysis; complexity and unpredictability of real system

   (b) Arrival rate; service rate; seating capacity; eating times; numbers eating

   (c) To provide insights into the way the system is behaving that may help with the writing of the program; to validate the computer model

2. (a)

| No. of arrivals | Frequency | Probability | Random numbers | No. of services | Frequency | Probability | Random numbers |
|---|---|---|---|---|---|---|---|
| 8 | 8% | 0.08 | 00 - 07 | 7 | 9% | 0.09 | 00 - 08 |
| 9 | 22% | 0.22 | 08 - 29 | 8 | 19% | 0.19 | 09 - 27 |
| 10 | 38% | 0.38 | 30 - 67 | 9 | 42% | 0.42 | 28 - 69 |
| 11 | 26% | 0.26 | 68 - 93 | 10 | 25% | 0.25 | 70 - 94 |
| 12 | 6% | 0.06 | 94 - 99 | 11 | 5% | 0.05 | 95 - 99 |

   (c) Depends on random numbers used in simulation but average queue length is likely to be in the range 10 - 15.

## Unit 45: Telephone hotline

1. (a) Difficulty of mathematical analysis; complexity and unpredictability of real system

   (b)

| No. of incoming calls per minute | Frequency | Probability | Random numbers |
|---|---|---|---|
| 0 | 720 | 0.60 | 00 - 59 |
| 1 | 300 | 0.25 | 60 - 84 |
| 2 | 120 | 0.10 | 85 - 94 |
| 3 | 60 | 0.05 | 95 - 99 |

| Duration of call (minutes) | Frequency | Probability | Random numbers |
|---|---|---|---|
| 1 | 216 | 0.30 | 00 - 29 |
| 2 | 130 | 0.18 | 30 - 47 |
| 3 | 108 | 0.15 | 48 - 62 |
| 4 | 72 | 0.10 | 63 - 72 |
| 5 | 65 | 0.09 | 73 - 81 |
| 6 | 50 | 0.07 | 82 - 88 |
| 7 | 36 | 0.05 | 89 - 93 |
| 8 | 29 | 0.04 | 94 - 97 |
| 9 | 14 | 0.02 | 98 - 99 |

2. Solutions are dependent on random numbers used; however, system becomes extremely congested with callers having to wait for long periods. (The assumption is that callers do not ring off before their call has been dealt with).

3. It is better to use the same collection of random numbers so that any differences between the two sets of results are then known to be due to changes in the system rather than due to changes in the random numbers.

4. The results of the simulation should provide evidence of the efficiency of utilising two hotline facilities; the average waiting time for callers is much reduced.

5. Run the simulation over longer time periods; use different sets of random numbers.

## Unit 46: Brand-switching

1.

| Event | Probability | Random numbers | | Event | Probability | Random numbers | | Event | Probability | Random numbers |
|-------|-------------|----------------|---|-------|-------------|----------------|---|-------|-------------|----------------|
| A to A | 0.5 | 0 - 4 | | B to A | 0.2 | 0 - 1 | | C to A | 0.1 | 0 |
| A to B | 0.3 | 5 - 7 | | B to B | 0.7 | 2 - 8 | | C to B | 0.5 | 1 - 5 |
| A to C | 0.2 | 8 - 9 | | B to C | 0.1 | 9 | | C to C | 0.4 | 6 - 9 |

2. (b) Proportions should tend to:  Brand A – 26% of the time

Brand B – 56% of the time

Brand C – 18% of the time

(c) Simulate the situation over a greater number of weeks; use different random numbers

## Unit 47: Program queueing

1. Results are dependent on simulation method and random numbers used. However, when two   minicomputers are used, the results are likely to indicate a doubling of the mean time that each   program spends in the system.

## Unit 48: Pseudo-random numbers

1. (a) There is no apparent link between seed and cycle length.

(b) Low numbers tend to generate low numbers.

2. (a) The mid-product method is more effective since two seeds need to repeat together before the cycle repeats; however, cycle lengths are still too short for practical purposes.

(d) This method, like the mid-square method, tends to favour lower numbers.

## Unit 49: Tables

1. (b) $7x + 3y \leq 600$     (Floor space)

$y \geq x$      (Number of each type)

$x \geq 30$      (Minimum number of Octos)

(c) Minimise:   $N = x + y$

2.

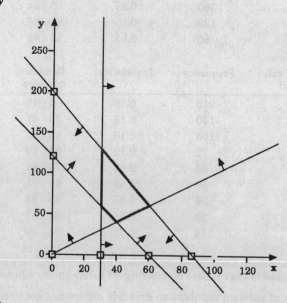

3. (a) 40 Quattros; 40 Octos

(b) (i)  480     (ii) 400 m²

4. (a) Minimise: $C = 140x + 6y$

(b) 30 Octos; 60 Quattros (Total cost £7800)

(c) 480

(d) Same number of people are accommodated but cheapest combination is 40 Octos; 40 Quattros  (Total cost £8000).

## Unit 50: Car Park

1. (a) $x + 3y \leq 180$ (Space)     $x + y \leq 80$ (Number of vehicles)

   (b) Maximise: $I = x + 2y$

2. (i) 30 motorbikes; 50 cars                    (ii) £130

3.

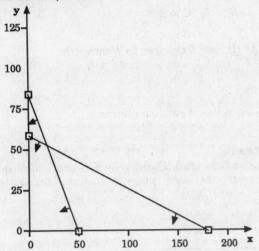

## Unit 51: Accommodation

1. (a) $10x + 3y \leq 360$     $5x + 4y \leq 280$     $x \geq 10$     $y \geq 20$

   (b) Maximise: $N = 4x + 2y$

2. (a) 24 houses; 40 flats

   (b) (i) 176          (ii) £2800000

## Unit 52: River pollution

1. (b) $5x + 9y + 6z \geq 800$                (c) Minimise: $C = 6x + 9y + 12z$

2. (a) Maximise $300X + 800Y$

   Subject to:        $2X + 5Y \leq 6$
                      $X + 9Y \leq 9$
                      $4X + 6Y \leq 12$

   (b) (i) Process 146.2 tons at BigCo
          Process 7.7 tons at MidCo
          Process 0 tons at LilCo

   (ii) £946.11

## Unit 53: File storage

1. (b)

| File type | Storage device | | | Storage requirements |
|-----------|-----------|-------------|------|----------------------|
|           | Hard disk | Floppy disk | Tape | |
| DTP | 16 | 40 | 68 | 140 |
| Spreadsheet | 4 | 12 | 18 | 100 |
| Database | 3 | 8 | 15 | 60 |
| *Storage capabilities* | 100 | 50 | 150 | |

2. (b) (i) DTP files:          Hard disc – 100; Floppy disc – 40

Spreadsheet files:      Tape streamer – 100

Database files:         Floppy disc – 10; Tape streamer – 50

  (ii)  Minimum time: 5830s

## Unit 54: Activity day

1. (b) (i)  School A:     30 children to Brooklands

          School B:     5 children to Brooklands; 10 children to Harper; 5 children to Wentworth

          School C:     10 children to Harper

          School D:     5 children to Harper

    (ii)   Minimum distance: 190 'child-miles'

2. School A:      30 children to Brooklands

   School C:      5 children to Brooklands; 5 children to Wentworth

   School D:      5 children to Harper

   Minimum distance: 120 'child-miles'

## Unit 55: Examinations

1. (c) (i)

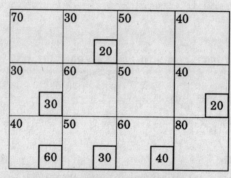

  (ii)   Minimum distance: 8600m

2. Change 'Store C - Sports Hall' route allocation to 10 tables.

   Minimum distance: 6800m

3. Optimum allocation:

Minimum distance: 8700m

## Unit 56: Swimmers

1. (a) Backstroke: F; Breaststroke: C; Butterfly: D; Freestyle: E

  (b) 261s

2. (a) Swimmer B: Backstroke; Swimmer F: Butterfly Swimmers C & D are interchangeable between Breaststroke and Freestyle

  (b) 4s slower

3. Backstroke: F; Breaststroke: B; Butterfly: D; Freestyle: C

Team time:    264s

## Unit 57: Compatibility

1.  (a) Several possible solutions; for example:

| A | B | C | D | E | F | G | H | I |
|---|---|---|---|---|---|---|---|---|
| e | a | c | b | d | f | g | h | i |

(b)  (i)  180          (ii)  20

2.  (a) Two possible solutions:

|     | A | B | C | D | E | G | H | I |
|-----|---|---|---|---|---|---|---|---|
| (1) | e | a | c | b | f | g | d | i |
| (2) | e | a | c | b | f | h | d | i |

(b) No effect

3.

| A | B | C | D | E | G | H | I | J |
|---|---|---|---|---|---|---|---|---|
| e | a | c | b | f | g | d | i | h |

## Unit 58: Inter-campus journey

1.  HXYZB is shortest path: 2800m

2.  Minimum time route:

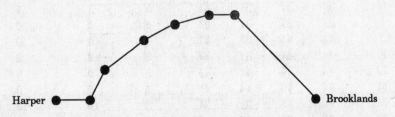

Time ≈ 10.2 minutes

## Unit 59: Telephone extension

1.  (a) 208m

(b) Minimum connector:

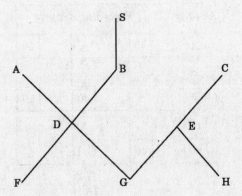

2.  (a) 35m

(b) As above, with additional connection from F to I.

## Unit 60: The Grand Tour

1.  Upper bound: e.g. N-A-B-S-G-R-L-T-C-D-P-N

Total distance ≈ 790m (depending on accuracy used in measurements)

Lower bound: Several possibilities e.g. ignoring node R, minimum connector ≈ 580m

Lower bound = 580 + 80 + 80 = 740m

## Unit 61: Sports complex

1.

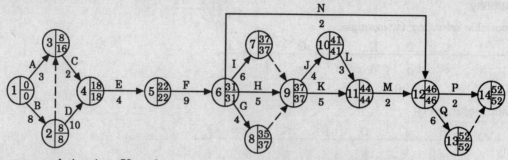

2. (iii) Minimum completion time: 52 weeks  (iv) Critical path: B-D-E-F-I-J-L-M-Q

3.

| Activity | Head EST | Head LFT | Tail EST | Tail LFT | Duration | Total float | Free float |
|----------|----------|----------|----------|----------|----------|-------------|------------|
| A | 8 | 16 | 0 | 0 | 3 | 13 | 5 |
| B | 8 | 8 | 0 | 0 | 8 | 0 | 0 |
| C | 18 | 18 | 8 | 16 | 2 | 8 | 8 |
| D | 18 | 18 | 8 | 8 | 10 | 0 | 0 |
| E | 22 | 22 | 18 | 18 | 4 | 0 | 0 |
| F | 31 | 31 | 22 | 22 | 9 | 0 | 0 |
| G | 35 | 37 | 31 | 31 | 4 | 2 | 0 |
| H | 37 | 37 | 31 | 31 | 5 | 1 | 1 |
| I | 37 | 37 | 31 | 31 | 6 | 0 | 0 |
| J | 41 | 41 | 37 | 37 | 4 | 0 | 0 |
| K | 44 | 44 | 37 | 37 | 5 | 2 | 2 |
| L | 44 | 44 | 41 | 41 | 3 | 0 | 0 |
| M | 46 | 46 | 44 | 44 | 2 | 0 | 0 |
| N | 46 | 46 | 31 | 31 | 2 | 13 | 13 |
| P | 52 | 52 | 46 | 46 | 2 | 4 | 4 |
| Q | 52 | 52 | 46 | 46 | 6 | 0 | 0 |

## Unit 62 – Concert

1. Possible precedence table:

| Activity | Preceding activity |
|----------|--------------------|
| A | — |
| B | A |
| C | A |
| D | A |
| E | A |
| F | A |
| G | A |
| H | A |
| I | D |
| J | C, D |
| K | J |
| L | D, G |
| M | D, H |

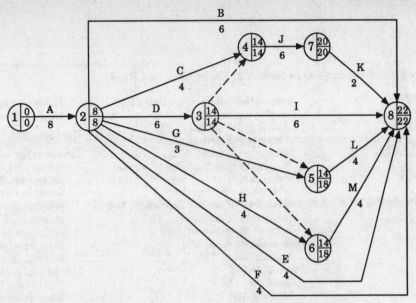

2. (iii) Minimum completion time: 22 weeks       (iv) Critical path: A-D-J-K

3.

| Activity | Head EST | LFT | Tail EST | LFT | Duration | Total float | Free float |
|---|---|---|---|---|---|---|---|
| A | 8 | 8 | 0 | 0 | 8 | 0 | 0 |
| B | 22 | 22 | 8 | 8 | 6 | 8 | 8 |
| C | 14 | 14 | 8 | 8 | 4 | 2 | 2 |
| D | 14 | 14 | 8 | 8 | 6 | 0 | 0 |
| E | 22 | 22 | 8 | 8 | 4 | 10 | 10 |
| F | 22 | 22 | 8 | 8 | 4 | 10 | 10 |
| G | 14 | 18 | 8 | 8 | 3 | 7 | 3 |
| H | 14 | 18 | 8 | 8 | 4 | 6 | 2 |
| I | 22 | 22 | 14 | 14 | 2 | 6 | 6 |
| J | 20 | 20 | 14 | 14 | 6 | 0 | 0 |
| K | 22 | 22 | 20 | 20 | 2 | 0 | 0 |
| L | 22 | 22 | 14 | 18 | 4 | 4 | 4 |
| M | 22 | 22 | 14 | 18 | 4 | 4 | 4 |

# Index

# Operating Systems
## Incorporating UNIX and MS-DOS

### C Ritchie

ISBN: **1 873981 32 5** • Date: **1992** • Edition: **1st**
Extent: **226 pp** • Size: **275 x 215 mm**

---

*Courses on which this book is known to be used*
BTEC Higher National and first and second year Computing degree courses; A Level and BTEC National Computing; Software Engineering and Mechanical Engineering degrees.

---

The aim of the book is to provide a course text for HNC/D and first and second year Computing degree courses. It covers the principles required by **general** Computing students.

The book illustrates theoretical concepts by showing their practical consequences in actual operating systems (UNIX and MS-DOS). Windows, GUI and many questions and practical exercises are included.

## Contents:

**Background** • Definition of Operating Systems • Overview of O/S Facilities Summary Description of UNIX and MS-DOS • **The Basics** • Relationship to Hardware • Use of Firmware • Functions of the Kernel • Introduction to Concept of 'Process' • User Interface • Types of 'User' • Command Languages, Graphical **User Interfaces** (GUIs) • Job Control Languages • System Calls • Introduction to UNIX Shell and MS-DOS Commands • **Process Management** • Multiprogramming, Multitasking and Multiprocessing • High and Low Level Schedulers • Resource Allocation • Scheduling Algorithms • Process States and State Diagrams • Introduction to Concurrency • **Memory Management** • Sharing Memory Space Between Processors • Relocatability • Types of Memory Allocation • Working Set Principle • Memory Protection • **Input – Output** • Relationship with Hardware • Problems of Speed Disparity – Buffering • I/O Procedures • Device Handlers • Device Independence • Error Handling • **File System Facilities** • Notion of 'File' • File Types • Filing System • Management of File Space and Free Space • System Services • **Interaction of Concurrent Processes** • Competing and Co-operating Processes • Deadlocks and Starvation • Semaphores and Monitors • UNIX Process Facilities • **Other Systems** • O/S Requirements for Networks • Introduction to Distributed Systems • Multiprocessor Systems • Virtual Machine Environments • **Security and Integrity** • Nature of Threats to System and Data • Access Controls • File Backup Techniques • Security in Networks • Viruses, Worms, Trojan Horses etc.

## Review Comments:

*'This is one of the most exciting, useful and lucid books on the subject that I have seen. I would have no hesitation in recommending it to students and colleagues. It's level of presentation and coverage is ideal for BTEC students and above.' 'Very readable book with difficult concepts presented in a clear, understandable way.' 'Excellent – I wish I had had it when I was a student!' 'Excellent book! Fills a big gap in giving a simple, easy-to-understand approach for BTEC/A Level students.' 'A very good foundation book in operating systems at a price I can expect students to buy.' – **Lecturers***

---

**⬆ Free Lecturers' Supplement ⬆**

# Local Area Networks
**P Hodson**

## An Active-Learning Approach

ISBN: **1 873981 33 3** • Date: **1992** • Edition: **1st**
Extent: **192 pp** • Size: **275 x 215 mm**

---

*Courses on which this book is known to be used*
BTEC Higher National Computing and Computing degree courses.

---

The aim of this book is to provide the course text for the Networking element required by most degree and Higher National courses in Computing.

There are many good texts providing simple descriptive treatment of local area networks, but the need was seen to provide understandable material on the important issues of internetworking as well as providing a framework for understanding key concepts in local area networks.

## Contents:

**Fundamentals** • Topologies • Signalling • Switching Technologies • Error Detection and Correction • Media • **Standards** • OSI Standards • 7 Layer Model • **LAN Signalling and Access** • Baseband • Broadband • Carrierband • P-persistant • CSMA • CSMA/CD • CSMA/CA • Token Ring • Token Bus • Slotted Ring • **Popular LANs** • IEEE 802.3 • 802.4 • 802.5 • 802.6 • 802.11 • FDDI • **Interconnection** • Repeaters • Bridges • Routers • Gateways • Brouters • Public Networks • **Interoperability** • Protocol Suites • Application Software • Operating Systems • **Performance** • Throughput • Tradeoffs • Reliability • **Network Products** • Commercial Products: Starlan • Arcnet • Appletalk • Ethernet • Token Ring • **Installation and Management Issues** • Installation Tips • Test Tools • Diagnostic Aids • Management.

## Review Comments:

*'There is no other book that covers these technical aspects with this clarity.' 'Excellent; will complement the new Operating Systems book well for our operating systems and Data Communications unit.' 'Excellent simple explanations rarely found in the difficult "technical" area.' 'Excellent coverage at level required.'* – **Lecturers**

---

**♠ Free Lecturers' Supplement ♠**

# Understanding Computer Systems Architecture

**M Lacy**

ISBN: **1 870941 81 0** • Date: **1991** • Edition: **1st**
Extent: **460 pp** • Size: **245 x 190 mm**

---

*Courses on which this book is known to be used*
BCS; HNC Software Eng; BTEC National; A Level; HNC/D Computer Studies; Modern Computer Foundations.
**On reading list of ICM**

---

The aim of this book is to provide a course text for HNC/D and first or second year computing degree courses variously called 'Computer Systems', 'Computer Architecture' and 'Computer Technology'.

The many good reference texts on the subject can be too intimidating and off-putting to be useful for the students mentioned above. What is needed, and this book aims to satisfy that need, is a book which assumes a knowledge of computer hardware and software to approximately GCSE level and provides students with the knowledge and skills to consult with confidence the advanced texts on this topic. In doing so, the text covers in detail the key concepts which are central to understanding computer systems at HNC/D and degree level

## Contents:

**The Processing Unit** • *Processor Basics:* A Simplified Processor • The Fetch/ Execute Cycle • Different Execute Sequences • *Towards Real Processors:* Multiplexer • Address Adder • General Purpose Registers • Flag Register • The Stack • *Microprocessors:* I8085 • Z80 • I8086 • **The Processor & Digital Logic** • *Logic Basics:* Gates • Physical Implementation • Combinational Circuits • Circuit Design • *Sequential Circuits:* Latches • Flip-flops • Sequencers • *Components of the Processor:* Registers • ALU • Control Unit • **The Computer as a System** • *System Components:* Memory • Interfaces • Controllers • *Communication Between Components:* Programmed I/O • Interrupt-driven I/O • Delegated I/O • Autonomous Devices • *The User Interface:* Assembly Language • Assemblers • Loaders • Linkers • **Higher Performance Systems** • *Increased Flexibility:* Microprogramming • Developments within the von Neumann Framework: Improved Technology • Memory Interleaving • Cache • Pipelining • CISC vs RISC • *New Directions:* Multiprocessor Classification • Interconnection Networks • Array Processors • Multiprocessor Systems.

## Review Comments:

*'Definitely the best book on the subject at this level.' 'Up-to-date – very well structured.' 'Well presented, clear coverage of an important area of computing. Should fill a previous gap in the market.' 'At last a book which allows the illustration of old concepts with modern day examples! Well done.' 'Refreshing approach.' 'Excellent value, a really useful addition to the course [BTEC National Engineering].' 'Very good coverage of current range of processors.' – Lecturers*

---

⬆ **Free Lecturers' Supplement** ⬆

# Convert to C and C++     *BJ Holmes*

**ISBN: 1 873981 20 1** • Date: **1992** • Edition: **1st**
Extent: **320 pp** • Size: **245 x 190 mm**

---

*Courses on which this book is known to be used*
BTEC National and Higher National
Computing; A Level Computing; BA Computing; MSc Computing and Info Systems; C & G 726

---

This book provides a complete course text book for students who already understand the fundamentals of programming in a high-level language, and are required to extend their knowledge of programming to include C and C++. The advantages of covering both languages in one text are:

☐ the major strengths and weaknesses of both languages can be compared and contrasted;

☐ since ANSI C is a subset of C++, the reader is encouraged, through the order of presentation, to learn about C before embarking on C++;

☐ the transition from ANSI C to C++ is taken in three easy
stages, covering enhancements to procedural programming, techniques for data abstraction, and object-oriented programming;

☐ the reader who can already program in an older, non ANSI, version of C can use the text as a refresher course in ANSI C, and quickly progress to learning C++;

☐ those who want a quick guide to C++ can turn to part two, knowing that revision material on ANSI C is available in part one, should it be needed.

The emphasis throughout the book is on the use of carefully chosen examples that highlight the features of the language being studied enabling students to convert to C and C++ in as short a time as possible. Explanation about the language follows from, and is put into context with, the example programs. A section of programming questions to test and reinforce students' understanding can be found at the end of each chapter.

## Contents:

### Part one – Convert to C
The Organisation of a C Program • Data Types and Input/Output •
Control Statements • Arrays • Files • Further Topics.

### Par two – Convert to C++
The Transition • Data Abstractions • Object-oriented Programming.

**Appendices** Answers.

## Review Comments:

*'Excellent book. Wide range of the language covered, well presented and at a very reasonable price.' 'Excellent progression for students from Pascal.' 'Excellent price, good coverage, straight-forward and readable.'*
*'Covering just the right ground and taking the right pace. Price and presentation good.' 'Appropriate levels of coverage for those who already know the language and are converting.' – Lecturers*

---

**⬥ Free Lecturers' Disk ⬥**

# Structured Programming in COBOL

*BJ Holmes*

ISBN: **1 870941 82 9** • Date: **1991** • Edition: **2nd**
Extent: **528 pp** • Size: **245 x 190 mm**

---

*Courses on which this book is known to be used*
Degrees in Computer Studies; BTEC National & Higher National Computer Studies; City & Guilds 424/425/726; IDPM; HND Commercial Systems; Programming Methodology.
**On reading list of ICM**

---

## Contents:

Computer Environment • Structured Design • Elements of COBOL • A Complete Program • Program Development • Picture Editing • Coding Data Files and Reports • Introduction to File Processing • Program Structures from File Structures • File Maintenance • Tables • Direct Access Files • COBOL- 85 • Program Implementation Techniques • JSP/COBOL – A Design Programming Tool • Miscellaneous Features.

This book is written around two themes: the design of structured computer programs based on the techniques from Jackson Structured Programming (JSP), and the methods available for coding these designs in the COBOL language.

**Notes on the Second Edition**

The contents have been reordered for this edition, with additional new chapters on Computer Environment, Structured Design, Program Development, COBOL-85 and JSP/COBOL – a design programming tool.

The author has used Standard COBOL in the translation of JSP program designs into COBOL code. The programs in the text have been compiled using an ANS 1985 COBOL compiler. Because of the subset of language statements used, it is also possible to compile the programs using older compilers that conform to the ANS 1974 Standard.

Note: With the lecturers' supplement is a free (and copyright free) PC-compatible disk incorporating all the illustrative programs in the text – saves keying in! Immediate use for demonstration and development purposes for lecturers and students.

(The disk needs to be compiled using either an ANS 1985 or ANS 1974 COBOL compiler.)

## Review Comments:

*'Wins on price and coverage.' 'Good coverage of COBOL, especially COBOL-85. JSP excellent, especially use of PDF.' 'Excellent in all respects.' 'Previously I hadn't been able to recommend one book.' 'Good on Jackson's Structures.' 'The author has brought together in a practical way the JSP philosophy with all the traditional areas of COBOL. At its price it offers unrivalled value for money.'* **– Lecturers**

*'A number of texts were mentioned, but the most popular seems to be BJ Holmes, Structured Programming in COBOL'*
**Report on COBOL on BTEC Higher National Courses, Manchester Polytechnic**

---

**♠ Free Lecturers' Supplement ♠**

# Pascal Programming

*BJ Holmes*

ISBN: **1 870941 65 9** • Date: **1990** • Edition: **2nd**
Extent: **464 pp** • Size: **245 x 190 mm**

---

*Courses on which this book is known to be used*

BCS Part 1; A Level Computing; BSc (Hons) Computer Studies; BTEC National and HNC/D Computer Studies; HNC Software Design; NDI; HEFC Info Tech; C & G 726/223.

**On reading list of ICM**

---

## Contents:

Computer Environment • Data • Instruction Sequence • Data Types • Selection • Repetition • Procedures • Program Development • Mathematics • Arrays • Sorting and Searching • Recursion • Text Files • Pointers • Dynamic Structures • Record Files • Common Extensions • Turbo Units • Object-oriented Programming (OOP) • Case Studies in OOP.

*Pascal Programming* can be regarded as a complete text on programming and the use of data structures. The aim of this book is to help the reader acquire and develop the skill of computer programming in a block-structured language and foster an understanding of the related topics of data structures and data processing.

**Note:** With the lecturers' supplement is a free (and copyright free) PC-compatible disk incorporating all the programs in the text – saves keying in! Immediate use for illustrative and development purposes for lecturers and students.

(The programs on the disk need to be compiled using Borland Turbo Pascal compiler version 5.5 or later.)

## Review Comments:

*'Excellent – no competition [BTEC ND Computing].' 'Affordable and Turbo Pascal and Syntax diagrams – great!' 'Far better than most books that are twice the price.'*
— ***Lecturers***

---

⬥ **Free Lecturers' Supplement** ⬥

# Modula-2

**BJ Holmes**

ISBN: **1 870941 31 4** • Date: **1989** • Edition: **1st**
Extent: **352 pp** • Size: **245 x 190 mm**

---

*Courses on which this book is known to be used*

BTEC National and HNC/D Computing; BTEC HNC/D Information Technology; BSc Computer Science; A Level Computing; HNC Software Engineering.

---

Within this single book there is enough information to provide a foundation for any reader who wishes to develop and implement a wide variety of systems in Modula-2.

**Note:** With the lecturers' supplement is a free (and copyright free) PC-compatible disk incorporating all the programs in the text – saves keying in! Immediate use for illustrative and development purposes for lecturers and students.

(The programs on the disk need to be compiled using 'JPI Top Speed Modula-2')

## Contents:

Computer Environment • Data • Instruction Sequence • Data Types • Selection • Repetition • Procedures • Program Development • Mathematics • Modules • Arrays • Sorting and Searching • Recursion • File Processing • File Maintenance • Pointers • Data Abstraction • Coroutines.

## Review Comments:

*'Ideal for our BTEC Higher Computer Studies course.' 'Its reasonable price, many examples, large answers section and complete coverage mean we will use it as a course text.'* – **Lecturers**

---

**♠ Free Lecturers' Supplement ♠**